PLUG IN

POWER!:

THE
COMPREHENSIVE
DSP GUIDE

By Ashley Shepherd

THOMSON
★
™
COURSE TECHNOLOGY

Professional ■ Technical ■ Reference

* 000263354 *

ISBN: 1-59200-953-0
Library of Congress Catalog Card Number: 2005929814
Printed in the United States of America
06 07 08 09 10 PA 10 9 8 7 6 5 4 3 2 1

THOMSON

★

™

COURSE TECHNOLOGY

Professional ■ Technical ■ Reference

Thomson Course Technology PTR,
a division of Thomson Course Technology

25 Thomson Place
Boston, MA 02210

http://www.courseptr.com

Publisher and General Manager, Thomson Course Technology PTR:
Stacy L. Hiquet

Associate Director of Marketing:
Sarah O'Donnell

Manager of Editorial Services:
Heather Talbot

Marketing Manager:
Mark Hughes

Acquisitions Editor:
Mark Garvey

Marketing Coordinator:
Jordan Casey

Project Editor:
Kezia Endsley

PTR Editorial Services Coordinator:
Elizabeth Furbish

Interior Layout Tech:
Sue Honeywell

Cover Designers:
Mike Tanamachi and Nancy Goulet

Indexer:
Kelly Talbot

Proofreader:
Steve Honeywell

*This book is dedicated to the people who have helped
me the most in making it a reality, my family:
Annette, Lottie, and of course Jas.
Without their patience and support,
I would not have been able to bring*
Plug-In Power! *to fruition.*

} Acknowledgments

I would like to thank the team at Course Technology for working hard to bring this book to the market. The editing staff is the largest asset I have in writing a book of this nature. Thanks Kezia, Mark, and Robert for your time and assistance.

I would also like to thank all the plug-in developers for helping me explore their world in-depth and for the technical guidance provided during the writing of this book. I would especially like to thank Yvan Grabit at Steinberg, Gilad Keren at Waves, and Michael Kurz at Native Instruments for taking the time to answer the interview questions found throughout the book.

} About the Author

A Berklee College of Music graduate, **Ashley Shepherd** has carved out a career in music and recording spanning 20 years. With Gold and Platinum record awards for engineering and an ADDY award for original music, Ashley has garnered major label production, recording, and mixing credits. His original music is broadcast worldwide, with a long list of television and cable broadcast titles, including *Everybody Loves Raymond, Seinfeld, 60 Minutes, Dateline, Chicago Hope,* and more. Ashley also works in film post-production with film scoring and sound design credits on independent feature films, such as *The Sixth Man, Pokémon: The First Movie,* and *Three Barbecues.* He has produced sound and music for gaming titles, museum exhibits, corporate installations, and a long list of independent musical artists, including Blessid Union of Souls, Emily Strand, Ryan Adcock, Buckra, and Noctaluca. Ashley is also the author of *Pro Tools for Film, Video, and Multimedia* (ISBN: 159200069X) and co-author of *Nuendo Power!* (ISBN: 1592003907), both available from Course Technology.

Operating Grandin Media, LLC, Ashley continues to produce music and audio for any number of uses, along with writing technical material, including Steinberg's Nuendo software manuals. Currently, he is embarking on the task of building his own studio facilities to enable a higher level of production quality and service flexibility while incorporating complete surround sound capabilities. Visit his Web site at www.picturemusic.com for up-to-date information or to contact him.

TABLE OF } Contents

xiii

❈❈❈

} Introduction

Welcome to *Plug-In Power!* This book is written to help provide users an in-depth understanding of the plug-ins that are used every day in audio software, digital consoles, and outboard digital audio processors. This book starts with the basics with an introduction to digital audio and continues to describe all the different types of digital audio processing as found in plug-ins and other digital audio processors. The level of detail will provide even advanced users a clearer understanding of how all these plug-ins work and interesting ways to apply them in real-world situations.

What You'll Find in This Book

In this book, you will find first a digital audio primer intended to create a basic understanding of digital audio theory that you can use every day to increase the quality of your recordings and troubleshoot problems that occur.

The digital audio and signal processing primer in Chapter 1 goes through the history, theory, and development of digital audio over the years. A basic explanation of sampling theory is explored. Specific parameters of digital audio signals and computer files are explained, along with some of the basic principles of digital signal processing, such as bit reduction and dither.

This section might be a bit technical in some ways, but please bear with these basic principles if you do not already have a firm grasp on them. This knowledge will allow you to fully understand all of the plug-ins available and maximize their potential for a given application, whether that is creating realistic ambience for replaced dialogue tracks in a feature film, tweaking out the most awesome kick sound for a hard rock mix, or putting that high-end sheen on an R&B lead vocal so it just shimmers above the rest of the track.

Understanding the basic digital audio principles will empower you to accomplish these tasks with ease and precision. Just because we all have these amazing digital tools does not mean that they are easier to operate than their analog counterparts. In some ways, digital audio is less forgiving about mistakes made along the way than analog recording and processing.

Next, the book examines all the different types of plug-ins there are today, from native processing such as VST to hardware-based plug-ins such as the UAD-1 and HTDM. The operating systems that host audio applications are examined to show their differences and similarities. Each system and protocol has its strengths and weaknesses. Once you understand these differences, using the plug-ins themselves becomes more straightforward.

Following this, a detailed explanation of each type of DSP plug-in (equalizer, compressor, reverb, and so on) is discussed in theory and in practice with examples from the most popular brands of plug-ins used today, including Waves, Universal Audio (UAD-1), TC Electronics (PowerCore), PSP and more on some of the most popular audio software including Pro Tools and Nuendo/Cubase.

Each processor type is explored in theoretical terms as to what it is supposed to do and then in real-world terms with examples of how each plug-in actually performs with real audio running through it. The real-world examples include tips and tricks to get the most out of your plug-ins. Conventional and unconventional techniques for music and multimedia/film are presented. You can try them out on your own productions and mixes.

Who This Book Is For

This book is intended for beginners to advanced audio engineers using DSP (Digital Signal Processing) to process audio in Digital Audio Workstations (DAWs), video-editing systems (such as Avid and Final Cut Pro), digital audio consoles such as Yamaha and Mackie, and outboard processors such as the TC System 6000 and Focusrite Liquid Channel.

Basically anyone who uses digital audio in some fashion can benefit from reading this book. The topics and techniques discussed run the gamut of audio situations from digital live reinforcement consoles, DJ setups, music recording and mixing, film sound, audio restoration and forensics, to home studio recording. Computer technology has leveled the playing field for audio equipment. It is possible for just about anyone to have a fully complemented studio facility in their bedroom or even sitting on the plane with a laptop and headphones.

However, this technological leap has only addressed one side of the coin. Insightful technique is the other side of that coin. That is what this book is attempting to rectify. A solid understanding of the basics helps you make better recordings than any amount of gear. With all of this power at your fingertips, it is also easy to overuse or abuse that power and minimize the results you can achieve. Twenty plug-ins on the lead vocal doesn't necessarily make it sound better, usually worse in fact.

How This Book Is Organized

This book is organized into two basic sections. The first sets the groundwork for understanding what digital audio is, how plug-ins work, and the different types of processing that plug-ins can provide. This section covers topics such as the different audio file formats, various plug-in technology, and theoretical descriptions of different types of signal processing. The digital audio and signal processing primer in Chapter 1 is intended to lay the groundwork for a firm understanding of digital audio basics, such as sampling rates, bit depth, dynamic range, and dithering.

The second section provides a detailed breakdown of each type of plug-in in theory and practice with real-world examples to help solidify your understanding of that type of signal processing. For example, Chapter 6 discusses compression in theory, defines its parameters, and uses the popular plug-in brands in real-world examples to illustrate how to use compression in various ways.

Most audio engineers of the past had to go through the processes of working as an intern at a big studio in order to gain the knowledge necessary to operate the recording studio and make great recordings. Watching the engineer and asking questions after a session provided this knowledge in a very special and hands-on manner. Today's recording enthusiasts and professional engineers don't have that opportunity as often, because of the reduction of larger studios and the focus of audio production moving into smaller, project-type studios. The chance to mingle and learn from a master engineer in the studio is becoming scarcer.

This book cannot replace an internship with a seasoned engineer, but it can serve as reference material for the aspiring engineer and professional alike. Because many younger engineers have never even used much of the analog audio gear that plug-ins often try to emulate, they might not even know what these units are supposed to sound like or are capable of doing. Hopefully, this book can provide some explanation of what these plug-ins are designed to do and also what other interesting and extreme things they are capable of doing outside of their analog counterparts.

No need to even bother with the analog toys; let's get on with the digital revolution!

1} Digital Audio and Signal Processing Primer

This first chapter lays the groundwork for a basic understanding of how digital audio works. It explains sampling theory, the Nyquist Theorem, and parameters of digital audio. This chapter is by far the driest of all of them. The chapters dealing with the plug-ins themselves are not as theoretical and have much more real-world examples, tips, and tricks. That being said, it behooves you, as the practical audio engineer, to have a firm understanding of the details involved in digital audio so that you can avoid simple mistakes along the way and thus create the highest quality audio.

Understanding the Audio Fundamentals

Understanding basic principles of sound and waveforms will aid you in understanding digital audio signal processing. Most types of DSP are based on processing in the analog domain for many years, including equalization and compression. But there are also many types of DSP that are most commonly done digitally, such as reverb, delays, pitch changing, time compression/expansion, and convolution (impulse modeling). Understanding these processes requires a clear understanding of the phenomena that is being manipulated, in this case, *sound*.

What Is Sound?

What you perceive as sound is really the fluctuations in air pressure caused by the vibration of air molecules. When an object such as a drum is struck and vibrates, it in turn moves the air around it,

Figure 1.1

Air molecules moving around and causing fluctuations in air pressure as a result of sound waves.

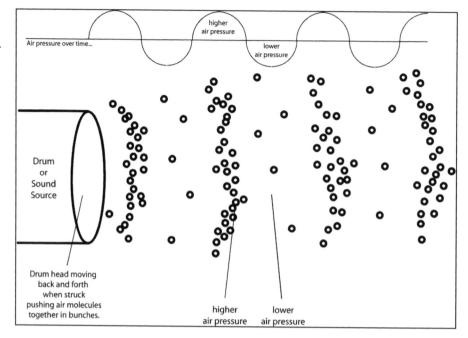

causing air molecules to bump into one another, which in turn causes minute fluctuations in air pressure, as shown in Figure 1.1. This action propagates through the air until it reaches your ears, much like the waves made by rock dropped into a pool of water. As the air pressure in your ear fluctuates, your ear turns these vibrations into nerve impulses that you understand as sound.

The point to understand here is that sound is the result of a fluctuation of air pressure. When the air is at rest (no sound), the air pressure remains constant. When sound waves are present, the air pressure increases to a positive value and then decreases past the normal constant to a negative value and then back again. This is important, because these air pressure changes must first be converted into electrical signals before they can become digital data.

✳ HUMAN HEARING RANGE

The common accepted range of human hearing is from 20Hz to 20kHz. Average hearing generally starts rolling off above 15kHz and can decrease with age. However, it has been demonstrated that, although we might not be able to discern steady tones above 20kHz, it is possible to notice changes in audible high frequency tones when their shape is altered. Altering the shape of a tone to something other than a sine wave will add harmonics to it that are above the human hearing range. This implies that frequencies higher than 20kHz do have an effect on our hearing. What that effect is and how it manifests itself in audio recording is debatable.

Transducers

An audio transducer is a device that converts air pressure into electrical signals or electrical signals back into air pressure. The two basic types of transducers are microphones and speakers. In essence, they are the same type of device working in opposite directions.

Microphones

The microphone is a transducer that converts air pressure changes into electrical signals. As the air pressure increases around a microphone, the resulting electrical output of the microphone is a positive voltage. When the air pressure decreases past the normal constant, the microphone outputs a negative voltage. This signal can be graphed as a function over time and might look like Figure 1.2.

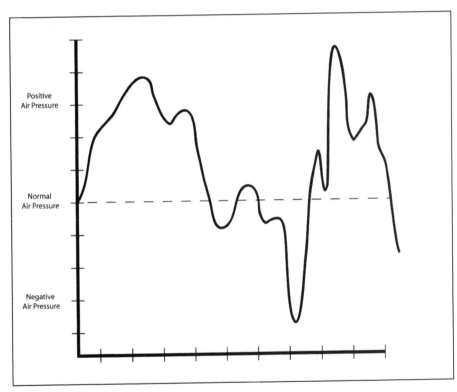

Figure 1.2
The graph of voltage output over time of a microphone shows a familiar waveform of sound.

Speakers

Speakers convert electrical signals back into fluctuating air pressure and sound. When no voltage is applied to a speaker, it is at rest. When a positive voltage is applied, the speaker cone moves forward or outward, causing air molecules to bump together, thus increasing the air pressure. When a negative voltage is applied, the speaker cone moves backward or inward, pulling air molecules apart and decreasing the air pressure.

> ✳ **SPEAKERS AS MICROPHONES**
>
> Speakers and microphones are very similar devices that operate in opposite directions. Microphones turn sound into electricity and speakers turn electricity into sound. You can actually use a speaker as a crude microphone. Try connecting speaker leads of a small woofer (6" to 8") to the inputs of a DI box and place it in front of a kick drum. Use it just like you use any other microphone. This makes for a very interesting low-frequency transducer and adds a solid thickness to the kick drum sound.

In between these two types of transducers lies the entire digital recording chain. What happens to signals in the digital realm is what this whole book is concerned with. In order to better understand the digital realm, you must first understand how audio signals become digital.

Exploring Digital Audio

Digital audio has had an interesting and long history dating back to 1928, when Harry Nyquist developed his sampling theorem. This provided a theoretical basis for digital audio, but the technological advances needed would not come about for many years.

In 1937, Alec H. Reeves, an engineer for International Telephone and Telegraph, invented the concept of *pulse code modulation* (PCM), which allowed digital information to be transmitted over wires and eventually stored on magnetic media such as the hard disk. The signal he developed uses a series of pulses to encode binary numerals into an electrical signal. The length of each pulse determines whether the digit is a 0 (short pulse) or a 1 (long pulse), as shown in Figure 1.3.

Figure 1.3

A Pulse Code Modulation (PCM) signal is used to encode binary numerals into electrical signals.

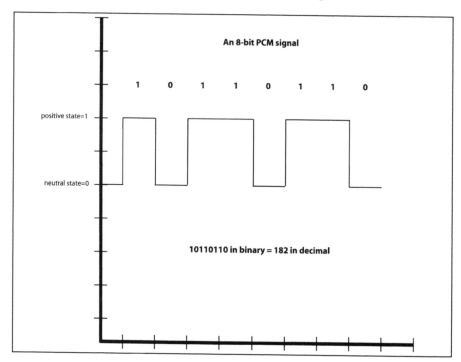

4
✳ ✳ ✳

The capability to store the data or numerical information that represents audio required the development of the computer and disk drive storage. IBM can be accredited with most of this development over many decades, resulting in the creation of computers capable of storing large quantities of binary data necessary for the storage and processing of digital audio.

Nyquist Theory

Harry Nyquist, born in 1889 in Sweden, was a mathematician and an electrical engineer for American Telephone and Telegraph from 1917 to 1934. During that time, he published a paper (Nyquist, Harry, "Certain Topics in Telephone Transmission Theory," 1928) that outlined the basic theory for digitization of analog signals, now known as the *Nyquist Theorem*. This theorem outlines a method whereby audio signals can be translated into numbers by observing the voltage level of the signal at regular timed intervals and quantifying that voltage into a number. These numbers can be stored and then used to reconstruct the waveform. This process of taking samples of the voltage level of a signal over time has come to be known as *sampling*.

Sampling

The Nyquist Theorem states that in order to capture the entire bandwidth of the signal being sampled, you must use a sampling frequency that is at least twice the highest frequency you want to capture, as shown in Figure 1.4. With audio frequencies, the lowest usable sampling frequency is 40kHz (2 × 20kHz). This allows sampling of signals up to 20kHz, the upper limit of human hearing. In practice however, the limitations of analog circuitry required in the converter itself necessitate the use of the higher sampling frequencies.

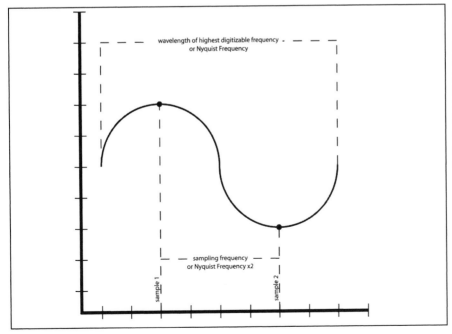

Figure 1.4

This graph shows the highest possible frequency that can be captured given a set sampling frequency. Notice that for one cycle of the waveform, two discrete samples have been taken, allowing the waveform to be reconstructed from the discrete samples.

❋ ❋ ❋

THE NYQUIST FREQUENCY

For a given sampling rate, the highest frequency that you can accurately capture and reproduce is half of the sampling frequency—known as the *Nyquist frequency*.

Any frequency above the Nyquist frequency that enters the digital converter system causes a phenomena called *aliasing,* whereby artifacts are generated in the digital data that when reproduced in analog form, create false tones in the audible range. Figure 1.5 offers a visual representation of how this occurs.

These ghost or alias frequencies are not desired, because they are fabrications of the sampling process and not part of the original audio signal. In order to remove the frequencies causing aliasing, a filter must be placed in the converter prior to the sampling stage that removes all frequencies above the Nyquist frequency. This is called an *anti-aliasing filter* and is critical to the performance of any analog-to-digital converter system.

Figure 1.5

Errors in interpolation of frequencies higher than the Nyquist frequency result in the creation of false, or aliased, tones in the audible band. A filter is placed before the sampling converter that removes frequencies higher than the Nyquist frequency to avoid this.

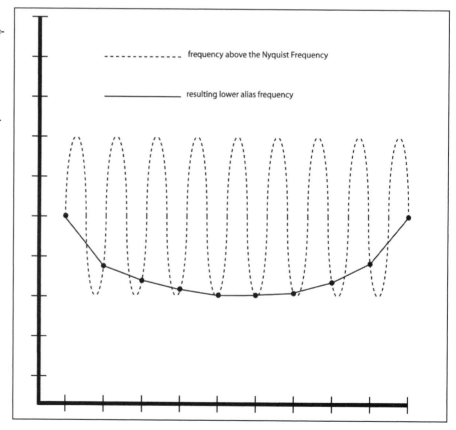

In order to create a digital audio system capable of recording frequencies as high as 20kHz, a sampling rate (or sample rate) of 40kHz or higher is necessary. A proper anti-aliasing filter for this system filters out any frequency above 20kHz. Because it's virtually impossible to create an analog filter of this nature a perfect, slightly higher sample rates were adopted so that the anti-aliasing filters don't have to be so severe in order to be effective. With a sampling rate of 44.1kHz, the anti-aliasing lo-pass filter can start rolling off as early as 18kHz, sloping until 22 or even 23kHz and still prevent alias tones from being audible. For more information on equalization and low-pass filters, refer to Chapter 5, "Equalizers and Frequency-Based Processing."

Grasping the Digital Audio Basics

From the theory created by Harry Nyquist, digital audio has evolved into the basis of most audio production and recording including music, film, and Internet media. As digital audio and multimedia have developed over the years, so has digital audio grown and changed. These changes require that any digital audio system be versatile in accommodating various formats.

To that end, there are two parameters associated with digital audio that define the basic fundamentals of any digital audio system. The *sample rate* affects a signal's frequency response and the *bit depth* affects its dynamic range. It is important to have a very clear understanding of these two aspects of any digital audio signal.

How Sample Rates Determine Frequency Response

Initially, the sampling frequency of 48kHz was selected to relax the requirements of the anti-aliasing filter and still provide 20Hz to 20kHz bandwidth. This has since become the standard sampling frequency for the video and film industry. During the development of the compact disc, the request was made that a CD should be capable of playing back Beethoven's 9th Symphony in its entirety without having to change discs. This required a slight reduction in the sampling frequency in order to increase the running time of a standard audio CD. The result: the 44.1kHz CD standard sampling frequency.

Because computer technology has become faster and less expensive, the adoption of higher sample rates is now widely used. Higher sample rates allow for a gentle curve in the anti-aliasing filters along with the ability to capture higher frequencies. Whether these higher frequencies affect our perception of the sound is a highly debated subject. However, the use of gentler anti-aliasing filters greatly improves the quality of the recorded audio. In addition, processing of higher sample rates results in higher degree of accuracy in the mathematical result. These benefits alone justify the use of higher sample rates when audio fidelity is the highest concern.

The higher sample rates are multiples of the two conventional sample rates:

❋ 88.2 and 176.4kHz are multiples of the CD standard 44.1kHz.

❋ 96 and 192kHz are multiples of the video standard 48kHz.

❋ Even 384kHz is in use as an experimental sample rate.

How Bit Depth Defines Dynamic Range

Each sample in a digital audio signal contains a numeric representation of the waveform's amplitude for that particular moment in time. There is a finite amount of numbers to choose from. The amount of available choices is determined by how many bits are used to represent each sample. This is called the *bit depth* of the audio sample.

> ❋ **BITS AND BINARY NUMBERS**
>
> When talking about bits and digital audio, I am referring to the binary system—numbers consisting of only ones and zeros. Binary numbers are simple to encode digitally, because ones and zeros are easily expressed with on or off conditions common to electrical circuits.

For example, in a three-bit system, samples can be represented by one of eight possible values ($2 \times 2 \times 2 = 8$). If you add one bit to the sample word, you double the amount of choices for sample values (4 bits yields 16 choices). With more values representing voltage fluctuations comes a greater accuracy in reproducing these dynamic fluctuations. As a result, the dynamic range of a digital signal is increased. See Table 1.1.

Table 1.1 Bit Depth Resolutions

Bit Depth	Number of Possible Amplitude Values
8-bit	256 possibilities (2^8)
16-bit	65,536 possibilities (2^{16})
24-bit	16,777,216 possibilities (2^{24})

The smallest number the binary word can represent (referred to as the *least significant bit* or LSB) determines the noise floor of the audio signal. Because the LSB is the smallest amount of change the digital signal can have, it also represents the change between silence and sound. If there are only 16 choices for the digital word, the quietest sound possible is 1/16th of the loudest sound possible.

This explanation is simplified for the sake of discussion; the math is more complex and involves decibels and logarithmic equations. Suffice it to say for the purposes of this text that the amount of bits in a digital audio signal determines the dynamic range that the signal can contain.

❋ DYNAMIC RANGE

The dynamic range of any audio system begins with the quietest perceptible sound and ends with the loudest sound the system can reproduce. The noise floor usually determines the low or quiet dynamics and clipping or distortion determines the loudest dynamics. With digital audio, the bit depth determines the theoretical dynamic range that the numbers can represent. Bear in mind that other elements in a complete audio system might not have the same amount of dynamic range as the digital audio stream. For instance, even though you are using a 24-bit audio signal, the speakers and amplifier you are listening to certainly will not have 144dB of dynamic range. Understanding how much dynamic range is available is powerful knowledge.

The theoretical maximum dynamic range of digital audio and the reality of its use in real-world situations are quite different and a source of confusion. Here's a list of typical dynamic range figures for common audio devices and acoustic situations.

* *96dB*—The theoretical dynamic range of 16-bit PCM digital audio signals.
* *144dB*—The theoretical dynamic range of 24-bit PCM digital audio signals.
* *80dB*—Usable acoustic dynamic range of most professional recording studios.
* *100dB*—World record studio dynamic range held by Galaxy Studios (www.galaxy.be).
* *40–60dB*—Dynamic range of a typical pop record.
* *3dB*—Dynamic range of the *chorus* in a typical pop record…just kidding.
* *80dB*—The Ultimate analog tape machine; a 2-inch 8-track.
* *50dB*—Typical analog multi-track machine at 30ips (without the use of Dolby SR noise reduction).
* *+100dB*—Professional mixing console.

❋ DECIBEL THEORY

For a complete discussion on decibel theory and dynamic range, refer to Chapter 4, "Gain Processing and Metering."

So why does digital have so much dynamic range when the real world doesn't even create it or need it? With 24-bit signals having 144dB of theoretical dynamic range, it makes it easier to set recording levels conservatively. Any creative performance, whether music, dialogue, or foley, can have unexpected signal peaks. Using 24-bit converters, recording levels can be set lower in order to accommodate these peaks without the use of limiting or compression to alter the sound.

Also, when using plug-ins and DSP in general, you need dynamic range to perform these functions. Having more dynamic range allows your DSP calculations to be more accurate and the results have a greater "space" to occupy. For example, when applying equalization to an audio signal that has a very high level, some amount of boost at a given frequency can cause digital clipping. Levels that are more conservatively set allow a greater amount of processing to be done before exceeding the dynamic range of the audio signal.

Understanding Audio Formats

There are several ways that audio data can be formatted for storage on a hard disk or transmitted over digital audio connections. This formatting has nothing to do with the computer file type, which is discussed separately.

PCM 16-Bit and 24-Bit

Pulse Code Modulation (Linear PCM) is the most common type of audio data format. The choices are only the sample rate and the amount of bits per word, or bit depth. In professional application, only 16- and 24-bit depths are used.

 USING 8-BIT SAMPLES

Some older sampler units and drum machines use 8-bit samples to conserve memory. Even though these units offer inferior sound quality, some recording artists prefer them for their "dirty" or "chunky" sound.

32-Bit Floating-Point Files

Certain audio applications such as Steinberg's Nuendo and MOTU's Digital Performer support the 32-bit floating-point format. This format consists of 24 bits of linear PCM data with addition of an 8-bit exponent, called a *mantissa*. The mantissa can be used to shift the range of the 24-bit PCM data up and down exponentially. The advantage of this format is the dynamic range of possible signals increases exponentially, resulting in theoretical ranges upwards of 1300dB. Now that's a lot of dynamic range!

In practice, however, the 32-bit floating-point data must eventually be reduced to linear PCM 16- or 24-bit data in order to be converted back into analog signals. Digital-to-analog converters can only accept linear PCM data. The advantage is that while the audio is still in data format, all sorts of DSP (such as plug-ins) can be applied without detracting from the dynamic range of the signal. A final gain adjustment might be necessary to return the level to something within the range of a 16- or 24-bit PCM signal.

Most often, you will find this format used for the internal signal path of certain software packages, including Nuendo/Cubase, SONAR, Pro Tools LE (not TDM), and others. The reason for this is that personal computers use CPUs that have built-in floating-point processors. It is economical to use floating-point processing with software that utilizes the CPU of the host computer for DSP operations.

NATIVE VERSUS HARDWARE-BASED PROCESSING

When audio software utilizes the host computer's CPU for processing audio, it is often referred to as native processing. Plug-in formats such as VST, RTAS, Audio Units, and MAS (Motu Audio System) are examples of native processing. TDM UAD-1, TC Powercore, and Pyramix plug-ins are examples of non-native processors and require a specific piece of hardware in order to run, such as a Pro Tools HD Process card in your computer. The advantage of native processing is economy. There is no need to purchase additional hardware outside of the host computer in order to use this type of processing. The disadvantage of native processing is that the host CPU is being taxed by the operations of the DSP. Hardware-based processors do not add any significant strain on the host CPU, because dedicated hardware does the processing. As personal computing power increases each year, this difference becomes smaller and smaller until there will be no processing benefit to dedicated hardware processors. Of course, plug-ins will become more powerful and require more DSP resources as well.

Recording to 32-bit floating-point is recommended only when digital processing is being applied during the recording or in an offline process. Recording straight audio without any processing to 32-bit floating-point is just a waste of disk space. Because 32-bit contains a 24-bit PCM word with the addition of an 8-bit exponent, audio directly from the converter's output contains 24 active bits of audio and eight zeros for the exponent.

When performing offline processing such as normalizing audio files already on disk, using the 32-bit format can be beneficial. The exponent bit is utilized for the gain change and the original 24-bit audio data is maintained, thereby preserving the original dynamic range.

Usually, the 32-bit format is available only in software that uses 32-bit internal processing, such as Wavelab. Applications such as Pro Tools HD, which uses fixed-point processing, cannot take advantage of the 32-bit format.

USING THE 24-BIT LINEAR PCM FORMAT

As a general rule of thumb, only use the 32-bit floating-point format file when you're doing a large amount of offline processing such as noise reduction, normalizing, or convolution. When you're recording audio directly from an analog-to-digital converter (straight recording), use the 24-bit linear PCM format. This saves on disk space while still retaining all the resolution available from the converter.

Single Bit Direct Stream Digital

In an effort to realize the highest potential in digital recording fidelity, Sony and Phillips have developed the high-resolution DSD (Direct Stream Digital) format. This format differs in very basic ways from linear PCM and 32-bit floating-point. It uses a 1-bit system so the only values possible for each word in DSD are 0 or 1. The sample rate is much higher, running at 2.8442MHz.

The principle is rather simple. When the converter sees an increase in amplitude, it spits out a 1. When it sees a decrease in amplitude, it spits out a 0. It does this 2,844,200 times a second (for a 2.8442MHz sample rate), providing a very detailed view of the waveform and capturing very high-frequency content. When the waveform is going down, the data stream is all zeros. When the waveform is going up, it is all ones.

> ※ **64X OVERSAMPLED SIGMA/DELTA**
>
> The data stream recorded using DSD is also known as *64X Oversampled Sigma/Delta*. Typically, modern analog-to-digital converters use this method when initially digitizing audio and then mathematically compute the 16- or 24-bit linear PCM data for the output. Because the DSD format does not perform any of this processing to the raw 64X oversampled signal, there is no need for anti-aliasing filters in the signal chain. This also helps audio quality for DSD.

DSD takes a large amount of disk space (four times more than the current CD audio format) to store and requires specialized equipment to process at this time. Pyramix provides solutions for DSD processing on its dedicated hardware. This book does not discuss DSD processing, only linear PCM and 32-bit floating-point, because those two are by far the most widely used in the audio industry today.

Audio Files Types

Many audio file types have been developed over the past two decades; most of them are compatible with the two most popular computer operating systems: Apple's OS and Microsoft Windows. These file types used to be incompatible across the two operating systems. Thankfully, this has changed somewhat and new standards have been introduced that are helping to minimize the gap between operating systems.

The following file types are the most commonly used with today's popular software:

* ※ *WAV*—This file type was created jointly by IBM and Microsoft and has become one of the most widely used audio formats today. Macintosh computers used to have difficulty reading these files but today with OSX, this is no longer an issue.

* ※ *AIFF (Audio Interchange File Format)*—This format has been popular with Apple systems and also are the same type that are found on audio CDs. Most professional audio applications support this file type on both platforms. It can support many sample rates and channel widths for multi-channel surround sound. These files can have .aif or .aiff as a file suffix.

* ※ *SDII (Sound Designer II)*—This file type was created by Digidesign, makers of the popular Pro Tools software. Originally intended for the Apple Macintosh operating system and Digidesign's Sound Designer software, this file type was proprietary and could not be used by other applications. Even though there are Windows applications that support SDII files, Windows operating systems have a tough time dealing with this file type even today. Because Pro Tools can now use other standard file types, it is likely that the SDII format is on its way to obsolescence. These files typically have an .sd2 file suffix. Beware on Windows systems, because this file type is often not recognized.

* ※ *BWF (Broadcast Wave File)*—The Audio Engineering Society (AES) and the European Broadcast Union (EBU) introduced the Broadcast Wave File format in 1996 in order to answer the needs of both radio and television audio professionals. It is intended to simplify the interchange of audio files between different computer workstations and was created with the input from audio professionals from various areas of audio production. These files can contain metadata that describes the author's name, title, artist, genre, and creation date. In addition, the files contain a SMPTE time stamp that identifies the start time of the

file so that is can be placed synchronously with other audio or video files in a post-production environment. Recommended by both the AES and EBU, this file type is quickly becoming the standard for today's professional applications. The Broadcast Wave File still uses a .wav extension, but contains additional metadata with time stamp and creator information.

✳ *MP3 (MPEG2 Layer 3)*—The very popular MP3 format has been adopted by consumers for playback on portable music players, such as the iPod, and for Internet transfer and playback on computers. This format is compressed for size at a typical ratio of 4:1 from uncompressed files of the same sample rate. Because plug-ins and most DSP functions need to be applied to uncompressed, linear, audio data, the MP3 format is not mentioned again in this book. It really is a format for final delivery, and not for processing. It should be noted that the MP3 format requires licensing in order to distribute files encoded this way. It is not a free format such as WAV or AIFF.

Understanding Bit Depth Reduction

One of the most important and misunderstood processes that digital audio constantly undergoes is the alteration of its bit depth. This is most apparent during mixdown and mastering when the audio signal is changed from 24-bit or 32-bit floating point to 16-bit in order to be compatible with the audio CD standards (44.1kHz/16-bit). During this step, it is important to change the bit depth carefully to avoid adding noise and distortion to the signal. In order to understand this, you must take a look at how the math works during bit reduction.

Truncation

The simplest method of reducing bit depth is to truncate the sample. Truncation is simply the removal of the lower or least significant bits of the sample. For example, reducing a 24-bit sample to a 16-bit sample requires getting rid of bits 17 through 24. That's it. Nothing else is done besides removal of the least significant bits. The next level of sophistication in bit reduction involves rounding off the value of the least significant bits (LSB) during truncation. This provide a very slight improvement in dynamic range of the resulting signal (on the order of 1/2 LSB). Truncation with or without rounding causes a type of distortion called *quantization noise*. This type of distortion is different from the more readily experienced type that occurs when signals exceed the maximum level that a device can produce and are clipped off. This type of distortion occurs at the very lowest levels of the digital signal and is the result of errors introduced by the truncation process. Because the distortion occurs at such low levels, it can be perceived as noise and is often referred to that way.

This noise is audible and affects the perceived dynamic range of the truncated signal. Low-level sounds and details in recordings can become masked by the quantization noise. Sounds such as the tail of reverb decay, room ambience, and the softer harmonics of instruments can all be obscured by quantization noise.

The errors that cause quantization noise are related to the audio signal itself because the error occurs when the signal passes into the range of the least significant bits that are truncated. The noise is correlated to the audio signal at that point. Even though this noise is at the very lowest level within the truncated signal (close to –96dB for 16-bit), it is more noticeable because it is tied to the signal itself, correlated.

You must do something to minimize this type of distortion or at least de-correlate it from the signal. This is where dither comes in.

What Is Dither?

In its most basic form, *dither* is a random noise signal added to other audio signals prior to truncation. Dither only affects the least significant bit in the resulting truncated bit stream. For example, when reducing the bit depth from 24-bit to 16-bit and adding dither, the last bit is randomly changed from 0 to 1 or 1 to 0, affecting the 16th bit, or LSB, of the 16-bit audio signal. The actual level of the dither signal is just below the LSB. That, plus the audio signal's level, work together to change the LSB in a random way that still includes audio signals.

The action of the dither signal on the LSB will de-correlate the resulting quantization noise from the audio signal. The de-correlation makes the noise less apparent to the listener. It also has the benefit of allowing audio signals at very low levels to become clearer because they are not being masked by audible quantization noise tied to the signal. Plus, the dither helps audio signals below the LSB to register in the truncated sample, thereby increasing the dynamic range even more.

In the real world, dithering helps low-level detail in your mixes be retained through the bit-reduction process. For example, reverb tails and low-level room reflections and harmonics become clearer when you use proper dither because such noises are not masked by audible quantization distortion. This, in essence, increases the resolution of the 16-bit signal, retaining more of the 24-bit information.

You would think that one kind of dither would work to reduce quantization noise. Well, as with anything related to audio, there are different opinions about what the dither noise should be. Different styles of music are sometimes better served by certain types of dither noise. The following sections cover several of the most popular types of dither and give some explanation as to how they work and what they are best suited for.

White Noise

Random noise without any modification is called *white* noise or TPDF (triangular probability density function) dither. If it is truly random, it will have energy at all possible frequencies over a given period of time. Although white noise serves the purpose of dither, it also adds noise to the signal. This noise can be audible because it is spread across the entire audible spectrum.

Noise Shaping

It is possible to equalize or shape the dither noise so that most of the energy is in frequencies that humans are less sensitive to. Typically, this means the higher frequencies between 18kHz and 22kHz in a 44.1kHz system. One of the more popular noise shaping dither algorithms is the Waves IDR dither, found in its popular L1 and L2 mastering limiter plug-ins (visit www.waves.com for more information).

Figure 1.6 shows the frequency curve of a typical noise-shaped dither signal. Notice that more energy is placed in the higher frequencies where the noise is less audible because human hearing is less sensitive in those areas.

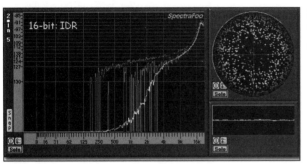

Figure 1.6
The frequency curve of Waves IDR 16-bit noise shaped dither as shown by SpectraFoo.

TOOLS OF THE DIGITAL TRADE

In Figure 1.6, SpectraFoo analyzes the IDR dither signal. SpectraFoo, made by Metric Halo Labs (see www.mhlabs.com) is just one example of the digital audio analysis tools that are available. In addition to the frequency analyzer seen here, SpectraFoo also contains a *bitscope*, which will display the activity of the bits in a digital audio stream. This can be very helpful in determining whether a plug-in or other digital device is performing as is should be or even as advertised. Sometimes processors alter the bitstream even when they are in "bypass" mode. Having tools like SpectraFoo can be invaluable when working with digital audio.

There are many variations on noise shaping curves made by different manufactures. There are also just as many opinions about which one sounds the best. The best option is to experiment and listen to each type of dither for a particular application, whether rock music or a film score.

Apogee UV22
Apogee has also developed a version of dither that is not entirely random. The signal is centered at 22kHz and is supposed to contain information from the lower eight bits. The claim is that the information is modulated into the 22kHz signal and therefore retained in the resulting 16-bit signal. UV22 is a very popular dithering signal that has been used in a variety of situations, from music mastering to film sound. Once again, you should use your ears to determine which dither is right for the situation at hand (visit www.apogee.com for more information).

POW-r
POW-r dither was created by a consortium of audio designers and manufacturers and uses noise shaping techniques that have not been made public due to patent issues. Suffice it to say that this is a very popular dithering solution that is widely available in popular audio software and as a plug-in.

It is useful in a wide variety of audio tasks and is highly acclaimed by audio professionals. Try it out and see for yourself. Figure 1.7 Shows the frequency curve of POW-r dither.

Figure 1.7

The frequency curve of POW-r dither as shown by SpectraFoo.

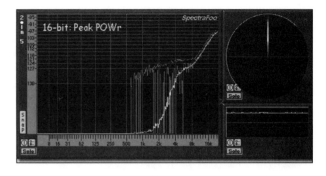

Crane Song Analog Dither CD

Crane Song is a maker of high-quality digital audio processors that try to emulate characteristics of analog processing and tube devices. The CD contains dither signals as audio files that can be placed in a DAW as another track of audio. When mixed in at the proper level, the audio files provide dithering that emulates a warmer, more analog sound. You must use your own ears to decide if this enhances your audio (see www.cranesong.com).

❋ LISTENING TO DITHER

Because dither affects very low-level details, it can sometimes be difficult to discern between different types of dither. One technique used to help you notice the effects of dithering is to use an audio signal that is very low in level and monitor it very loud. Try this: Put one of your favorite mixes in your DAW. Turn its level down by 40dB or so by using the channel fader. By adjusting the fader, you have applied a DSP function and caused a calculation to be performed on the audio signal, thereby increasing its word length. In order for the signal to be played back through your converters, the bit depth must be reduced back to its previous size. Turn on the internal dither (if available) or insert a plug-in on the master channel of your DAW that has dithering (Waves L1 or L2, POW-r, UV-22, and so on). You will have to turn up your monitor system to hear the audio at a reasonable level. This will bring up the level of the dithering result.

Now you can listen to the result and determine which type of dither yields the most detail and best sound for that type of program material. Rock music might sound better with a certain type of dither than does classical piano, for example. Also, try turning the dither off and see what a difference straight truncation makes. This can be a very revealing experiment. For additional information and some actual audio files demonstrating various dither techniques, please visit: http://www.mtsu.edu/~dsmitche/rim420/reading/rim420_Dither.html

---

Dithering and DSP

Whenever DSP is performed to an audio signal, mathematical functions such as addition, multiplication, and others are applied to the data stream. Each time a function is applied to the number stream, the results can, and usually do, have a greater bit depth than the original signal. These extra bits must be dealt with in order to return the signal to its original bit depth. Truncation, with or without dither, is the usual method of accomplishing this.

The point to understand in all of this is that whenever *any type of alteration, processing, or bit reduction* is applied to a digital audio signal, truncation occurs afterwards. If properly done, dithering should be part of this step. Without it, noise and distortion can be added to the signal. This applies to plug-ins as well. Because plug-ins alter audio signals, they require truncation before moving on to the next plug-in or section of the audio software mixer.

Many plug-ins have internal processing depths that far exceed the depth of the audio software you are using. For example, many of the plug-ins made by Waves use internal processing at the 48-bit level. Once audio has been processed, the 48-bit signal must be reduced to the native bit depth in order to continue through the audio software.

Quite often, no dither signal will be added when working in 24-bit systems as signal passes through various stages of processing within the DAW. The inherent noise in most audio signals is sufficient enough to dither a 24-bit signal by itself. Also, dithering requires DSP resources and, if possible, developers prefer not to use any resources that are not necessary.

Digital Audio Signal Processing (DSP)

In addition to being able to store audio in the form of numbers, digital audio can also be used in mathematical equations in order to manipulate the numbers for various purposes. For example, if an audio signal passing through a channel in a DAW's virtual mixer has its gain modified in any way (the fader has been moved away from the null point of 0dB), a mathematical process has been applied to that signal.

Any time the numbers that represent audio signals are modified in any way, by mathematical manipulation, digital signal processing has been performed.

There are several types of audio processing that can be grouped together as a function of what elements of the audio signal are altered. Understanding what processors are similar in this fashion can help you use them to their fullest extent, and even help you create new types of processors by using standard ones in non-standard ways. Here are the commonly grouped processor types.

Gain Processing

Gain processors affect the volume of audio signals in various ways. They can do so as a function of time, frequency, or statically.

The simplest form of this type of processor is a static gain adjustment such as a fader on a mixing console (or virtual mixer in a DAW). By changing the volume of an audio signal passing through that channel, you are applying gain processing. By adding gain (moving the fader up), you are increasing the values of each sample of audio that passes through this processor.

REDUCING THE WORD LENGTH

Most any computation of an audio signal results in a numeric remainder that must be included in the data, thereby increasing its word length. At some point, word length reduction must take place in order for the signal to return to its previous bit depth.

Gain processors that adjust the gain as a function of the input signal over time are called *dynamics processors*. They range from plug-ins that reduce the overall dynamic range, such as compressors and limiters, to ones that increase the dynamic range such as gates and expanders.

There are even more specialized dynamics processors that only affect certain frequencies, such as de-essers and multi-band dynamics processors.

Frequency Processing

Frequency processing is the adjustment of the level of frequency bands within the audio signal itself. The most obvious example of this is the equalizer. Equalizers selectively increase or decrease the volume of certain frequencies and tonal areas of sound. There are several types of equalizer filters that do various types of adjustments. Each one is explored in Chapter 5.

Recent development in plug-in technology has also led to processing that can analyze the effects of outboard equipment such as analog equalizers. The result can be stored as a preset and used to process digital audio. The Waves Q-Clone plug-in is the best example of this. Figure 1.8 shows the frequency response curve of an external equalizer that Q-Clone has analyzed. That response curve is then applied to any signals going through the Q-Clone plug-in.

Figure 1.8

The Waves Q-Clone plug-in displaying the response curve of an analyzed external equalizer.

Time-Domain Processing

Time-domain processing involves the temporary storage of portions of the audio signal in order to be replayed at a later time. The simplest form is the delay or echo effect. This processor, at its most basic level, stores a copy of the audio signal for a certain time and then plays it back, usually mixed with the original signal to form the echo effect.

Reverb processors work under the same principles, but create many thousands of delays to achieve the reverb effect of a room or hall sound. More complex forms of this processor type include *pitch-shifting,* which involves speeding up or slowing down the stored audio very quickly in order to change its pitch.

Convolution and Modeling

One of the more recent developments in audio DSP is the convolution or modeling processor. Convolution processors can mimic the sound of actual analog devices or acoustic spaces. They do this by using what is known as an *impulse response.* An impulse response is a recording of the actual device or acoustic space. This recording is analyzed by the convolution processor and then applied to incoming audio signals. The result is audio that sounds like it was played through the device or in the acoustic space itself.

Combination Processors

Many of today's plug-ins use more than one type of processing to achieve the desired effect. For example, multi-band dynamics processors use a combination of frequency processing and gain processing to control the dynamics of different frequency bands. A complex plug-in such as the UAD-1 Nigel guitar amplifier simulator can use all types of processing to achieve realistic guitar sounds. Gain, EQ, room sound (reverb), and even convolution modeling might be used to create a specific guitar tone.

As there is no one way to group these types of plug-ins; descriptions of different combination processors are found throughout this book as they relate to the topics at hand.

Summary

Digital audio has come a long way since Harry Nyquist began formulating his theories on sampling. The technology has revolutionized how audio is created and manipulated. On of the most revolutionary technological advances has been the evolution of plug-ins. No longer is one developer responsible for creating an entire audio-processing chain within one application. With plug-ins, many developers can join forces to provide more and better DSP tools for every DAW.

2 Plug-in Technology

Plug-in DSP technology has expanded into many different audio production tools. From the familiar computer workstations such as Pro Tools and Nuendo, to digital consoles such as the Yamaha 01V96 and the Mackie DXB, DSP plug-ins are being used everywhere. With so many different ways to apply DSP, there is a lot of confusion between the different formats. With VST, RTAS, and Audio Units to HTDM, UAD, and PowerCore, plug-ins vary from platform to platform, each one having its own strengths and weaknesses. This chapter explores each plug-in host format in detail and discusses the merits of each.

Understanding the Plug-In Formats for PCs

Personal computers that run the Microsoft Windows operating system are commonly referred to as "PCs." This is from the original name of the first IBM personal computer release called the "PC." For the purposes of this book, whenever references to "PCs" are made, it is directed to computers that are using a Microsoft operating system, most commonly Windows XP.

VST

Steinberg created their Virtual Studio Technology (VST) for early versions of Cubase. This technology allowed digital audio to be processed within the computer in many varied ways. It can be used to create audio from pre-recorded samples, generate synthetic sounds using wavetable synthesis among others, and process any of this audio with DSP such as faders, equalizer, delays, and more.

VST is probably the most widely used audio DSP technology today. With so many applications supporting the VST specification and the proliferation of Windows-based computers, VST has many users across the globe. The VST specification is available to anyone who wants to create his or her own VST plug-in. This opens up the playing field to developers from all areas of audio. There are a great many varied VST plug-ins out there. There are free ones, expensive ones, bad ones, good ones, efficient ones, and not so efficient ones.

Q & A WITH YVAN GRABIT OF STEINBERG ON VST TECHNOLOGY

Q: How did you get into designing audio DSP technology?

A: After my studies in engineering for electronics and image processing in Paris, I worked for three years at Aerospatiale (the French equivalent of NASA) on imaging DSP. Then I had the possibility of moving to Hamburg, Germany and working at Steinberg (originally, the motivation for the move was a German woman). That was my first contact with audio processing. Then I helped develop plug-ins and surround tools for Nuendo 1.0 (around eight years ago).

Q: Who came up with the idea of VST and why?

A: The initial application was Cubase Audio, which ran with TDM, then with the Yamaha CBX-D5, and later on the Atari Falcon. Then the first PowerPC Macs arrived (clocked at 60MHz) and the idea came up to use this power and built-in audio hardware for native audio processing. The graphics were also enhanced and we added some effects. It was like a logical evolution, with more processor power meaning more integration of studio features in the computer.

Q: Were plug-ins part of the original design? If not, when did they come about?

A: The VST programming interface was designed because there were repeated functions when we did the very first effects (reverb, chorus, stereo echo, and autopanner). So initially it was just for use as a development tool within Steinberg. Later, the VST plug-in interface was made public. It allowed anyone to create VST plug-ins very easily.

Q: What was the major problem to overcome during this process of creating VST?

A: Processing power, memory limitation, and disk streaming, to name just a few. I think we've got those sorted now, though.

Q: How long did it take to develop VST from the initial idea to complete product?

A: Coming over to native processing from TDM was a continuous process. The idea of VST as a way to describe a number of components based on native processing such as mixer, graphics, and effects arose in around 1994. In a way, it was a complete product then, but of course a lot has happened since those early days—mainly opening up the interface, and the appearance of VST Instruments with VST SDK 2.0—to further enhance the virtual studio right up until the present day.

Q: Did you anticipate how VST technology would take off? Was it surprising?

A: Yes and no. When we had our first complete "studio" with audio tracks, the mixer, and effects running natively we felt this had to be a revolution. But it was surprising how incredibly well the VST plug-in API was received (as mentioned above, it was not initially planned for public use). The hundreds of plug-ins that were released in a very short time exceeded even our expectations.

Q: What inspires you to create new technology like this?

A: Just have look at the price and the limitations of hardware such as mixers and effect hardware. The inspiration was and is to rebuild a studio in a computer (Virtual Studio Technology) and make it better and more flexible to give the musician more space for their creativity.

Q: What technology are you following in anticipation of the next great DSP idea?

A: That's difficult to say, but I think we have to follow a lot of technology direction from CPU evolution (like multiple core processors) to wavelet tools, with perhaps some neuronal networking.

Q: Do you feel that native processing is the future or dedicated hardware-based?

A: Steinberg's philosophy was always built around the concept of native processing and with the evolution of the processor power and networking; I will say that native processing is only at the beginning of a very long life.

Q: What is the most important tool for the DSP designer?

A: There are many, but perhaps the most used is Matlab (or equivalent like Octave) and a good host application like WaveLab, for example.

> ❄ *Q: Do you think plug-ins and computer audio have improved audio productions?*
>
> A: Plug-ins and sequencers have allowed more creativity by opening up new ways of creatively working with sound. They also allow more complexity, such as working with lots of automation, and they also allow many user-friendly features such as Undo/Redo. All this allows a different approach to composing, arranging, and mixing music. And an another big change is that a non-musician is now capable of making music without any specific skill in audio and without having to invest a lot of money.
>
> *Q: What has been the largest effect of VST and other computer audio technology?*
>
> A: At Steinberg as VST Sampler effect I will say HALion and all its derived products (TheGrand, StringEdition).
>
> *Q: What are the negatives of plug-in technology?*
>
> A: . . . [hum] . . . perhaps the success of VST and the large number of available plug-ins which are not all of high quality.
>
> *Q: What have you enjoyed the most about creating and improving VST?*
>
> A: Probably the feedback from users of VST and from developers. It's a great feeling that we share something together like a big family.

All VST Instruments and effects pass audio data along in 32-bit floating-point data . There is no limit as to the sample rate. In the VST 2 specification, support was added for surround sound and the capability to use MIDI input to trigger audio events for VST Instruments and MIDI tempo synchronization to help set delay times and other parameters to musical values.

There are many audio applications that support the use of VST plug-ins. Figure 2.1 shows the mixer in Nuendo, Steinberg's flagship DAW.

Figure 2.1

The Mixer window in Nuendo. Nuendo supports the VST specification and has a 32-bit floating-point audio engine.

Here are a few of the more popular applications:ere are a few of the more popular applications:

* Cubase/Nuendo
* Cakewalk Sonar
* Samplitude
* Wavelab
* Sound Forge
* Vegas
* Ableton Live
* Mackie Tracktion
* Acid Pro

It is possible to use VST plug-ins in other applications using what is known as a *wrapper*. The wrapper is a piece of software that translates the VST plug-in into whatever the host application can use. Audioease (www.audioease.com) has created VSTWrapper that translates VST plug-ins into MOTU Audio System (MAS) plug-ins for use in Digital Performer. FXpansion (www.fxpansion.com) has created VST wrappers for Apple's Audio Units and Digidesign's RTAS plug-in formats. With so many VST plug-ins available, these wrappers have allowed the use of VST to extend to other audio platforms.

Audio applications that use VST for plug-ins typically use the host computer's CPU for processing. The speed and power of that CPU will determine how much DSP or how many plug-ins can run on the system. Bear in mind that each plug-in uses a different amount of DSP resources. For example, a basic equalizer such as the NuendoEQ shown in Figure 2.2, uses very little CPU power, whereas the impulse modeling plug-in, SIR, uses a great deal of CPU power to convolve audio, shown in Figure 2.3.

Figure 2.2

The NuendoEQ uses a fairly small amount of DSP.

Figure 2.3

The SIR impulse modeling plug-in uses a great deal of DSP power.

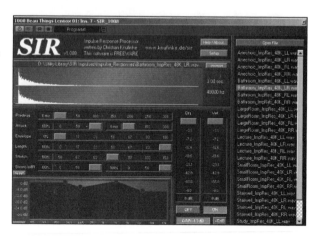

The following lists some valuable resources on the Web for learning more about VST plug-ins and instruments:

❋ List of free VST plug-ins—http://www.sadglad.com/freevstplugins6.html

❋ Information resource for VST plug-ins and instruments—http://www.kvraudio.com/

DirectX (DX)

DirectX technology was created by Microsoft to enable software designers to interact directly with the hardware of a computer without having to write machine code. For audio, DirectX allows access to special processors within the computer, especially the floating-point processor, for audio DSP. The advantage of DirectX is that just about any application running on a Windows operating system has access to hardware-level processing without writing tricky specialized code. Just about every audio software tool that runs on a Windows machine can use DirectX plug-ins.

Using Plug-In Formats for Apple Macintosh

Apple computers running Macintosh operating system have long been known for their preference among creative people. With the early adoption of the Graphical User Interface (GUI) and the mouse, Apple was at the forefront of modern computer operating systems. Apple computers come preloaded with many multimedia applications ranging from photography libraries to audio and video editing. GarageBand and SoundTrack are the latest additions to Apple OSX's audio software.

There are two plug-in types that are exclusive to the Apple operating system (OSX): Apple's own proprietary audio plug-in format called Audio Units and another made by Mark of the Unicorn, developers of Digital Performer.

Audio Units

Audio Units is a plug-in protocol made for OSX. It takes advantage of OSX's built-in audio technology (CoreAudio), and the audio hardware included with all Apple computers. Using CoreAudio, the plug-ins written using the Audio Unit protocol become available to any OSX application, similar to DirectX on Windows machines.

The Audio Units protocol supports sample rates up to 192kHz, and support multi-channel audio streams with 24-bit depths. The idea is that the audio system and plug-ins are integrated to the operating system rather than added to individual audio software, making them usable by any application in the computer, such as video editing software. Having the audio system available to this type of application can help video editors create more sophisticated soundtracks. Most plug-in developers have created Audio Unit versions of their plug-ins.

MOTU Audio System (MAS)

Mark of the Unicorn (MOTU) has been making MIDI and audio software since 1984 with the debut of Performer in 1985. Through the years, MOTU has been a leader in MIDI and digital audio software, providing the first integration of audio and MIDI in one application on an Apple computer with the advent of Digital Performer.

Digital Performer, shown in Figure 2.4, has its own proprietary plug-in technology known as the MOTU Audio System, or MAS for short. MAS plug-ins only run inside Digital Performer on Apple computers. The internal processing of MAS is now up to 64-bit floating-point, providing a high degree of fidelity and resolution. Most plug-in developers create MAS version of their plug-ins, but the variety of MAS is not nearly as wide as VST.

Figure 2.4

The Digital Performer Mixer window.

VST Mac

Steinberg has made the VST specification compatible with OSX operating systems and CoreAudio. VST, combined with ASIO drivers for audio hardware, creates a powerful mix of DSP facilities on Macintosh computers.

Pro Tools

And who could forget Pro Tools? Well, no one can at this point. Digidesign has been at the forefront of digital audio technology from the debut of their application, Sound Designer, in 1985. Originally created as a sample editor for the EMU-II samplers, Sound Designer took off and became a full-fledged two-track editing station widely used in professional recording studios. Over the years, Digidesign evolved their technology and created some of the most industry changing products in audio. Pro Tools (originally called Sound Tools) was the first known "tapeless studio" where all recording and mixing was done "in the box."

In 1994, Pro Tools III was released offering plug-in support for third-party plug-ins. This opened the floodgates for all types of DSP developers to create interesting plug-ins for a very popular application. This arrangement allowed for greater innovation among developers because they did not have to deal with maintaining the application, only creating one small piece of DSP code that could be used within Pro Tools. That is what we are here to talk about: Plug-ins.

TDM

Time Division Multiplexing is the technology that has allowed Pro Tools to become the versatile audio editor, recorder, and mixing system all in one. The TDM technology allows PCI cards in a computer to route audio between the hard disks, mixer channels and DSP without using the host CPU for these tasks. With this modular approach, audio can be routed through Pro Tools hardware cards and processed in a variety of ways with the added capability to scale the size of the mixer when needed. This is done through the use of dedicated audio processing PCI cards.

Each card contains several Motorola DSP chips that perform various DSP functions based on the setup of the current audio session. The chips themselves do the processing, not the host computer. One chip might be running the mixer engine and another might be running several plug-ins. If more processing power is needed, simply add more DSP cards to the system. None of these DSP functions tax the host CPU at all. All the work is performed on the DSP cards. In Figure 2.5, the DSP usage of a Pro Tools HD2 system is displayed. You can see how plug-ins are spread out over several DSP chips on the Pro Tools Core and Accel cards.

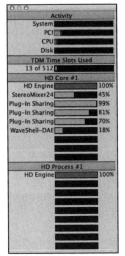

Figure 2.5

The Pro Tools DSP Usage Display showing plug-in usage across several DSP chips.

Digidesign did the smart thing and opened up the TDM technology to third-party developers to create various plug-ins that can be used on the proprietary hardware. This has helped Pro Tools become a leader in the industry. Many plug-in designers created TDM plug-ins for Pro Tools. Some developers do this exclusively and do not release their plug-ins in other formats, such as VST. Eventide, Princeton Digital and others have created plug-ins exclusively for TDM systems. Although host-based systems are gaining in speed and DSP capacity every day, hardware-based systems such as TDM still have an advantage when tremendous amounts of DSP are required without additional latency.

Audiosuite

Audiosuite plug-ins are Pro Tools plug-ins that are performed offline, not in the mixer. They do not get processed in real-time as do plug-ins in the mixer. Audiosuite plug-ins actually create new audio files on disk. The only time the CPU is used is while the new file is created. Once the audio file is written to disk, the CPU resources are available again.

Usually, there are Audiosuite versions of all plug-ins in a Pro Tools system. There are also some plug-ins that are only Audiosuite because of the nature of their processing. The main example of this is the Time Compression/Expansion Audiosuite plug-in shown in Figure 2.6. Because this plug-in changes the length of audio files, it cannot work in real-time because its processing algorithm affects timing.

Figure 2.6

The Time Compression/Expansion Audiosuite Plug-in in Pro Tools.

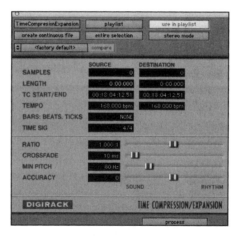

RTAS (Real-Time Audiosuite)

As the name implies, RTAS plug-ins work in real-time within the Pro Tools mixer. Unlike TDM plug-ins, they use the host CPU for processing. RTAS plug-ins were originally developed for Pro Tools LE, which runs entirely on the host CPU.

The use of RTAS plug-ins is limited in two ways. The speed of the host CPU determines how many plug-ins you can use before the entire system is taxed to its limits. In the hardware setup of Pro Tools, shown in Figure 2.7, the user can determine how much of the CPU can be used for host processing. Limiting the CPU usage can help minimize problems in other areas of the software such as screen redraws and general sluggishness of a system performing at its limits.

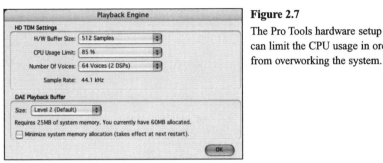

Figure 2.7

The Pro Tools hardware setup window, where you can limit the CPU usage in order to avoid errors from overworking the system.

The second limitation of RTAS plug-ins occurs when using them on a TDM system. They can only be used prior to TDM plug-ins on disk tracks. They cannot be used on Aux tracks or Master faders. The reason for this is that in order to compensate for the CPU delays that RTAS plug-ins generate, the audio must be pre-loaded or buffered earlier in order to remain in time with the other audio signals in the mixer. Once the audio has entered the TDM realm, it cannot be processed by RTAS plug-ins.

HTDM

HTDM (Host TDM) plug-ins are simply TDM plug-ins that can be run on the host CPU. They use a gateway from a TDM chip to go to the host CPU to be processed and then return back to the TDM chips. The benefits of HTDM are that the limitations of RTAS are no longer there. HTDM plug-ins can be used on Aux tracks and Master faders and can be inserted after other TDM plug-ins. Also, unlike RTAS they can accept external side-chaining inputs. HTDM provides the user with a way to utilize the host CPU power without sacrificing the flexibility of TDM routing.

The only detractor of HTDM plug-ins is they generate latency that cannot be compensated for in the Pro Tools mix engine.

Dedicated Hardware DSP

There are other hardware DSP solutions out there. Pro Tools is not the only DAW that can use dedicated DSP cards. Products from Universal Audio, TC Electronics, and Waves all provide DSP to computer-based audio software. In addition, digital mixing consoles also have DSP capability. They can have onboard effects processors, equalizing and dynamics on every channel. There are even network-based systems to distribute DSP over several computers.

UAD-1

Universal Audio brought innovation to the DSP market when creating the UAD-1 Powered Plug-in DSP card. It is a single PCI card that processes audio and returns it to the host application. UA makes a proprietary line of plug-ins that run on the UAD-1 card shown in Figure 2.8. These plug-ins gained popularity in VST systems that being host-based, were sorely in need of some hardware solutions to increase the amount of processing that was done on one system.

The UAD-1 card is compatible with Windows and Mac OSX operating systems. Additionally, through the use of a software wrapper, the UAD-1 can be used with Pro Tools as RTAS plug-ins.

Figure 2.8

The UAD-1 PCI card by Universal Audio processes plug-ins designed just for this card.

With its long history developing some of the greatest audio gear made, UA was in a unique position to start creating plug-ins that emulated older analog equipment that has stood the test of time, such as the 1176 Limiting Amplifier shown in Figure 2.9. UAD-1 powered plug-ins sound and look like their hardware counterparts. Meticulous modeling of the functions in classic hardware processors led to their innovative plug-in designs.

The emulation of vintage equipment is something that you see with a growing number of plug-in developers. By all accounts, the UAD-1 does a fine job emulating such vintage favorites as the LA-2A Opto Compressor and the legendary Fairchild 670 Compressor.

Figure 2.9

The famous 1176 Limiting Amplifier as modeled by Universal Audio for the UAD-1 card.

UA has not only limited development of plug-ins to just vintage equipment, but also creates stunning all-new plug-ins such as the Cambridge EQ and the Precision Limiter. These plug-in tools take full advantage of the resolution of modern digital recording.

TC PowerCore

TC Electronics has been making digital audio equipment for over 20 years. With their work in delay, reverb and other time-based processing, a DSP card with TC algorithms is a must for any professional studio to have. To that end, TC created the PowerCore line of DSP processing. The original PowerCore PCI card works in much the same way as the UAD-1 card does. The DSP operations take place on Motorola DSP chips on the card thereby relieving the host CPU of those demanding tasks.

TC has expanded the PowerCore line to take advantage of FireWire technology with the PowerCore FireWire and PowerCore Compact units, shown in Figures 2.10 and 2.11. Both of these units connect to the host CPU via FireWire connections. This allows easier connection and disconnection without having to open the computer to put a PCI card in or take it out. It makes for a more portable and flexible solution.

Figure 2.10
The TC Electronics PowerCore FireWire DSP processing unit.

Figure 2.11
The more portable PowerCore Compact unit.

Yamaha Digital Mixers

No discussion of DSP technology is complete without talking about digital hardware mixers. Yamaha has been making digital mixers since 1986 with the introduction of the DMP7, and has broken ground with some of the most innovating products such as the original 02R digital mixer.

Inside any digital mixer is a whole plethora of DSP including mixing (gain), equalizing, compression, delay, and reverb, plus many other specialty processors. Digital mixers perform many of the same functions as a DAW in terms of DSP and mixing. Each channel on the Yamaha 01V96, shown in Figure 2.12, has an equalizer, gate, compressor, and delay built-in.

Figure 2.12

The Yamaha 01V96 digital mixer.

In addition to the built-in channel processing, the 01V96 has four effects processors that can do anything from reverb and delays to distortion modeling and dynamic filters. These effects can be used as send effects or as inserts for channels, buses, and outputs. Digital routing makes the console very flexible and every setting can be stored for instant recall.

In addition to the effects that come with Yamaha digital mixers, optional effects packages can be purchased and added to the console as a software package. An optional Waves processing card (Y56K) brings the renowned sound of Waves plug-ins to the hardware world of digital mixers. Simply putting this card in an available Mini-YGDAI slot allows the console to utilize many Waves plug-ins as inserts on channels or as send effects. The flexibility of digital hardware allows for this type of expansion and upgrading.

❋ **YAMAHA PACKAGES**

Software updates and optional add-on effects packages are available for the entire line of Yamaha digital mixers at http://www.yamahaproaudio.com.

❋ **YAMAHA AND STEINBERG'S STUDIO CONNECTIONS PROJECT**

In the interests of fully integrating studio setups to include all hardware used during a session, Yamaha and Steinberg have joined forces to create a system by which all settings for each piece of hardware in a studio can be saved within the song or session file stored on the computer. To that end, Yamaha digital mixers can be connected to the host computer via USB or MIDI and communicate directly with DAW software such as Nuendo. All parameters of the console become addressable by the computer so that each can be saved along with the Nuendo data to one file on the computer. When opening the project file at a later date, all settings can be returned to their saved values eliminating the tedious process of resetting mixers and other outboard gear each time a project is worked on. As more vendors join, more pieces of gear can become integrated in the studio setup, requiring less work from the engineer. Visit www.studio-connections.com for more information.

Mackie DXB

Since the advent of the D8B, Mackie has been invested in digital consoles and DSP technology. The next generation Digital X Bus (DXB) console, shown in Figure 2.13, reflects the added freedom that open architecture designs can have. In addition to being able to mix and process audio with Mackie's own DSP algorithms, the DXB also supports VST plug-ins from Waves and Universal Audio. The UAD-1 card can actually be installed inside the DXB.

Figure 2.13

The Mackie Digital X Bus Console featuring VST and UAD-1 plug-in support.

The DXB is configurable with different input and output cards to meet the needs of a particular studio. Also, every component that is related to the sample rate is upgradeable to meet future audio requirements such as DVD post-production and hi-resolution audio.

Focusrite Liquid Channel

Focusrite has a fine history in audio. Their outboard gear is found in the cream of the crop studios around the world. In an effort to create the next generation of outboard gear using digital technology, they created the Focusrite Liquid Channel.

The Liquid Channel uses convolution technology to model classic and vintage mic preamp and compressors to create the ultimate recording chain that changes as the session dictates. Need a warm tube preamp coupled with a classic Neve compressor? Dial it in and you're ready to go. For more information, visit http://www.ffliquid.com.

Waves Network Box

Waves plug-ins are probably the most popular of plug-in brands out there and with good reason. Waves has been at the forefront of plug-ins technology, creating the plug-ins that we have all come to enjoy and use everyday. In staying on the edge of the latest technology, Waves has created a dedicated DSP processor box that runs their plug-ins on custom designed DSP chips. This helps eliminate the strain on the host computer's CPU while mixing with a large amount of Waves plug-ins.

The APA32, shown in Figure 2.14, and APA44-M work over standard Ethernet connections. Multiple units can be used to increase the amount of DSP power available. With multiple units, several computers on the network can share the DSP power. Any of the Waves plug-ins can be run locally on the host CPU or transferred to the remote DSP box.

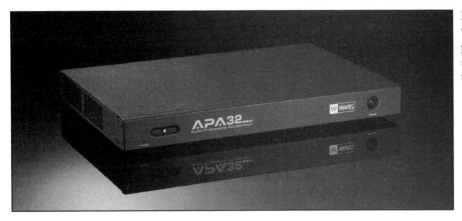

Figure 2.14
The Waves APA32 dedicated plug-in processor works on standard Ethernet connections.

❈ DISTRIBUTED AUDIO PROCESSING

Both the Waves AMV and FX Teleport are examples of distributed processing, where tasks are split up among multiple processing devices. You might be familiar with the SETI screensaver program (SETI at Home: http://setiathome.ssl.berkeley.edu/), by which your personal computer can be used by SETI to process a small bit of radio telescope data to search for any signals that might be a sign of life elsewhere in the universe. Millions of personal computers have been used during their idle times (while the screensaver is on) to process an immense amount of telescope data for SETI without incurring significant costs. The same holds true for audio processing. Multiple processors to distribute the DSP load can increase any systems capacity for plug-ins. FX Teleport allows up to four computers to process plug-ins for one DAW system using Ethernet. Granted, each computer costs money, but older systems that might otherwise go unused can now be utilized to add DSP power to one main system (do you have an old computer lying around collecting dust?). This approach might be the future of audio processing.

FX Teleport

FX Teleport (www.fxteleport.com) is a unique system of plug-in processing that uses networked computers to process plug-ins for a host DAW system. It uses standard Ethernet connections to send audio and MIDI data to connected computers for audio processing. No audio hardware or other DAW software is required on the slave computers. The system currently only works with Windows operating systems and VST plug-ins. The plug-ins themselves must be installed on the slave computer along with the FX Teleport software.

With several computers networked together, a great deal of DSP power becomes available to the host DAW system. Older computers that might otherwise be unused can now add power to another computer without any additional hardware.

Latency in Host versus Hardware DSP Systems

Any DSP operation takes time, processing time. The speed of the chip and how many other operations it is doing at the same time determine how long a certain DSP operation takes. This amount of time is referred to as *latency*. As more DSP operations are added, latency can increase if no more processing chips are available. On host-based systems, this is a concern when recording live musicians, because the delay can cause timing errors. With DSP card systems like Pro Tools and hardware mixers such as the 01V96, the latency is minimized by adding dedicated DSP chips so that each additional DSP operation is handled by another processor instead of causing more latency and delay in the host processor. The trade-off is cost. Adding multiple DSP cards or a digital mixer to your system can get costly, whereas faster CPUs are getting less expensive every day.

With host-based systems such as Nuendo, additional DSP operations are handled by multiplexing data through the processor asynchronously, and then re-aligning the audio after processing. Each additional DSP operation is handled by using more CPU cycles and thereby increasing the delay. Theoretically, any amount of DSP can be performed this way, but the reality of the increased delays and the memory needed to store or buffer the audio while processing cycles take place limit the amount of DSP that one processor can handle.

Plug-in Processing Delays and Compensation

The other issue at hand here involves delays within the audio mixer that can affect the phase relationships between multiple tracks in a mix. If you route a signal, such as a snare drum, to two mixer channels and process one channel with a compressor plug-in that causes a certain amount of latency, the processed one will be delayed by this amount relative to the unprocessed channel. Combining these signals can cause unintended results, such as comb filtering or even audible delay in systems with high latency amounts.

Now, contemplate a large complex mixdown configuration with multiple signal paths, auxiliary returns, plug-ins inserted on individual channels, groups, and master outputs with all the delay possibilities. The results can be overwhelming. Channels that are precisely related to one another, such as drum microphones, might lose those relationships once plug-ins have been inserted on one or more of those channels.

To continue with this example, if the overhead microphones of a drum kit recording are processed by a plug-in that causes any amount of latency, the sound of the drum kit can change drastically. In an extreme case, the overhead sound might be audibly delayed from the close mic sounds, causing slap-back, or echo effect, in the drum mix. Unless this is desired, it might be necessary to avoid processing at all.

In the past, audio engineers had to compensate for these delays or limit their routing flexibility in order to avoid problems mixing. This involved measuring the latency caused by certain plug-ins and then adding delays to other channels to keep them in line with the processed audio tracks. As you can imagine, this was complex and tedious, not to mention harmful to creativity in the studio!

All the calculation necessary for compensating for plug-in delays can be automated by the host application. Nuendo was the first popular DAW to implement plug-in delay compensation. The audio engine is notified whenever a plug-in is inserted on any channel. Because the latency of most plug-ins is known, it can be reported to the engine, which in turn delays all other audio streams so that they stay in perfect time alignment with the processed signals. In more complex mixer arrangements, this calculation can get very complicated. Because the calculations are handled by software, it appears seamless to the user. Most professional DAWs (Pro Tools, Nuendo, Digital Performer, SONAR, and so on) currently have plug-in delay compensation.

Native versus Hardware DSP

With all this technology available, DSP solutions exist for most audio professionals' needs. The future holds nothing but promise for even more DSP capacity and diversity, allowing advanced audio processing in more places and with less trouble than ever before. Native processing is fast becoming as powerful as the best dedicated hardware and the future lies in the personal computer. The capability to change with the technology gives native processing the advantage over time. Computer technology evolves so often that having to change dedicated hardware can be costly and not necessary. However, today's hardware systems, most notably Pro Tools HD, still have more power and less latency than the best native systems. So, for those with a no-compromise approach, consider the power hardware systems have to offer.

Summary

Thankfully, the issue of plug-in delay compensation has been addressed for both hardware and native systems, allowing for a more even comparison between the two. Mixing outboard analog gear with internal DSP is also now a possibility with both types of systems. The integration of studio hardware and computer software continues to grow each day.

Plug-in technology will continue to expand and, with ideas such as distributed processing over multiple CPUs, the access to greater amounts of DSP will pave the way for more sophisticated plug-ins and fewer restrictions on their use. As native CPUs gain in speed and power, the need for dedicated DSP hardware will diminish. In essence, the host CPU and any networked CPUs will become the dedicated hardware.

3 } Plug-in Developers

Plug-in developers are the people who write the code that makes the plug-in. This is where the action is: with the plug-ins themselves. There are so many plug-in developers out there that this book cannot possibly cover them all, but the major developers are discussed as real-world examples of plug-in power and how this power can make your productions better.

Here is a rundown of some of the major plug-in developers and a brief background into what their plug-ins provide. For detailed information and usage tips, each of the following chapters use examples from these plug-ins to demonstrate the various forms of DSP (compressors, equalizers, and so on) and their functionality.

> ❄ **PAINTING WITH SOUND**
>
> Having a diverse collection of plug-ins helps mixes have a diverse and in-depth sound. Using the same plug-ins on all of your tracks can lead to a one-dimensional, flat sound. Having plug-ins that color the sound in unique ways can help provide separation among tracks in a mix. Even lower-quality effects can provide a welcome change in a mix with many other high-quality plug-ins. Having a collection of freeware plug-ins to add in the mix can provide you with a unique sound found nowhere else. Mixing can be like painting; you don't want to use just one color.

Waves

As mentioned before, Waves is arguably the largest and most popular plug-in developer around. Its line of plug-ins cover the entire spectrum of audio processing, from EQs to convolution reverbs using impulse modeling. From its early partnership between two men trying to make a digital vocoder, to the creation of the first audio plug-in, the Q10 Equalizer, and on to the entire line of Waves plug-ins, the story about Waves is an interesting one and best told by Gilad Keren, one of the founding partners, pictured in Figure 3.1 with Meir Shashua, the other founding partner.

Figure 3.1
Meir Shashua (left) and Gilad Keren (right), founders of Waves.

❄ Q & A WITH GILAD KEREN, FOUNDING PARTNER OF WAVES

Q: How did you get into making DSP plug-ins?

A: Waves was founded by Meir Shashua and myself. We met more than 20 years ago when I was a recording engineer and Meir was a musician. We both had been educated as engineers and were fascinated by vocoders and the new possibilities opened up by DSP [digital signal processing] technology, which was very new at the time.

We wanted to build a vocoder, and we realized that first we needed to create good digital filters, so we focused on digital filter implementation and ways to design them to work in real-time. That was around the time the first 24-bit audio DPS chip, the Motorola 56000, was launched, which enabled the kind of quality we were after. So we started work and came up with a product that evolved into our first plug-in, the Q10 equalizer.

That first product worked under Microsoft Windows version 2.0 on the PC, using a Motorola ADS board and Ariel A/D and D/A. When we first showed it at AES in 1990, the established manufacturers didn't want anything to do with an equalizer controlled by a graphical interface. In fact, many of them said that computers would never make it in the recording studio.

Meir and I worked briefly for a start-up company that was never able to bring the product to market, and they folded. We then realized that to create the kind of tools we wanted to make, we had to start our own company, so Waves was founded in 1992.

Q: Who came up with the idea of an audio plug-in?

A: It was an idea we worked out with Digidesign. They were very open to the idea of working with third-party software vendors who could make use of Digidesign hardware to provide added value for Digidesign system owners. With that encouragement, we took the product we had and turned it into the first ever audio plug-in, the Q10, released at the 1993 AES convention in New York.

Q: Did graphic programs like Photoshop influence you in this?

A: Yes, but the graphic program that used plug-ins and which influenced us at the time was Autocad.

Q: What was the major problem to overcome during this process of creating the first plug-in?

A: The business issues were the hardest, as no company wanted to let us have our own "widget."

Q: How long did it take to develop Q10 from the initial idea to complete product?

A: We had the Q10 concept around 1986. We had the code working by 1988 under DOS and later under Windows 1.0. We finally released Q10 as a plug-in in 1993, so the total development time was about seven years.

Q: What made the Q10 so unique at the time?

A: The Q10 was the first audio tool ever with a Graphical User Interface (GUI), and at the time people didn't realized how powerful that could be. We took advantage of using color in the interface, which added another level of control. With a GUI, you can gang controls and create complex EQ curves by dragging the dots around. This was impossible on any traditional interface. Our design proved so useful that now there are dozens of plug-ins that use the style of GUI we invented. Another innovation was that, unlike hardware, presets could be stored and also supplied with the product. In the case of the Q10, an extensive preset library was created by the late Michael Gerzon, one of the most highly regarded pioneers in audio. Michael also wrote the documentation. That library is still there, and is part of what makes the Q10 a classic tool.

Q: Did you anticipate how plug-in technology would take off?

A: Yes.

Q: Was it surprising?

A: No, but it was surprising that it would take over 10 years for the industry to really accept it.

Q: What inspires you to create a new plug-in?

A: We look to the past for inspiration from classic processors, including the sound of great classic hardware, and recently, great guitar amps and effects. We are also inspired by the future that digital technology enables—audio tools that are impossible to create in hardware. The L3 Multimaximizer is a good example.

Q: What technology are you following in anticipation of the next great DSP idea?

A: Michael Gerzon, who was a close friend, left a wealth of theoretical papers which we often look to for technological direction. Michael was ahead of his time with many of his ideas.

Q: What is the next great plug-in idea?

A: A digital smell processor.

Q: Do you feel that native processing is the future or hardware-based?

A: A combination of both. That's why we created our APA series. This allows people to connect one or more APA hardware units to their native system using standard Ethernet; the APA unit then handles the Waves plug-ins, taking a load off the CPU. I think the future is in solutions like this, where the processing power is handled by networked outboard units.

Q: What is the most important tool for the plug-in designer?

A: Mathematics, and a great understanding of the physics of sound and the psychology of hearing, otherwise known as psycho-acoustics.

Q: Do you think plug-ins have improved audio productions?

A: Yes, but they have also enabled people to go too far and to use powerful tools to abuse sound!

Q: What are the negatives of plug-in technology?

A: There is a staggering amount of information that we need to comprehend to build and use plug-in technology. This is not a minus—just a fact.

Q: What have you enjoyed the most about creating the Waves plug-ins?

A: I enjoy serving this industry, which I think is the most fun industry to work in. I also enjoy getting feedback, both good and bad, from our users.

The Waves line of plug-ins can separated into several categories, with common traits among each group.

The Basic Waves Plug-Ins

The basic group of Waves plug-ins includes tools that any audio engineer needs during the course of a typical audio project. They cover the basics.

The first Waves plug-in was the Q10 equalizer, shown in Figure 3.2, a fully parametric equalizer with high resolution and accuracy. This EQ is designed to be neutral in its sound and highly controllable for surgical EQ work.

Figure 3.2

The Waves Q10 Parametric Equalizer.

The C1 Parametric Compander, shown in Figure 3.3, is a fully controllable gate and compressor that has side-chain capabilities. This powerful tool does not color the sound but merely does whatever is needed to the dynamics of incoming signals. Capable of de-hissing, ducking, compression, limiting, expanding, side-chained de-essing, and more, the C1 is a quietly powerful DSP tool.

Figure 3.3

The Waves C1 Parametric Compander.

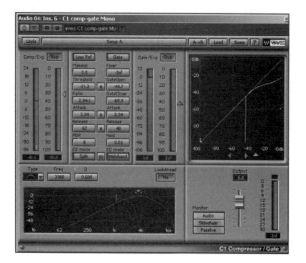

Continuing with basic tools, the DeEsser, shown in Figure 3.4, is a very useful plug-in, especially when working with vocals. Quite often, the high frequency EQ used on pop vocals can lead to excessive "s" sounds. The DeEsser is capable of compressing just those frequencies typical of human "s" sounds (4kHz–8kHz). It is a very fast compressor so that its artifacts are not as audible in the rest of the signal.

Figure 3.4
The Waves DeEsser.

For room simulation and reverb there is the TrueVerb plug-in, shown in Figure 3.5. This plug-in allows you to determine the reverb sound by setting the room size, frequency response, or damping, and the distance the listener is from the source. With those parameters, realistic room sounds, including early reflections, are created.

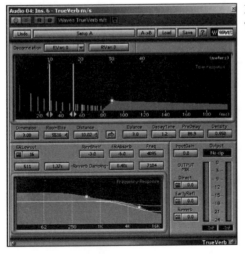

Figure 3.5
The Waves TrueVerb plug-in.

The L1 Ultramaximizer, shown in Figure 3.6, is a well-known limiting plug-in used primarily on finished mix files to increase the overall level without disturbing the dynamics of the audio. The L1 lets you remove transients in the signal that reduce the average level of the recording. By removing these peaks, the overall level can be brought up dramatically in many cases. The L1 also includes dithering for bit reduction of a final master file.

Figure 3.6
The Waves L1
Ultramaximizer.

THE LOUDNESS WARS

There is much discussion in the audio community about the overuse of the mastering limiter type of processing such as the L1. In the quest for louder and louder master recordings, limiters like this can be abused, creating overly distorted sound that has become the norm for popular music and even movie trailers. Producers have historically felt that the public perceives louder sounds as better. Radio stations have built-in processing that tries to maximize the broadcast signal of their station by doing many horrible and ugly things to the audio signal. When an overly compressed and limited record is broadcast through that same processor, bad things can happen. As a general rule of thumb for the L1, be careful not to have more than 3dB of gain reduction for most peaks to avoid distortion in your mix. The newer L2 processor is capable of more gain reduction without noticeable distortion, but many well-respected mastering engineers advise moderation.

The C4 Multi-band Compressor, shown in Figure 3.7, is a very powerful dynamics tool for shaping the overall sound in profound ways. It divides the signal into four frequency bands, each having a dynamics processor for compression or expansion. It is similar to having an equalizer that reacts dynamically to the audio signal. Each band can be compressed in different ways, thus providing control in one area without sacrificing the fidelity in another band.

Figure 3.7
The Waves C4 Multi-band
Compressor.

Waves Renaissance Series

The Waves Renaissance series of processors is one of the earliest attempts to emulate the sound of vintage analog equipment in plug-in form. This met with great success and it has become one of the most popular lines of plug-ins available.

The Renaissance Equalizer, shown in Figure 3.8, provides up to six bands of parametric EQ with a warmer, vintage sound. The filters are designed to respond like traditional analog and tube equipment. This is a workhorse of a plug-in that is useful on a variety of sounds.

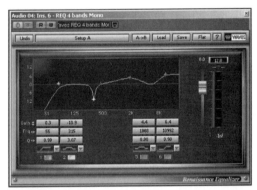

Figure 3.8

The Waves Renaissance Equalizer.

The Renaissance Compressor, shown in Figure 3.9, is designed to emulate vintage analog compressors, including the type of detector circuit used. In traditional analog compressors, either an optical or an electric circuit was used to detect the signal used for gain reduction. This detector had a great impact on the sound. The Renaissance Compressor allows you to choose which detector circuit you want, along with all the other standard compressor controls.

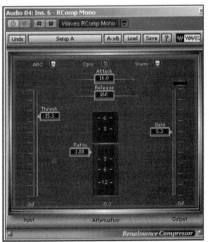

Figure 3.9

The Waves Renaissance Compressor.

Waves Linear Phase Mastering Tools

Adjusting an equalizer does more than change the levels of certain band of frequencies. Each gain change in one frequency has an effect in other frequencies. When using large amounts of EQ, the overall sound can suffer from the phase distortions. High-quality filter design can overcome these issues by creating minimum phase filters that do not disturb the internal phase relationships of an audio signal. This requires more DSP horsepower but can be very useful in mastering situations where conserving the overall quality of sound is paramount.

The Linear Phase series of plug-ins from Waves are designed with this in mind. The Linear Phase Equalizer, shown in Figure 3.10, has five general bands of EQ, plus a specialized low frequency filter. The sound of this plug-in is very transparent, perfect for equalizing full mixes.

Figure 3.10

The Waves Linear Phase Equalizer.

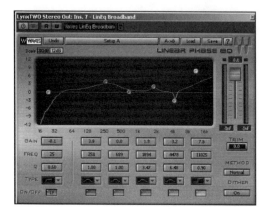

In keeping with the linear phase model, the Linear Multi-band plug-in, shown in Figure 3.11, works just like the C4 Multi-band compressor, but with linear filters that minimize phase distortion. This is another great tool for mastering.

Figure 3.11

The Waves Linear Multi-band plug-in.

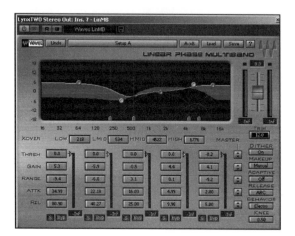

Last but certainly not least in this series is the L2 limiter, shown in Figure 3.12, successor to the L1 Ultramaximizer. This plug-in increases the overall level without creating audible distortion artifacts. By using linear phase filters, greater amounts of peak gain reduction can be achieved (upwards of 6dB or more, please see note about over-limiting masters) with less distortion. Also included are advanced IDR dithering options for bit depth reduction of a final mix.

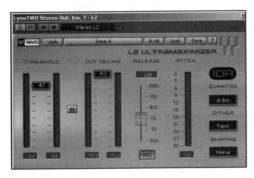

Figure 3.12

The Waves L2 limiter and dithering plug-in.

Waves Convolving and Modeling Plug-Ins

Recent additions to the Waves line involve convolution processing and impulse modeling. Using actual recordings of acoustic spaces and outboard gear allows modeling plug-ins to recreate their effects in the digital domain.

The IR-1 Parametric Convolution Reverb, shown in Figure 3.13, represents the most controllable impulse reverb yet. With adaptive analysis that separates early reflection from reverb tails in the impulse, the capability to shape the room sound to the needs of the moment has never been this flexible. The early reflection times can be altered to create the illusion that the room is larger or smaller without altering the reverb signature of the space. The actual impulse can be lengthened or shortened by modeling to alter the sound. There is also the IR-360, which is a multi-channel surround version of the IR-1.

Figure 3.13

The Waves IR-1 Parametric Convolution Reverb.

Using a patent-pending technology similar to impulse modeling, the Q-Clone plug-in, shown in Figure 3.14, can capture the sound of outboard equalizers and then recreate that setting in the plug-in. This allows one outboard EQ to be used on many tracks within the DAW. This can effectively give you an unlimited number of outboard EQs at your disposal.

Figure 3.14

The Waves Q-Clone modeling EQ plug-in.

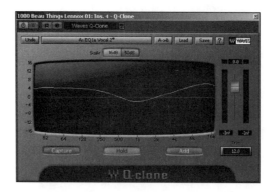

It works by sending a test signal through the outboard EQ, which accurately captures the response of the settings as they are. Once this test is done, the outboard gear may be removed from the signal chain and Q-Clone will take its place, sounding just like the real piece of gear. Now that's pretty cool.

Waves Restoration Tools

The Waves restoration tools are comprised of four plug-ins; X-Hum, X-Click, X-Crackle, and X-Noise. Each plug-in is designed to remove different types of noise. You can use them by themselves or as a team on really tough restoration or forensic audio processing.

The X-Hum tool, shown in Figure 3.15, contains a set of eight harmonically related *notch filters* (which are very narrow, frequency-specific equalizers) that can be tuned to AC line noise, air conditioner hum, and other constant sounds. Not only does X-Hum remove the fundamental hum sound but also removes the harmonics of that base tone so that all remnants of hum are removed.

Figure 3.15

The Waves X-Hum plug-in.

The X-Click tool is used to remove pops and clicks arising from old vinyl records or digital switching errors. It can be used in automatic mode or, for the best results, manually.

The X-Crackle tool is usually used after X-Click, to remove scratchiness, crackles, and surface noise from vinyl records.

Finally, the X-Noise tool, shown in Figure 3.16, removes broadband noise dynamically. It analyzes a sample of the noise floor in a recording, such as during a pause in the dialogue or before a musical passage. The analysis creates a noise profile for the recording. Then, using some of the standard dynamics controls, the noise is "gated" out and removed. Consider X-Noise to be a multi-band gate with a large amount of bands. Only noise in certain frequency bands is removed as needed, leaving the rest of the signal unaltered, thus preserving clarity.

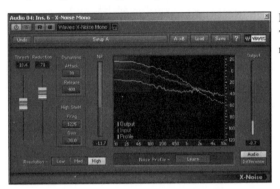

Figure 3.16

The X-Noise broadband noise reduction plug-in.

Waves Surround Tools

Surround sound provides its own set of challenges for DAW systems and plug-ins. Waves has created a suite of plug-ins to address many of these issues, including multi-channel compressors, limiters, panning tools, and bass-management monitoring tools.

The M360 Manager plug-in, shown in Figure 3.17, is designed for the master fader of a five channel or 5.1 channel mix. It allows calibration of surround speaker setups, including bass management for

Figure 3.17

Waves M360 Master Channel Surround plug-in.

satellite systems and the LFE channel. When subwoofers share duties of LFE and bass augmentation of smaller speakers, confusion can arise when calibrating these setups. The M360 also provides gain and delay settings for each channel so that speaker placement can be compensated for. Working in concert with the M360 Manager is the S360 Panner and Imager. These plug-ins precisely place sounds within a 360-degree soundstage. The Panner provides divergence, width, and rotation controls. The Imager uses early reflection modeling to place signals at certain distances within the surround soundstage.

Multi-channel dynamics processors are needed for surround mastering. The C360 is a surround compressor, whereas the L360 is a surround peak limiter based on the L1 and L2 technology. Each provides linked controls so that the same processing is applied to all channels in the surround mix. Channels can be grouped or unlinked as needed.

The R360 surround reverb and the already mentioned IR-360 provide modeled and convolution-based reverb and ambience for surround mixing. Each plug-in creates an enveloped soundstage with de-correlated channels. It is difficult to make a surround reverb using multiple stereo plug-ins due to the correlation factor. Using the same settings, the two stereo reverbs will have such a similar sound with the same source material that the surround reverb field will lose the three-dimensionality it can have. De-correlated channels provide envelopment that truly places you "there."

Waves Modulation and Delays Plug-Ins

For chorusing, flanging, delays, and other modulation toys, Waves offers several plug-ins. The Enigma plug-in, shown in Figure 3.18, is basically a modulated comb filter with resonance. You can create some very interesting effects with this beast.

Figure 3.18

The Waves Enigma plug-in.

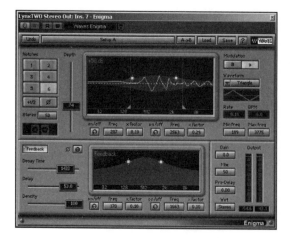

For delays, the SuperTap plug-in is a complete solution. With six individual delays up to six seconds long, the plug-in has Q10 filters for each tap and Waves unique rotation control to pan sounds throughout and beyond the stereo field. Feedback and resonance modulation controls expand the possibilities from a mere delay plug-in.

MondoMod takes advantage of the rotation processing where the phase of low frequencies is shifted or shuffled to create a moving sound source that can be subtle or drastic. There are modulation controls for the rotation settings and the plug-in can follow tempo information from a DAW.

Metaflanger does just what its name suggests; flanges, phases, choruses, emulates tape flanging, and more. There are presets for vintage boxes, such as the Mutron and MXR flangers.

UltraPitch is a six-voice pitch shifting plug-in designed to create harmonies or chorusing effects using multiple pitch shifts along with subtle delays and *formant* correction to reduce the "chipmunk" effect.

✳ FORMANTS

The *formant* of someone's voice is basically the harmonic structure of its sound. When pitch-shifting vocals, the formant usually shifted shifts right along with the pitch. This produces the familiar "chipmunk" effect when moving up in pitch, for example. Antares' Auto-Tune is an example of DSP that compensates for the formant shift and returns it to the original composition in order to retain the vocal character even during severe extreme pitch shifts (more than five semi-tones). Conversely, it is also possible to alter the formant without affecting the pitch, which will changes the character of the voice without tuning it. You could can make a woman sound like a man by lowering the formant range or make a tenor sax sound like a baritone in the same fashion.

Another interesting plug-in is the Doppler processor, shown in Figure 3.19. By using pitch shifting, subtle delays, panning, and gain changes, the effect of a sound source passing by with the Doppler effect is created. This plug-in is fully automated, so fly-bys can be accurately recreated during a mix.

Figure 3.19

The Doppler plug-in.

Waves Transform Tools

The Transform Tools from Waves involve radical processing such as making synthesizers talk, changing the length of a voice-over without altering its pitch, or turning up the pick sound of an acoustic guitar without using EQ.

The Morphoder is a highly adjustable vocoder using formant-correction techniques. Vocoding is the process of modulating one sound (usually a synth sound) with a human voice to make that instrument "talk." *No Parking On the Dance Floor* immediately comes to mind as the classic example of vocoding, but I've dated myself here. With an adaptive release system, more voice characteristics can be impressed onto the vocoded sounds.

The SoundShifter plug-in allows you to alter the length of sound files without changing the pitch or, vice versa, to alter the pitch without changing the length or timing. This can be a helpful tool when synchronizing various drum loops together in a track or aligning other instruments together. The plug-in does not destroy the punch or clarity of sounds like so many earlier plug-ins of this type did.

The TransX plug-in, shown in Figure 3.20, is a dynamics processor that allows you to adjust transients and sustain separately. It is possible to turn up the room sound of a recording or reduce the transients of an acoustic guitar track. TransX can control the perceived mic placement by altering the relationship between transients and sustained tone. There is a four-band version and a broadband version for quick fixing.

Figure 3.20

The TransX multi-band transient processor.

There are even more Waves plug-ins that are related to the ones discussed here. For complete information on all Waves plug-ins, visit www.waves.com.

Universal Audio

Universal Audio has a line of plug-ins associated with its UAD-1 DSP card. These plug-ins are aimed at recreating vintage equipment, but also offer modern plug-ins that escape the notion of vintage very quickly. Some of their plug-ins can run on Pro Tools TDM systems without the use of the UAD-1 card. Any native system can use the plug-ins with the UAD-1 DSP card installed on the computer. Installed as VST plug-ins, the UAD-1 card is accessed when any of the plug-ins are used, without taxing the host CPU.

Universal Audio continues to expand its line of plug-ins, with new additions regularly becoming available. Here is a look at the current lineup of UAD plug-ins.

CS-1 (Channel Strip)

The CS-1 Channel Strip, shown in Figure 3.21, is an all-purpose plug-in with EQ, dynamics, and some spatial processing included. Each component of the CS-1 is also available as a separate plug-in should you want to conserve DSP. There are three basic components combined to make the CS-1—the EX-1 EQ and compressor, the DM-1 Delay Modulator, and the RS-1 Reflection Engine.

Figure 3.21
The UAD CS-1 Channel Strip plug-in.

The EX-1 combines a five band parametric EQ with a vintage style compressor to give you full control over tonality and dynamics in one package. The DM-1 Delay Modulator provides a surprisingly large amount of stereo delay options, ranging from chorus to ping-pong delays. The powerful RS-1 creates early reflections based on 22 shapes, from springs and plates to halls and imaginary fractal patterns. For such a DSP light plug-in, the CS-1 packs a lot of useful features.

1176LN and LE

Universal Audio first made the hardware version of the 1176 Limiting Amplifier in the 1960s. At the time when tube technology was at its height, its FET (Field Effect Transistor) circuitry gave it a unique sound that is still sought after today. The 1176LN plug-in, shown in Figure 3.22, faithfully emulates that sound with the same controls as the original. Even the non-standard "all buttons in" mode is recreated in the software version.

Figure 3.22

The UAD 1176LN plug-in.

> ## ALL BUTTONS IN
>
> The "all buttons in" mode for the 1176LN refers to a non-standard setting that the original hardware unit was capable of. Discovered by accident, when you push all ratio buttons down so they lock, the unit exhibits a very aggressive sound with added distortion and fast attack and release time. This has been used to create unique sounds for guitars, drums, and other instruments. The software version faithfully emulates this setting as well.

LA-2A

And now for something completely different, check out the all-tube, LA-2A optical compressor/limiter, shown in Figure 3.23. This very popular compressor uses an optical detector circuit for gain changing. The software version emulates the sound this type of circuit makes. With very simple controls, this compressor adds smoothness and a warm character to the sound. It has slower attack and release times and they are not adjustable.

Figure 3.23

The UAD LA-2A plug-in.

Fairchild 660

The Fairchild is perhaps the most esoteric and expensive of vintage audio gear. Fetching around $30,000 US on the market, these units are highly sought after by vintage equipment connoisseurs. The unit houses 14 transformers and 20 vacuum tubes for a total weight of 65 pounds. Maintenance nightmares, these compressors provide a sound that we have all heard and enjoyed. The UAD software version, shown in Figure 3.24, is modeled after Allen Sides favorite unit at Ocean Way Studios. UA has also provided additional controls not available on the standard hardware unit, but that correspond to typical modifications that have been used with the 660 over the years.

Figure 3.24
The UAD Fairchild plug-in.

Cambridge EQ

The Cambridge EQ, shown in Figure 3.25, is a workhorse of a plug-in. Equalization is perhaps the most used type of DSP, and having great tools for this is an absolute must. The Cambridge EQ is designed to be a full-featured equalizer with five fully parametric bands, including two shelving filters and high and low pass filters with 17 possible slopes. The EQ has three filter types that alter the bandwidth response to emulate popular console EQs. There are also two channels of EQ that can be switched back and forth for comparison or by automation during a mix. The sound quality is excellent and the flexibility is unsurpassed. This is a "go-to" EQ in my book. A typical DAW running at 44.1kHz can have up to 28 Cambridge EQs with all filters active on one UAD card. The DSP efficiency of this plug-in makes it indispensable for any native DAW.

Figure 3.25
The UAD Cambridge Equalizer—an excellent choice

Precision Limiter

In creating professional mastering tools, Universal Audio developed the Precision Limiter, shown in Figure 3.26. This dynamics processor provides brick-wall limiting with a detector that "looks ahead" for peaks in order to have a zero attack time. This prevents clipping from occurring at any time. This plug-in functions in a way similar to the Waves L1 and L2 processors.

Figure 3.26

The UAD Precision Limiter.

Precision Equalizer

The Precision Equalizer, shown in Figure 3.27, is designed as a mastering EQ. With stepped controls and wide Q values, this plug-in looks and sounds like traditional analog mastering EQs. The sound quality is the priority with a program equalizer, and the Precision Equalizer meets this requirement easily. Universal Audio uses up-sampling to achieve greater accuracy with this plug-in. Up-sampling to 192kHz provides more precision with fewer distortion artifacts. And, because the mastering process usually requires fewer individual processors, the extra DSP needed for the higher sampling rate should be available.

Figure 3.27

The UAD Precision Equalizer for mastering.

❄ UP-SAMPLING

Up-sampling is the process of mathematically deriving a higher sampling rate signal for the purposes of processing. Certain plug-ins use this technique internally to increase the precision of the result. By using higher sampling rates, Nyquist filters can be gentler, causing fewer phase problems. Likewise, filters can be designed to handle the extreme low and high frequencies with improved results. Once processing is done, the bitstream can be down-sampled back to the original sample rate to return to the mix engine. Many mastering engineers routinely use up-sampling for all digital processing and then down-sample at the end of the signal chain just prior to dithering and truncation, when going to the final 44.1kHz/16-bit audio file. This way, all other processing computations take place at higher sample rates; more samples per second equals more accuracy for DSP.

Pultec and Pultec-Pro

The Pultec EQP-1A program equalizer is a legend in analog equipment. Famed for its capability to adjust the tonal shape without adversely affecting other frequency ranges, this unit is quite valuable. The UAD plug-in emulation uses up-sampling and modeling techniques to create a great sounding plug-in version of the classic unit. Figure 3.28 shows the Pultec-Pro version where the EQP-1A is married to the MEQ-5 midrange unit of the same vintage. Together, they make an excellent full-range vintage EQ processor.

The controls on the EQP-1A are unique in that the low frequency controls allow both a boost and a cut to happen at the same time. One might speculate that these two would cancel each other out. However, the original unit uses a passive circuit in which the interactions between the boost and cut controls were not symmetric. The result is that different tonal shaping can occur when both the boost and cut are applied to the low end. More details on how this works are found in Chapter 4.

Figure 3.28

The UAD Pultec-Pro plug-in emulation of the classic program EQ.

RealVerb

The RealVerb plug-in gives the user a complete palette from which to design an acoustic space, including shapes, sizes, materials, and morphing between two unique spaces. This type of control can be daunting at first, but starting with the presets can get you a long way to understanding the interactions between the many parameters of this plug-in. RealVerb provides discrete controls for early reflections and diffuse reverb along with three-band tonal damping controls, which gives you an almost limitless variety of possible reverb and ambience settings.

DreamVerb

Shown in Figure 3.29, DreamVerb is the logical continuation of the RealVerb idea. With more variations in materials including air types, DreamVerb takes it to a whole new level. Five bands of resonance shaping and envelope adjustments for early reflections and reverb give even more possibilities for this powerful plug-in. Plus, the sound quality is up several notches from the RealVerb algorithm but at a cost in DSP power. One UAD card can run eight stereo RealVerbs but only five DreamVerbs. Having both plug-ins available can help you allocate DSP resources more effectively.

Figure 3.29

The UAD DreamVerb plug-in.

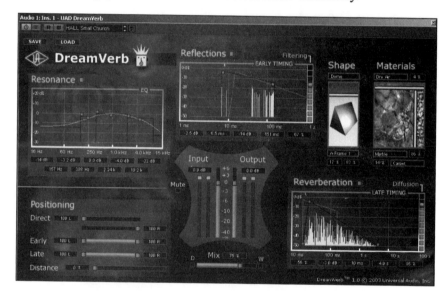

Plate 140

Made in 1957, the EMT 140 was the first plate reverb to become commercially available. The sound is created by stimulating a large metal sheet or plate and then placing transducers at various locations on the plate to pick up the vibrations made as sound resonates through the metal. This unique sound has made its way into many popular recordings even today. By recreating this wonderful tool in the Plate 140 plug-in, shown in Figure 3.30, Universal Audio has brought a very expensive, bulky, and fickle piece of audio gear into everyday use as a plug-in.

Figure 3.30

The UAD Plate 140 plug-in.

Nigel Amp Simulator

With so many nuances provided by tube guitar amplifiers and speaker cabinets interacting with each other, emulating an accurate plug-in version is difficult. However, the Nigel guitar processing plug-in, shown in Figure 3.31, does a fine job of bringing amp-modeling tools to the convenient arena of plug-ins and DAWs.

The heart of Nigel is the Preflex module, which emulates guitar amps and can morph between two amplifier types to provide new tonalities not possible with physical amps. The cabinet type and mic positions can be chosen for a variety of guitar tones just to start with. The Nigel also provides a slew of typical guitar effects, from phasers and modulation filters to tremolo and delay effects. Each module is also available as a separate plug-in for DSP conservation. With all these modules, the complete Nigel eats up quite a bit of DSP; one third of the whole UAD-1 card, to be exact.

Figure 3.31

The Nigel guitar processor plug-in.

Roland CE-1

Roland is famous for guitar stomp boxes and the Boss CE-1 is one of the first chorus effect pedals made. It has become the classic guitar and bass chorus sound ever since. Universal Audio was commissioned by Roland to recreate this vintage effect as a plug-in. Faithfully adding warm analog color, the CE-1 plug-in, shown in Figure 3.32, can be set up in classic mode where the left channel is dry and the right channel is wet, or it can be run in dual mode, whereby each channel has a separate chorus processor for

Figure 3.32

The UAD Boss CE-1 stomp box emulation.

maximum stereo spread. Because the real units are hard to find, the plug-in emulation is a great tool to have for mixing. Try it on vocals!

TC Electronics

TC Electronics has been making digital audio devices for many years and has earned a reputation for excellence. The PowerCore line of DSP processors and plug-ins appear in many DAW computers in the top studios. Although TC's strength lies in time-domain processing, they have also made some excellent plug-ins for equalizing and dynamics control with their line of Finalizer hardware units. With all that experience, the plug-ins that run on the PowerCore do not disappoint. They have also allowed other third parties to develop plug-ins for the PowerCore processors. Sony Oxford makes a line of top-notch plug-ins that run on the PowerCore systems as well.

24/7C Limiting Amplifier

The 24/7C Limiting Amplifier, shown in Figure 3.33, is TC's version of the 1176. Although not a direct copy of an 1176, the resemblance and control layout is unmistakable. The famous *four-button* mode exists on this plug-in in the same fashion as the UAD 1176LN. By comparison, this plug-in seems to have slower attack and release times and perhaps a slightly edgier sound than the UAD version.

Figure 3.33

The TC 24/7C
Compressor/Limiter plug-in.

❋ SO MANY PLUG-IN CHOICES

With so many types of EQ plug-ins available, how do you choose? The pleasure in having all these choices is that the character of each of these plug-ins is different. Each sound source might benefit from using one EQ plug-in over another. Also, DSP resources might affect decisions about which EQ to use. Priority might be given to certain sources such as the lead vocal over certain background parts when it comes to applying DSP. Spend more DSP dollars on the things that count and if you must scrimp on something, make it a less significant part of the overall mix. Having many EQ plug-ins to choose from is a blessing when helping to shape a complex mix and allocate DSP resources efficiently.

EQSat

EQSat, shown in Figure 3.34, is TC's full-featured channel EQ, featuring five filter bands, three fully parametric mid bands, and two shelving filters, all with graphic feedback of the response curve. EQSat features a unique saturation setting, which adds harmonic content to emulate a warm, analog sound.

Figure 3.34
The TC EQSat five band equalizer plug-in.

PowerCore Vintage CL

The TC Vintage CL plug-in is another vintage compressor/limiter plug-in for use on a variety of sounds. It is more DSP efficient than the 24/7C, because 28 of them can be run on one PowerCore Element card. The standard compressor parameters are there, plus a separate limiter section. This plug-in is modeled after the classic dbx brand of compressors.

PowerCore VoiceStrip

The VoiceStrip is an example of a combination processor. It includes several types of processing that all relate to vocal sounds. There is a high-pass filter to remove rumble and other low-frequency sounds, a vocal contoured EQ section along with a vintage compressor, a de-esser and a noise gate to round out the strip. With one preset of this plug-in, you can save all the vocal-processing parameters or recall them. You can bypasse each section if you don't need it.

MasterX3

The MasterX5, shown in Figure 3.35, is the software version of the now famous Finalizer hardware mastering unit. Basically, the X3 is a three-band dynamics processor similar to the Waves C4. However, there are separate settings for compression, limiting, and even expansion of each band. Also included are dithering and bit reduction settings to complete the mastering process.

Figure 3.35

The TC Master X5 mastering plug-in.

Dynamic EQ

Along the same lines as the MasterX3 and X5 is the Dynamic EQ plug-in. This four-band processor is like an EQ and multi-band compressor all in one. It is possible to apply EQ curves with dynamic control. Also, the side-chain bands can be un-linked, allowing one frequency band to control the dynamics of another band. This is a very interesting and powerful processor. Chapter 6 discusses multi-band dynamics in greater detail.

ChorusDelay

The ChorusDelay plug-in for PowerCore recreates the sound of the 1210 Spatializer hardware unit, also made by TC. The plug-in provides chorusing, flanging, slap delay, and other effects that help spread the stereo image wider. Sound quality is excellent. The controls are adequate and familiar.

ClassicVerb

The ClassicVerb is a basic, low DSP usage reverb that still retains the quality expected from a TC product. More useful for smaller spaces, it has relatively simple controls and makes it easy to get a good reverb tail going.

MegaReverb

MegaReverb is TC full-featured reverb plug-in. As you can see in Figure 3.36, the control and parameter selection is diverse. Based on the M5000 hardware unit algorithms, MegaReverb can create big, dark, rich spaces with ease.

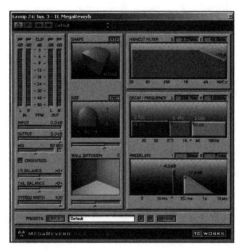

Figure 3.36
TC's MegaReverb plug-in.

DVR2 Digital Vintage Reverb

The DVR2 plug-in is the PowerCore version of TC's System 6000s (their powerful hardware unit) EMT 250 Plate reverb emulation. Users of the System 6000 will appreciate TC's attention to detail in converting this processing algorithm into a plug-in. There are special goodies such as the Input Transformer option, which emulates the addition of a physical transformer on the input signal, imparting a warmer sound.

Tubifex

Tubifex, shown in Figure 3.37, is a guitar amp modeling plug-in with some unique features. There are three tube stages, each of which can have different supply voltage settings, gain, and "body." The voltage controls provide a unique way of altering the type of linearity each tube stage has. The two controls together determine exactly how the tube will distort. These expert adjustments make Tubifex a very useful and creative tool for amp modeling.

Figure 3.37

The TC Tubifex amp modeling plug-in.

TC Thirty

If you ever have had the pleasure of playing or listening to a classic Gibson Les Paul Jr. with P90 pickups plugged into the legendary Vox AC30 amplifier with the Top Boost option, you will appreciate the TC Thirty plug-in even before you hear it. Used by many rock bands through the years, most notably the Beatles, this amplifier has become synonymous with the "brown sound" or "that sound." Whatever you choose to name it, it is a wonderful, beautiful thing. The TC Thirty, shown in Figure 3.38, has all the same features as the classic AC30, including the top boost or treble booster option that many AC30s have in them. TC also has made a special "no latency" operation mode for this plug-in to be used while recording live.

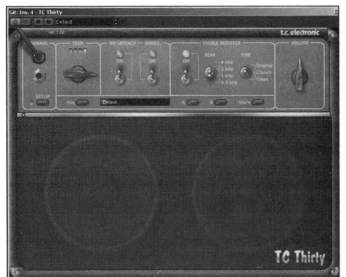

Figure 3.38
The TC Thirty emulation of the classic Vox AC30 amplifier.

Intonator

The TC Intonator plug-in is one of several pitch-correction plug-ins that allow automatic correction of vocal and instrument pitches using a preset scale.

❋ PITCH CORRECTION

Vocal pitch correction has become a hot topic in relation to its usage in pop recordings. The use of this type of plug-in can be subtle or very heavy-handed. With careful use, pitch correction software can improve a great performance without being noticed. It can also be used to "create" a performance out of thin air. Sound designers can also benefit from creative use of this type of processing to create new and intriguing sonic textures. Chapter 8 is dedicated to pitch correction plug-ins and their use.

PowerCore 01 Synthesizer

The PowerCore 01 plug-in is a sound generating device. It takes incoming MIDI signals and, via DSP, generates sounds. This plug-in is an emulation of the Roland SH-101 bass synthesizer often used in electronic music styles such as techno, and drum and bass.

❋ VIRTUAL INSTRUMENTS VERSUS AUDIO PROCESSING

Any plug-in that generates sounds from incoming MIDI signals is commonly referred to as a software instrument. In the case of VST technology, these are called VSTi (Virtual Studio Technology instrument). There are a multitude of software instrument developers out there and because this book is more precisely concerned with audio processing and not audio generating, this entire universe of awesome plug-ins cannot possibly be explored here. It would be a book all unto itself. Chapter 13, "Virtual Instruments," covers the technology only on the surface level.

Sonalksis

The Sonalksis line of plug-ins use what they have termed "steady-state" modeling to recreate classic high-performance audio gear. Started by some folks who used to work at Neve, you can bet that the quality of these plug-ins is first-rate. Dealing in the basics, Sonalksis has created a line of dynamics- and frequency-based DSP that can form the foundation of a great mixing system.

SV-517 Equalizer

The SV-517 equalizer, shown in Figure 3.39, is another workhorse of a plug-in. With four parametric bands, two switchable to shelving, and two filters, high and low pass, this EQ has all the basics of a full-featured console EQ. The bell curves of the parametric bands have three filter shapes and the shelving filters have two shapes. The functionality is complete and the sound is top-quality. There is nothing better than a high quality, full-featured EQ to start your day off right.

Figure 3.39

The Sonalksis SV-517 Equalizer.

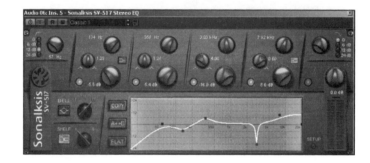

SV-315 Compressor

The Sonalksis SV-315 compressor, shown in Figure 3.40, features a fully adjustable compressor with several unique controls and a simple limiter. This plug-in looks deceptively simple, having advanced features such as variable knee adjustments, two detector circuit types, and the unique Crush and Hold parameters. With incredible fidelity, this compressor can put some bone-crushing gain reduction on a signal while still retaining high frequency detail often lost with poorer quality compressors.

Figure 3.40

The Sonalksis SV-315 Compressor/Limiter.

CQ1

The CQ1 Multi-band Compander, shown in Figure 3.41, is designed primarily as a multi-band dynamics processor. Because it has complex features such as upwards compression and downwards expansion for each of four bands, it can be a bit confusing to set at first. With a variable side-chain filter, this device can compress or expand one frequency band based on the dynamics of any other frequency range. The CQ1 is capable of very aggressive dynamics manipulation.

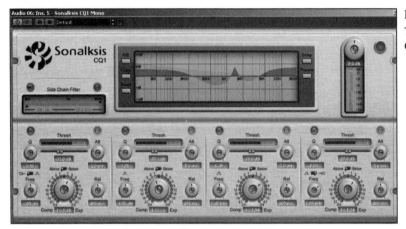

Figure 3.41

The Sonalksis CQ1 Multi-band Compander.

DQ1

The companion plug-in to the CQ1 is the DQ1 Dynamic Equalizer, shown in Figure 3.42. The DQ1 differs from the CQ1 in that it is designed primarily as a dynamic equalizer, gently shaping sounds with dynamic filters. The CQ1 is more of a dynamic processor with selectable bands capable of more severe dynamic alteration.

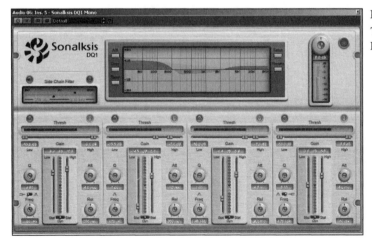

Figure 3.42

The Sonalksis DQ1 Dynamic Equalizer.

Basically, the DQ1 can apply a certain amount of gain (positive or negative) in a frequency band as that band exceeds a threshold. At the same time, it can also apply a positive or negative gain to a frequency band when that band is below another threshold. With these two possibilities on each of four bands, the tonal shaping possibilities are quite large.

Voxengo

Alexsey Vaneev released the first Voxengo plug-in, CurveEQ, shown in Figure 3.43, in 2002. This linear phase equalizer allows *spectrum modeling,* which involves using the frequency response of one particular sound or mix to modify another audio source. A possible application for this is *music mastering,* which is the process of trying to make several distinct songs blend together with a similar sonic signature within an album. The frequency response of one tune modifies the spectrum of another to match. This equalizer has a unique approach that includes a comprehensive visual feedback system, including spectrum displays of both input and output waveforms superimposed upon one another. The spectrum view can be an interesting tool for learning how equalizers work and shape sound.

Figure 3.43

The Voxengo CurveEQ with spectrum display.

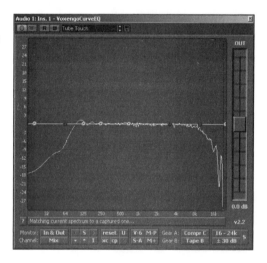

PHA-979 Phase Adjuster

The PHA-979, shown in Figure 3.44, is a valuable tool for any recording or mix engineer dealing with multiple microphone recordings. When two microphones capture the same sound source (such as multi-micing drum kits), the phase of signals in each microphone might not be the same. In fact, they are most likely not in phase with one another to varying degrees. This can be beneficial in some cases and detrimental in others.

The PHA-979 plug-in allows you to incrementally adjust the phase of a signal or one side of a stereo signal in order to realign signal for more desirable results. It also can be used to separate signals within the stereo field by phase manipulation for effect. This is a deceptively powerful tool with very simple controls.

Figure 3.44

The Voxengo PHA-979 Phase Adjustment plug-in

Voxengo offers a complete line of plug-ins for various applications with the same unique approach to DSP. Visit www.voxengo.com for a complete list of plug-ins.

Nomad Factory

The Nomad Factory began as a search for plug-ins that emulated tube equipment. Bernie Torelli resorted to creating his own plug-ins that did just that. In 2002, The Nomad Factory began producing the Blue Tubes line of plug-ins for the public.

The PEQ2A, shown in Figure 3.45, is modeled after classic tube equalizers with simple controls and a tubey sound. DSP resources are minimal with these plug-ins, keeping CPU resources available for other tasks. There are 19 individual plug-ins in the Blue Tubes line. The Nomad Factory has several other plug-in lines, including the Liquid Bundle and the Essentials Bundle. (Visit www.nomadfactory.com for more information.)

Figure 3.45

The Nomad Factory Blue Tube PEQ2A vintage EQ plug-in.

URS (Unique Recording Software)

Formed in 2003, URS is the brainchild of Bobby Nathan, former partner in New York's famed Unique Recording Studios. With many gold and platinum records on the wall and tons of technical achievements in audio technology, Bobby Nathan knows a thing or two about audio. The URS plug-ins are basically emulations of the classic analog "go-to" equalizers that the hit makers use everyday.

From the N Series EQ (a model of the classic Neve 1073 console EQ) shown in Figure 3.46, to the S Series EQ modeled after the Solid State Logic (SSL) console EQ, engineers who have had the pleasure of working with the world's best analog consoles will be right at home with URS's faithful remakes of these wonderful audio tools (see www.ursplug-ins.com).

Figure 3.46

The URS N Series EQ modeled after the Neve 1073.

Bomb Factory/Digidesign

The Bomb Factory lines of plug-ins are emulations of vintage equipment. Each interface has been modeled after the actual piece of gear that it models, such as the green face of the Joe Meek "Meequalizer," shown in Figure 3.47. The sound of these plug-ins is colored the way many of the vintage pieces affect the sound. The Bomb Factory line includes emulations of the Fairchild, LA-2A, 1176, Moog dynamic filter (MoogerFooger), and even the Tel-Ray delay effect.

Figure 3.47

The Bomb Factory emulation of the Joe Meek equalizer.

Sony Oxford

The team that creates the Sony Oxford line of plug-ins has been together for over 20 years, amassing more than 200 man-years of pro audio experience. The result is a set of first-rate plug-ins derived from the flagship Sony OXF-R3 or "Oxford" digital mixing console. Oxford has also moved beyond that early digital console and created plug-ins that offer unique processing capabilities, such as the Inflator plug-in, shown in Figure 3.48. The Inflator plug-in increases apparent loudness of a mix without some of the damaging side effects of traditional peak limiting.

Figure 3.48

The Sony Oxford Inflator plug-in.

Another plug-in that has made the Oxford line so successful is the Oxford EQ with the GML option, shown in Figure 3.49. The normal Oxford EQ is the same as the original console EQ with the addition of the GML (George Massenberg Labs) option. The analog GML 8200 parametric EQ has become one of the best channel EQs ever made. Found in many high-end studios, this unit provides minimum phase EQ with incredible sound quality. Having this George Massenberg-approved option in a plug-in is a very desirable thing.

Figure 3.49
The Sony Oxford EQ with GML option.

PSP

PSP has made some award winning plug-ins, including the PSP VintageWarmer, a multi-band, tube emulated program compressor/limiter, shown in Figure 3.50. This plug-in offers increased loudness along with an imparted tube warmth and harmonic content. It does add distortion and, as such, can be dangerous when abused. With judicious application, it can enhance many digital recordings.

Figure 3.50
The PSP VintageWarmer award-winning mix processor.

PSP is also known for their remake of the famous Lexicon PCM-42 digital delay. Using a variable sampling technique to imitate the way the PCM-42 works, the PSP 42, shown in Figure 3.51, can replicate many of the "trick" sounds used by mix engineers for many years. There is a unique modulation section that allows an LFO or the actual input level to modulate the delay time, creating dynamic and interesting delay effects.

Figure 3.51

The Lexicon PSP 42 delay modeler.

iZotope

iZotope is an audio research company from Boston that primarily licenses technology to other developers. They also have several interesting plug-ins available for all native formats.

Ozone is a mastering plug-in that has several processors combined into one interface, including an equalizer, a limiter, a multi-band dynamics and imaging processor, and a unique multi-band harmonics generator shown in Figure 3.52. Users have commented that the dithering options available in Ozone are preferable in many cases.

Figure 3.52

iZotope's Ozone mastering plug-in.

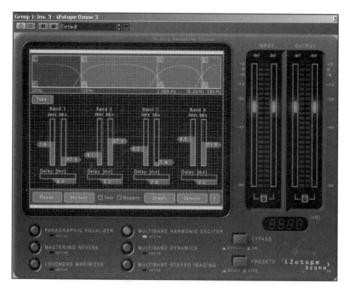

Spectron is a unique delay plug-in that can delay various frequency bands by differing amounts. For example, 200Hz can be delayed by 100ms. 1kHz can be delayed by 200ms. The resulting sound is quite remarkable; check it out. (Visit www.izotope.com for demo versions.)

Trash is a plug-in designed to offer ways of destroying signals with distortion, speaker modeling, compression, and various delay types. Vinyl offers a way to add artifacts common to old vinyl records into your signal, including record scratches, hum, and groove noise. Sometimes in the ultra-clean world of digital audio, it's helpful to add a little noise and grunge.

Antares

One of the unique effects that audio DSP has provided is the capability to alter the pitch of an audio file without altering much of anything else, including time or length and the harmonic content or formant. This effect paved the way for the vocal tuning plug-ins, most notably Auto-Tune, shown in Figure 3.53, made by Antares.

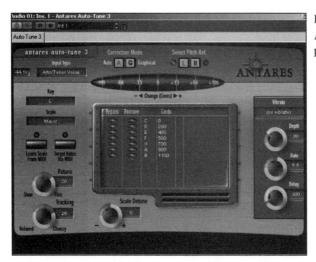

Figure 3.53

Auto-Tune pitch-correction plug-in.

Auto-Tune has two modes: auto and manual. With the auto mode, you can define a tonal center (the key) and a scale of notes (major, minor, and so on) and the plug-in will alter the pitch of any note that does not fall within certain boundaries of one of the designated pitches. If this is performed in an extreme manner, you can create interesting effects such as the ones heard in popular music by Cher and other artists.

Used in manual mode, Auto-Tune can be subtle. An otherwise great performance that may have a few out of tune notes can be adjusted without any adverse effects. There is quite a debate in the music production world about how much auto-tuning is too much. Powerful tools can have powerful effects when used to extremes.

Celemony's Melodyne

Although Auto-Tune has become synonymous with pitch correction, even becoming the generic term for it (*autotuning* someone's vocal), there are other tools for the same purpose. Celemony's Melodyne software is a very sophisticated tool for pitch correction. Either as a stand-alone application or as a plug-in within a DAW, Melodyne, shown in Figure 3.54, is capable of independently altering pitch, formant, length, and timing of individual notes in a performance. This affords you a massive amount of control and even the capability to "create" another performance from the original. For instance, you can use a lead vocal to create a harmony track using Melodyne. You could even use multiple copies of one vocal to create a whole chorus of vocals, each with a unique harmony note. This pushes the envelope of the infamous term "fixing it in the mix."

Figure 3.54

Celemony's Melodyne software for pitch correction and more.

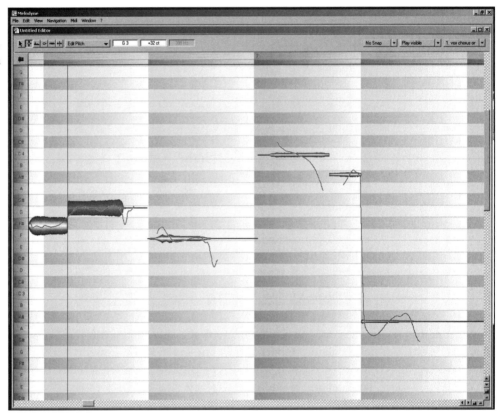

Algorithmix

Algorithmix is a German company founded in 1997 that has spent a great deal of time creating DSP algorithms that have been used in other products, including digital mixing consoles, rack-mount outboard processing, virtual instruments, and even technology used by other plug-in developers. They also have developed a line of professional audio DSP plug-ins including ScratchFree, a broadband noise-reduction plug-in similar to Waves's X-Noise.

Algorithmix also makes reNOVAtor, a unique restoration and forensic tool for removing isolated noises such as cell phones, car horns, bird calls, and more from the background of a recording.

This fascinating plug-in can do this while program material is occurring at the same time with minimal disruption to the desired audio. Chapter 10 explores this plug-in fully.

Native Instruments

Native Instruments is almost synonymous with the world of software plug-in instruments. With a complete line of software samplers, synths, and modeling instruments, this company has forged new paths into virtual instrumentation. With plug-ins such as the B4 Hammond Organ plug-in, once expensive, vintage instruments are now available to anyone with a computer.

Kontakt Virtual Sampler

Kontakt, the flagship sample instrument shown in Figure 3.55, is even used by sample library developers to deliver sample libraries in a self-contained plug-in. Many libraries come as complete plug-ins using the Kompakt sample player engine.

Film composers use this type of technology to create virtual orchestras for scoring films. In many cases, the virtual orchestra is the one you hear in movies. With smaller budgets, composers might not be able to afford to hire a 200-piece orchestra to record the film cues. The virtual orchestra is an amazing feat of this sort of technology.

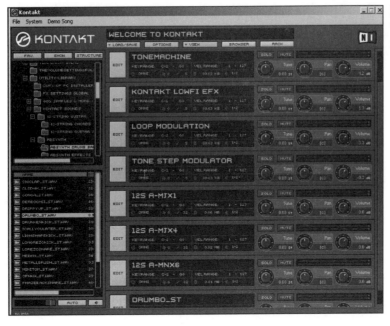

Figure 3.55

The Kontakt virtual sample player instrument.

Guitar Rig

Native Instruments has also released an audio processing tool for guitar effects and amplifier modeling shown in Figure 3.56. Guitar Rig has a virtual rack where various amplifiers, effects, and speaker emulators can be placed to create the ultimate guitar tone in a plug-in.

Guitar Rig is also designed to be used in a live performance context. An external MIDI controller can be used to alter presets and change various parameters of the plug-in in real-time. Native Instruments offers a foot controller designed to work with Guitar Rig.

Figure 3.56

Native Instruments Guitar Rig.

IK Multimedia

IK Multimedia is an international company founded in 1996 with the goal of providing tools that take advantage of the then-emerging virtual recording technology using personal computers. IK Multimedia creates virtual instruments, guitar processing tool (Amplitube), sample players in various forms, and a set of mastering tools known as T-Racks.

Summary

All these amazing tools provide the chance for everyone to create stunning audio productions. But the tools are not the reason that this can happen. The knowledge that the user possesses is the key. Understanding how all of these plug-ins work within the context of an actual audio production requires an in-depth look at how each one works.

With the advent of the home and project studio facilitated by the computer audio revolution, many things about audio production have changed. It has empowered new users with tools that they did not have in the past. Just the physical size of some of the old analog equipment is prohibitive. Now, anyone with a digital audio workstation can have a 24+ track studio in his or her bedroom.

This also has taken something away from audio production: the ideas of apprenticeship and team-work. Traditionally, audio engineers had to start out as runners or assistants in larger recording studio in order to gain the knowledge necessary to become a full recording engineer. There was no other way to gain access to the equipment. Working with an experienced engineer, the novice learned how to use the equipment before getting the chance to experiment alone.

Today, with the computer studio, access to the equipment or tools has become ubiquitous; everyone has the goods! What is missing is the knowledge and experience gained by working with others. The following chapters attempt to bridge that gap by providing explanations of the tools and some studio tricks that have been used over the years to create appealing sounds and productions.

4 } Gain Processing and Metering

The most important and often overlooked DSP operation is the mixing and panning of audio channels. This is what creates the mix. Mix engines can use fixed-point or floating-point math and can have varying bit depths. Systems that use floating-point math are less vulnerable to internal clipping than fixed-point systems. Even within a specific software tool, there can be various bit depths in different parts of the signal path. The information that a meter provides you is critical to maximizing the performance of your system.

Panners are also a form of gain processing. And with surround sound, panning becomes a somewhat complex subject. A 5.1 surround panner controls the level between five speakers channels together and a discrete subwoofer channel called the LFE channel.

Mixing faders, panners, and meters are all DSP operations that are fundamental to any DAW. It is important to have a clear understanding of how they function and what their limitations are. Mixing and level control are the most basic DSP functions that a virtual mixer can provide.

The most basic DSP processing is *gain-changing* or altering the amplitude of an audio signal. This is also the most important type of processing, because it forms the basis for any type of audio mixing and can make or break the sound quality of a mix. All audio must pass through some sort of gain stage or simple gain device such as a master fader if it is being processed. When discussing gain changes, the term *decibel* is most often used. Decibels are one of the most misunderstood topics in audio.

Understanding Decibels (dB)
Audio gain is measured in decibels, or dB. The decibel represents one tenth (deci) of a *Bel*, which was the amount of signal loss that Alexander Graham Bell measured over one mile of telephone line. The tricky thing about decibels is that they are not absolute values, like a centimeter or a pound. A decibel is a measure of relativity: how loud one sound is compared to another sound. It can be described as the ratio between two measurements of power. One unit of power is considered the reference and is 0dB. The second unit of power is relative to the first and is expressed in a logarithmic ratio or decibels.

For example, audible sound in the air is measured in decibels relative to the threshold of hearing. All sounds are measured relative to that absolute level. This is expressed in terms of sound pressure or Newtons per square meter. The actual measurement of the threshold of hearing is 2×10^{-5} Newtons/m^2. This is called 0dB SPL (sound pressure level). Any sound above the threshold of hearing has a positive value, such as 70dB SPL, which is the sound of a busy street.

* 0dB SPL—Threshold of hearing.
* 10dB SPL—Quiet meadow with insects buzzing.
* 50dB SPL—A two-person subdued conversation.
* 80dB SPL—Acoustic guitar one foot away.
* 110dB SPL—Electric guitar amp "on eleven,"—six inches away.
* 120dB SPL—Threshold of pain or someone yelling directly in your ear. Also one trillion times the power of the threshold of hearing.
* 160dB SPL—Right next to a Jet engine.

The decibel is a logarithmic scale. Decibels are used to compare extremely large differences in numbers. For instance, twice the acoustic power is 3dB. 100 times the power is 20dB. And 1,000 times the power is 30dB. With this in mind, the capacity of human hearing is quite large. From 0dB SPL, the threshold of hearing to 120dB SPL, the threshold of pain, humans can hear things comfortably between one and one trillion times in power, or a dynamic range of 120dB SPL.

The following list shows common decibel calculations that are handy to remember.

* Every additional 3dB of gain is a doubling in power—6dB is four times the power, 9dB is eight times the power, 12dB is 16 times the power, and so on.
* 10dB is also 10 times the power. In order for a sound to be *perceived* as twice as loud as another sound, it has to be around 10dB louder.
* 120dB, the dynamic range of human hearing, is one trillion times the power. This is just fun to know but not really practical in day-to-day audio work.
* In acoustic spaces, whenever the distance from a sound source is doubled, the volume goes down –6dB or one quarter the power. This is known as the *inverse square law*.
* Two identical audio signals (two phase accurate 1kHz sine waves, for example), when added together, increase the level by 6dB or four times the power.
* Two audio signals having the same amount of power but that are not identical (two channels of de-correlated pink noise for example) will increase the level by 3dB, exactly twice the power. For example, two trumpet players sound approximately 3dB louder than one trumpet player.

Understanding Dynamic Range
This capacity for hearing can be described as the *dynamic range* of human hearing. Dynamic range is defined as the area in between the softest perceivable sound and the loudest sound that can pass through a device, such as an analog-to-digital converter or a system, such as human hearing.

The threshold of hearing can be equated to the noise floor of an audio device. The threshold of pain can be equated to the onset of distortion for an audio device. Understanding these boundaries, even in the digital world, can help prevent audio catastrophes and improve overall quality. It is a common misconception that digital has so much dynamic range and lack of noise that proper gain staging is not necessary. With digital audio, the issues are just different than analog. In many ways, analog recording and mixing are much more forgiving than digital. When something goes wrong in digital, the outcomes are usually quite bad. Analog equipment can take some abuse and odd settings without going completely off the deep end and ruining everything.

Decibels are used to measure features like dynamic range, the noise floor, and maximum level before distortion. Because decibels are always relative, each decibel measurement must be made relative to some absolute value. There are many of these values used and without knowledge of them all, the decibel numbers can be meaningless.

The most important decibel scale for plug-in technology relates decibels to the loudest sound that a digital signal can output without distortion. This level also corresponds to the highest number that a digital word can represent or *full scale* (all ones and no zeros). Decibels Full Scale (dBFS) will always be zero or a negative number because the 0dBFS is the highest value possible. This is absolute because digital is a numeric system and it is not possible to have a number higher than the highest number the bits can represent. See Table 4.1.

Table 4.1 Common Audio-Related Decibel Scales

Decibel Scale	Meaning
dBm	Electrical decibel scale reference to the power of one milliwatt as dissipated across a 600-ohm resistance. 0.775 Volts across 600 ohms is one milliwatt. Any voltage/impedance pair that results in one milliwatt is 0dBm.
dBVU	VU meters (volume units) were originally used for radio broadcasters as an indication of how much of the total legal broadcast signal modulation the station could output. 0VU equals 100% signal modulation. Any levels above 0 were marked in red and illegal to broadcast with. The same meters were placed in the first tape machines and the VU scale continued life as the tape recording scale. However, analog tape could handle more than 0VU in level without distortion and that capacity continued to grow over the years as tape formulations improved. This level above 0VU is called *headroom*. This parlance has been overused to describe aspects of many types of equipment, including digital audio gear, which technically has no *headroom* whatsoever, just dynamic range. Remember that decibels are always relative.
dBFS	Digital Full Scale decibels refer to the loudest signal that the numbers in a digital audio stream can represent, with 0dBFS being the loudest signal level. There is no headroom or positive dB, because there are no numbers above the highest possible number. This is absolute.
dBv	L scale is relative to 1 volt and is used for electrical measurements.

(continued on next page)

Table 4.1 Common Audio-Related Decibel Scales *(continued)*

Decibel Scale	Meaning
dBA, dBC	These are both SPL scales that are weighted in terms of frequency to compensate for human hearing and perceptions. They are most often used for loudspeaker calibration and acoustic noise assessment.

The dynamic range of digital audio depends on how many numbers or bits are used in the signal. 24-bit audio has around 144dB of dynamic range. This far exceeds that of human hearing at 120dB and should be sufficient for all needs. 32-bit floating-point audio has a much higher dynamic range through the use of the 8-bit exponent. The exponent can be used to shift the first 24 bits of PCM data up and down the dB scale to provide upwards of 1300dB of dynamic range. Obviously, no recording or playback system exists that can reproduce the entire dynamic range, but the exponent is very useful in maintaining the full 24-bit dynamic range while processing audio with plug-ins and the DAW mix engine.

❋ RECORDING 32-BIT FLOATING-POINT FILES WITH NATIVE DAWS

Analog-to-digital converters cannot create a true 32-bit floating-point output. Modern converters use a 24-bit linear PCM format. Some Native DAWs are capable of recording in 32-bit floating-point format. The DAW adds the 8-bit exponent to the original 24-bit signal. The exponent during recording is always eight zeros and adds no additional information to the signal.

It is possible to process audio as it is being recorded in some DAWs, such as Nuendo. If any processing has occurred during recording, the exponent will only then contain some information. If you are not processing audio while recording it, using the 32-bit floating-point format does not help and will only take up more disk space.

Once audio has been recorded, offline processing such as normalizing or time stretching can be done in 32-bit floating-point and will retain more information than quantizing back to 24-bit. Also, exporting mix-down files can benefit from using the 32-bit floating-point format. If the output level of the final mix has not been optimized to have the highest peak just under 0dBFS, printing a 32-bit file will help retain more detail. A mastering engineer who can import the 32-bit file directly can then have more information to work with prior to creating a final 16-bit file for a music CD for instance.

A rule of thumb is that if you are recording the direct output of an analog-to-digital converter in a native DAW, use the 24-bit format. If the audio stream is being processed by the native DAW, using the 32-bit format can retain more information.

16-bit audio has an un-dithered dynamic range of 96dB. However, with the use of proper dither, the actual dynamic range (including signals that are audible below the noise floor) can be as high as 115dB. Because dynamic range is more a measure of perception, the effects of dithering have an impact on low-level sounds and can increase the perceived dynamic range.

Metering and Analysis

With decibels being one of the most misunderstood topics in audio, the next concept in line is high-quality metering. Knowing how many of those dB you are using at any given point in time is a valuable piece of information. Additionally, knowing how that energy is spread out in the audio spectrum and stereo sound field is very valuable.

Metering comes in many varieties, from standard digital peak meters and digital over indicators, to old school VU-type meters and third octave analyzers. With digital systems, other types of analysis tools are needed, such as "digital over" counters and bit depth information. Understanding how each type of meter works gives you a higher understanding and level of control over the audio itself.

Level Meters

There are two basic types of level meters: digital peak meters and RMS or VU level meters. They differ in how fast they respond to signal peaks. The digital peak meter responds quickly and the RMS or VU-style meter responds more slowly. Each meter displays a different type of information. Sometimes, both metering types are shown together in one meter display.

Digital Peak Meters

Digital peak meters respond instantaneously to every peak in a signal. These meters are the most common types in digital equipment because they are paramount for detecting digital clipping during recording or mixing. Unless a system is capable of handling levels higher than 0dBFS, such as pure 32-bit floating point processing, any level that exceeds 0dBFS will result in distortion, and not the pleasant kind. Digital distortion from clipping is one of the most audible and annoying types of distortion and should be avoided like the plague (unless you happen to be Trent Reznor).

The level meter in Wavelab, shown in Figure 4.1, has two meter types superimposed on one another plus some additional information. The light blue bar represents the average or RMS level, reading around –15.5dBFS. The green bar is the peak meter, reading around –9dBFS. Also, the small red hash marks indicate the highest recent peak reached at –2.3dBFS. The red and blue numbers at the very right display the highest value for the peak and RMS meters since the meter was last reset. These indicators give you a mini-history about the level of this audio file.

Figure 4.1
The Wavelab
level meter
showing both
RMS and
peak levels.

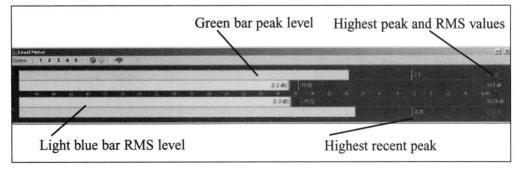

Green bar peak level   Highest peak and RMS values

Light blue bar RMS level   Highest recent peak

Notice that the scale of this meter includes positive values. This is possible because Wavelab is a native application that is capable of dealing with 32-bit floating-point files. As stated before, these files can contain levels above 0dBFS. However, those levels cannot be played back through digital-to-analog converters without clipping. They can only exist virtually in the computer. Gain processing is needed to reduce the level at or below 0dBFS in order to avoid distortion during playback.

Peak meters are best used to avoid digital clipping. Using this meter, peaks that exceed 0dBFS can easily be found using the highest peak value at the right side of this meter. In this case, the highest peak was at –0.1dBFS. Digital clipping has not occurred.

> ### ❊ HOW HOT IS TOO HOT?
>
> With so much dynamic range available to you with a 24-bit signal, there is no reason to push the recording level of incoming signals close to 0dBFS. The particular meter reading shown in Figure 4.1 was taken from a mastered music cut that had been meticulously processed to achieve a high level without clipping in order to be used for a commercial CD release. In day-to-day recording, levels can be set much more conservatively without worrying about loss of dynamic range.
>
> With regard to music CD mastering, it is common practice to limit the peak output level to −0.1dBFS. This small increment prevents many consumer CD players from overloading their analog outputs. Even though a digital signal at 0dBFS will not clip the converter, the analog circuitry that comes after it could possibly distort. The −0.1dBFS provides a safety net for consumer systems.
>
> Film sound rarely gets close to 0dBFS. In fact, most theatrical releases have an average RMS level of −20dBFS with peaks of −10dBFS. Only in extreme cases where very loud sound effects are used will the level approach 0dBFS, and that should only be for a moment. The judicious use of dynamic range adds excitement and drama.

RMS Meters

Human hearing perceives volume or loudness as a function of energy over time. The instantaneous peak level of a particular sound does not have as much effect on our perception of its loudness as its sustained level over time. Figure 4.2 shows a waveform of a high-peaking sound that is not perceived as very loud compared to the waveform in Figure 4.3. The shaded area underneath the waveform is the measure of power that a signal has; the larger the area, the louder the perceived sound. The mathematical way of defining this area over time as an average is called the *Root Mean Square* or RMS method.

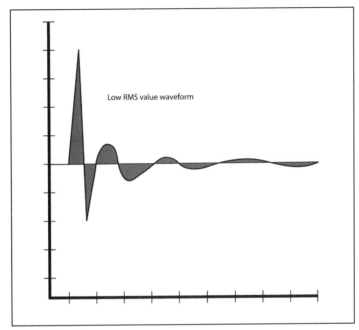

Figure 4.2
A highly transient waveform that will have a relatively low RMS value. The shaded areas indicate the actual power the waveform has and how loud it will be perceived.

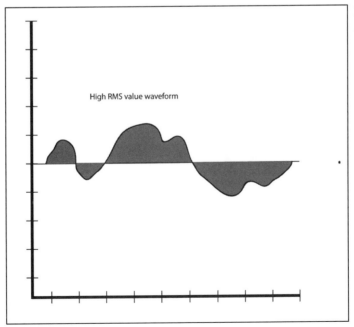

Figure 4.3
A high-RMS value waveform that has greater amounts of energy or power, as shown by the shaded areas. Even though the absolute or peak level is lower than in Figure 4.2, this waveform will be perceived as louder to the human ear.

A meter that displays this average value of a waveform is called an RMS meter, such as the InspectorXL as shown in Figure 4.4. RMS metering is valuable because it describes the perceived effect of loudness on the listener. Watching a peak meter all day will not give you an accurate idea of how loud a signal will be perceived. Peak meters are very good for avoiding clipping because they indicate every absolute level the waveform has.

❄ THE CREST FACTOR

The *crest factor* of any given signal is the ratio of its instantaneous peak level to the average or RMS level. In many modern pop music releases, the crest factor is very low, indicating the overuse of dynamic range compression and limiting. In older CD releases, on vinyl records and in theatrical sound, the crest factor is much higher and provides a more dynamic listening experience.

Because film sound is based around a calibrated mixing and playback system, the tendency for movies to have a much higher crest factor is prevalent. The difference between dialogue levels and the sound of T-Rex crashing through the woods is in the realm of 20dB. That's 1000 times the power between the average and highest level in an action movie. The hope is that popular music practices will evolve and increase the crest factor of the average music CD, thereby improving the overall quality of such releases.

As an experiment, import two music tracks from different decades and compare the relative levels in the speakers and on RMS and peak meters. It is truly amazing how overall levels have risen on commercial music releases.

Figure 4.4

Elemental Audio's Inspector XL's K-System meter with integrated RMS and peak metering.

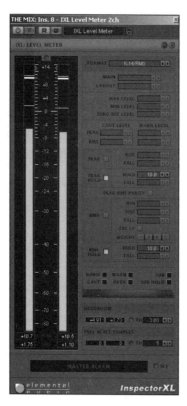

Spectral Metering

In addition to knowing the overall level of a mix, it can be very beneficial to know how that level is spread across the frequency spectrum. This requires a spectrum analyzer. Figure 4.5 shows the Elemental Audio Inspector XL 2 channel Spectrum Analyzer. This plug-in displays the frequency content of signals as a graph of frequency versus dBFS.

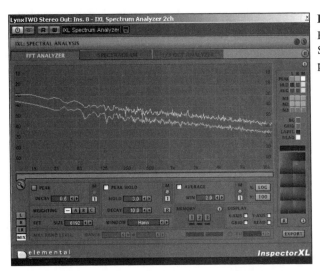

Figure 4.5

Elemental Audio's Inspector XL Spectrum Analyzer displaying pink noise.

The highest peak level for each frequency is displayed in the upper line, whereas the average level is shown in the lower line. There is also an instant peak level that moves quickly (and would be confusing in a figure). With this information, you can identify specific frequency areas that are causing difficulty and then address them with EQ or other solutions. Identifying them is the first big step to fixing such problems.

You can adjust the peak hold times and the averaging time to provide a more readable graph depending on the program material. You can apply frequency weighting to the display for speaker calibration and other tests.

There is also an FFT size parameter. FFT stands for *Fast Fourier Transform*. This is the method of analysis the Inspector uses to separate the audio signal into its component frequency parts for display. Basically, the plug-in analyzes one chunk of audio at a time. The size of this chunk is determined by the FFT size. Smaller sizes provide a quicker meter response. When analyzing speaker response, the shorter FFT avoids errors due to low frequency anomalies in the room. A larger or longer FFT size (it is measured in samples) provides more accuracy in the low-end readings. The longer wavelengths of lower frequencies require a longer FFT for accurate measurements.

The window type (Hann, Blackman-Harris, Flat Top, and Boxcar) determines the way the audio chunk is separated from the rest of the audio stream. Simply cutting a small audio chunk out of a whole stream takes it out of context and leads to inaccurate results in certain areas, depending on the window used. For a complete understanding of FFT analysis and windowing techniques, another book would be required. Here are some guidelines for how common FFT windows are used. (For more information on FFT, visit http://en.wikipedia.org/wiki/Fourier_transform.)

* *Hann* or *Hanning*: This window type is good for most mixing tasks, having a blend of good resolution of peaks versus decent rejection of false readings for non-integer values of the window size.

* *Blackman-Harris:* This window type has been used in many FFT analyzers and is a common reference for FFTs.

* *Flat Top*: This window type is good for analyzing spectral peaks in which interference from adjacent frequencies is not an issue. This is good for analyzing a swept sine wave in a speaker system. Only one frequency at a time is analyzed. It provides a highly accurate amplitude measurement.

* *Boxcar*: Using this window provides higher frequency resolution.

Those for whom this list takes geekdom to new heights, just set it on Hann and enjoy watching the display. In all but the most demanding analysis tasks, the Hann window works just fine.

The Inspector XL also provides a spectrogram, which basically takes the FFT graph and imposes it over a time-based graph. This way, you can see resonances and other audio phenomena that a normal FFT would have difficulty showing. Figure 4.6 shows the spectrogram of someone singing. The color represents the level of a given frequency at that time. The darker areas in blue are for quiet sounds and the lighter areas are mid-level, with red being very loud. You can see the patterns of the melody echoed in the fundamental tones between 125Hz and 500Hz and relative harmonics in the upper frequencies. You can identify almost 20 various harmonics of the voice. They get closer together as the frequency goes up. Looking at various elements of a mix with the spectrogram is always an eye-opening experience, because you can see how much of a sound's character is contained in its harmonic content.

Figure 4.6

Jason Ludwig from the band Noctaluca sings a passage from "On A Roll" in this spectragram. Harmonics define the character of most sounds. The spectragram is in color and shows blue as low level and red as the highest level.

Finally, the third-octave analyzer is a standard reference tool for calibration and testing. It is very similar to the FFT except that it is limited to the number of bands it analyzes. Surround sound speaker calibration, especially for the LFE channel (the .1 in a 5.1 configuration), benefits from the use of the third-octave analyzer. Measurements made with a calibrated test microphone are more accurate using the third octave analyzer instead of a simple SPL meter. For more information on surround-sound system calibration, refer to Chapter 11, "Surround Sound." Figure 4.7 shows the Inspector XL's third-octave analyzer measuring the output of a subwoofer in a surround sound speaker setup.

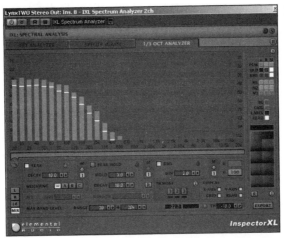

Figure 4.7
The Inspector's third-octave analyzer showing the response of a subwoofer.

Stereo Image Metering

When mixing stereo or surround material, the question of how much information is panned away from the center versus the information in the middle of the sound field can be answered by a stereo correlation, balance, and image meter as shown in Figure 4.8. The balance between middle and side energy is the measure of width in a mix. This can also help determine what the mono compatibility

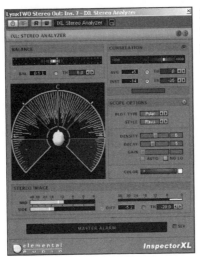

Figure 4.8
The Inspector's stereo analyzer plug-in.

will be of various stereo sources. The more out-of-phase information there is in a stereo signal, the less mono-compatible it is. If the correlation meter is showing significant negative numbers, a mono mix will lose some information and the balance will change.

Clip and Digital Over-Detection

Most digital peak meters have a clip indicator that lights up whenever the signal exceeds 0dBFS. Unfortunately, the clip indicator only informs you that a clip has occurred. It is possible and more than likely that if one clip occurred, several clips have gone by since the first one has happened but there is no way to tell from the simple clip indicator. When mixing and working on other tasks, it is not always possible to keep an eye on every meter in the studio. Keeping a count of clips, also called *overs*, is a mundane task that is best left to a plug-in.

Once again, Elemental Audio's Inspector XL has a wonderful tool for doing just that. The clip statistics plug-in, shown in Figure 4.9, keeps count not only of the simple digital overs but also of clips as they are defined by the user. It has been commonly accepted that not all digital overs are audible. In fact, up to ten samples in a row that exceed 0dBFS might not be heard as distortion. The Inspector lets you define what activity is considered a clip. Typically, three samples in a row that exceed 0dBFS should be considered a clip. In addition, if you are mastering for consumer CDs, samples that exceed –0.1dBFS are considered clips.

Figure 4.9

The Inspector's Statistics plug-in used for clip and over-detection.

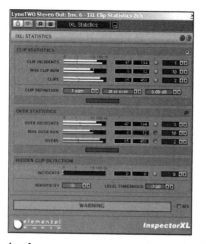

Once the clip definition is clear, you can set up alarms in the Inspector to indicate the number of clips that have occurred. Again, the user defines the number of clips that sets off the alarm.

A unique feature is the capability to detect clips that have occurred earlier in the production process. Called *hidden clips,* these are distorted waveforms that are the result of earlier processing and due to gain changes while mixing, and might not be evident at the very loudest part of the dynamic range. However, the Inspector can look for clipped waveforms within the mixed audio in a range that is determined by the user. Using two parameters, sensitivity and level threshold, the Inspector examines audio above the level threshold for clipped waveforms. The sensitivity determines how easily the clip detector is set off. With lower settings, hidden clips are detected more often than using higher settings. Clips can be very short or longer if they are more severe. The sensitivity setting affects how long hidden clips need to be in order to be tallied in the hidden clip counter.

The K-System Monitoring Calibration

For many years now, mastering engineers have been dealing with the phenomena of ever-increasing loudness in popular music releases. This stems from the era of vinyl records where getting a hot level on the vinyl was tricky and important for a good signal-to-noise ratio to be achieved. Also, at that time, the louder the vinyl was, the more positive the response was from consumers and radio listeners. Now, with the advent of the CD, the signal-to-noise ratio is less of a problem and radio stations routinely level-adjust their output to maximize each recording's level to the highest legal broadcast strength permitted by the FCC.

It has come to the point that major label releases on CD with 96dB of dynamic range end up only using maybe 10dB to 20dB of what is available in order to compete with the apparent loudness of most other commercial releases. In order to do this, the mastering engineer must compress and limit the final mix by absurd amounts, causing distortion and loss of sound quality. This might not be a huge issue for the casual listener in a car, using a portable radio, or listening to MP3s on an iPod, but for the home listener on a quality playback system, the results are disappointing.

Many of today's home playback systems are also the home theater playback systems capable of the greater dynamic range needed for film sound. After watching a movie that used a calibrated monitoring system to mix and had a lower average level and higher crest factor, a commercial music CD placed in the same DVD drive without adjusting the volume will assault the listener with a much louder signal. There is no need for this to be the case.

The K-System utilizes three separate calibrated monitoring levels depending on the material being mixed or mastered. A pink noise signal is set to a fixed volume using an RMS or K-System meter and then each speaker is calibrated to 83dBC using an SPL meter such as the Radio Shack model shown in Figure 4.10. The SPL meter should be set to C weighting with a slow response for an

Figure 4.10
The Radio Shack SPL meter.

accurate measurement. The C weighting avoids error due to the lack of low frequency response of smaller speakers and the modal interference of smaller (less than 3500 cubic feet) mix rooms.

Using a volume level of 83dBC SPL also helps the human ear to perceive the frequency spectrum in a more even way. This is due to the effect that loudness has on our spectral perception. The Fletcher-Munson curves, shown in Figure 4.11, depict how our hearing changes as the overall volume of sound goes up and down. As the level increases, our perception of the bass increases as well. If mixing occurs at a monitoring volume that is too high, not enough bass will be added so that at normal listening levels, the mix will seem thin or bass-light. Also, at lower levels, mixing can add too much bass because our hearing is less sensitive to bass at lower levels. Mixing at 83dB SPL will help produce a more even spectral balance that better translates to various playback levels.

Figure 4.11

The Fletcher-Munson equal loudness curves show how the sensitivity to various frequencies changes as the volume changes.

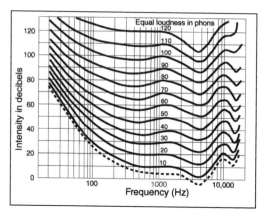

Consumers will tend to adjust their playback level to a comfortable listening level regardless of how loud the level is on CD. If most CDs were mixed using a calibrated mix level, the consumer would not have to constantly adjust the playback volume for comfort. Plus, headroom can be retained to provide a better listening experience.

Mix engineers often check mixes on various sets of speakers and different volumes but should be able to quickly return to the calibrated K-System setting. Keeping in mind the Fletcher-Munson loudness curves, having a reasonable monitoring level should also improve the quality of many mixes.

The K-20 reference, which corresponds to the current theatrical standard, is used for films, classical music, and hi-fi 5.1 popular music that is becoming available in the new DVD-Audio and SACD formats. The pink noise is set at –20dBFS, yielding 20dB of "headroom" above the reference level for peaks. This allows mixing and mastering engineers to take full advantage of the incredible dynamic range afforded by the latest consumer digital technology.

The second K-System level, K-14, uses a lower monitoring level and is appropriate for pop music and other high-energy audio. With pink noise set at –14dBFS and calibrated to the same 83dBSPL, the monitors are actually lower in volume than for K-20. This still affords 14dB of headroom for peaks and should be plenty for great-sounding pop music.

The last K-System spec is K-12 and is reserved for audio that is to be broadcast only. This is used for radio and TV commercials, which are typically the loudest mixes ever created! Have you ever been watching a movie on TV and then during the commercial break, have to turn the TV volume way down? You have experienced the results of non-calibrated mixing at its finest. Advertisers are always interested in having their message "heard" at the loudest possible volume. Unfortunately, this often results in the consumer actually turning the TV down during commercial breaks, because the volume is so disparate from the movie or show they are watching. The law of diminishing returns has set in.

Figure 4.12 diagrams the dynamic range of digital audio for various systems including the K-System. It shows an overview of how all the various references relate to one another. For more information on the K-System, visit mastering engineer Bob Katz's website at www.digido.com for a complete set of articles on this issue.

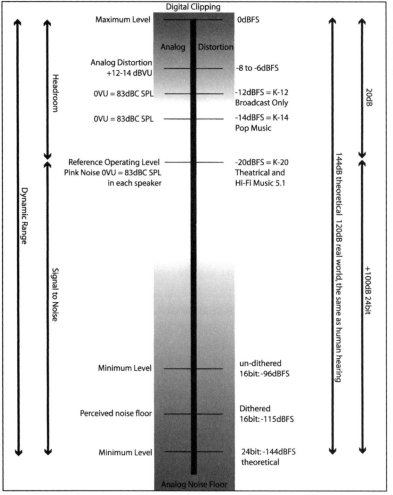

Figure 4.12

A chart of dynamic range and different decibel scales including the K-System monitoring calibration specs.

Faders

The term *fader* refers to the linear sliders found on most conventional analog mixers since the 1960s. They can control the relative level between multiple signals that are being combined or the level of auxiliary signals that are being routed to effects such as reverb or headphone mixes. A fader can also control the overall level of a group of signals that are already combined, referred to as a *master* fader. In audio software, such as a DAW or plug-in, any control that affects the overall level of a signal, whether by a linear slider or rotary control, is referred to as a fader or gain control in this book.

Most faders in DAW software also have a numeric readout of decibels for very accurate gain adjustments as seen in Figure 4.13. Faders are usually set in a logarithmic scale. In other words, as the fader is moved down, gain lowers faster and faster for each equal movement of the fader. Human hearing is exponential and as such, fades that sound smooth and even, are actually moving in a logarithmic scale, the scale of the decibel. The closer the fader gets to silence, the faster decibels are removed. It is very difficult to execute a smooth fade on a linear fader. Move a fader in any popular DAW and watch how the gain reduces faster as you pull the fader down at an even pace.

Figure 4.13

A fader in Nuendo's mixer window with a numeric readout that can be used to directly enter gain values or to display the current gain of the fader. Nuendo's faders move on a logarithmic scale.

It is often necessary to group several faders together for the purpose of mixing. Groups of faders should maintain their relative levels while grouped regardless of the overall gain of the group. If fader A in the group has a gain of 0dB and fader B has a gain of –7dB, when the group is pulled down by –10dB, fader A should be at –10dB and fader B should be at –13dB. That way, the sonic relationships between the signals in the group are maintained. This should sound the same as if the channels in the group were routed together on a bus (Pro Tools) or Group Channel (Nuendo) and then the Auxiliary Input (Pro Tools) or Group Channel (Nuendo) is pulled down. The audio relationships remain intact. In the past, some audio software had been improperly designed and fader groups did not maintain their relative levels. A simple experiment can determine if this is true or not.

1. Create three audio channels and set their levels numerically to 0dB, –3dB, and –10dB.
2. Group the faders together.
3. Pull the fader set at 0dB down by –3dB.
4. Check to see that the numeric readout of the other two faders is –6dB and –13dB, respectively.

5. Pull the original fader down another 3dB to –6dB.

6. Check to see that the other two faders are set at –9dB and –16dB, respectively.

7. Set the first fader to +3dB.

8. Check to see that the other two faders are set to 0dB and –7dB, respectively.

If this test worked correctly, the DAW software is designed properly as far as channel grouping is concerned. If not, there could be a problem when you use grouped faders to mix.

Offline Gain Processing

Offline processing, such as gain changing or normalizing, is another type of gain processing. The only difference is that offline processing is applied to a file and the file itself is permanently changed or a new one is created. Gain changing in the mixer happens in real-time and does not affect the actual files on disk.

Normalizing is an offline process offered in most DAWs and audio editors. When you choose to normalize an audio file, the file is analyzed to find the maximum peak signal level it contains. Gain is then added to the entire audio file until the highest peak level is also the maximum level the digital file can have or a preset level determined by the user, as seen in Figure 4.14.

For instance, if an audio file has a peak level of –4dBFS, normalizing to a value of 0dBFS adds 4dB of gain to the entire file so that the maximum level is now 0dBFS. If more gain were added, the signal would be clipped, which would add distortion and would not be desirable. The idea is to maximize the potential level of an audio file without adding distortion.

Figure 4.14

The offline normalizing process window from Nuendo showing the user-definable maximum peak level setting.

Normalizing is typically used to increase the level of poorly recorded audio files. This can be very helpful with live recordings that are less than optimum or film production audio that was recorded with too much dynamic range. The softest passage of dialogue can be recorded with levels so low that they are impractical to use in the mixer.

Normalizing audio files with low levels will bring the audio signal up to a more usable level depending on the peak content of the file. The downside to normalizing is that more precision (a higher bit depth) is needed to add gain. Adding gain increases the word length of the audio file. This excess word length must then be reduced to the original bit depth in order to be stored back on disk. Hopefully, the audio application will add proper dither during this process in order to maximize the apparent resolution and avoid quantization noise. The addition of the dither can increase the noise floor a bit and if the normalizing process is poorly implemented, rounding or truncation distortion can be the result.

Modern DAWs have a higher internal resolution that is capable of adding gain without the distortion and loss of resolution associated with some offline normalizing algorithms. Use the internal gain capabilities of your DAW when possible, including plug-ins, to bring up the level of poorly recorded material. Normalizing does not increase the resolution of audio files. It merely brings the same dynamic range up to a higher *absolute* level. Normalizing should be a last resort effort when other processing techniques are not possible.

Certain DAWs, such as Nuendo, allow each audio region or event to have a real-time gain applied to it. Figure 4.15 shows an event in Nuendo's project window and the volume handle, which is used to adjust the gain of that particular portion of audio. Using this type of gain processing can avoid the pitfalls of normalizing while maintaining the full resolution of the original audio file. Dither is added only at the very end of the mixing chain, thus avoiding the additional dither noise needed for normalizing.

Figure 4.15

The volume handle of an audio event in Nuendo can be used to adjust the gain of that portion of audio up to +24dB or down to —infinity. This should be enough to adjust the level of even the lowest recording audio to a range that is useful in the mixer.

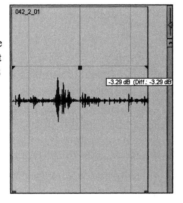

Summing or Mixing

After you have adjusted the individual levels of various sounds, these levels are combined to form the complete mix, whether a piece of music or a complete film soundtrack. The process of combining all the signals together is called *summing* and requires DSP with a greater precision and bit depth than the source audio in order to retain the highest quality and flexibility in routing for the engineer.

32-Bit Floating-Point Summing

The very nature of 32-bit floating point DSP allows summing to occur with a great deal of headroom and precision. You can sum multiple signals at various levels and still have headroom to add many more without ever getting close to the maximum level that 32-bit floating-point is capable of. All the detail of lower level signals is retained in the mix as well. No truncation is necessary at this stage.

After all the signals have been combined, you must turn the final result into a fixed-point number in order to play it back via digital-to-analog converters. This step requires dither and truncation. Do this only at the very last step in order to minimize their. When you do it this way, the results of 32-bit floating point summing are excellent. With proper dithering, a 16-bit result can be obtained with up to 115dB of dynamic range.

Fixed-Point Summing

Fixed-point math requires additional word length in order to sum multiple signals without any quality loss. Pro Tools HD, for example, uses a 48-bit summing algorithm for the mix bus. It allocates these bits in a way that provides as much flexibility for the engineer while retaining the highest resolution possible. Table 4.2 shows the way the Pro Tools mix bus bits are allocated. Room is left on both ends of the dynamic range to ensure that there is sufficient headroom for louder signals and larger precision in the lower area to retain low-level signal details.

Once all signals have been combined in the 48-bit summing bus, they then must be dithered and truncated down to a 24-bit result in order to pass through master output plug-ins or out of the mixer to analog converters. The Pro Tools Master fader is used to scale the final 48-bit result to an appropriate level in 24-bit. In other words, use the master fader to set the final level of your mix in Pro Tools so the maximum detail and resolution will be retained. Using proper dither, the 24-bit result can then be truncated to 16-bit for CD mastering and still retain up to 115dB of dynamic range.

Table 4.2 Pro Tools 48-Bit Mix Bus Yields Close to 288dB of Available Dynamic Range

Bit Range	Description
40–47	The top eight bits are reserved for headroom. 128 full-level coherent audio channels would sum to bit 46. The last bit is available because there is an additional 6dB of gain available from each channel fader. These eight bits provide close to 48dB of available headroom above 0, before the mix bus clips.
16–39	One 24-bit channel of audio, with its fader set to 0, uses bits 16–39. When the master fader (if present) is set to 0, these bit also represent the main output, before any mix bus plug-in processing or dither is added. These 24 bits represent close to 144dB of available dynamic range. A second full-scale channel with coherent audio (say, a pair of sine waves with identical frequency and phase) would sum to bit 40. In order to avoid clipping the mix bus, the user needs to pull the channel faders down 6dB, create a master fader, or use a aux track as a sub-group, without the output fader set to −6dB. In any of these three examples, the full precision of each channel is maintained and no bits are lost.
0–15	These lower 16 bits preserve audio data when the channel faders are pulled down below 0, or unity gain. These 16 bits allow a channel's fader to be pulled down to −96dB and still contribute to a full 24 bits of precision audio to the mix bus.

> ❄ **AWESOME DAWSUM CD SAMPLER**
>
> Lynn Fuston of 3D Audio in Nashville has created a set of CDs called the *Awesome DAWSUM Sampler* that contains the results of a carefully conducted test of many digital mixing platforms from Pro Tools and Nuendo to Yamaha 02R and the Mackie D8B consoles. There has been a great deal of debate on the Internet now for years about the summing and mixing engines of various software and hardware. This experiment was an attempt to conclude if there are any differences and what they might be. Visit http://www.3daudioinc.com/ for more information on the Awesome DAWSUM Sampler CD, including its results and other interesting audio test CDs.

Spatial Positioning

If you have ever viewed the Disney movie, *Fantasia*, you have heard the first example of multi-channel audio utilizing a device that would eventually become the pan control. In the 1930s, Walt Disney asked his chief engineer, William Garity, to design a device that would allow the movement of sound across three speakers positioned in the front of the projection screen. Soon after, the *panpot* was born.

Ever since the advent of stereo recording and playback, the capability to place sounds within a wide sonic field has been possible. In the earliest days of multi-channel audio, this was simply accomplished with a three-position differential circuit, which allowed the engineer to place a sound in the middle or in the left or right positions. Today, we have a continuous control that affords positioning of the source in many places between the left and right speakers.

Continuing the development of multi-channel theater sound systems started by Disney, surround-sound went from the movie theater into the home with the advent of low-cost multi-channel playback systems. Designed for film soundtracks, these consumer playback systems are capable of a wider dynamic range and have five or even seven directional speakers, plus dedicated low-frequency drivers known as subwoofers. Controlling the position and motion of sound between all these speakers is the task of the surround panner. Simple left and right positioning has given way to divergence and vector controls along with the LFE channel for low frequency effects.

Stereo Panners

Once the blend of audio signals is created, the stereo or surround image must then be created. Panners are gain devices used to do just this. The most basic panner is a stereo gain device that proportions the signal level between the left and right channels of a stereo mix. The tricky part about panning is keeping the overall level of the signal the same as it pans between the speakers and across the stereo field.

In theory, when two signals with equal power are added, the overall level increases by 3dB. If those two signals are absolutely identical (the same signal), adding them together will add 6dB to the overall level. When a sound is panned directly in the middle, the same signal is sent to both speakers. This should theoretically increase the overall volume in the room by 6dB. However, as a result of the interference created by reflections within the typical listening room, the volume will realistically go up by about 3dB. Maybe in a perfect acoustic environment such as an anechoic chamber (a room that has no reflections or echoes), a center-panned signal would actually go up by 6dB. The reality of most listening environments, including many sound studios, is that only a 3dB increase will result from two speakers playing the same exact sound.

To compensate for this, panpots are designed with a reduction in gain as the signal is panned to the center. This is called the *pan law,* and has several variations. The most common implementation of the pan law involves a 3dB reduction in gain when signals are center-panned. In typical listening rooms, this results in sound that retains the same perceived loudness regardless of where it is panned in the stereo field.

Opinions vary on how much reduction is needed to achieve smooth, even panning. Solid State Logic implemented a standard –4.5dB panning law on its famous analog consoles. Pro Tools adopted this standard as well in the digital world. Most DAWs now offer the option to change the panning law to suit your own tastes. Nuendo offers pan law choices of 0dB (no pan law, center panned sounds will be louder), –3dB (standard on most DAWs), –4.5dB (SSL standard), and –6dB (the theoretical ideal).

Keep in mind that unless you are using dynamic or moving pans while mixing, the pan law itself might not have any effect on your mixes. If you follow certain mix procedures, the pan law could have a significant effect. Many top music mix engineers prefer to blend signals in mono in order to hear more clearly the effects of masking between instruments. Once a blend is created this way, panning the individual sounds left and right of center should not alter the balance that was created in mono. The pan law will affect this.

✵ **MONO COMPATIBILITY**

Always check your mixes in mono. There are innumerable things that you can avoid by checking mixes in mono. Varying room acoustics among other things can differ the stereo playback from the mono mix. Making sure that balances remain intact in mono ensures that your mix will translate over radio and other broadcast media that can result in a mono sound for the consumer. Having a clear idea of how loud the center image is in relation to the hard left and right is paramount. You can resolve the effect of masking (where one sound in a similar frequency band covers another sound in the same band) more quickly by listening in mono where the effects are more pronounced. You can also hear and resolve phase issues that result in a level loss in mono, along with address many other mixing issues.

Surround Panning

Today's home theater systems have typically five discrete speakers and one dedicated subwoofer speaker that handles the LFE channel in a 5.1 mix and in many cases, low frequency content from the other five speakers. Coordinating how sounds are heard within this six-channel sonic panorama is the duty of the surround panner.

Shown in Figure 4.16 is the Nuendo surround panner in the default setup. Like most surround panners, the Nuendo one uses a joystick-type of interface, thus allowing the user to grab the virtual image of the sound's position and move it freely around the soundscape. The surround panner uses this visual information to adjust the level of the five individual speakers to achieve the desired "position" of the sound source.

Figure 4.16

The Nuendo surround panner.

For complete information on surround sound, 5.1 speaker setups, panning, and bass management plug-ins, please refer to Chapter 11.

Summary

Understanding gain, including how it works and the tools used to alter the fixed gain of signals, is critical in audio mixing. Organizing the gain structure of any mix configuration is critical to the final outcome. Controlling the dynamic range and understanding the effects of peak signals versus perceptually louder RMS signals in a mix is one of the things that takes a whole career to learn and use well. Discussion of decibels, signal to noise ratios, headroom, and crest factor is the foundation upon which the rest of audio processing is based.

The one thing that all plug-ins have in common is some sort of gain structure. Manipulating this is the key to delivering the highest quality audio possible in any DAW or audio software. The next chapter deals with an intimately connected subject: frequency processing and equalizers.

5 } Equalizers and Frequency-Based Processing

Equalizing plug-ins can add or reduce the gain of various frequencies in an audio signal. This might sound simple, but is in fact an amazing feat. In a complex audio signal, there are many frequencies interacting with each other to form the composite waveform. An equalizer can zero in on a band of frequencies and adjust the volume of that band without affecting the rest of the signal's frequencies.

> ❋ **FREQUENCY BANDS**
>
> A *frequency band* is a group of frequencies in one area of the spectrum defined by the centermost frequency. It is not possible to affect just one frequency with any equalizer, so the term *band* is used to identify certain groups of frequencies. Bands are often measured in octaves. An octave is a doubling of frequency. An octave above 50Hz is 100Hz. Spectrum analyzers and graphic equalizers are often calibrated in octaves or third-octaves. In a third-octave graphic equalizer, there are 31 bands of EQ to cover the entire audible range of 20Hz to 20kHz (10 octaves of frequencies in the audible spectrum).

Well, there is the rub. Avoiding adverse effects to the rest of the signal is the hardest part about equalizing. Different equalizers affect the rest of the signal in various ways, depending on the type of equalizing going on and how extreme the settings are. The thing to understand is that the only way to change the level in one frequency band is to alter the relationships of other frequency bands. Two things happen as a result of equalization.

❋ Frequencies close to the affected band will ring and have a resonance, or there will be a ripple response in frequencies adjacent to the chosen band. This is *frequency error*.

❋ The transients in a signal will get smeared as a result of phase shifts in the component frequencies. This is *time domain* or *phase error*.

Phase response of equalizer filters is a complex subject. Although this book does not intend to cover all aspects of filter design compromises, the main points are reviewed so you'll have a better understanding of why different equalizers sound different to the ear even when the settings remain the same.

Every complex audio waveform can be broken into a series of simple sine waves at various frequencies. This is the *Fourier* transform law (named after the French mathematician Joseph Fourier) at its most basic level. When combined, the interaction of all these sine waves produces the complex waveform. Figure 5.1 shows a very basic example of what this might look like. The sine wave A is a harmonic frequency of the sine wave B. When the two are combined, they form the complex waveform C.

The point to clearly understand is that every possible audio waveform, and therefore every sound you have ever heard, is made up of many simple sine waves combined in various ways to yield every sound possible.

Figure 5.1

Two simple sine waves, A and B, make up the complex waveform C.

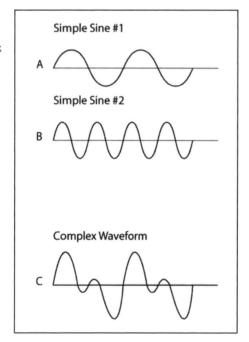

When an equalizer operates, the time relationship between these two sine waves will be altered in some way. The example in Figure 5.1 is very simplified for the sake of discussion. In the real world, a sound could be made up of hundreds or thousands of sine waves. The extremely complex relationships between them all are disrupted by the use of equalization. These are time domain or phase changes. The relative phase between each component sine wave must be altered in some way when an equalizer is used.

Figure 5.2 shows the same two sine waves with a different time relationship. This change is the result of some amount of equalization or filtering. The resulting waveform is altered. Because *transients* (sharp peaks in amplitude of a waveform, the smack of a drum for instance) are made up of many sine waves with harmonic relationships, using an equalizer affects transients as well. The transient portion of the waveform is altered because component sine waves of that transient have been shifted in time or phase. The timings of the various component sine waves have changed and the resulting transient can be blurred or smeared.

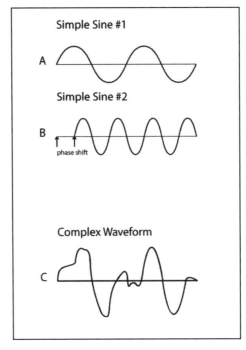

Simple Sine #1

A

Simple Sine #2

B

phase shift

Complex Waveform

C

Figure 5.2
Sine wave B has been shifted in time in relationship to sine wave A. The resulting complex waveform C will not have the same transient components as before.

❊ LINEAR PHASE EQUALIZERS

Only *linear phase equalizers* do not alter phase relationships between sine waves. They avoid doing so at the cost of other factors discussed later in this chapter.

Do not let the technicalities of all this overwhelm you. The thing to remember is that there is no way to avoid altering the sound while equalizing in other ways that affect the phase relationships of component sine waves and therefore the transient response. Equalization is always a tradeoff between accurate frequency response and accurate time-domain or transient response.

The good news is that all the horrible things that equalization does to audio is something that we are all used to hearing everyday. In many cases, these alterations are pleasurable and desirable. It is just a good idea to understand what it is that you desire and how to achieve those results with the best compromise between frequency and phase response.

Implementing Filter Designs

It is not possible to design a (digital, or especially, analog) filter that has perfect frequency and time properties. To have a perfectly accurate frequency filter, the time domain will be affected. To have a perfectly accurate response in the time domain, there will be errors in the frequency spectrum. This is why all digital (and analog) EQs sound different. The designers have made various tradeoffs between frequency and time domain errors to arrive at a particular filter design.

Digital filters can be implemented in two ways: by *convolution* (also known as *Finite Impulse Response* or FIR) or by *recursion* (also known *as Infinite Impulse Response* or IIR). These two methods have benefits and disadvantages. Most of the time, any specific EQ plug-in will use a combination of both types of processing to achieve the desired effect. Suffice it to say, most developers are loath to tell you just how their plug-in is designed for obvious reasons. The following section takes a look at these designs and examines their traits so you might better understand what the equalizer is doing to the audio.

Basic Filter Types

In both analog and digital designs, there are four basic filter types used in combination to create equalizers you know and use everyday. They are high-pass, low-pass, band-pass, and band-reject filters. Each filter is used to separate frequencies from one another so they can be altered in amplitude. These four filter types, in various combinations, yield all the different kinds of equalizers used today, from fully parametric to wideband program EQs, such as the Pultec, to graphic-style EQs, such as the URS A10 shown in Figure 5.3.

Figure 5.3

The URS A10 is a graphic style EQ that has 10 fixed frequency bands. It is modeled after the classic API console graphic EQs.

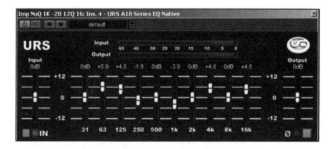

Each filter has three basic areas of interest that determine its sound. The pass-band is the area of frequencies that the filter is supposed to let through and not affect. The stop-band is the area of frequencies that is supposed to be suppressed in the output of the filter. The transition-band is the area between the pass-band and stop-band where the frequencies are affected but not necessarily suppressed all the way. The transition band determines the slope of the filter. These three areas are shown in relation to a low-pass filter in Figure 5.4.

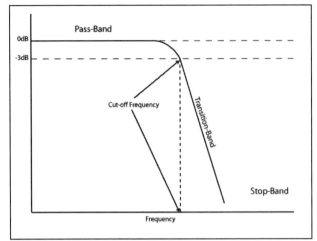

Figure 5.4
The three frequency areas of a low-pass filter.

The high-pass filter is a mirror image of the low-pass filter. In fact, simply inverting the polarity of every other audio sample while processing a low-pass filter algorithm can create a high-pass filter. It is a kind of inversion of the mathematical process.

Figure 5.5 shows the anatomy of a high-pass filter. The turnover frequency or cutoff frequency of the high-pass (or low-pass) filter is most often defined as the frequency at which 3dB of gain reduction has occurred, or the 3dB down point.

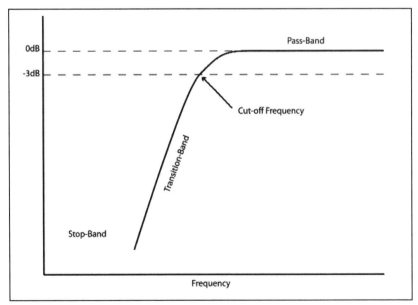

Figure 5.5
Anatomy of a high-pass filter. Note the cutoff frequency or 3dB down point.

When you combine a high-pass and low-pass filter together in series, you create a band-pass filter as seen in Figure 5.6. If the cutoff frequency of the high-pass filter is lower than the cutoff frequency of the low-pass filter, the frequencies that remain are the pass-band of the band-pass filter.

Figure 5.6

Combining a high- and low-pass filter in series creates the band-pass filter.

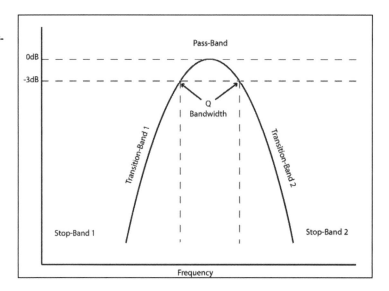

To create the fourth filter type, the band-reject or notch filter, high- and low-pass filters are combined in parallel. The signal is split into two paths, one that is high-pass filtered and the other that is low-pass filtered. The two resulting signals are then combined to create the band-reject profile, as shown in Figure 5.7.

Figure 5.7

A band-reject, or notch filter created by parallel processing of high- and low-pass filters.

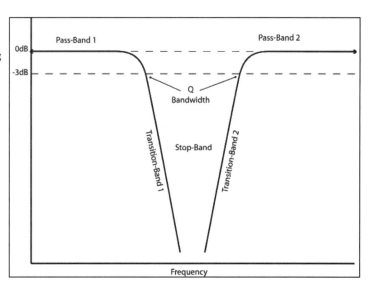

These four filter variations are used together to create equalizers. By using filters to separate frequencies in a signal, each component can be added back in varying amounts to create gain changes in specific frequency bands.

With all the phase and amplitude relationships being altered in each filter type, imagine how this becomes amplified in a complex filter like a parametric equalizer with many bands (such as the Voxengo Curve EQ shown in Figure 5.8).

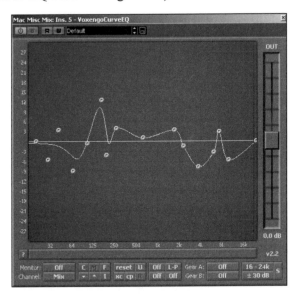

Figure 5.8

The Voxengo Curve EQ can have many individual bands of EQ, thereby exponentially increasing the amount of phase and the amplitude-altering processes.

Filter Shape

One of the most critical aspects of filter design is the resulting shape of each area of the filter, pass-band, transition-band, and stop-band. The method of calculation determines how a particular filter will sound in terms of frequency response. Each filter shape is displayed as a low-pass filter for comparison because it is the most basic type of filter.

Butterworth

The Butterworth shape is very common and is referred to as *maximally flat* due to the fact that there is no disturbance in the pass-band until just before the cutoff frequency. Figure 5.9 shows a Butterworth low-pass filter's frequency response. The roll-off of frequencies begins just slightly before the 3dB down point and then continues through the transition-band all the way to the stop-band.

Figure 5.9

The shape of a Butterworth low-pass filter is called maximally flat.

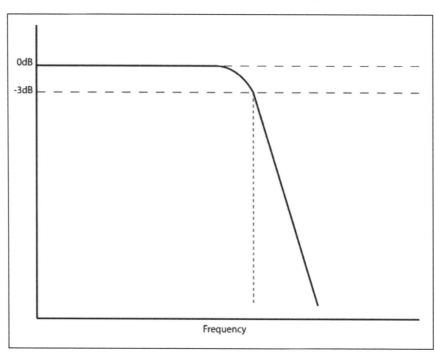

❊ FILTER SLOPE

The angle of the transition-band determines how much frequencies are reduced as the frequency increases. This is commonly called the slope of the filter. Slope is measured in decibels per octave, or dB/8ve. If the cutoff frequency is 50Hz and the slope is 24dB/8ve, 100Hz will be −24dB below 50Hz, 200Hz will be −48dB below 50Hz, and so on.

The tradeoff with Butterworth filters is that, in order to keep the flat pass-band response, the phase response is altered. Transients that are processed with a Butterworth filter are smeared as a result. The degree of smearing depends on the severity of the filter slope. The steeper the slope, the more phase alteration occurs.

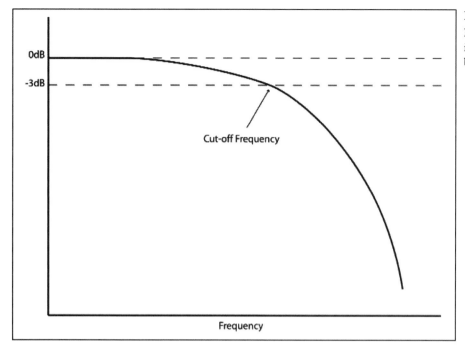

Figure 5.10
Bessel low-pass filter showing a long gradual roll-off
before the cutoff frequency.

Bessel

Bessel filters are similar to Butterworth filters except that they slope earlier and very gently towards the cutoff frequency. Figure 5.10 shows the shape of the same low-pass filter using the Bessel calculation. Bessel filters affect more frequencies than Butterworth, but often have a more natural sound to them, similar to moving a microphone farther from the source. Once in the transition band, Bessel filters react in the same manner as Butterworth filters.

Bessel filters have a much better phase response than Butterworth at the expense of the gentle slope in the pass-band. This type of filter might be better for drums and percussion than a Butterworth. Conversely, the Butterworth filter is better for organ sounds or strings, which have fewer transient components than percussive sounds.

Chebychev

Chebychev filters exhibit what is known as *pass-band ripple* prior to the cutoff frequency. The frequency response varies in both positive and negative gain as it approaches the cutoff frequency.

Figure 5.11 shows the response curve of a Chebychev filter. The pass-band ripple effect is something we are all used to hearing and is not necessarily a bad thing. It just depends on the circumstances.

The pronounced peak just before the cutoff frequency is a common artifact of equalizers that can be desirable in certain situations. For example, when rolling off the high end from an electric guitar track, the cutoff frequency might be 6kHz. Using a Chebychev filter, the area around 4–5kHz could be increased, giving the sound a bit of an edge in this area while removing frequencies above. This might help the guitar to stand out in the mix without interfering with other high-frequency elements such as the cymbals or sibilance in vocal tracks. It might eliminate the need to use an additional filter to add these frequencies. Each filter type has its purposes.

Figure 5.11

The Chebychev filter shape, including pass-band ripple just before the cutoff frequency.

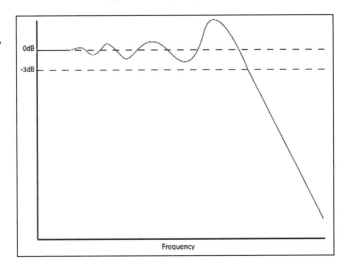

Elliptical

Elliptical filters are more severe in nature, with odd response occurring in the stop-band and pass-band ripple as well. The stop-band does not exhibit an even reduction at all frequencies. Figure 5.12 shows how the response is curved and uneven as the frequency increases. However, elliptical filters are capable of very extreme performance in the transition band without complex filter design.

The UAD Cambridge EQ has an elliptical filter, as seen in Figure 5.12. This high-pass filter slopes very steeply in the transition band, allowing for a greater control in separating frequencies. The tradeoffs are in the response of the stop-band, more pass-band ripple, and poor phase response. Elliptical filters are good in extreme cases where quick attenuation in the transition-band is desired to separate frequencies that are close together.

Linear Phase Filters

The linear phase type of filter is very accurate in the time domain as far as phase distortion is concerned. However, in order to get a linear phase response, frequency domain errors must be equally spread out both before and after transients. In other words, there will be a "pre-ring" and "post-ring" to the filter that can be noticeable in extreme cases.

❀ ❀ ❀

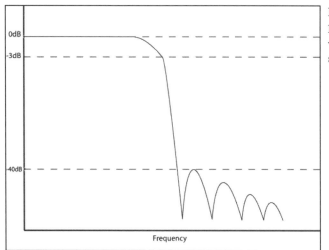

Figure 5.12
Elliptical filter response with odd effect in the stop-band.

This pre-ring occurs just before the initial steep waveform begins. A small amplitude variation occurs, leading up to the transient spike. In most cases, this should be inaudible. With extreme gains of low frequencies, this pre-ring can become more noticeable. Figure 5.13 shows what happens when a simple digital spike is processed by Waves Linear Phase equalizer with a very steep notch filter to emphasize the ringing effect. You can see both the pre-ring and post-ring in the waveform on either side of the spike.

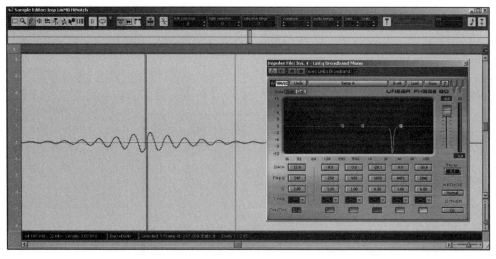

Figure 5.13
The Waves Linear Phase Equalizer exhibits a "pre-ring" effect as a result of FIR linear phase filter processing when excited by an impulse or transient.

These sections covered all these filter types and their ramifications in order to demonstrate how equalization affects audio signals. When you're using equalizers, bear in mind that the phase distortion consequences of many of the filters described are not always detrimental to the audio itself. It depends on the type of signal and the settings of the filter. Most analog filters have terrible phase response and have been used in audio for decades. Many of these types of filters are preferred to their digital linear phase counterparts in some audiophile circles. You must always use your ears to decide what sounds good.

Equalizer Basics

Equalizers, as we know them, are a combination of many filter types. From the treble and bass controls on a home stereo to a fully parametric five-band channel EQ, every type of frequency adjustment is based on the filter types mentioned earlier.

Complex Filter Types

In addition to the simple low- and high-pass filters, there are two complex filters that are common in equalizers. Each one is made up of several basic filters, plus gain staging and summing to create the final result. These are the items that are normally considered the parts of an equalizer.

For example, a signal being fed into an equalizer is divided into two paths. One is high-pass filtered and the other remains untouched. The two signal are then recombined. The level of the high-pass filtered signal determines the gain of those frequencies in the output of the equalizer. If the polarity of the high-passed signal was reversed, adding it to the original would reduce the level of those frequencies through phase cancellation. This would create a basic shelving filter with positive and negative gain.

Shelving Filter

Shelving filters increase or decrease the gain of a large number of frequencies, starting at a turnover frequency (often called the *corner frequency*) and continuing upwards in frequency or downwards in frequency. Their frequency response curve looks like a step or shelf, hence the name, shelving filter.

Figure 5.14 shows the PSP MasterQ with a high-shelving filter boosting frequencies starting at 5.01kHz and above by 4.59dB. All frequencies above 5.01kHz are not equally boosted. This is due

Figure 5.14

The PSP MasterQ with an active shelving filter boosting 5kHz and above.

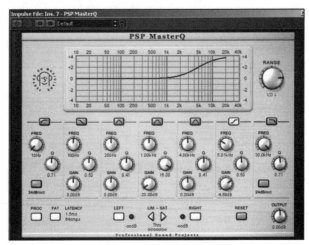

to the transition band of one of the basic filters used to create the complex shelving filter. Some shelving filters, such as the MasterQ, allow adjustment of the slope of the transition band. This determines how steep the curve is. In addition, some pass-band ripple can be present in the area close to the corner frequency, depending on the steepness of the slope.

When adjusting the slope of a shelving filter, the control is often referred to as slope, Q, or shape. Steeper slopes often result in a dip in the area just before the corner frequency, as seen in Figure 5.15 with the TC EQSat plug-in. This is the result of a steep high-pass filter that results in pass-band and stop-band ripple.

Remember that this can be a desirable trait for a high-shelving filter because it clears out a frequency range just below the now-boosted region. This can help emphasize the higher frequencies even more, thus requiring less gain from the shelving filter.

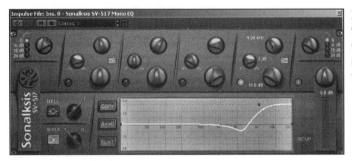

Figure 5.15

The TC EQSat high-shelving filter with a steep slope exhibiting stop-band ripple effect close to the corner frequency.

You can use low-shelving filters to remove unwanted rumble and subsonic material from tracks or just to make a voice sound more distant by reducing lower frequencies. They are mirror images of high-shelving filters, as seen in Figure 5.16. This filter is set to reduce the muddy elements in a hi-hat track below 400Hz. The slope is very gradual, thus minimizing the phase distortion of higher slopes and preserving the transient of the hi-hat attack.

Figure 5.16

The Waves Renaissance EQ set to a low-shelving filter, removing unwanted lower frequencies from a hi-hat track.

Parametric EQ

The *Parametric* EQ, first coined by audio guru George Massenburg in the early 70s, is a complex filter that affects only one band of frequencies. The term *parametric*, meaning all parameters, stems from the ability to control the three characteristics of the filter independently: gain, center frequency, and bandwidth, or Q.

The simple band-reject, or notch filter, is one example of what a parametric is capable of. The parametric filter can also boost a band of frequencies. The center frequency of the band is where the maximum gain is applied. All adjacent frequencies have a lesser amount of gain applied, depending on the slope, or Q of the filter.

The slope of a parametric filter affects two areas, one below the center frequency and one above the center frequency. These are the two transition bands of the filter. This slope is more often referred to as the Q or bandwidth of the filter. The Q, or Quality Factor, determines how wide the "bell" shape of the filter is. It is measured as the ratio of the center frequency to the bandwidth between the two −3dB down frequencies, as seen in Figure 5.17.

Figure 5.17
The Q, or Quality Factor, is a ratio of the −3dB down bandwidth to the center frequency.

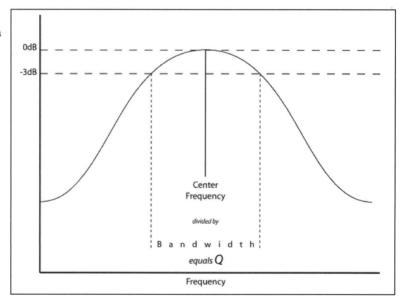

The point to remember about Q is the higher the Q number, the narrower the bandwidth of the filter. Figure 5.18 shows two parametric filters, one with a low 0.6 Q and the other with a high 4.99 Q. The higher Q filter is much narrower. Extremely narrow filters can exhibit more ringing and ripple than wider filters. Narrower Qs also suffer from poorer phase response in the time domain.

Figure 5.18

Two parametric filters. Filter A has a Q of 0.6 and filter B has a Q of 4.99.

Filter Parameters

Most filter types share a set of parameters that you can adjust. You can tune the frequency or adjust the bandwidth, slope, or Q factor to change the shape of the curve. And for all filters except the high- and low-pass ones, the gain adjustment can be positive or negative.

Frequency

The frequency parameter allows you to choose the target frequency around which the filter will operate. In the case of the parametric filter, it is the center frequency. High- and low-shelving filters have the turnover or corner frequency, which is defined by a gain change of +/–3dB. Figure 5.19 shows the Sonalksis EQ with a low-shelving filter boosting 5dB with a corner frequency of 100Hz.

Figure 5.19

The Sonalksis EQ shelving filter in action with a corner frequency of 100Hz.

Bandwidth/Slope/Q

Bandwidth, slope, Q, and shape are all ways of describing the transition band of any filter. With high- and low-pass filters and shelving filters, there is only one slope involved. With parametric filters, the slopes occur on both sides of the center frequency to create the bell shape. The parameter remains the same. Higher Q values translate into steeper slopes with more dB per octave transition.

Figure 5.20 shows the Waves Renaissance EQ with a high-shelving filter set with a steep slope that results in a large amount of pass-band ripple just prior to the turnover frequency of 10kHz. The slope or Q of a filter can also affect the frequency response around the filter, as seen in the Waves example in Figure 5.20. With a steeper slope, the filter exhibits a stronger ripple heading into the transition band than with a gradual slope. The frequency response dips prior to sloping upwards through the transition band. This is a typical response that emulates the behavior of vintage equalizers.

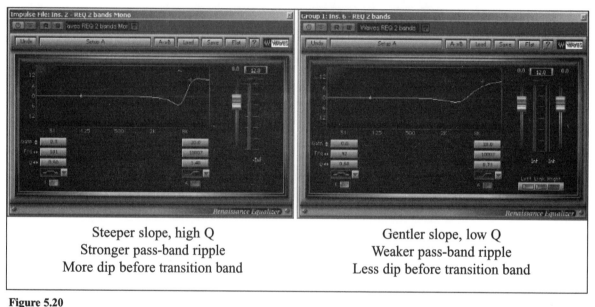

Steeper slope, high Q
Stronger pass-band ripple
More dip before transition band

Gentler slope, low Q
Weaker pass-band ripple
Less dip before transition band

Figure 5.20

The Waves Renaissance EQ with a steep slope and gradual slope high-shelving filter at 10kHz.

Gain

Once you determine the slope and frequency, you can set the gain. This is only true for shelving and parametric filters. High- and low-pass filters only roll off frequencies. No gain setting is required.

With parametric filters, the gain setting applies directly to the center frequency. If 3dB of gain is added at a center frequency of 1kHz, only 1kHz will actually be 3dB louder. Frequencies around 1kHz will also be affected, but only as determined by the Q or slope of the filter.

Gain and Q Dependency

Some equalizers have the option of changing the dependency of the Q factor as the gain is increased or decreased. The Sonalksis, Cambridge, and Sony Oxford EQs all have several filter types that react differently for a given set of gain and Q parameters. The reason for this is that certain favored analog designs of the past had frequency responses that would alter the Q of a filter as gain was increased, usually making the bandwidth narrower. This had an influence on how the equalizer was used creatively. Recognizing this fact, designers such as Sonalksis and Sony Oxford have included various gain/Q dependencies as options within their equalizers.

Sony Oxford

The first type (Type 1) has minimal gain/Q dependency and is best used for very precise adjustments. As gain is changed, it can often be necessary to manually adjust the Q in order to maintain a similar perceived tonal change. This type of EQ often gets labeled as "harsh," although it is only a relationship of the gain-dependant Q. This style of EQ closely relates to early SSL 4000 console EQs.

The Oxford Type 2 exhibits the only asymmetrical gain curves. Figure 5.21 shows the positive and negative gain curves. The positive gain has the same gain/Q dependency as Type 1. The negative gain curves exhibit a constant Q design, which keeps the bandwidth the same regardless of gain settings. This can be helpful for removing unwanted resonance in percussive instruments, while retaining the capability to gently add positive EQ shaping within the same EQ plug-in. Positive gains have a wide Q setting, whereas negative gains use a much narrower Q.

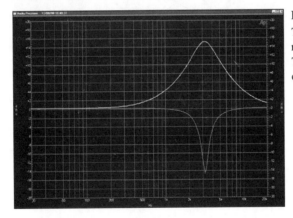

Figure 5.21

The positive and negative response curves of the Oxford R3 Type 2 equalizer with asymmetrical gain/Q dependency.

The R3's Type 3 EQ has a moderate amount of gain-dependent Q. As the gain is increased, either positively or negatively, the bandwidth becomes narrower or the Q values increase, and the slope becomes steeper. This response is similar to the revered Neve and newer SSL G series console EQs.

The Type 4 EQ has a much larger amount of gain/Q dependency. It is suited more for mastering applications where wide, gentle adjustments are needed to shape entire mixes. The area under the response curve remains the same at various gain settings. As the gain approaches 10dB, the Q narrows into a notch-type filter.

The shelving filters on the Oxford R3 do not change with the EQ type. Their slope shape is controlled by the Q setting. When the shelving option is selected, as shown in Figure 5.22, the Q control becomes a shape control for the shelving filter. Lower settings have a smoother curve with no reduction in the pass-band area. As the Q is increased, a dip in the frequencies just below the corner frequency occurs. This can be beneficial when trying to emphasize higher frequencies by removing mids just below the cutoff frequency.

Figure 5.22

Selecting the shelving filters changes the Q control to a shape control for the shelf.

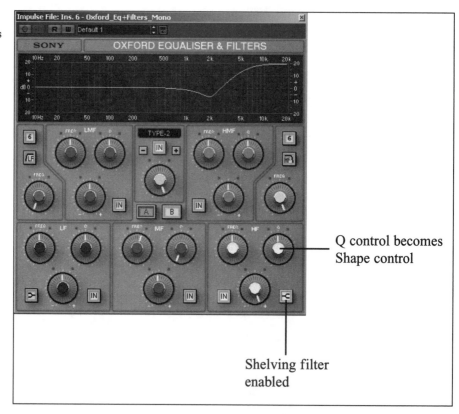

Q control becomes Shape control

Shelving filter enabled

Sonalksis SV-517

The Sonalksis EQ has three settings for the parametric bands and two for the shelving filters. In addition, both the parametric and shelving filters have a switch determining the symmetrical aspect of the filter. With these two options, the Sonalksis can achieve quite a few unique equalizer curves.

The three bell curve (parametric) types have similar responses to the Sony.

* Type I has a moderate amount of gain/Q dependency similar to Sony's Type 3.

* Type II has the most gain/Q dependency where the bandwidth narrows quickly as gain approaches the maximum.

❅ Type III is the constant Q design similar to the Sony Type 1, where the Q does not change regardless of gain change. This is the most clinical EQ type.

The symmetrical buttons determine how the shape behaves in negative gain values. For each bell curve type, the symmetrical and asymmetrical negative gain shapes are different. When the button is lit, the curves are symmetrical. Without the symmetrical curve option on, the negative gain curves are different than the boost, usually with a narrower bandwidth. The designers at Sonalksis have determined that many of the analog equalizers that the SV-517 emulates have asymmetrical bell curves. The combination of the three dependency types and the symmetrical button yields six variations for just the parametric bands.

There are two shelving types with the Sonalksis:

❅ With Type I, the response contains a dip in frequencies just before the corner frequency that increases as the slope is increased. See Figure 5.23.

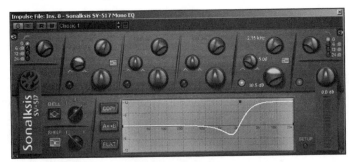

Figure 5.23

The Sonalksis Type I shelving filter with a relatively steep slope, showing the characteristic dip in the area just before the corner frequency.

❅ With Type II, there is a dip just as with Type I, but also a peak at the end of the transition band, as seen in Figure 5.24.

Figure 5.24

The Sonalksis Type II shelving filter with a dip on one end of the transition band and a peak on the other end.

The shelving filters also have a symmetrical curve option. If not used, the negative response curves will vary from the positive gain curves. By default, the symmetrical curve option is on.

UAD Cambridge EQ

The UAD Cambridge EQ also has several choices for gain/Q dependency and shelving response. The parametric bands have three types.

* Type I is a constant Q design.

* Type II is asymmetrical. The positive gains increase the Q value as the gain goes up, resulting in narrower bandwidths at high-gain settings. The negative gain settings have a constant Q response.

* Type III has symmetrical gain/Q dependency with increasing Q values as either positive or negative gain is applied.

Even the shelving filters have three variations in shape, as seen in Figure 5.25. Each shelving filter has a button next to it to determine what shape the filter will have: A, B, or C. These three options determine where the resonant peak will be located in the response to the shelving filters.

* Shelving shape A has a resonant peak at the end of the stop-band.

* Shape B has the resonant peak at the edge of the pass-band or shelf.

* Shape C has both resonant peaks at the edges of the transition-band.

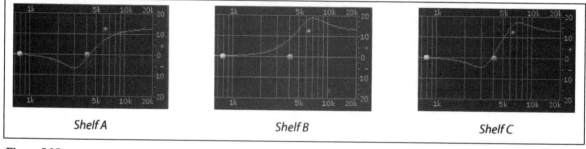

Figure 5.25
The three shelving shapes of the Cambridge Equalizer.

There are quite a few variations that are possible with these controls. It is truly a great thing to be able to have so many EQ curves possible with one plug-in, whether the Sony, Cambridge or Sonalksis. It would take several high-end outboard analog EQs to match this kind of diversity. In the area of equalization, digital processing has advanced to the point of being a viable alternative to the best analog processing at a fraction of the cost, but with so much more versatility.

Applying Equalization

Taking advantage of all the possibilities with modern EQ plug-ins will help simplify equalization tasks. One type of filter will invariably yield better results in less time than the others in a given situation. This section deals with understanding what each filter type is capable of and what sort of situations warrants their use.

Selecting a Filter Type

When approaching an equalization task, the first issue is determining what you need to do with the equalizer. Are you trying to fix some error in the recording or odd resonance? Maybe you are trying to creatively alter the character of an instrument to complement another sound. Sometimes, gentle tonal shaping is all that is needed. Knowing what filter type to select will help achieve results quicker.

Fixing a Problem

So much of equalization is fixing problems in the recording. If every track were recorded perfectly, would there even be a need for EQ? EQ can be used to counteract undesirable aspects of a recording technique or sound source.

One of the most common problems encountered in recording is a less than optimal recording space that may contain one or more room resonances or modes. Depending on the dimensions of the space, room modes occur at specific frequencies that relate the wavelength to one dimension of the space.

For example, if the recording room has a lengthwise dimension of 10 feet, there could be resonant peaks and dips at various locations in the room around 100Hz. This is caused by sound reflecting off one wall and then bouncing between the two walls. Because those walls are 10 feet apart and that is also the wavelength of 100Hz, when the sound wave bounces back upon itself, it creates large amplitude variations at different places in the room, as shown in Figure 5.26.

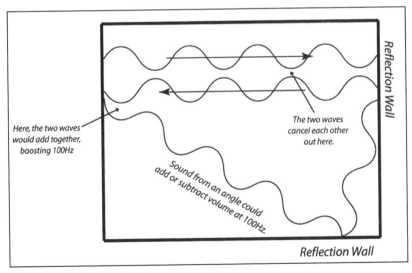

Figure 5.26
How a 100Hz mode affects room resonance at various positions.

If a drum set was being recorded in this room and a microphone was placed at a point where 100Hz was amplified by the room mode, the recording will be colored by a predominance of 100Hz. Conversely, the microphones can be placed at a point where cancellation of 100Hz occurs, leaving the recording deficient in that tonal area.

An equalizer can be used to compensate for this anomaly. The filter of choice in this case would be a parametric band. The band can easily be tuned to 100Hz and a negative gain applied to reduce the resonance of the room mode. The critical adjustment is the Q setting so as not to affect any other frequencies besides the resonant one. Using your ears is the best way to determine the correct frequency and bandwidth size (Q).

The second example is more common in video and film production. Often the environment on a film set is less than optimal for audio recording. The presence of high-powered lights, fans, camera equipment, and other audio hazards can wreak havoc on dialogue recordings. The most common issue is the introduction of 60-cycle hum into the audio signal from other electrical sources. This can be the result of overlapping cables or improperly grounded circuits, among many other causes. This is also commonly experienced in home studio with less than optimal wiring and electrical supply.

✻ EXACTLY 60 CYCLE HUM OR NOT?

60Hz relates to the carrier frequency of Alternating Current (AC) power in North America. The frequency is not always exactly 60Hz due to variances in power stations. Some fine-tuning (59Hz to 61Hz or so) of the filter might be necessary to properly remove this noise. Be aware that in Europe, the carrier frequency is 50Hz. Also, film transfers alter the speed and pitch of production audio by 0.1% for NTSC transfers and 4% for PAL transfers. You have to adjust the filter frequencies to compensate for this speed change.

In addition to the basic 60Hz tone, harmonics of 60Hz can also be created, causing a more complex issue. A simple notch filter at 60Hz might do the trick but if the harmonics are relatively loud, the hum signature might still be audible. In this case, it is necessary to identify the harmonics and filter them out as well. Fortunately, tools exist to facilitate harmonic filtering.

Figure 5.27 shows Elemental Audio's Eqium equalizer plug-in set to filter 60Hz and seven of its harmonic frequencies. The harmonic filter is just one of 11 filter types available in Eqium. The harmonic filter can affect the even, odd, or all harmonics with various curves and bandwidths.

Figure 5.27

Elemental Audio's Eqium equalizer set to a harmonic filter at 60Hz.

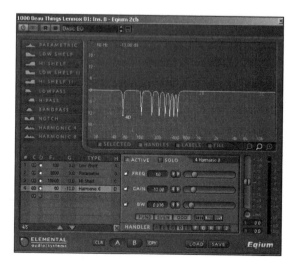

✻ ✻ ✻

High-pass filters are very useful for removing many kinds of noise and problems in recordings, from wind noise in outdoor recordings to mic stand rumble in studio recordings. Clearing out the low end in individual tracks can really help create space in a mix. It is advisable to listen to individual tracks and filter out any unwanted low-frequency material prior to mixing to avoid cluttering up the low end and using up valuable energy that can be used elsewhere in the spectrum.

❊ PHASE CONSEQUENCES

Remember the phase consequences of certain types of high-pass filters. Bessel curves offer the best phase performance, but have gradual slopes. Elliptical filters are the steepest, but alter the signal's phase the most.

With any recording problem that you are faced with, take the time to determine what filter type is the best for the job. Diving in headfirst and tweaking several filter bands to achieve a goal that could be done with one filter of the right type can eat up DSP resources and cause unwanted phase issues. Careful selection of filters yields better mixes in the end.

Contouring

Once you have eliminated any problems in frequency response, the usual next step is contouring of sounds to complement each other in a mix. This can involve anything, from broad parametric filters and shelving to emphasize various areas of the spectrum to more focused bands to alter the character of a sound. The choice of a filter in these situations is more dependent on the program material itself.

For starters, the broad Q parametric filters such as The Oxford Type 4 and Sonalksis Type II will have a more musical response, coloring gently without altering phase too much. The *character* of an EQ comes into play when dealing with contour and shaping. To that end, some plug-ins from URS can be very helpful.

Figure 5.28 shows the URS N series EQ, which is closely modeled after the classic a much sought-after Neve 1073 module. This five-band EQ has a unique sound that is useful in a number of ways. Even though it is not as precise or versatile as some of the other parametric EQs mentioned earlier, the sound quality offers a distinct *color* palette to use.

Figure 5.28

The URS N Series EQ is useful for contouring. The parameters are limited to fixed values, except for gain.

The frequency choices for each band are limited to fixed values. The frequencies are musical choices that should not hinder most contouring duties. The mid-band is the only parametric band available but only has two choices for Q, a broad setting and a "Hi Q" setting when the button is engaged. The high and low bands are shelving only without any shape adjustment. There are also two additional filters, one high-pass and one low-pass, with several frequency choices. Only the gain has a continually variable adjustment. On the original Neve 1073, even the gain controls had discrete settings—only certain gain settings were possible.

This semi-parametric EQ is what can be called a "decision maker" due to its limited settings. Sometimes having an unlimited amount of choices in a complex task such as mixing can overwhelm the engineer. Having some limitations can be a good thing. One frequency setting might sound preferable to another and because there is no in-between choice, the decision is made.

Another famous contouring equalizer is the Pultec EQP-1A, modeled by Universal Audio in the UAD plug-in shown in Figure 5.29. This program EQ is designed to contour entire mixes or elements within a mix. Its very gentle shelving curves and tube circuitry yield a warm sound that has been celebrated for many years.

However, using the Pultec can be confusing due to its archaic control system, which is also part of its charm. In the low-frequency band, there are two separate gain controls, one for boost and one for attenuation. The frequency control is labeled CPS for cycles per second. The boost and attenuation controls can work together at the same frequency setting due to their asymmetrical gain curves.

Figure 5.29

The UAD Pultec program equalizer.

Applying a boost at 60Hz, for example, adds a tremendous amount of energy throughout the low-end spectrum, as far up as 200 or 300Hz, depending on the amount of gain. This will add a great deal of size to the signal, but can easily muddy things up as well. Keeping the boost set, you can turn up the attenuation control to alter this boost. The result is a clearing out of lower mid frequencies where much of the mud can be found, thus complementing the size added by the boost. In this fashion, many contours can be created with this rather simple equalizer.

The high-frequency controls are slightly different. The boost and attenuation controls have separate frequency settings. The boost control has a frequency control and bandwidth setting. The bandwidth can have a rather narrow Q at its lowest setting and gets very broad and sweet at its highest setting. This is an ideal filter for adding "air" to a vocal without thinning it too much.

If too much sibilance results from a high-frequency boost, the attenuation controls can provide a somewhat narrow cut at 5kHz, 10kHz, or 20kHz. This cut interacts with the boost in nonlinear ways. Experimentation is the best route. Always let your ears show you the way.

Analytical Equalizers

Another method of contouring the entire sound has only become possible with plug-in technology. In mastering applications, it is often needed to alter the spectrum of an entire mix to match that of another piece. There are now plug-ins that can do this by design.

Elemental Audio's Firium is an analyzing equalizer. It can "learn" the spectrum response of one signal and apply it to another. This is done in two stages. Figure 5.30 shows Firium analyzing the spectrum of one signal as the source sound. This spectrum is what you want the equalizer to emulate. Once the source spectrum is gathered, the spectrum of the signal to be processed or target signal must be analyzed. Firium compares the two spectrums and creates a set of filters that alters the original spectrum to match the target.

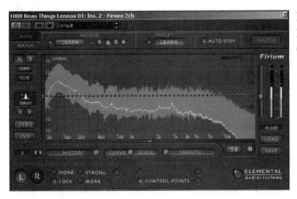

Figure 5.30

Elemental Audio's Firium analytical equalizer.

TC Electronics Assimilator, shown in Figure 5.31, is a similar type of plug-in. It can create two comparative filter sets that can be morphed together to create a composite third set. Go ahead and make your R & B tune sound like a cross between Peter Gabriel and Joss Stone!

Figure 5.31

TC Electronics Assimilator analytical equalizer.

Another useful task this type of plug-in can perform is the matching of dialogue recorded on the set with ADR (Automated Dialogue Replacement recorded later in the studio). In film production, dialogue recorded on the set might be contaminated with AC hum, wind, and air-handling noise, camera and motion control noise, airplanes—you name it. Directors often find themselves in a situation where the on-set dialogue is not acceptable.

Actors and actresses are brought into the studio and watch the footage onscreen while they mimic their dialogue performance. Obviously, the studio environment does not sound like the location environment. It is the job of the dialogue re-recording mix engineer to match those sounds seamlessly in the final mix. An analytical equalizer can be used to examine the spectrum of the on-set dialogue and apply it to the studio recording.

Creating Energy

Equalizing can add energy to tracks just by emphasizing certain frequency areas and harmonics. Usually this is a boosting of frequencies rather than a cut. In popular music, the higher frequencies of most instruments are not natural at all. They have a "hyped" sound to them that can be exciting if done well.

Unless you are using a linear phase filter such as the Waves Linear EQ, some degree of phase shift will always occur with filters. Certain phase response of specific filters can lend themselves more to boosting than others, providing more energy without transient loss. The URS A10 graphic equalizer is a good example of this when used with drums.

Modeled after the classic API console graphic EQs, the A10 is a 10-octave-band graphic equalizer with fixed frequencies and Q settings. Each frequency is an octave of the other. Figure 5.32 shows the EQs frequencies as 31Hz, 63Hz, 125Hz, 250Hz, 500Hz, 1kHz, 2kHz, 4kHz 8kHz, and 16kHz, all which are multiples of one another. This is a musical configuration for an equalizer. Some graphic EQs have third-octave bands for a total of 31 bands. The A10 has a wide enough bandwidth per band to exert a great deal of control over any signal.

Figure 5.32

The URS A10 equalizer, modeled after the API 560 Graphic EQ.

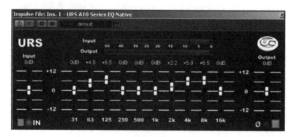

Particularly when boosting, the A10 imparts a great deal of energy into drum sounds, providing attack in the 2kHz to 8kHz range and impressive size and impact in the 63Hz to 250Hz range. Judicious use of this equalizer on pop kick and snare tracks can be a good start at creating energy.

Another URS plug-in modeled after the famous SSL EQ is the S Series shown in Figure 5.33. This equalizer has more versatility than many modeled EQs due to the fact that the SSL is a more modern console with more features in their equalizer. The EQ has two fully parametric mid bands and two semi-parametric shelving/peaking bands for highs and lows. Also included are high- and low-pass filters.

The shelving filters are especially interesting because they provide a high degree of coloration to the sound. The high-end sheen found in many pop background vocals can be achieved with this plug-in. Using the high-shelving filter to extremes will bring a very unnatural sound that has become ingrained in the ears of pop music listeners over the years. You turn the knob and say, "Oh, that's how they do it."

Figure 5.33

The URS S Series EQ modeled after SSL console EQs. The high-shelving band has a unique color that can be useful.

Finding the right equalizer to add just the kind of coloration is a wholly different task than choosing a filter for more surgical tasks such as removing room resonances. Having a wide variety of plug-ins to choose from can provide your mixes with various tonalities that help separate instruments and give things unique sonic perspectives. Also, using the various filter shapes can help you arrive at better EQ settings without the hassle of constantly adjusting the Q settings for different gains.

The search for the right contour can be a lifetime journey. Fortunately, the vast array of plug-ins can bring those choices closer. Affording all these tools in the analog world is prohibitively expensive for most budgets. The world of plug-ins exposes more users to the palette that once were only had by the few.

Creating Space

In today's world of audio where the DAW is king, the issue of having a limited amount of tracks for any production has become meaningless in all practical terms. A typical pop music mix can easily have 48 tracks of instruments and vocals, with any number of effects returns and other grouping channels. In the film world, it can get plain ridiculous. The film *Blackhawk Down* used 450 audio tracks at mixdown. This was after the film's editors had created pre-dubs from all the sources tracks. The use of the DAW has opened Pandora's box in terms of track count.

With so many tracks that are routinely created for audio productions, creating space for them in the final mix is imperative. Many of these decisions are production issues about whether to include some tracks in the final mix. Even after extraneous tracks have been weeded out, the mix engineer can be left with many tracks that need to fit into the final mix at any given point in time. This is affectionately known as a *wall of ho-ho* for those who have experienced it.

Finding one's way through the maze of sounds to arrive at the perfect blend and sonic mix is trying and requires diligence and the proper use of equalization. Equalizers are the perfect tools to create the space needed for any track within a mix. By carefully allocating areas in the spectrum for various sounds, a large number of tracks can be blended together and still be clear and cohesive. This is the art of mixing, and the equalizer is one of the main tools.

Instruments that sound just fine by themselves might have trouble in a mix if other sounds are sharing the same spectrum area. An equalizer can be used to shift the predominant spectrum of a sound to another region in order to make space.

For example, the kick drum in popular music occupies much of the same spectrum as the bass guitar or bass synth part. Figure 5.34 shows the spectrum response of an un-equalized kick drum. Notice the amount of energy between 20Hz and 150Hz. Figure 5.35 shows the response curve of a bass guitar playing a low G. Its fundamental is around 50Hz or so, with the first harmonic at 100Hz. Mixing these two signals together might cause a problem, because one instrument will mask the sound of the other, depending on their relative levels.

Figure 5.34

The spectrum of the un-equalized kick drum.

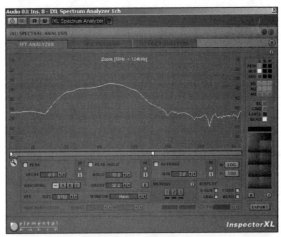

Figure 5.35

The spectrum of a bass guitar playing a low G.

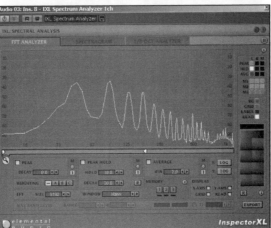

To avoid the masking effect, the energy spectrum of each instrument can be shifted using an equalizer to make some space for both sounds. Figure 5.36 shows the equalization applied to the kick drum. The dip at 120Hz opens up an area for the first harmonics of the bass guitar. The boost at 40Hz adds energy to the lowest octave to compensate for the dip higher up. This should make the kick drum fuller with more low-end punch while also creating a space for the bass.

Figure 5.36

The equalization curve applied to the kick drum in order to make space for the bass guitar.

The bass needs to shift some energy higher in the spectrum so as not to muddy up the kick drum and still have good presence in the mix. Figure 5.37 shows the EQ curve applied with a steep high-pass filter at 48Hz and a boost at 120Hz or so. This shifts the energy up into the first harmonics of the bass and reduces the lower octave information that might interfere with the kick drum.

Figure 5.37

The equalization curve applied to the bass guitar to shift the energy up into the first harmonic range and remove unwanted lower octave material.

Figures 5.38 and 5.39 show the resulting spectrum response for the kick and bass after equalization was applied. The kick drum has an obvious peak around 40Hz and then a relatively clear area above 80Hz. This is the space for the bass guitar. The bass guitar response curve shows the fundamental 40Hz is lower than the first harmonic at 80Hz. The energy has been shifted upwards and out of the kick region.

Figure 5.38

The equalized spectrum of the new kick.

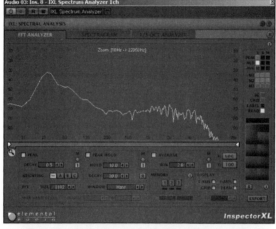

Figure 5.39

The equalized spectrum of the new bass.

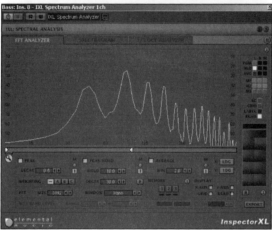

Hopefully, the ears will agree and reveal that this has cleared up the low end in the mix while providing more clarity for both instruments. These examples are exaggerated for the sake of visual representation and discussion, but the ideas remain the same. Always let your ears decide if the technique is working. Do not let a spectrum analyzer make mix decisions for you.

Tuning the Filter

Choosing the right frequency for any filter is probably the most important task in equalizing. There are several techniques for finding the right frequency setting. Each technique has benefits and problems. It depends on the task the EQ is performing and your experience at identifying various frequencies by ear.

To Sweep or Not To Sweep

For removing resonances, a common technique is to set a parametric filter to a high Q value or narrow bandwidth and boost by a large amount, say +8dB or so. Then, while listening to the program material, sweep the frequency control up and down the spectrum until the resonance that you are after is boosted prominently. Once identified, the gain can be reduced to a negative value to remove the unwanted frequency. With practice, this technique can also help train your ear to identify frequency ranges unaided.

The downside to this method relates to how human hearing adapts quickly to changes in the environment. Human hearing is quite capable of quickly identifying changes in surroundings by hearing echoes, room resonances, and many other cues. Once identified, the brain can then ignore these sonic anomalies in order to concentrate on sounds within that environment.

For example, if you are having a conversation with another person while walking across an open park and then enter a cathedral as the conversation continues, your hearing must reconcile the acoustic differences between the outdoor park and the huge reverberant sound of the cathedral in order to maintain intelligibility of the conversation. This analysis and reconciliation takes place in a fraction of an instant without your knowing about it.

When sweeping an equalizer, our hearing is attempting to reconcile the spectrum changes in order to ignore them and pay attention to the musical performance instead. It can become difficult to identify resonant areas that are subtle because our hearing system is constantly compensating for changes in the spectrum almost instantly. It is better to toggle two static states, or use A/B comparisons, to judge differences in EQ. When using a constantly moving EQ change, the ear is more likely to adapt to it and reduce its sensitivity to the change.

If your hearing is trained and experienced in identifying various frequencies, trying to set the frequency of a filter without any gain being applied can help make better EQ choices. When setting the equalizer, first take a guess as to what frequency needs adjustment. Then adjust the gain in the appropriate direction and see if the result is pleasing.

Most EQ plug-ins, such as the Cambridge shown in Figure 5.40, have the capability to turn off individual bands. Once the band has been set, turn it off and then on again to determine whether the adjustment is making a real improvement on things. This avoids your ears being tricked with the sweep and forcing them to compensate for dynamic changes in the spectrum. Additionally, once you've made a complete EQ setting, you can bypass the entire plug-in to see if the sound is an improvement.

Figure 5.40

The UAD Cambridge EQ has individual enable switches for each band of the equalizer.

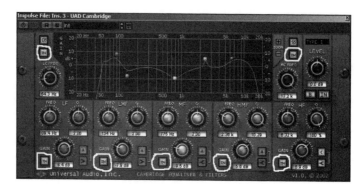

Another issue is the added volume that EQ can generate. Sounds that are louder tend to excite the senses and appear "better" than the softer sound. When you engage a boosted band of EQ, the added volume can be perceived as improved quality even though the EQ setting may not be the best. Most EQ plug-ins also have a master gain control, such as the Sony R3 shown in Figure 5.41. The master gain can be used to compensate for added or reduced volume as a result of equalization. When comparing the EQ'ed version of a sound to the unprocessed version, try to match the perceived volumes with the master gain control on the equalizer. This will allow you to make accurate decisions on EQ choices.

Figure 5.41

The Sony Oxford R3 with master gain control that can be used to gain-match equalized and un-equalized signals for better comparison.

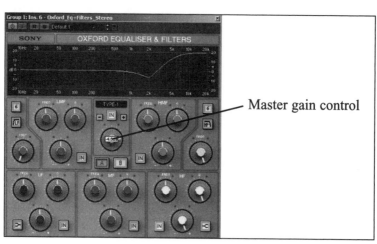

Master gain control

A third, more creative, technique involves identifying two instruments that are prominent in the mix and that need to have a complementary relationship, such as the lead vocal and acoustic guitar in a folk song. The technique requires diverting attention to the sound that is not being EQ'ed while making changes in the other sound. For example, you adjust the equalizer for the acoustic guitar while concentrating on the lead vocal to see how changes affect the relationship between the two instead of one instrument by itself.

Removing Excess Bandwidth

Once you have identified a frequency and set the gain, you need to adjust the Q or bandwidth control for the proper bandwidth. When removing resonances, the Q will most likely be narrow to avoid affecting other frequencies around the resonance. Contouring will usually require smaller Q values, affecting wider frequency areas.

Take advantage of the filter types with variable gain/Q dependency to help adjust the Q values as you change gain. The asymmetrical gain curves of some equalizers can help find the correct Q setting.

The point to remember is that extreme EQ settings are more precise, but they also come with a price in the time domain: poor phase response. Less gain and wider Q values have better phase response. The tradeoffs between phase and filter accuracy can only be measured by the best sound analysis tools in the world: your two ears.

Ringing

When equalizers are set to extreme settings, resonances can be created within the filter that causes a ringing. This is usually due to a parametric filter set with a very high Q setting and large amounts of boost, as shown in Figure 5.42. This effect can be desirable in certain situations, such as when creating a radio vocal or megaphone effect.

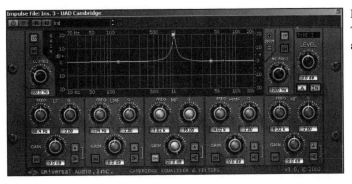

Figure 5.42

The Cambridge EQ set to create an obvious ringing filter.

If it seems like the only way to control some aspect of a signal is with a tight filter such as this, you should experiment with various plug-ins using similar settings to see whether one produces better results than the other. If better results cannot be found with any plug-in, it is time to figure out if you should be boosting at all.

To Boost or To Cut

To boost or to cut: That is the real question. Opinions vary on this subject. Some opinions suggest that first attempting to work exclusively with cutting or attenuation will yield the best results. Cutting of frequencies creates more space and signal headroom in general than boosting. Creating space first seems like a sensible idea.

All sounds cannot be equalized by merely attenuating frequencies. At some point, boosting becomes necessary. Boosting can add energy to lifeless tracks and provide that processed or unreal sound that many pop music records have. The key is to avoid over-EQ'ing things. If you can achieve the same result with one or two filters, there is no need to use all five bands plus filters on every EQ.

Summary

Becoming proficient at equalizing requires a lifetime of listening and experience in front of the speakers. Understanding the tools helps you experiment and learn more about equalizing the audio spectrum. The incredible variety of tools that plug-ins provide gives you hands-on experience with things that, only a few years ago, would not be available to most audio engineers. Take advantage of this by trying out many different plug-in equalizers and seeing how they alter the way you address equalization in general.

6 Dynamics Processors

Dynamics processors are gain processors that operate as a function of the input signal and time. The gain adjustment changes over time, depending on several variables. Dynamics processors analyze the incoming signal and adjust the gain of that signal accordingly.

The most common dynamics processor is the compressor. As the name implies, it is used to "compress" the dynamic range of a signal. In effect, more of the signal is at the same or similar level. Compressors control signal levels. Louder passages can be brought down and quieter passages can seemingly be brought up in level. This has the effect of bringing a sound forward in the mix and making lower level detail more audible. Side effects include the capability to create more punch in a sound or flattening out of a signal's dynamics. Large amounts of compression tend to dull the high frequencies a bit.

The limiter is the same thing as a compressor, only with a very high ratio. The basic premise for using a limiter is to prohibit a signal's level from exceeding a certain point. The traditional application for this was in radio stations to control the broadcast signal. The limiter would not allow the station's broadcast strength to exceed the legal limit imposed by the Federal Communications Commission (FCC). Limiters have their own sound characteristics and each plug-in has its merits. Some plug-ins offer look-ahead detection not possible in the analog world. This eliminates the possibility of signals exceeding the maximum allowed level.

Expanders work in the opposite direction of compressors. Above the threshold, they add gain (upwards expansion). Below a threshold, they reduce gain (downwards expansion). They create more dynamic range. You can use expanders to add liveliness back into tracks or for specific noise reducing operations like gating. Gates are downward expanders that turn a signal off when it is below the threshold. Gates are commonly used to remove background noise from sounds by setting the threshold just above the noise floor.

You can use dynamics processors in conjunction with equalizers to adjust the dynamics of a band of frequencies independent of the rest of the signal. The prime example of this is a de-esser, which reduces the level of sibilant frequencies often found in vocals.

Apart from controlling the level of sounds, most compressors, limiters, and other dynamics processors impart a sonic characteristic to the sound that is just as important as their level controlling capabilities, sometimes even more so.

Using Compressors and Limiters

Compressors and limiters are dynamics processors that only reduce the gain of incoming signals. By doing so, they reduce the dynamic range of signals or limit their maximum output level. As the input level gets louder, the compressor or limiter reduces gain, thereby controlling the average loudness by keeping the signal level within a certain range. The standard dynamics parameters are threshold, ratio, attack, and release. There are additional controls that some plug-ins use and they will also be reviewed after the basic controls.

Threshold

Whenever a signal's amplitude exceeds a certain level, called the *threshold*, gain reduction begins. If the threshold is set very high, gain reduction occurs less often. If the threshold is set very low, some amount of gain reduction will occur all the time a signal is present. The threshold can be thought of as the trigger for the compressor to start working. Any signal above the threshold triggers the compressors reaction. Signals below the threshold do not trigger the action of the compressor.

Ratio

The amount of gain reduction is dependent on the ratio. For every dB the signal exceeds the threshold, the compressor will apply an amount of gain reduction as determined by the ratio. For example, if the ratio is 2:1 (read 2 to 1), the compressor will bring the gain down by 1dB for every 2dB the signal exceeds the threshold. If the signal exceeds the threshold by 4dB, the compressor will reduce the gain by 2dB. The output of the compressor therefore only goes up by 2dB as a result: 4dB in, 2:1 ratio yields 2dB of gain reduction, as shown in Figure 6.1.

Figure 6.1

This graph represents how the ratio affects the output level of a compressor. In this example, the ratio is set to 2:1. Above the threshold point, the output of the compressor goes up only 1dB for every 2dB of input level. The shaded area shows the amount of gain reduction.

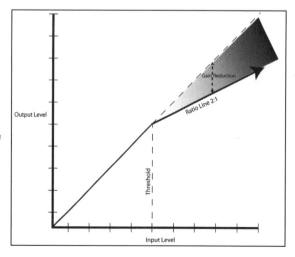

If the ratio were 6:1, it would take 6dB of signal level above the threshold to get 1dB more signal level from the output of the compressor. At ratios of 10:1 or higher, the output of the processor barely increases at all when the signal goes beyond the threshold point. At this point, the device is called a *limiter* because it basically "limits" the signal level to the threshold point, as seen in Figure 6.2.

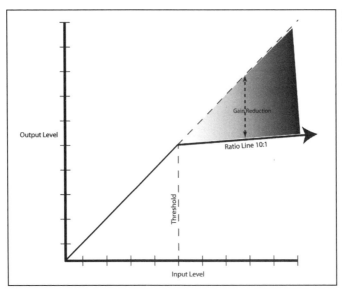

Figure 6.2

The IO graph of a limiter showing a ratio of 10:1. Ratios above 10:1 are considered limiting and not compression.

Attack Time

The other two main parameters of compression have to do with time. Because no analog processor can quite instantaneously reduce the gain due to physical limitations, there has traditionally been a lag time before gain reduction occurs. This is called the *attack time* and you can adjust it on most compressors. It is usually measured in milliseconds but many older analog units do not have a scale to represent the actual attack time. Plug-ins that emulate vintage units might not have a measured time scale either. Most plug-in compressors can set their attack time numerically for more precise adjustments.

The attack time has a lot to do with the sound of a given set of compression parameters. Slower attack times let transient signals pass through without gain reduction, sometimes creating a sense of "punch" to the sound. Conversely, very fast attack times remove transients from signals, smoothing or flattening out peaks.

WHY ANALOG?

The analog units are only mentioned here because so many of today's plug-ins are designed to emulate older or vintage audio equipment. The UAD-1 compressors are classic examples of this with the LA-2A, 1176, and Fairchild models. As you can see in Figure 6.3, the LA-2A does not have controls for attack and release times. This plug-in models the behavior of the original Teletronix unit, which had its own peculiar time response depending on the input signal.

Figure 6.3

The UAD-1 LA-2A plug-in interface. There are no controls for attack or release times. The ratio can only be set between "compress" and "limit" by using the switch on the left.

Release Time

The release time determines how fast gain reduction is removed once the signal passes back below the threshold. Sometimes called *recovery time,* this setting is measured in milliseconds. On some vintage style plug-ins, however, there might not be a timescale displayed.

Release times also affect the sound of a compressor. Faster release times tend to bring up the low level detail of a sound. Faster release times can also create a "pumping" effect if the signal is constantly triggering the compressor and then releasing quickly. Release times must be set musically to complement the sound's rhythmic nature.

Soft or Hard Knee

Most analog compressors exhibit slightly odd behavior just around the threshold point. The ratio fluctuates in a small arc around the threshold point. The shape of this area is called the *knee* of the compressor. A sharp knee compressor has a quick transition from 1:1 ratio to the above-threshold ratio as set by the user. Soft-knee compressors gradually increase the ratio as the signal passes the threshold, as seen in Figure 6.4. Some plug-in compressors, such as the Sonalksis SV-315, have an adjustable knee setting.

Non-Standard Compressor Parameters

Some complex plug-in compressors have other more "esoteric" parameters available. Where these parameters are available, tweaking the sound gets even more fun as the character of the compressor itself becomes something you can adjust.

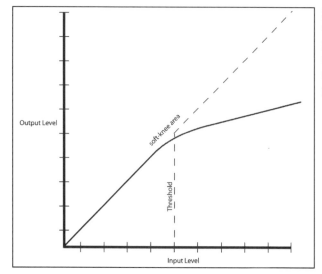

Figure 6.4
The ratio graph of a soft-knee compressor showing the gradual increase in ratio right around the threshold point.

Hold

Both the Sony Dynamics and Sonalksis compressors have a hold parameter that keeps the gain reduction in place for a period of time after the signal goes below the threshold. As seen in Figure 6.5, the Sony Dynamics plug-in measures this in seconds.

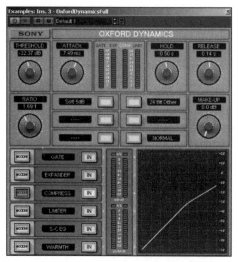

Figure 6.5
The Sony Dynamics plug-in showing the hold parameter set to 50 milliseconds.

The Sonalksis SV-315 compressor uses a percentage value for the hold parameter and must have the release set to automatic in order to function. This hold function is more complex than a simple time value. The Sonalksis hold parameter is a function of input material. The idea is that certain program signals, such as two very closely spaced peak signals, can cause a normal hold parameter to create odd distortion artifacts. Allowing the SV-315 to control the hold time automatically will avoid this type of coloration.

Side-Chain Filtering

Compressors split the incoming signal into two paths. One path is directed to the level detection circuit, which tells the compressor when and by how much to compress. This is called the *side-chain signal* and it can be treated in certain ways that will affect the outcome and sound of the compression. The other path is the actual audio signal that will be compressed.

Filtering of the side-chain signal can yield different compression characteristics. Most analog compressors had some sort of filtering in their side-chain paths to create a desired response in the compressor. The PSP MasterQ compressor has the capability to control the filter response of the side-chain as seen in Figure 6.6. When various frequencies are removed from the side-chain signal, the compressor will only react to the frequencies that are left. This allows you to "weigh" the action of the compressor in favor of certain frequency bands. In other words, if you filter out all the low frequencies from the side-chain, the compressor will only be triggered by high frequencies. This allows you to create a high-frequency compressor tuned to your own specific needs very easily.

Figure 6.6

The PSP Master Comp plug-in has high and low-shelving filters for the side-chain signal. Clicking on the filter icon changes it from high- or low-pass to high- or low-shelving boost. The monitor button allows the user to hear the side-chain signal after filtering.

The Waves C1 comp-sc allows side-chain filtering that is a bit more flexible with high- and low-pass, band-pass, and band-reject filters, all with adjustable frequency and Q controls, as seen in Figure 6.7. Using this filter, you can direct the compression at a specific portion of the audio spectrum. For example, if you have a guitar tone that is particularly harsh in the 800Hz to 1kHz region, you could set up the C1's side-chain to filter out other frequencies besides this region. When you adjust the threshold of the compressor, the compression is then focused on this frequency area.

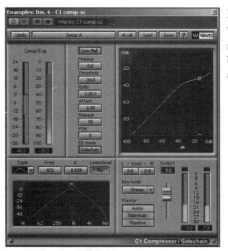

Figure 6.7

The Waves C1 comp-sc compressor with the side-chain filter set to band-pass the area between 800Hz and 1kHz.

Level-Detector Modes

The Sonalksis SV-315 also has two level-detection modes that alter the way the compressor reacts to dynamics. Mode I models classic compressors by allowing the attack and release to have more signal-dependent coloration. This has the effect of giving more bite and crunch in the compression sound when really clamping down on a signal with a lot of compression. In Mode II, the compressor behaves more like a modern unit that has less coloration of the sound as the program transients change. This mode is good for more transparent compression with fewer artifacts.

The Waves Renaissance Compressor also has two operation modes, Electro and Opto. In the Electro mode, the release time gets faster the less compression there is (<3dB). As compression increases, so does the release time. Electro mode is recommended for increased loudness applications such as voice-overs. When the compression amount is around 3dB, the Electro mode will add a great deal of RMS volume to the signal.

The Opto mode does just the opposite. When there is more compression, the release time is quicker and, as compression decreases, the release time slows down. This effect sounds great on drums and sounds that need quick short-term release times with longer, leveling properties as well.

Mid-Level Compression

Often what is needed with compression is the capability to bring up detail in the middle and lower portions of the dynamic range while still maintaining peak transients. Both the Waves C1 and the Sonalksis SV-315 have the ability to compress mid-level signals and still retain peak transients.

With the C1, this curve is built-in to the plug-in. As you lower the threshold, you will see that the IO curve of the C1 returns to a 1:1 ratio at a certain point, as seen in Figure 6.8. Basically, as the signal passes the threshold, compression kicks in until it reaches a much higher level where the compression ceases. At that point, the highest-level signals do not get compressed. By compressing only the mid-level signals, a sound may be made perceptually louder without losing its transient components.

Figure 6.8

The Waves C1 showing the mid-level compression curve.

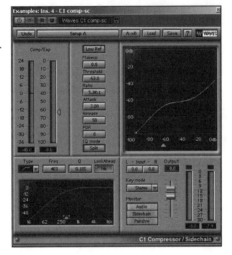

The Sonalksis SV-315 approaches this issue with a different control, Crush. The Crush control is designed to emulate the effect of a level detection circuit becoming saturated and cannot trigger more compression. This phenomenon occurs in analog compressors and has the same effect as mid-level compression in the C1. In Figure 6.9, the SV-315 has the Crush control set to 10%. The lower the Crush setting, the more transients that will escape compression.

Figure 6.9

The Sonalksis SV-315 with Crush set to 10%. The mid-level compression curve can be seen.

It should be noted that when the ratio returns to 1:1 above the mid-level compression curve, gain reduction does not stop. It just ceases to change any more. If gain reduction has gone to –5dB by the time the signal has gone above the mid-level compression zone, it will stay at –5dB and not change as the level increases. When the level returns to the mid-compression zone, the gain reduction change again.

Look-Ahead Peak Limiters

Digital audio and plug-ins have made some seemingly impossible things possible. The "look-ahead" peak limiter is one of them. Because no analog limiter could ever possibly react quickly enough to ultra-fast transients to actually control them, there was always the chance that even in a limiter levels could exceed a certain value, even if only for less than a millisecond. In the world of analog tape machines and other forgiving electronics, this was acceptable.

Now in the digital era, any signal that exceeds 0dBFS will definitely cause distortion. Digital distortion is also not very pleasant and can damage speakers and hearing easily. Having a peak limiter that can instantaneously control peak transients, even anticipate them, is a good thing. The "look-ahead" peak limiter can do this. Also known as a "brick-wall" limiter for the fact that no signal will pass through it above the set level, peak limiters such as the Waves L2, shown in Figure 6.10, the UAD Precision Limiter, and the TC BrickWall Limiter all are "look-ahead" limiters.

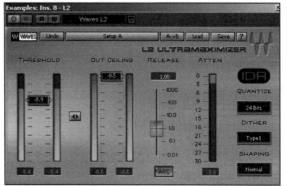

Figure 6.10
The Waves L2 Peak Limiter.

In order to "look ahead," the limiter must be able to analyze the audio signal before processing it. This is done by delaying the output of the plug-in by a small amount in order to allow the limiter to perform the analysis needed to gain-process the signal. Whenever a peak signal is encountered, the limiter can identify it and apply gain reduction in such a way that no signal exceeds the set maximum level.

HOW TO SET THE L1 AND L2 ULTRAMAXIMIZERS

The Waves L1 and L2 peak limiters use a system that automatically adjusts the output gain of the limiter to compensate for any gain reduction that occurs. This can be confusing when you're first using the plug-in because there is no indication that the output gain is being adjusted automatically. If you pull the threshold down by 3dB, the output gain of the L2 invisibly and automatically goes up by 3dB. The only other gain control available is the Out Ceiling. This determines the maximum output level the L2 will generate. Because it is a brick wall limiter, it is possible to determine exactly how much level the L2 will output.

In practice, the L2 is typically used at the end of the mixing chain after all other plug-ins to increase the overall level or RMS level of the mix. If the particular mix is for an audio CD, a fairly loud final level will be appropriate, especially for pop music. To do this, simply pull down on the threshold control and watch the "Atten" (attenuation) meter, which indicates how much gain reduction has been applied. The numeric readout at the bottom of the "Atten" meter shows the maximum gain reduction the L2 has applied. This can be reset by clicking on the number. As you pull down on the threshold, the volume of the material will get louder as a function of the automatic gain adjustment. At some point, the attenuation meter will register some gain reduction. Depending on the material itself, 3–6dB of peak limiting is about the maximum attenuation you can achieve with no degradation of the sound. There might be certain peaks in the program that are much louder than others. If there are only a few of these peaks in a mix, it could be just fine if they require more limiting (–10dB or so). The idea is to avoid constant limiting above 3–6dB.

The L1 and L2 use an Automatic Release Control (ARC) process that optimizes the release time of the limiter based on the input signal. Unless the material is unique, the manual setting is not needed. The ARC provides the smoothest sounding limiting for the majority sources.

The amount of attenuation shown in the L2 indicates how much you have raised the relative RMS level of the program. The threshold setting indicates how much you have changed the absolute level of the material. Careful use of the L2 (or L1) can dramatically increase the overall loudness of just about any program material without significant degradation of the sound.

This look-ahead processing also allows the plug-in to tailor the release times and attack slope to minimize audible distortion that might be created by a large amount of peak limiting (–6dB or more). The idea is that the sound of the peak limiter should be as transparent as possible.

This type of peak limiting is most often used at the very end of the mixing chain to increase the RMS level of the final output. However, it can also be very effective in doing the same thing by limiting only portions of the mix that contain the most transients, namely the drums. Creating a drum sub mix for the purpose of peak limiting is a common practice among pop music mix engineers. By controlling peaks as close to the source as possible, the remainder of the mix can avoid being affected by any artifacts the peak limiter might add to the whole mix.

✳ **PEAK LIMITING AND THE LOUDNESS WARS**

Mastering engineers use peak limiting, among other techniques, to match the perceived loudness of masters to that of competitive recordings in the same genre. This is also the source of much contention in the audio community about abuse of peak limiting in the race for the "loudest" master recording. This has also bled over into the more conservative movie-mixing community with the sound of movie trailers. The next time you see a feature film in a commercial theater, get there in time to see the trailers and compare the loudness of the trailers to the actual film. Because the trailers are advertisements and might also be used for television and other media, the clients often request that they are as loud possible. In a calibrated listening environment such as a movie theater, this can be a deafening experience. The use (or abuse) of peak limiters has a lot to do with this loudness war. Hopefully, future standards such as the K-System calibrated monitoring will help mitigate these issues. Client education is the only way to win the volume wars and bring back the idea of good-sounding audio to these amazing digital formats.

Using Expanders

Expanders perform the inverse operation to compressors and limiters. They extend or expand the dynamic range of a signal. They can do so in two ways.

- ✳ You can add gain to signals above a threshold, thereby increasing their level (called *upward expansion*).
- ✳ You can reduce the gain of signals below a threshold c, thereby lowering their level even more (called *downwards expansion*).

Both types of expanders add dynamic range but do it on opposite ends of the range of dynamics. In a nutshell, downwards expansion makes quiet sounds quieter and upwards expansion makes loud sounds louder. The most common application of expansion is the noise gate.

Gates

A gate is the opposite of a compressor. A *gate* is a downward expander, reducing the gain of signals below the threshold. As the name implies, a gate is normally used to keep unwanted sounds out (to gate them) and keep desired sounds in. Noise and low-level information is usually what is being "gated" out of the signal. Signals above the threshold are not altered, whereas signals below the threshold are attenuated. The graph in Figure 6.11 shows how this appears as a function of input level versus output level.

Figure 6.11

The IO graph of a gate.

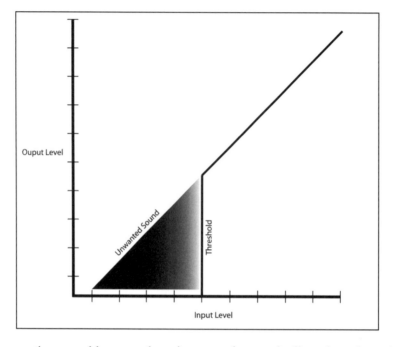

Most gates do not have a ratio control because there is no need to gradually reduce the gain. The ratio of the gate is very high. Once a signal passes below the threshold, the gain should be reduced to nothing or next to nothing in most cases. The ratio in these instances is 40:1 and above. The Pro Tools Expander/Gate, shown in Figure 6.12, is set to a ratio of 100:1. What replaces the ratio and functions in a similar fashion is the range or noise floor parameter. This setting determines the maximum gain reduction that the gate can apply. In other words, signals below the threshold will only be attenuated by the range amount.

Figure 6.12

The Pro Tools Expander/Gate set for 100:1 gating.

The Waves C1 gate calls this the floor parameter, as seen in Figure 6.13, where it's set to –50.3dB. By looking at the IO graph in the C1, you can tell that the signal will be attenuated at the threshold point. Then, as the signal level passes above the threshold point, the ratio returns to 1:1; no more attenuation. The purpose of this setting is to minimize the obvious sound of the gate. If a gate is opening and closing 100dB every time, this could be audible, especially with fast attack and release times.

Figure 6.13

The Waves C1 gate has a floor parameter that sets the maximum gain reduction possible from the gate.

Gates also have attack and release times, which do basically the same thing as they do on a compressor. Quick attack times are most often desirable with percussive sounds so that the attack of the sound is not lost due to slow opening of the gate. Extremely fast attack times can lead to a popping sound that is not natural. When a gate opens too fast, it can create its own transient in the form of an artificial pop sound. This usually only happens with attack times less than one millisecond.

Setting the attack time effectively should yield a normal envelope for the sound in question. The combination of attack and threshold is critical when setting the gate. With lower thresholds, the attack time can usually be quicker without unwanted pops or missed transients. As the threshold gets higher and closer to the actual level of the desired sound, attack times become more critical and touchy. It might be necessary to slow the attack time down a bit in order to avoid artificial pop sounds as a result.

 MIX TIP: GATING THE BASS, DISCOVERING THE "POP"

Try setting a gate on a bass instrument. Crank up the threshold with a fast attack time until you start hearing the "pop" or "tic" sound of the gate opening up too quickly. Adjust the attack time to smooth away the pop. This exercise helps you identify the sound of a particular gate when it is opening too quickly and creating a pop. Using a bass instrument makes the pop sound more obvious.

The release time on a gate determines how long it takes, once the signal has passed below the threshold, for maximum gain reduction to be reached. This setting is dependent on the program material. For example, a cowbell could have a very fast release time on the gate and not cause problems. A delicate synth pad, on the other hand, would need a longer release time in order to avoid clipping off the sustain of the pad sound. Release should also be set in conjunction with the threshold as the two interact.

The unique time factor for hi-end analog and most plug-in gates is the hold time. The hold time determines the amount of time after the signal has passed below the threshold before the gain reduction begins. Figure 6.14 illustrates the three time parameters of a gate.

Figure 6.14
This graph shows the different time factors of a typical gate: attack, hold, and release.

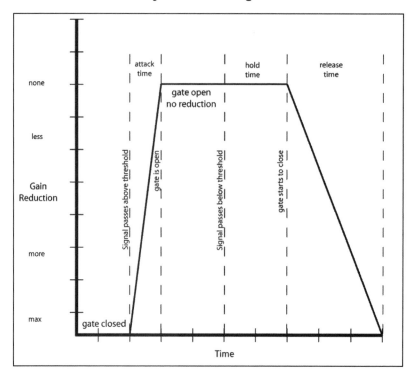

> ❄ **DAWS AND GATING**
>
> It should be noted that you will not find many dedicated plug-in gates on the market. This is due in part by the capability of the DAW to minimize the need for gates at all. Each track in a DAW can be edited to remove any unwanted noise or lower level signals in a very quick and painless way. Most DAWs have an option to detect the softer portions of an audio file and, using a set of parameters, strip the silence or unwanted portions of audio as a series of edits to the track. Each edit can then be altered to have just the right attack and release profiles that you desire without the need to waste DSP on a gate plug-in. Of course, quickly setting a gate can sometimes be faster than the editing method.

Normal Expanders

Normal expanders extend dynamic range just like gates, but with milder ratios. They are not commonly used because most of the time mixing is a matter of reducing the dynamics of recordings to fit within the context of a whole mix. Upwards expansion will add dynamics back to audio that has been overly compressed. Gentle downwards expansion can help suppress noise without the extreme action of a gate.

Transient Shaping

One of the more recent developments in plug-in DSP has been the capability to shape the transients of signals in a more accurate way than before. Transient modeling allows control over the transients in any signal, turning them up or down without affecting the rest of the program. Transient modelers can be considered a type of expander when used to amplify transients in the signal.

The Digitalfishphones plug-in, Dominion, is an example of transient modeling. This free VST plug-in (visit www.digitalfishphones.com for more information) allows the individual control over the level of transients or "attack" and the sustain of signals. Even the duration of the transient is adjustable by the length parameter, as shown in Figure 6.15.

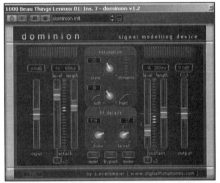

Figure 6.15
The Digitalfishphones Dominion free VST transient modeling plug-in.

Waves also has its transient modeler with the TransX plug-in shown in Figure 6.16. The TransX plug-in can model the transients in various frequency bands. This level of control makes for some interesting effects, removing transients from one band and adding more to another band. In the age of over-compression, the capability to enhance or expand the transients in a signal can be helpful.

Figure 6.16
The Waves TransX transient modeling plug-in.

Noise Suppression

Expanders have been used to suppress noise for a long time. The gate itself is really a noise reduction device in most cases. However, using frequency-dependent expansion can be a more effective tool to suppress typical hiss and noise from the desired audio signal.

The Waves C1 expander with side-chain filtering can be used to suppress noise in a specific band. Two things you need to know: you can turn the gate into an expander by pressing the gate button at the top of the parameter display for the gate. The side-chain has three modes: Wideband, Sidechain, and Split. Wideband is used for normal gating. The Sidechain mode allows filtering of the side-chain input to target gating by frequency bands. Split mode is unique because not only can you alter the side-chain input with the filter, but only those frequencies are gated or expanded. The rest of the spectrum does not have gain applied to it.

Here's how to set up a noise-suppressing expander for the Waves C1 comp-gate.

1. Insert the Waves C1 comp-gate plug-in onto the track in question.
2. Unless you also want to compress this signal, disable the compressor.
3. In the gate section, change the Gate function to Expander.
4. Enable the side-chain filter to Split mode, as seen in Figure 6.17.
5. Adjust the filter to center on the frequency band that contains the noise to be suppressed.
6. Adjust the floor parameter to something between –6dB and –12dB or more. This will be the total amount of noise suppression in the band that will be possible.
7. Adjust the thresholds, both upper and lower, until a desired effect is reached.
8. Adjust attack and release times, if needed.

Figure 6.17

The Waves C1 comp-gate set for high frequency noise suppression.

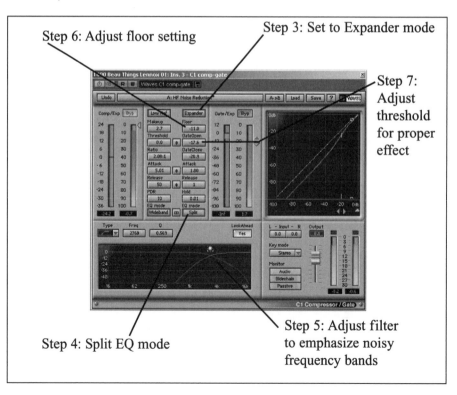

Step 6: Adjust floor setting

Step 3: Set to Expander mode

Step 7: Adjust threshold for proper effect

Step 4: Split EQ mode

Step 5: Adjust filter to emphasize noisy frequency bands

There are also a number of presets that come with any Waves installation that have similar settings. The idea is to understand what each setting is doing in order to tweak the plug-in for maximum results.

Side-Chaining or Keying

The side-chain signal has been discussed as it relates to filtering of that signal. It is also possible to have other external signals feed the side-chain input and trigger gain changes in a compressor or gate. This is called side-chaining or *keying* the compressor or gate externally. The side-chain or key signal is fed to the detector portion of the processor. Any gain change is then applied to the main incoming signal. Unique effects can be created this way.

> ❋ **MIX TIP: SYNTH-CHOPPING EFFECT**
>
> One interesting trick that is done using side-chaining of a gate involves taking any sustaining sound such as a synth pad and insert a gate on its channel. Then, using the key input to the gate, route a percussive sound, such as a hi-hat, into the key input. Set the gate to trigger off of the key input and you have created a "synth-chop" effect with the synth pad pulsing in the same rhythm as the hi-hat. This technique is common to electronic dance music. It is but one example of the many techniques that are possible with side-chained dynamics processors.

One common application of keying is called *ducking*, where one signal is used to feed the side-chain input of a compressor for another signal. Whenever the first signal is present, it causes the second signal to become attenuated. The classic example of this is using a voice-over to key the music bed in a commercial or TV show. Whenever the announcer says something, that voice is used to key the side-chain of a compressor on the music track, thereby having the music lowered as soon as the announcer speaks. When the announcer stops speaking, the compressor returns to normal gain, bringing the music back up in level.

In music mixing, the technique of keying the bass guitar with the kick drum has been used to tighten up an otherwise loose performance. By ducking the bass each time the kick is hit, it gives the impression that the kick and bass are more in sync with one another.

Applying all sorts of crazy processing to a side-chain signal can be a source of experimentation during mixing. Try applying distortion to a side-chain signal and see what happens. The compression curve might be more desirable in certain situations.

The ability to have external side-chains is dependent on the DAW itself. Pro Tools has side-chaining ability. Logic has side-chains with its built-in compressor plug-in. Any DAW that uses VST does not have the direct ability to use external side-chains in the VST 2.0 specification. There are some workarounds involving specific plug-ins, such as the dbAudioware compressor (www.db-audioware.com) or the older TC Electronics Native Compressor/De-esser. These plug-ins can communicate the side-chain signal between two instances of the plug-in.

There is a technique by which you can create a side-chain compressor or gate in a VST application such as Cubase SX, using the Waves C1 and a somewhat convoluted mix routing involving a Quadro Group Channel. For those situations where you absolutely must have keyed side-chain dynamics, here are the steps to set it up in Cubase or Nuendo.

The Quadro bus is a four-channel surround-sound bus that routes signals through two stereo C1 compressors. Each compressor compresses one side of the stereo music signal. The trick is to use the internal Key mode of the C1 to have the right channel key the left channel. Using surround routing, the key signal (in this case a voice-over) is sent to the right channels of each C1 and the music is sent to the left channels. The output of the bus only has the two left channels and so only the stereo music is heard, after being key-compressed by the voice-over. The voice-over is heard on its own channel. The key signal is fed to the C1s through an aux send.

1. Edit the two audio tracks, the music and voice-over, so that they are properly placed on their own tracks, as seen in Figure 6.18.

Figure 6.18

Music and voice-over tracks edited and ready for key side-chain compression.

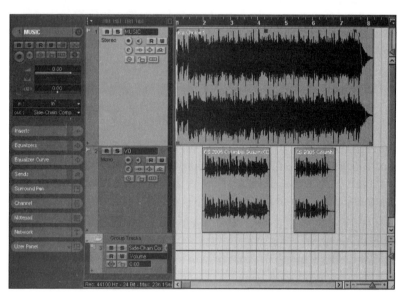

2. Create a Quadro Group Channel. This channel has four sound paths within it and is normally used for surround mixing.

3. Insert on the Group Channel in this order, a MixerDelay plug-in (for tricky routing), two instances of Waves stereo C1 comp-gate, and then one more instance of MixerDelay, as shown in Figure 6.19.

Figure 6.19

The order of plug-ins in the side-chain Quadro Group Channel.

4. Open the channel setting window for the Quadro group channel and switch the inserts view to routing, as seen in Figure 6.20. Here, you can move the second C1 from the left and right channels to the left and right rear channels.

Figure 6.20

The group channel settings window with the inserts view set to routing.

5. Double-click on the routing tabs for the second C1, which will open the plug-in routing window, as seen in Figure 6.21.

Figure 6.21

The plug-in routing window for the second C1 compressor.

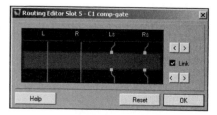

6. Using the arrow buttons, move the plug-in so it is inserted on the Ls and Rs channels, as seen in Figure 6.21.

7. Route the music track to the Side-Chain group channel and, using the surround panner, pan it to the front two channels only, as seen in Figure 6.22. The key signal, the voice-over, will be panned to the rear two channels to act as the side-chain. It will all make sense at the end.

Figure 6.22

The Music track is panned to the front two channels of the Quadro group channel.

8. Set up the first MixerDelay to route channel 2 to channel 3 and vice versa, as shown in Figure 6.23. The channel routing is found at the bottom of the plug-in window as a pull-down menu. If you pull down channel 2 and select channel 3, it will automatically route channel 3 back to channel 2. This is how to trick the two plug-ins into acting as one stereo plug-in.

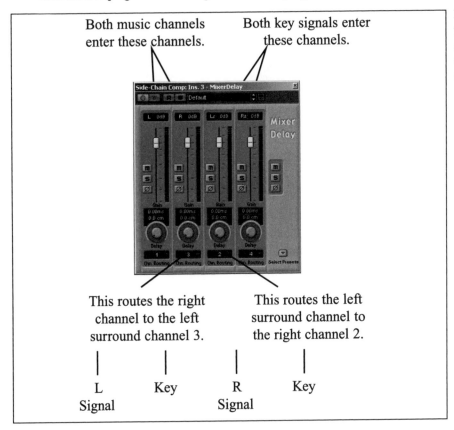

Both music channels enter these channels.

Both key signals enter these channels.

This routes the right channel to the left surround channel 3.

This routes the left surround channel to the right channel 2.

L Signal   Key   R Signal   Key

Figure 6.23
The MixerDelay plug-in shown routing channel 2 to channel 3 and channel 3 to channel 2.

9. Set the second instance of MixerDelay in the same fashion as in step 7. This will reverse the crossed channels back to normal and allow the music to be heard back in stereo again.

10. Using an aux send from the voice-over track, route it to the Side-Chain group channel. Open the group channel settings window and switch the sends view to routing in order to access the surround panner, as seen in Figure 6.24.

Figure 6.24

The voice-over track channel settings window with the sends view set to routing. This allows access to the surround panner for that aux send.

11. Open the surround panner for the aux send and pan the voice-over signal to the rear channels, Ls and Rs. This routes the voice-over to both right channels of the two C1 compressors.

12. In each C1 compressor, set the Key mode to R>L as seen in Figure 6.25. You can also use the other settings for the compressor seen in Figure 6.25 as a starting point for a ducking setup.

Figure 6.25

The Waves C1 set for R>L Key mode and basic settings for a ducking compressor.

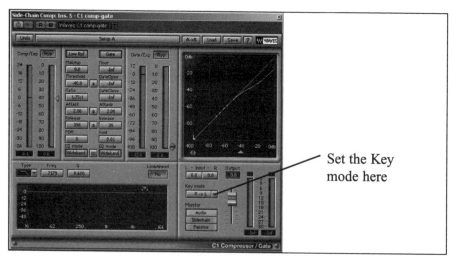

Set the Key mode here

13. Play the project and watch the gain reduction meters on both C1s. When the voice-over comes in, both compressors should have gain reduction applied to the music track. You should notice the music become quieter. Some adjustment to the threshold and ratio may be necessary for proper operation.

This example is just one way you can use creative routing techniques to get the most out of everyday plug-ins. Once you have an understanding of the basic principles of how each type of processor works, the permutations of what is possible become almost infinite.

Using Frequency-Dependent Dynamics

Using filtered side-chains, frequency-dependent dynamics processors can be created easily. Many plug-ins are designed this way to make controls simpler and more user friendly. Some more complex designs in this genre are next to impossible to create with creative routing and would eat up great amounts of DSP to operate. To avoid all this, many developers have created tools that incorporate many types of frequency-dependent dynamics plug-ins.

De-Essers

The most basic and often used frequency-specific processor is the de-esser. As the sound of the name implies, it is used to reducing the volume of sibilant frequencies in vocals that are part of the "s" sound. These sibilant sounds include t's, c's, and sh's, among others. Their frequency range is fairly limited to the area roughly between 3kHz and 10kHz. The specific band depends on the gender of the voice and the particular harmonics it generates.

A de-esser is created by using either a high-pass or band pass filter on the side-chain signal of a compressor or limiter. The ability to tune this filter is important to the operation of the de-esser. Ideally, the de-esser should zero in on just the sibilant frequencies and compress or limit them without affecting the rest of the spectrum.

The Waves Renaissance DeEsser, shown in Figure 6.26, is a fine example of a highly adjustable de-esser that demonstrates most operating parameters found on any de-esser. The interface shows a visual representation of the spectrum and the side-chain filter along with a shaded area that indicates the area in which the de-esser operates.

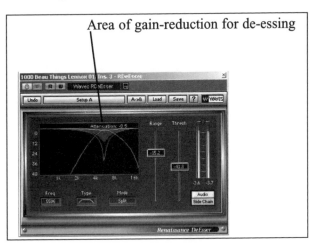

Area of gain-reduction for de-essing

Figure 6.26
The Waves Renaissance DeEsser.

The two main controls are on sliders to the right of the visual display. The Range control works much like the range control on a gate, determining the maximum amount of gain reduction the processor can apply. The Thresh (threshold) control is the level of sibilant frequencies that trigger the onset of gain reduction. Between these two controls, most of the basic operation of the de-esser is complete.

The Renaissance DeEsser can adjust the side-chain filter in frequency and filter shape using the controls at the bottom-left side of the plug-in. The frequency sets the turnover frequency of the filter. The Type determines the type of filter used in the side-chain. The choices are high-pass and band-pass.

The high-pass filter uses a larger amount of frequencies to trigger gain reduction. This is the default and will work in many cases. The band-pass filter can be used to fine-tune the sibilant area in order to prevent undue gain reduction that can result in a dulling of the vocal sound.

The monitoring mode can be helpful in tuning into this frequency band. When the monitoring mode, found in the lower-right corner, is set to Audio, the de-essed signal is heard at the output. If the mode is changed to Side Chain, the filtered side-chain signal will be heard at the output, allowing you to tune the filter to the most strident frequency areas. Once the filter has been tuned, return the monitoring mode back to Audio in order to hear the results.

The operation mode, found in the bottom center, can be used to determine what part of the spectrum is affected by the gain reduction. In Split mode, only the frequencies determined by the filter have gain reduction applied to them. The rest of the signal remains unchanged. In Wideband mode, the entire signal is affected. Obviously, affecting only one area of the signal logically makes the most sense, although, sometimes wideband compression with the filtered side-chain yields the best de-essing results. Experiment with each vocal to see what works best.

MIX TIP: DE-ESSING OTHER INSTRUMENTS

De-essers are not just for vocals. They can be used on other instruments that have high-frequency transient peaks that you want to remove. A good example of this is sliding fingers on an acoustic guitar strings. Guitar players often have to move their fingers rapidly over the fret board in order to get to the next chord position. In doing so, it is possible to create a high-frequency scraping sound as the fingers slide across round wound strings found on many acoustic guitars. This sound can often be undesirable. A de-esser tuned to those frequencies can be effective at reducing their volume in a very pleasant way without dulling the sound of the acoustic in the mix. Fret clacking on bass guitars is another sound that can be addressed with a de-esser. Always be creative with the use (or abuse!) of plug-ins. Sometimes doing something extreme or unorthodox with a particular plug-in can lead to astonishing results.

Dynamic Equalizers

The next level of frequency-dependent dynamics is the dynamic equalizer. Instead of applying a static gain change to a specific frequency band like a normal equalizer, a dynamic EQ can make that gain fluctuate as a function of the input level just like a compressor but only on one frequency area. This type of processing opens up a whole other world of possibilities for tonal shaping.

For example, you can use the TC Dynamic EQ to add detail and punch to the attack of the kick drum in a mix of an entire drum kit. The high frequency boost that is needed to add the attack to the kick must only be triggered by the kick drum and not every other drum in the kit.

The TC Dynamic EQ has the ability to separate the side-chain signal from the EQ band to perform just this sort of tricky processing. Figure 6.27 shows the Dynamic EQ set to add high-end detail to just the kick drum in a mix of a drum set. Band 4 has a boost at 3.476kHz of +12.2dB. This boost is entirely dynamic, that is, it will only occur when the side-chain signal exceeds the threshold of –34dB.

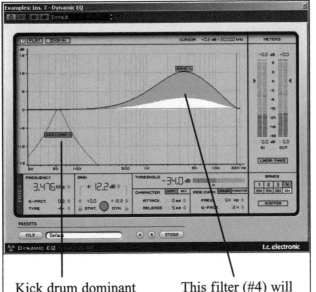

Figure 6.27

The TC Dynamic EQ set to add high-end detail to the kick drum in a mix of a drum kit.

Kick drum dominant frequency 54Hz

When the level of the side chain band exceeds the threshold of –34dB, it will trigger the dynamic response of filter #4. This will happen predominantly when you hit the kick drum.

This filter (#4) will boost high frequencies when the side-chain signal exceeds the threshold. Because this will happen when you hit the kick drum, the filter will add attack to just the kick drum.

The trick here is that the TC plug-in allows the side-chain filter for that band to be set to a different frequency band. In the lower-right area of the plug-in is the side-chain control. The unlink button has been enabled allowing the side-chain filter to be tuned to a narrow band of frequencies centered at 54Hz, where the kick drum is mostly by itself. The side-chain EQ curve can be seen in the lower half of the visual display to the left.

Whenever the signal at 54Hz exceeds the –34dB threshold, a boost at 3.476kHz will happen, adding high-end detail to just the kick drum attacks. This is a pretty slick and sophisticated bit of DSP. To perform this little bit of processing in the analog world would be very difficult and time consuming and might not even be all that possible given the normal type of gear found in a typical studio.

The Sonalksis DQ1 dynamic equalizer has some unique controls, as seen in Figure 6.28. For each band, there are two thresholds, a lower and upper one. For each threshold there is an adjustable gain response. When the signal is below the low threshold, gain can either be added or removed. Additionally, when the signal goes above the upper threshold, gain can also be added or removed independently. The frequency and Q of the band is adjustable along with attack and release times for the dynamic filter.

Figure 6.28

The Sonalksis DQ1 Dynamic Equalizer.

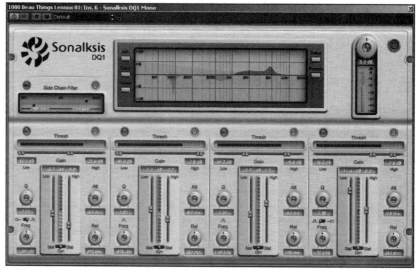

In a similar fashion to the TC Dynamic EQ, the side-chain signal of the DQ1 can be filtered. High and low-pass filters are provided for the side-chain signal, allowing the dynamic action of the DQ1 to be controlled by a specific frequency band. Unlike the TC's multiple side-chain filters (one for each band), the DQ1's bands all share the same side-chain filter.

The possibilities of processors such as these are mind-boggling in their variety. Dynamic EQs are one of the areas in which digital processing has far exceeded the possibilities of analog. Although, hopefully this type of tricky processing is not needed everyday, it is nice to know that it is possible when the need arises.

Multi-Band Dynamics

The multi-band dynamics processor is very similar to the dynamic equalizer. It processes various frequency bands with dynamic gain changes such as compression, limiting, or expansion. The exact difference is somewhat of a grey area because they are so similar. Dynamic EQs are primarily concerned with changing the tonal character of a sound, whereas multi-band dynamics processors are dealing with the dynamic range of various frequency bands.

Multi-band dynamics processors have become very popular in the project-studio mastering world because of their convenience and quick results when trying to maximize the level of master recordings. TC Electronics debuted the Finalizer hardware multi-band DSP processor and changed the way home recordists finished their mixes in a major way. Figure 6.29 shows the MasterX5, the big brother plug-in to the original Finalizer.

Figure 6.29

The TC Electronics MasterX5 multi-band dynamics processor.

The MasterX5 is a five-band multi-band dynamics processor with low-level expansion, mid-level compression, and peak limiting on each frequency band. This exerts an iron fist of control over the dynamics of any signal. The potential for overuse is clear and present. Much can be gained by the careful manipulation of the dynamics of program material. However, mangling of the internal dynamics in various bands with the intention of creating an incredibly loud master recording can result in disaster.

※ MIX TIP: MASTERING ENGINEERS AND MULTI-BAND DYNAMICS

Avoid using multi-band processors on final mixes that will also be worked on by a mastering engineer. Although these processors are wonderful for references and listening copies, masters that have been overly processed by multi-band compression and limiting are difficult to work with in the mastering studio. The process cannot be undone. When using this type of processing on the master bus, always print an unprocessed version as a backup. Even if you are mastering the recording yourself, having an unprocessed backup can be helpful if you decide to re-master the mix at some later date. This is most important when another professional is going to be working on your material. Leave enough headroom in the mix so that the mastering engineers can do their job effectively.

The Sonalksis CQ1 is another multi-band dynamics processor capable of expansion and compression of tunable frequency bands either above or below the threshold. One of the things the CQ1 is capable of enhancing the high- or low-frequency content of a signal without the muddiness or harshness associated with equalization. This is done using below-threshold compression. In order to emphasize the high frequency content of a drum set, for example, the high band of the CQ1 can be set to a shelving filter with below threshold compression of 3:1 or so and the threshold set fairly low (–26dB), as shown in Figure 6.30. This would bring up high frequencies when the signal goes below the threshold, adding high-end detail to the overall sound of the drums but without affecting the sound of the kick and snare transients.

Figure 6.30

Settings of the high-frequency band of the CQ1 to add high-end detail to a drum set without adding harshness to the transients.

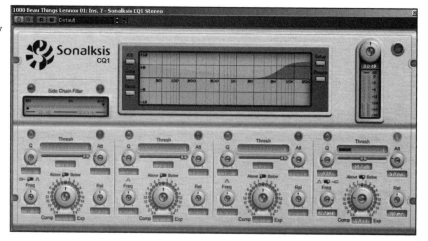

The lineage of the Waves Ultramaximizer, beginning with the original L1 and growing into the renowned L2, has now embraced the multi-band method with the L3 Multimaximizer, shown in Figure 6.31. The L3 is a multi-band peak limiter using a single peak limiter that reacts to a composite side-chain signal made up of the individual frequency bands that have been weighted and prioritized according to an optimization algorithm. In other words, its a proprietary system that utilizes a multi-band approach to peak limiting. The result is a louder signal that has fewer artifacts associated with brick-wall limiting.

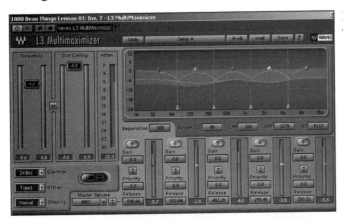

Figure 6.31

The Waves L3 Multimaximizer.

The Waves L3 can be adjusted in a simple fashion for most situations just like the L1 and L2 using the threshold and output ceiling controls. If more control is needed, the L3 has full parametric controls over each band including gain, priority, and release for each band. Additionally, each band's frequency spectrum is adjustable, affording a great deal of flexibility for fine-tuning.

Setting a Compressor: A Creative Approach

Setting compressors has always been a bit of a black art in the audio world. Beyond the need to control the dynamic range of instruments, compressors add sonic character to a mix in ways that EQs cannot. They can make things sound aggressive without distortion and can create the illusion of size even on small speakers. In pop music, we all have been listening to all kinds of compression on records for many, many years now and the sound of it has become ingrained into the society of radio, rock and roll, and popular music. What started out as a very technical tool for maintaining legal broadcast modulation levels for radio stations has evolved into a creative sculpting tool for the mix engineer.

Because the compressor has become more of a creative tool, the approach to adjusting compressors should also be more creative. Instead of just looking at the gain reduction meter to see that a certain amount of compression is occurring, this approach almost disregards the meters in favor of listening and creative knob twisting to arrive at a compressor setting.

MIX TIP: EARS, NOT EYES

As with any plug-in technology, the temptation is to work with your eyes instead of your ears. Computers are primarily visual devices that require you to look at them in order to operate them. For audio engineering, this can be problematic in certain situations. Obviously, editing audio with visual assistance is incredibly efficient. However, mixing and processing audio visually is not always beneficial.

One major issue is the Graphic User Interface (GUI) that all plug-ins and audio software must have in order to function in the computer. The GUI forces us to look at the screen in order to maneuver the mouse pointer onto various controls to make adjustments. It is not possible to close your eyes and "feel" your way around a compressor or equalizer setting. Even when a control has been selected, it is often necessary to continue to watch to make sure the mouse does not lose control of the parameter.

Hardware control surfaces such as the Mackie Universal Control shown in Figure 6.32 give you access to plug-in parameters via real knobs and sliders. This can free up your mind for more creative and important tasks other than watching the mouse.

Figure 6.32

The Mackie Control Universal hardware control surface gives you physical control of plug-in parameters.

A/B Comparison of Compression Settings

Compression is a much more subtle sonic attribute to listen to than equalization. The ear can easily be tricked into perceiving things with just a change in volume. Because compressors, limiters, and other forms of dynamics processors all affect volume, the ear can play tricks on you while trying to adjust settings. The only way to minimize this is to constantly use A/B comparisons to determine if your settings are an improvement.

When you set up a compressor to some initial settings, use the bypass switch on the plug-in to turn off the processing and compare it to the unprocessed sound. Use the output gain control to match the perceived level of the compressed sound to the uncompressed sound. Then, using the bypass control, compare the two sounds back and forth, A and B, to see if you are achieving the best result. This process might take time, but in the end it will be a more accurate way of adjusting compressors and can actually save you time by not having to go back and change settings later.

Start with Extremes

Hearing the effects of compression and especially the attack and release times of a compressor can be difficult when the compression amount is subtle. Start out by setting the compressor to its most extreme settings with a high ratio, low threshold and fastest attack and release times. This will exaggerate the compression sound, making it audible while you make some adjustments. Keep in mind that with certain vintage modeled compressors such as the UAD 1176LN shown in Figure 6.33, the threshold is fixed. Therefore, in order to get more gain reduction, you must turn up the input and adjust the output gain accordingly to match the unprocessed signal.

Figure 6.33
The UAD 1176LN has a fixed threshold. Getting more gain reduction is possible by turning up the input level.

Start with Time Constraints

With severe compression going on, it is much easier to hear the attack and release times of a compressor. Start with the attack time and decide how much attack you want to hear. Try to ignore the pumping effect the compressor will have with extremely fast release times and focus on the attack. Obviously, this choice is a matter of taste and is program-dependent, but having lots of compression going on will help you hear the effects of various attack times.

Once you determine the attack time, move on to the release time. In most cases, the release time should be set as long as possible to avoid pumping effects and other obvious signs of compression unless those effects are desired. It is tempting to set the release faster in order to have the perceived loudness come up. Make sure you constantly adjust the output gain so that A/B comparisons can be made and that the added volume does not trick your ear into believing the louder sound is also the better sound.

With more advanced compressors such as the Sonalksis SV-315, there are other parameters that directly affect the compression curve such as the detector type, crush, hold, and soft-knee amount. Although the compression is still strong, adjust these parameters as well to determine which setting is more pleasing to the ears.

Control Versus Size

The ratio and threshold parameters will have the most effect on the control and size of the sound. The more control you exert over the sound in terms of level control, the less size it will have. The tradeoff between the two is the creative choice you have.

Start with the ratio. As you lower the ratio, the size should increase and the amount of control should decrease. With lower ratios, the sound can get looser, with more varied dynamics. Higher ratios yield more control at the cost of size. Finding that happy medium is your creative choice.

Finally, the threshold can be set to complete the compression adjustment. Common practice suggests that there should be some point during the program or song that the compressor is not acting on the signal at all, presenting a 1:1 picture of the sound. A quiet passage in a tune or a dramatic moment in a film can present a moment where the compressor should not be affecting the sound. This keeps the action of the compressor working in a dynamic way. If the threshold is too low, the compressor will never stop working on the sound and, to some extent, its effects will be minimized. Sometimes, the side-chain signal can become saturated resulting in a 1:1 ratio with extreme threshold settings even though the gain reduction meter shows massive amounts of compression. It ends up being the same as turning the fader down. Compressors and limiters need to move in order to be effective. A compressor that is always compressing the maximum amount and not changing is not doing anything to enhance the quality of the sound.

If the compressor is always working around its threshold point, the effects will have the most movement or bounce, thus creating a more interesting sound in many cases.

> ❋ **MIXING WITH YOUR MIND**
>
> It should be noted that much of this material on compressor settings is inspired by the book *Mixing With Your Mind,* mentioned earlier. This book contains a fascinating approach to audio mixing, concentrating on mental states rather than all the gear or plug-ins at your command. It is well worth the read for mix engineers trying to improve their art.

Controlling Dynamics in the Mix

One of the toughest tasks in audio mixing is controlling the dynamics of a mix. Reigning in control over the dynamic range of individual sounds and the overall program is extremely important to the success of any mixdown. Compressors, limiters, and other forms of dynamics processing provide many tools for doing this.

Every type of mix has its own needs for dynamics control. Each situation is different.

- ❋ *Pop Music:* Very controlled dynamics that are musical and yet compete in a world where the "loudness wars" cause mastering engineers to exert maximum control over peak levels. Also, radio stations employ dastardly, evil processing to maximize their broadcast levels. If a mix is over-compressed before going to the radio station, it will surely come out butchered once the broadcast processor gets a hold of it. Sometimes less is more with radio mixes.

- ❋ *Movie Soundtracks:* This is almost the opposite of pop music dynamics because the listener is in a calibrated listening room, the theater. Mixes are created using a reference playback level and full use of the available dynamic range is encouraged and needed in order to not have listening strain affect the audience. Because movies are much longer than most pieces of music, use of the full dynamic range is necessary to keep the interest up and the fatigue down.

❋ *Broadcast Television/Satellite/Cable:* Broadcast mediums all have some sort of dynamics chain involved in the distribution of the program material. TV stations have compressors and limiters to maximize their broadcast level and keep the level between programs more even. Also, television often is heard through very small speakers with limited high and low frequency response, requiring the mix engineer to make sure the necessary material can be heard in the middle bands. Clients often want their commercial to be the loudest thing on TV so that everyone knows about their product. Sometimes this comes at a price when viewers automatically turn down the commercial sections of a broadcast due to the annoying volume compared with the show they are watching.

❋ *DVD*: DVD video and audio has become the latest chance for high-quality audio to be delivered to the home listening environment. The dynamic range and fidelity available from the DVD format is great and (hopefully) the industry will take advantage of that and put out great quality material in this format. Still, you must take into consideration that not all home playback systems are created equal, thus a certain dynamic control must be maintained in order for most audiences to enjoy the material.

Reference Levels

Mixing with reference levels is always a big help. Keeping the volume at a reasonable level will help your ears make better decisions. Monitoring the peak versus average or RMS levels with a high-quality meter (such as the Elemental Audio's InspectorXL shown in Figure 6.34) can help you keep an eye on where the dynamics sit in your mix. Knowing the relative difference between the peak and RMS levels in a mix is the first step to controlling them.

Figure 6.34

The InspectorXL level meter set to K-14 metering for pop music mixing.

Some common practices have evolved over time for various mix scenarios. Certainly with film mixing, there are standards in place that require calibration of mix studios so that mixes created in them translate well to the majority of theaters. The Dolby and THX standards are the most common form of reference for film mixing.

For pop music mixing, the difference between the RMS and peak levels in a mix prior to mastering should be anywhere between 10 and 20dB. Sometimes there will only be one particular instance where the peak level is significantly higher than during the rest of the song. Careful investigation as to the cause of the highest peak can often lead to the discovery of a bad edit or other technical reason for the peak that could be rectified, allowing the overall program level to be increased without use of a peak limiter.

In film and dramatic television mixing, conservation of headroom is often the requirement. There always needs to be room for the one scene with all the big effects and loud booming sounds. If the dialogue is pushed louder during the rest of the program, there will be no headroom left for the big sound effects scene. DVD authoring levels usually have conversational dialogue around –25 to –27dBFS RMS with peaks going up to –8 or –5dBFS maximum. Even the loudest dialogue shouldn't be as loud as an explosion or a falling building.

The trouble is the real world has so much more dynamic range than we are used to hearing in movies and music. Plus, most playback systems are nowhere near capable of reproducing all of that dynamic range. It is the job of the mixer to decide how to allocate the available dynamic range to achieve the best effect. You can use compression to create the illusion of more dynamic range by bringing up low level sounds to a more reasonable listening level and also reducing transient peaks that use up so much valuable dynamic range.

Transients
Transients are the beasts that will use up dynamic range the quickest. A small peak that is barely audible can eat up 10dB or more and not add anything sonically to the mix. Tracking down these non-critical peaks will open up the dynamic range for other purposes. Here are two examples of how this might occur.

Drums in a Pop Music Mix
The drums in a pop music mix are the single largest source of peaks. Their peaks can also combine with various other peak signals in the mix to create higher peaks that are a combination of the two. Find out how much of these peaks are eating into your dynamic range and then address them with some careful peak limiting in order to get rid of non-critical peaks and have more room for the rest of the mix.

To begin, make sure you can see a meter that has both peak and RMS or average meter readings on it and is measuring the entire mix. This is something that should always be present in every mix session in order for the engineer to gauge the dynamics of the mix at all times. Also, having the drums sub-grouped together on an auxiliary channel can help this process immensely.

Make note of the current average and peak levels. Go back and play the same section of material, this time with all the drums muted. Make note of the peak and RMS levels again. The difference in peak levels between the whole mix and the mix minus the drums should be dramatic. The difference in RMS levels should be less so.

Next, insert a peak limiter on the drum subgroup. For this example, the Waves L1 was used. With the L1's automatic makeup gain function, making adjustments to the threshold changes the overall level of the drums. This might upset the balance between the drums and the rest of the instruments and vocals. In order to avoid this, pull the threshold and output ceiling down by the same amount. In this case, let's use the measured difference in peak levels between the two measurements taken earlier as a starting point for peak reduction.

As seen in Figure 6.35, using the center control on the L1 will adjust the threshold and output ceiling at the same time, making this rather easy. Both the L2 and L3 have similar controls. Lower the center control by the measured difference in peak levels of the mix with and without the drums. Doing so will bring the peak level of the drums down to the same level as the rest of the mix.

Use this center control to adjust the threshold and output ceiling at the same time

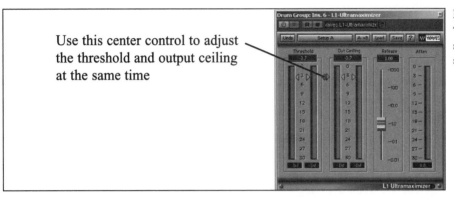

Figure 6.35

The Waves L1 peak limiter set to reduce the peaks on a subgroup of drums.

Check the peak and RMS levels of the mix with and without the peak-limited drums. You should have a significant amount of headroom available. This setting might be too extreme and you will have to use your ears to make final adjustments to the amount of peak limiting. The rule of thumb is 3dB of peak limiting should not be detrimental to the sound. Over 6dB of limiting will have some amount of distortion artifacts and can be undesirable. Once again, use your ears to make the call.

Dialogue in a Film Mix

The dialogue in a film mix is the most important thing. It tells the story and conveys the emotion of the actors and actresses on the screen. It has quiet moments as well as loud moments. The human voice is very dynamic. Because films are trying to convey reality, or at least suspend your disbelief that the movie is not reality, full use of dynamics makes sense and helps us connect with the reality of the soundtrack.

Due to the fact that not even the best film sound system in the world is capable of recreating the complete dynamic range of reality, some amount of dynamics control must be used in order to create a useful soundtrack. Much of this dynamic control is accomplished by the mixing of the various tracks themselves. But some amount of dynamic control can be exerted by a compressor or limiter.

Obviously, large amounts of compression are not useful for film dialogue, because it would not sound realistic. It might sound like a great pop vocal sound, but not dialogue in a movie. More often, a carefully set peak limiter on the dialogue group channel will greatly assist in controlling the dynamic range. Using a peak limiter, the dialogue mixer can then bring up the level of dialogue in certain appropriate scenes and not have to worry about eating up too much headroom for the big sound effects.

Setting a brick wall limiter around –5 or –6dBFS, and then mixing at the calibrated monitor volume, should allow you to mix the dialogue as you want to hear it in the theater. The occasional erroneous peak will get taken care of by the limiter. During a scene with a heated argument between two people, the dialogue levels can rise naturally but the peak level stops at –5dBFS by the limiter. This will help keep the dialogue mix under control while allowing the mix engineers flexibility in following whatever their ears are telling them to do.

A common technique for this is to use one group or aux channel for all the dialogue tracks to feed into. This channel can then have one brick wall limiter inserted on it to control the dynamics for the entire dialogue mix. Figure 6.36 shows the TC BrickWall Limiter set to limit to –5.5dBFS. This setting is appropriate for film mixing and mixing for DVD releases. Granted, the level of dialogue should rarely reach this point. When it does, it should only be for a short period of time, such as during a particularly loud scene with yelling and shouting. The peak limiter will prevent anything from exceeding –5.5dBFS.

Figure 6.36

The TC BrickWall Limiter set to stop any levels from exceeding –5.5dBFS.

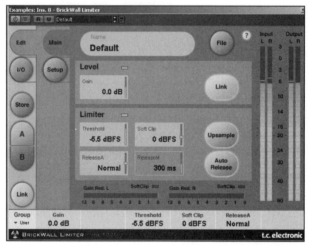

When converting film mixes for release on DVD, it might also be necessary to reduce the overall dynamic range to something more appropriate for home playback systems. This becomes the job of the DVD mastering engineer. The original film mix can be delivered as stems containing various mixed elements that, when combined at unity gain, create the entire soundtrack. The DVD mastering engineer can then individually address the dynamic range of the various stems with compression and limiting to make them more appropriate for DVD authoring. This usually means a reduction in the overall dynamic range because the film mix is designed for the powerful, full-spectrum playback system in movie theaters.

Figure 6.37 shows the Waves C360 Surround Compressor. It's an ideal tool for the DVD mastering engineer to use to reduce the dynamic range of a film mix for release on DVD.

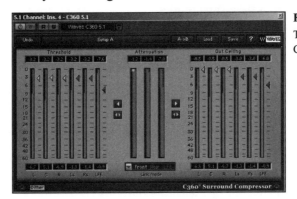

Figure 6.37

The Waves C360 Surround Compressor.

Reference Monitors

Attack and release times are so critical to the sound of a compressor or limiter that being able to hear them accurately is very important. Compressors alter the transient signals in a mix, changing their duration and volume. Attack slopes are changed along with the timbre as more compression and limiting is added.

Being able to hear all of these factors accurately requires a high-quality playback system. This goes beyond just frequency response into the dynamics of a speaker system itself. An accurate reference monitor system needs to be capable of recreating the sharpest of transients so that decisions to change the attack times on compressors can be made clearly. High-current power amplifiers with large amounts of reserve energy for instantaneous peak response are needed to really hear what a compressor is doing, especially on a whole mix.

Many modern speaker systems available to project and home studios have traded efficiency for distortion and poor transient response. Amplifiers in active systems must be made smaller and lighter to be practical. Sometimes the tradeoff is in transient performance or distortion artifacts. A proper speaker design with a powerful amplifier capable of good transient response and damping will give you an eye- (and ear-) opening listening experience.

When shopping for a speaker system, make sure you find a set that does not make everything sound great. Poor quality should sound poor in a reference system. You should be able to clearly discern faults in your mixes with monitor speakers. Create an audio CD that contains material that you know sounds both good and bad from experience on many other systems. Take this CD with you when auditioning monitor speakers. If you can easily discern the good audio from the bad audio, the speakers will help you. If the entire CD sounds great in a pair of speakers, chances are they will hamper your ability to create great mixes.

The frequency response of a speaker is of course very important. What is often overlooked is the time-domain response of a speaker—the way it handles transients. This affects your ability to accurately place sounds in the stereo field (imaging) and how dynamics are affecting your mix (transient response).

Summary

Dynamics are possibly the most important aspect of audio in any form. Control and manipulation of them is an art form that takes a great deal of understanding and experience to master. Plug-ins have allowed untold advances in dynamic control that just were not possible in the analog world. Just think about dynamic equalizers and look-ahead peak limiting.

With all this control at your fingertips, you need to take time to experiment with various dynamics processors and try to create new sounds that push the envelope. The tools are so complex that some noodling around is needed to find out just what the plug-ins are capable of.

7 Time-Based Processing

Time-based processing is built around the simple delay. Flanging, chorusing, echo, reverb, time compression, and pitch-shifting are all based on the delay processor. Time-based processors are traditionally associated with "effects." Most of the cool, neat things you could do in an analog studio were based around delay processing. In the digital world, the delay is the simplest form of processing and is the basis for all kinds of interesting plug-ins.

Using Time-Based Processors

The earliest example of a delay processor is the tape echo. The vocal sound made famous in the 50's by Elvis Presley was created using a tape machine setup to make a short delay of 50–100 milliseconds (ms). The vocal signal was fed to the input of a 2-track tape machine that was in record and the tape was running. Professional tape machines use different heads for recording and playback. The record head comes before the playhead in the tape path, so, when the vocal signal is being recorded, it can immediately be played back while the tape is running from the playhead, all at the same time.

Depending on the speed of the tape (7 1/2 ips [inches per second], 15ips, or 30ips) and the distance between the record and playheads, the vocal signal would be delayed by some amount, usually 60ms or so. When the playback signal was mixed back in with the original at the console, the echo effect was created and the dawn of outboard gear began.

Simple Delays

A DSP plug-in delay is very simple. All you need is a small amount of memory to store audio samples until the delay time is reached. Then the samples are played back. In a straight delay, the signal is not modified, just played back at a different time. The effect that a simple delay creates only happens when it is mixed together with the original signal.

Delay Time

The effect a delay creates can be anything from comb filtering caused by phase cancellations in very small delays to slap-back and echo effects. This is all determined by the delay time, which is usually measured in milliseconds. The following list illustrates the effects various delay times create.

- 1–8ms—Comb filtering or flanging with modulation
- 8–20ms—Imaging or chorusing with modulation
- 20–120ms—Slap-delay or tape echo with modulation
- 120–500ms—Short delay
- +500ms—Echo and phrase sampling

Delay times can also be measured in musical terms using quarter notes, eighth notes, bars, and beats. Many DAWs have the capability to communicate tempo information to the delay plug-in so that the delay time will automatically be synchronized with the tempo of the song.

Figure 7.1 shows the PSP42 delay plug-in that is modeled after the classic studio-standard Lexicon PCM 42. All the controls are faithfully reproduced in this excellent delay plug-in. Notice that the mode switch is in the CLK position, indicating the delay time will be based on the MIDI clock information coming from the DAW software. The display shows "1 4," indicating a quarter note delay time will be used. The actual delay time depends on the tempo of the song. If the tempo changes, so will the delay time. This makes it possible to set delays more musically.

Figure 7.1

The PSP42 delay plug-in modeled after the classic Lexicon PCM 42. The delay time is set to MIDI clock quarter notes.

❋ MIX TIP: MUSICAL DELAY TIME CALCULATION

If you do not have a delay plug-in that accepts MIDI clock information and want to set a delay time that correlates to the tempo of the song, there is a simple formula you can use to generate the appropriate delay time. 60 divided by the song tempo in beats per minute (BPM) gives you the exact delay time for one beat or a quarter note in seconds. Unless the tempo is very slow, this value is usually less than 1 second.

Using a calculator to find the quarter note delay time for a song at 112 BPM, you input 60 and then divide by 112, which yields 0.53577142. Because this is measured in seconds, you must convert it to milliseconds. Move the decimal point to the right three places and round off the remainder. This gives the answer 536ms. When rounding, decide whether you want the delay to push or pull the tempo. This is a musical decision that affects the sound of the delay, even with small differences. Altering the delay time even further enhances the push or pull of the delay.

Calculated delay times in milliseconds:

- ❋ Quarter note: 60/BPM × 1000
- ❋ Eighth note: Quarter note ÷ 2
- ❋ Sixteenth note: Quarter note ÷ 4
- ❋ Half note: Quarter note × 2
- ❋ Dotted quarter note: Quarter note × 1.5
- ❋ Dotted eighth note: Quarter note × 0.75

When a delay is set using the MIDI clock option, its time will be accurate to the musical time selected. Using a calculator and a manual delay setting offers more control and subtle expression if the delay is not perfect. The calculator will give you the exact rhythmic time, which you can then modify to your taste. For example, try making a quarter note delay time longer by a few milliseconds. This allows the echoes to lag behind ever so slightly, creating a relaxing vibe to the sound. Conversely, quickening or shortening the delay time adds a sense of urgency or tension, depending on the music.

Perfection can be beautiful, but sometimes a little imperfection is more interesting. Delay times are an area in audio mixing where subtle imperfections might just make perfect sense and better mixes.

The musical delay times are a great start. However, some delay plug-ins, including the PSP42, allow you to create a delay time using the MIDI clock information and then convert that into a manual delay time in milliseconds that you can tweak to the desired setting. With the PSP42, merely switching the mode to CLK and then back to DLY will set the delay to the quarter note value of the current tempo in the song. Once back in DLY mode, you can freely change the delay time.

> ❋ **GUI TIP: PSP42 DELAY TIME SETTING**
> Place the cursor over the delay time in the PSP42 and drag up or down to quickly change the delay time. Dragging left and right slows the rate of the delay time. There is another invisible slider found just in between the up and down arrows. This is much faster than clicking the up and down arrow buttons.

Feedback

A simple delay creates only one delayed sound—one echo. In order to have more than one echo, the delayed signal must be fed back into the input of the plug-in. This is called *feedback* and is measured in a percentage of the feedback signal or in dB.

If the signal is fed back into the input at full volume (0dB or 100%), the delay cycle will go on and on forever. Usually, the delay signal being fed back into the input is much lower than the input signal. This creates a fading echo effect that we have all heard a million times. The amount of echoes is controlled by the amount of feedback; each echo becoming quieter until they fall below the noise floor.

Some delay plug-ins, such as the Waves SuperTap delay shown in Figure 7.2, allow independent delay of the feedback signal. In other words, you can delay the feedback signal separately prior to its being routed back into the plug-in's input. You can create unique rhythm effects in music mixes using this technique.

Figure 7.2

The Waves SuperTap delay with additional feedback signal delay control.

Damping

It is also common to process the feedback signal with a low-pass filter. This is called *high-frequency damping* and enhances the illusion that the echo is fading away. In a real echo situation, such as yelling in a canyon, each echo must bounce off some surface. Every bounce reduces the high-frequency content of the sound, making it duller. Low-pass filtering the feedback signal achieves this effect.

The Nomad Factory Liquid Delay has separate low-pass filter adjustments for each delay output channel, as seen in Figure 7.3. This is not the same as filtering the feedback signal. Each echo will have the same sound, just softer in volume. Using the PSP42's hi-cut filter, shown in Figure 7.4, makes each progressive echo become duller because the filter is on the feedback signal itself, not on the output of the plug-in.

Figure 7.3

The Nomad Factory Liquid Delay with dual low-pass filters for just the output signal.

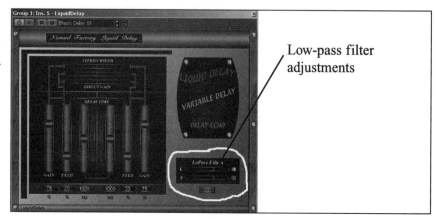

Low-pass filter adjustments

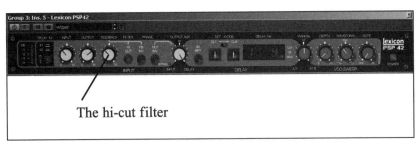

Figure 7.4

The PSP42 has a hi-cut (low-pass) filter on the feedback signal. This filter cuts down on the high-frequency content of each progressive echo.

The original PCM-42 was based on a sample and hold circuit in which the sample rate was varied to change the delay time. By using the MANUAL control in conjunction with the x1, x2 switch on the left, you can alter the delay resolution and virtual sampling rate of the PSP42 plug-in in the same fashion. This gives the PSP42 the same unique sound that the original PCM-42 had.

The x1, x2 switch effectively reduces the sample rate by one half in order to generate longer delay times. The PSP emulation of this remains faithful using interpolating algorithms to mimic the variable sample rate of the original device. The MANUAL control further varies the sample rate and delay time continuously from x.5 to x1.5 the sample rate. This unique control allows you to speed up and slow down the delay time in real-time, affecting whatever sound is currently in the buffer. This control alters the pitch and speed of the audio in the buffer allowing for some interesting effects.

When the sample rate is at its lowest (x2 switch in and MANUAL set to x1.5), the Nyquist frequency of the delay circuit is lowered. This creates a form of low-pass filter that works as a function of the sample rate. Each progressive echo starts to have a grainy sound to it as well as being dulled by the continuous re-sampling of the echoed audio. To hear this clearly, set up the PSP42 as shown in Figure 7.5. The hi-cut filter should be off to expose the sound of the re-sampling noise as much as possible. This unique sound has been used countless times on many records throughout the years.

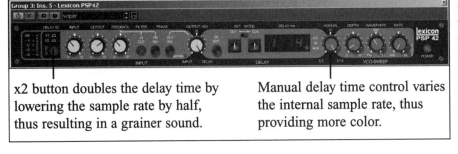

Figure 7.5

The PSP42 set to maximize the grainy sound of lo-res delay re-sampling.

x2 button doubles the delay time by lowering the sample rate by half, thus resulting in a grainer sound.

Manual delay time control varies the internal sample rate, thus providing more color.

Delay Modeling

Since the creation of the first tape-based delay effect, many other techniques have been used to make different delay effects. Guitar players, among others, have used these various effects boxes over the years to create memorable sounds that are hard to recreate without the original equipment. Some plug-in developers have tried to fill that gap with delay modeling plug-ins, such as the Bombfactory Tel-Ray delay shown in Figure 7.6.

Figure 7.6

The Bombfactory Tel-Ray delay plug-in.

This plug-in mimics the sound of a very odd device made in the 60s known as the *oil can delay*. It used a circulating belt made of insulating material to store a magnetic charge created by a charged brush as it passed by. The electrolytic oil was used to prevent the charge from escaping the belt as it traveled around the can. The sound that it produced was very wobbly and lacked in frequency response.

The kind of echo that it created was unique and sought after by guitarists. They are very rare today and maintenance is very difficult. The Tel-Ray delay plug-in is a substitute that will never break or fall apart but still delivers that crazy, wobbly sound of the original unit.

The Line 6 EchoFarm is a discontinued plug-in for Pro Tools TDM systems that emulated many vintage delay effects including so many of the classics:

* Maestro EP-1 and EP-3 Tube Echoplex
* Roland RE-101 Space Echo
* Boss DM-2 Analog Delay
* Electro-Harmonix Deluxe Memoryman
* TC Electronics 2290

Owning this collection of classic delay lines would cost a fortune in the analog world. Plus, EchoFarm was only available for Pro Tools TDM users. However, many of the effects that these classic units were famous for can be somewhat recreated with careful adjustment of other delay plug-ins.

One of the most apparent aspects of the tape delays is the presence of wow and flutter in the echo signal. *Wow* and *flutter* are words that describe the inherent physical speed changes that tape transports exhibit, thus resulting in subtle pitch changes in the delay signal. In order to create these various speed changes, you must modulate or change the delay time. A low-frequency oscillator changes the delay time in a regular fashion, creating the illusion of tape wow and flutter. Further discussion about how to set this up takes place in the next section.

iZotope's Spectron and Trash plug-ins offer unique delay modeling that is hard to describe easily. These plug-ins are a combination of several types of DSP processors that interact and create some very interesting results. Spectron is capable of delaying certain portions of the spectrum independently of others. For example, Figure 7.7 shows Spectron delaying one band at 747Hz by 816ms and another higher band at 8kHz by 122ms. The feedback signal can be filtered and the delay times can be modulated by an LFO or by an envelope follower. There are numerous other options in this fairly complex plug-in. The spectral delays alone are very intriguing and can provide you with hours of endless tweaking and fun.

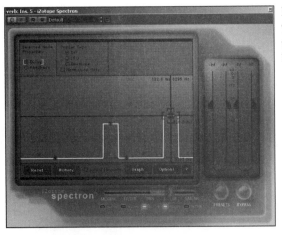

Figure 7.7

The iZotope Spectron plug-in set up to delay two frequency bands by different delay times.

The iZotope Trash plug-in has several delay tones that model classic delay signatures. In Figure 7.8, the Trash plug-in is set to a *Lo-Fi Digital* delay, which mimics the sound of early digital delay lines that had poor high-frequency response. This dark, murky delay can be useful when a perfectly clear delay sound does not have the right character. The *Broken Bit* delay adds a certain type of digital

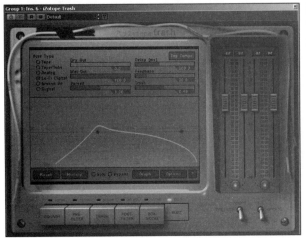

Figure 7.8

The iZotope Trash plug-in with several delay modeling types.

distortion to the signal similar to the sound of a digital system that is not working properly. The Trash parameter in both cases determines how much of this effect is added to the signal.

Modulated Delay Times

Modulation of the delay time (changing its value over time) is a method commonly used to create effects such as flanging, chorusing, and warbling echoes reminiscent of tape delay systems. Modulation is usually accomplished through the use of a Low Frequency Oscillator (LFO) that controls the delay time. The settings of the LFO determine how fast and how much the delay time is changed.

Figure 7.9 shows the PSP42's modulation section (VCP-SWEEP) with depth, waveform, and rate controls. Here, you can create all sorts of modulated delay effects from chorusing to whacked-out wiggly echoes and more. Start with small delay times (less than 10ms) and adjust the modulation section until you start hearing a change in the sound. As you increase the depth control, you'll hear more pitch variation. The higher the rate, the faster the pitch change occurs.

The unique parameter in the original PCM-42 and the PSP42 is the continuous waveform control. It has the capability to gradually change from sine wave to the envelope follower (ENV) and on to a square wave. The envelope follower varies the delay time as the input signal gets louder. This creates a neat effect when using small delay times and rather obvious pitch-changing delays with longer delay times.

Figure 7.9

The PSP42's modulation section with the unique Waveform control and envelope follower.

Flanging

The original flange effect was created literally using the flange of a tape reel. A tape reel flange is the wheel (typically metal) that's placed on either side of the tape and prevents the tape from falling off the center hub.

To create a flanging effect, the engineer would record a section of audio onto another tape machine, usually a 2-track master recorder. The tape would be edited to a certain location, such as the downbeat of a musical section. The original tape would be played back and then, at just the right moment, the engineer would start the second tape machine in order to get the two to play in sync.

Once the two machines were playing in exact time, the engineer would place a finger on the tape reel flange and gradually slow down the second tape machine, creating a very short delay that was constantly changing. When this was heard mixed together with the original audio, it created the *flanging* sound we are used to today. The tape could also be sped back up by pushing the flange around faster, creating a different flange effect.

This is how a modulated delay creates a flanging sound. A small delay, about 1–8ms, is modulated by a small amount creating a pitch change in the delayed signal that, when mixed in with the original or dry signal, creates the flanging sound. Another component of the flange effect is comb filtering, which occurs at high frequencies with such short delay times. Comb filtering is caused by phase cancellations between the dry and delayed signals similar to how room modes (discussed in Chapter 5, "Equalizers and Frequency-Based Processing") behave, but only at higher frequencies. These phase cancellations are harmonically related and, as the delay time changes, the harmonic comb filtering shifts in frequency, adding to the flange effect.

Chorusing

Figure 7.10 shows the UAD Roland CE-1 classic chorus pedal effect. Chorusing works in the same fashion as flanging, except the delay times are longer, in the range of 10–20ms. The difference between flanging and chorusing is somewhat of a grey area and is up to personal taste. They are both forms of modulated delay effects. Chorusing is more related to the pitch change of the delay rather than the comb filtering effect. Usually, chorusing requires a larger depth of delay change, creating more pitch change in the delayed signal.

Figure 7.10

The UAD Roland CE-1 classic chorus pedal plug-in.

> ❋ **GUI TIP: ROLAND CE-1 MODE**
>
> The UAD Roland CE-1 chorus has two modes: dual and classic. In the classic mode, the delayed signal comes out of the right channel and the dry signal comes out of the left channel. A stereo chorus effect is achieved when the delayed and dry signals are heard together in stereo. In dual mode, two separate delayed signals are created and panned left and right. Dual mode provides a more balanced stereo image but classic mode has a stronger signature. Options are good.

Wobbly Tape Echoes

As the delay times get longer, modulation creates more pitch wobbling and starts to sound like tape machine wow and flutter. This can be used to create a tape-based echo sound. The various wave shapes that LFOs can have will change the sound of any modulated delay. Experiment with the possibilities for each plug-in, and you will find something interesting every time.

Multi-Tap Delays

Multi-tap delay plug-ins, such as the SuperTap shown in Figure 7.11, are simply plug-ins with multiple delay signals and times. With SuperTap, you can pan each delay signal to a different location and apply different filters to each delay line, or "tap." Even the feedback signal can have its own delay time. A stereo delay can be called a two-tap delay, as long as each side of the delay can have its own delay time.

Figure 7.11

The Waves SuperTap 6 multi-tap delay plug-in.

Reverb

Reverb is sound bouncing off of various surfaces in a room and returning to the listener along with the direct sound itself. Every space has some reverb to it, with the one exception being an anechoic chamber used for acoustic research testing. Even the inside of your car has some amount of reflected sound in it. The sound of a particular reverb is very complex, with thousands or even millions of individual reflections that each can sound slightly different and arrive at different times. Various algorithms have been developed to calculate various reflection patterns that mimic the sound of rooms, halls, and even plate reverbs used in analog studios.

❄ **WHAT IS PLATE REVERB?**

The *plate reverb* is made by mounting a large metal plate, usually a rectangular 3' by 6' shape, in a suspension that allows it to vibrate in a certain fashion. Transducers are mounted on the plate that will stimulate the plate into vibration when an audio signal is applied. Additional transducers or pickups are used to capture the vibrating sound of the plate at various locations once it has been excited. That sound is plate reverb and has been used in studios since 1957 with the introduction of the EMT 140 plate reverb so faithfully reproduced in the UAD-1 Plate 140 plug-in, shown in Figure 7.12.

Figure 7.12
The UAD Plate 140 reverb plug-in.

Direct Sound and Critical Distance

The sound of reverb can be broken into several distinct elements. The first element is the direct sound from the source. The direct sound arrives at the listener's ears first and is usually the loudest element. In most large rooms and halls, when the distance from the source to the listener reaches a certain point, the direct sound and early reflections have the same volume. This is known as the *critical distance* in acoustics.

The ratio of direct to reverberant sound can be controlled within the reverb plug-in itself or by blending the dry and wet signals on two separate mixer channels. The Waves Renaissance Reverb has three level controls for blending the elements of reverb, as shown in Figure 7.13. The wet to dry balance, early reflections, and diffuse reverb all have independent level controls.

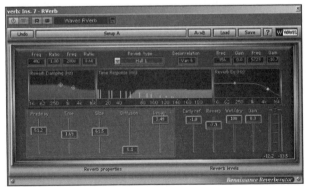

Figure 7.13
The Waves Renaissance Reverb blend controls allow adjustment of the wet to dry balance, early reflection, and diffuse reverb levels.

Typically, reverb is used as a send effect, with separate channels for dry and processed signals, described earlier in this chapter. In this case, the direct sound should not be heard through the plug-in. The effect balance should be 100% wet. If the reverb plug-in is used as an insert effect, the balance of wet to dry signal will take place in the plug-in itself.

The ratio of direct to reverb signal is one of many factors that determine the perceived distance the listener is from the source. The critical distance is the point where direct and reverberant sounds are equal in volume. This usually defines the maximum distance the ratio of wet to dry signals can create. Other factors must be used to further increase the perceived distance.

Pre-Delay

The first reflection arrives after the direct sound. The time between the direct signal and first reflection is called the *pre-delay*. The pre-delay gives the ear its first impression of the space the sound is occupying. With longer pre-delays, the ear perceives the sound emanating from a larger space (because it takes more time for the sound to travel in this space before it reaches your ears). The Plate 140, shown in Figure 7.12, has a pre-delay parameter that was not original to the EMT 140. A delay had to be patched in order to create a pre-delay for the original plate reverbs.

❊ WHAT IS IN A NAME?

Some manufacturers and developers use different terms for their plug-in parameters. For example, the pre-delay parameter in Waves Renaissance Reverb is the amount of time between the direct sound and the onset of diffuse reverb, not early reflections. For this plug-in, pre-delay is useful for exposing the early reflections by moving the diffuse reverb later in time. You have to use an additional delay plug-in before Renaissance Reverb to give the early reflections a pre-delay as well.

Early Reflections

After the pre-delay, there are a series of strong echoes known as the *first reflections* or *early reflections*. These early reflections last between 10 and 300ms and play a major role in determining how the ear perceives the size and character of the room. Most reverb plug-ins allow control over the first reflections separately from the rest of the reverb sound. First reflections define the ambience of the space.

Figure 7.14 shows the RealVerb plug-in for the UAD-1. It displays the early reflection pattern and can adjust the volume and duration of the early reflections. The various room shapes change the pattern of room reflection times.

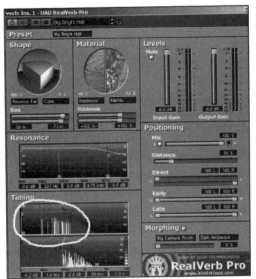

Figure 7.14
The UAD RealVerb plug-in displays the early reflection pattern.

Reverb Decay

The remainder of echoes in the room blur together to form the diffuse reverb decay. Individual echoes are not readily discernable in the reverb decay. The length, spectral content, and stereo image of the reverb decay all affect the overall reverb sound. This is the sustaining signal that is associated with reverb. Diffuse reverb does not help much in localizing the source signal like early reflections do. Rather, it creates the sense of largeness and depth by sustaining notes and sounds.

Typically, reverbs have a high-frequency damping control that determines the rate of decay of the high end of the spectrum relative to the lower frequencies. The more damping that is used, the darker the reverb will sound. Plug-ins such as DreamVerb, shown in Figure 7.15, have controls for the entire spectral shape of the diffuse reverb. The resonance controls in DreamVerb allow control over damping of any frequency band in variable amounts. You can tailor the response of the reverb to meet your needs, thus removing unwanted resonances or adding sustain at various frequencies.

Resonance control and damping are different than simply using an equalizer after a reverb plug-in. However, inserting an equalizer after a reverb plug-in affords a different kind of control over the spectral balance of reverb and may be more effective in certain situations.

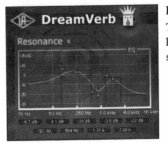

Figure 7.15
The UAD DreamVerb plug-in has resonance control for spectral adjustment of reverb.

Diffusion

Diffusion is related to the types and variance of surfaces within an acoustic space. If the walls are smooth, hard marble, there will be little diffusion in the reverb decay. If a room is made with various materials and has surface variations such as corners, crevices, relief patterns, and obstructions, there will be more diffusion. With less diffusion, reverb sounds more metallic, resonant and noticeable. With more diffusion, reverb is smoother and subtle. Think of diffusion as the focus of a camera lens. When things are in sharp focus, diffusion is low. With a soft focus, diffusion is high.

The TC MegaVerb plug-in uses a visual image to show the effect of diffusion. Figure 7.16 shows the image first with a low diffusion setting and second with a higher diffusion setting.

Figure 7.16

The TC MegaVerb plug-in diffusion display showing low diffusion and then high diffusion settings.

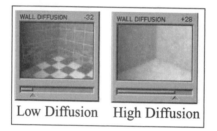

Pitch-Shifting

Real-time pitch-shifting is accomplished by using a small delay time and rapidly changing its play-back speed to change the pitch of the delayed sound. This is over-simplified for the sake of explanation as plug-ins use complex algorithms to smooth out this process. Using real-time pitch-shifting such as the Waves UltraPitch, shown in Figure 7.17, always induces a small amount of delay as a result of this processing. DAWs with plug-in delay compensation (PDC) will adjust for this delay and keep all signals in correct alignment. Sometimes this processing delay can be an element of the effect itself.

Figure 7.17

The Waves UltraPitch induces a very small amount of delay between the input signal and the pitch-shifted signal. In many cases, this can become part of the effect.

Formants

The side effect of pitch-shifting is the alteration of the formant. The *formant* is the harmonic content of a particular sound such as the human voice. Each person has a unique set of harmonics that make up their vocal quality. When the pitch of a voice goes up and down, the harmonics normally remain the same as the pitch changes. Using a pitch processor, the formant or harmonic content shift along with the pitch. The result is best demonstrated by the "chipmunk" effect.

Speeding up analog tape recordings of normal voices created the classic cartoon voices of the chipmunks. The resulting voice formant was shifted along with the pitch, resulting in the unnatural sound of the chipmunks. This might be well and good for animated cartoons, but when a natural voice quality is desired, the formant must be modified when pitch changing occurs in order to maintain a natural voice quality.

Startling results can be achieved when formant processing is performed along with pitch changing. Artificial harmonies can be created from one vocal track that are quite believable in a mix. The best pitch changing usually comes from offline processing because the signal can be examined outside of the normal flow of time. With this careful analysis, the pitch-change can be performed with the least amount of sonic damage.

Pitch Correction: "Auto-Tuning"

Pitch-shifting technology has led to the capability to correct for tuning errors in musical performances. The Antares Auto-Tune plug-in has become synonymous with pitch correction of singers in pop music and has led to the generic phrase *auto-tuning the vocals,* implying various forms of pitch correction. Figure 7.18 shows the Auto-Tune GUI in manual mode, where each note in a performance can be adjusted for pitch in very subtle ways.

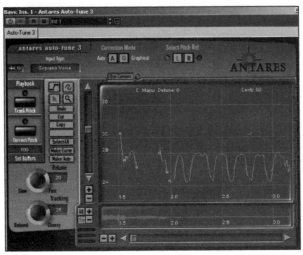

Figure 7.18

The infamous Auto-Tune plug-in.

Auto-tuning is a complex subject and is covered in detail, including step-by-step methods for tuning bad vocals without the telltale sound of Auto-Tune in its automatic mode, in Chapter 9, "Pitch Correction and Adjustment." Precise pitch correction can be achieved while minimizing the obvious signs of processing when done correctly.

Time Compression and Expansion

Time compression and expansion are the sister processes to pitch changing. Speeding up a sound changes its pitch and shortens it. Conversely, slowing a sound down lowers its pitch and lengthens it. The trick is to shorten or increase the length without altering the pitch. The same goes for pitch changing; when you raise the pitch, the speed increases and the length shortens. When you lower the pitch, the length increases. Figure 7.19 shows the Nuendo Pitch Shift process window. Notice the Time Correction check box that compensates for the speed change of the file.

Figure 7.19

The Nuendo Pitch Shift process window with the Time Correction check box.

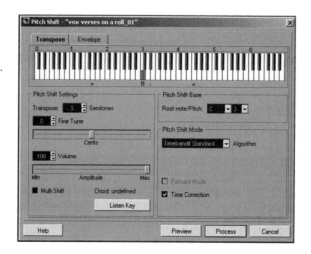

Pitch-shifting and time compression/expansion are related processes that often work together, compensating for one another. When pitch-shifting a sound higher, the speed increases and the length is shortened. Time expansion reverses that effect so the pitch has been raised without the length changing. Conversely, when you time-compress an audio file, it raises the pitch. Pitch-shifting must be used to return the pitch to normal after the length has been altered.

You can perform time compression and expansion in real-time. However, the quality will suffer because such a large amount of DSP is needed to do it well. For the best fidelity, time compression and expansion should be performed as an offline process by creating a new sound file.

There are various algorithms for time compression and expansion that are tailored to different source material. Vocals can benefit from a different algorithm than drums, for instance. Most DAWs and plug-ins offer several algorithms for time compression and expansion. Figure 7.20 shows Nuendo's options in the Time Stretch process window.

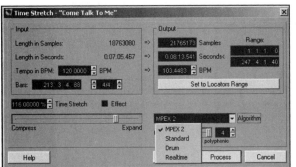

Figure 7.20

Nuendo's Time Stretch window with four algorithm options.

Using Time-Based Processing

Time-based or time-domain processing dominates the arsenal of effect used during mixdown. The applications range from acoustic space creation to drum loop tempo changes and vocal tuning. Time-based processing is one of the "big three" aspects of audio: frequency, amplitude, and time. Altering the time element of audio can create all sorts of interesting results. The following are some real-world examples of how you can apply time-based processing.

Delay Times

Delays are the most basic form of time-based processing and are the basis for all the other time-based processors. Delays are very discrete and specific, requiring more precise settings and careful implementation. They can be very powerful at creating space and identity for various sounds in a mix. They provide color and dimension to otherwise plain sounds. They can also add bounce and rhythm to music.

Tempo-Based Delay

As discussed earlier, many delay plug-ins feature the capability to set the delay time musically by following tempo information relayed to the plug-in from the host DAW. If you know the tempo of the music, a calculator can give you delay times related to the musical beat.

Many delay plug-ins offer yet another method of deriving the delay time from a tempo: tap tempo. Figure 7.21 shows the Spectron delay plug-in tap tempo screen. Placing the cursor over the tap button and clicking it in time with the music will generate a delay time based on how fast the tap button was clicked. This is a very quick method of calculating a tempo-based delay time. Sometimes a live performance will not have a steady tempo and the tap tempo option is the only way to come up with a reasonable setting.

Figure 7.21

The Spectron Tap Tempo screen.

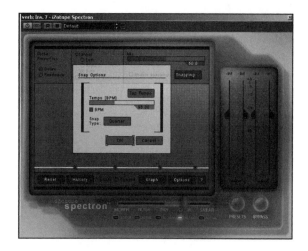

The classic quarter note delay that falls on the beat is a very common delay setting that creates a rhythmic echo. Eighth notes create more of a slap back sound depending on the tempo. Sixteenth notes do more of the same. As you increase the delay time to half notes and whole notes, the echo becomes more of a repeat, catching whole phrases and repeating them back in time. Sometimes creating more than one delay with a different musical value can provide more options for rhythmic variation.

Setting a delay time to an exact musical time yields a very accurate delay. Try adjusting the delay slightly away from the perfect setting to create additional moods. Lengthening the delay time can create a looser, more relaxed feeling to the echo. Quickening the time can give the echo a sense of urgency. Experiment creatively with subtle adjustments of musical delay times to get the sound you are looking for. Perfect delay times set to exact musical beats are not always the best delay times.

MIX TIP: THE MARCH OR PING-PONG DELAY SETTING

The classic ping-pong or "march" delay is created using to different delay times based on the tempo of the song. Usually, the delay times are a quarter note, or one beat, and a dotted quarter note, or a beat and a half. For example, a song at 120bpm has a quarter note delay time of 500ms. The dotted quarter note value is 750ms. Dotted musical notes are one and a half times the value of the undotted note. Each delay is fed back upon itself to create a stereo balance between the two. Usually, the quarter note delay needs a bit more feedback to echo as long as the dotted quarter note delay. One delay is panned hard left and the other is panned hard right. When rhythmic musical phrases are sent into the "march" delay patch, a bouncy back and forth rhythm is created. Drums can be sent through the march to create a "dub mix" feel, among other things.

Early Reflection Delay

One use of the delay that is often overlooked is the use of an imaging delay. By using short delay times (less than 100ms), you can create an early reflection echo to place a sound within some sort of acoustic space. The engineer's first response to this might be to use reverb to create an acoustic space, but often the early reflection single delay can be more effective. Reverb tends to fill space up where a delay is discrete, leaving more space for other instruments or sounds.

The single delay can be panned away from the original sound in order to create a wider image. Use feedback signal filtering to alter the brightness of the acoustic space or simply put an EQ on the delayed signal. The amount of feedback can also increase the apparent size of the space. To start off, use a delay time of 60ms and then adjust to taste. Also, using a high-pass filter on the output of the delay makes it sound more like a true echo.

❄ MIX TIP: INSERT EFFECT VS. SEND EFFECT

There are two basic ways to apply effects to audio signals. The first method, the insert effect, places the plug-in directly on the audio channel in order to process the entire signal. The second method uses a parallel path to send the signal to another channel where it is processed, allowing more control between the dry (original unprocessed signal) and the wet (processed signal). Both methods have advantages and disadvantages. Insert effects can only be applied to the audio channel they are inserted on. Send effects are available to every channel in the mixer.

A compressor is an example of a processor that is most often used as an insert effect to control the dynamics of one signal. A reverb is a good example of a send effect. Many signals can be sent to a reverb plug-in at once using aux sends. Figures 7.22 and 7.23 illustrate the two types of effects routing.

Typically, plug-ins that create a separate signal that is to be added in various amounts back with the dry signal, such as delays and reverbs, will benefit from a send effect signal flow. Plug-ins that process the original signal and are meant to replace the original signal completely are better suited for insert effect routing, such as equalizers and compressors.

Another benefit to send effects is that you can process the effect signal by itself separately. For example, it is very common to want to put reverb on an echo delay return. That way, each echo has its own ambience. Also, the wet signal can be panned to a different position than the dry signal, offering more stereo and surround possibilities.

Many plug-ins have a way to control the amount of dry versus wet signal in their outputs. Some plug-ins have separate gain controls for the dry and wet signals. Others use a single blend control to vary the balance between wet and dry signals. The point to remember is, when using the send effect routing shown in Figure 7.23, make sure the balance is 100% wet signal. If there is dry signal in the mix, level sent to the plug-in will also add level to the original dry signal, thus altering the balance.

Figure 7.22
Insert effect signal routing.

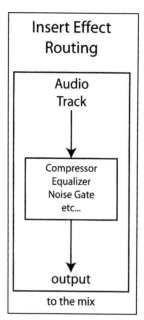

Figure 7.23
Send effect signal routing.

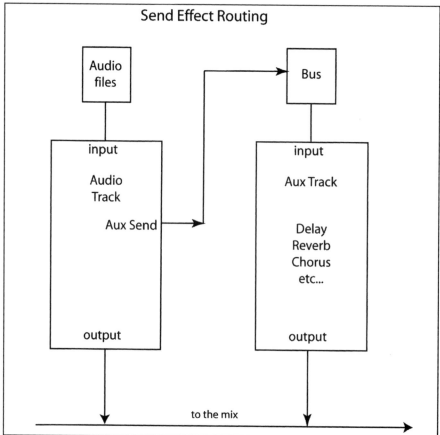

Creating a Feedback Loop

It is also possible to create your own feedback loop for a delay so that you can apply various types of processing to the feedback signal. To create a feedback loop, you need to create another path for the signal coming out of the delay plug-in to be routed back into the delay after being processed. Here is one way to do it in Pro Tools. Certain native DAWs can pose more difficulties in setting up this kind of signal flow. It might be necessary in those cases to use the DSP mixer in your audio hardware to create a feedback loop signal flow.

To create a feedback loop in Pro Tools, follow these steps:

1. Create two Aux tracks in Pro Tools: one for the delay processing and another for the feedback signal processing.

> ❋ **AUX TRACKS IN PRO TOOLS**
>
> Aux tracks in Pro Tools are open ended audio paths. They can have various input sources from physical inputs to buses. A similar audio path in Cubase is the Group Channel. The Group Channel can be fed by multiple audio tracks via direct routing or aux sends. Aux tracks and Group Channels are used for creative audio routing of all sorts. Most DAWs have audio similar paths available.

2. Insert a delay plug-in on the first Aux track.

3. Set it up for the proper delay setting. Understand that there will always be a small amount of additional delay in the feedback signal due to processing time. On a TDM system, this should not be noticeable. On a native system, there might be some noticeable additional delay. For most feedback applications, this should not be an issue because these effects are meant to be extreme.

4. Insert plug-ins on the feedback Aux track that you want to process the feedback signal with. This can be an equalizer, compressor, or even a distortion generator. Try anything. Experimenting here can be the source for many inspiring effects. A compressor such as the UAD LA-2A is a common choice. Compressing the feedback signal will cause the delay to repeat longer but in a more controlled fashion. This is dependent on the actual settings of the compressor.

5. From the audio channel you want to apply this delay effect to, create an aux send to route the signal to the input of the feedback Aux track.

6. On the Delay Aux track, create an aux send that also is routed to the feedback Aux track. This is the actual feedback connection. The level of this aux send is a critical one to determining the amount and length of the feedback. If it is turned up too much, very loud signals can be created, causing signal clipping and possible damage to speakers and other equipment. Always be careful when working with feedback loops. A brick wall limiter on the output of the feedback channel can prevent accidental feedback spikes from damaging other equipment.

7. Finally, route the output of the feedback Aux track to the input of the delay Aux track. The fader level controls the level sent to the delay. If all other aux sends are at 0dB (unity gain), the feedback will be at 100% and should echo almost infinitely depending on the processing that is inserted on the feedback aux track. Figure 7.24 shows how the signal flow works. Dynamics processors on the feedback aux track will greatly affect the amount of feedback generated. Experiment to find some interesting settings.

Figure 7.24

The signal flow diagram of a delay feedback processing chain.

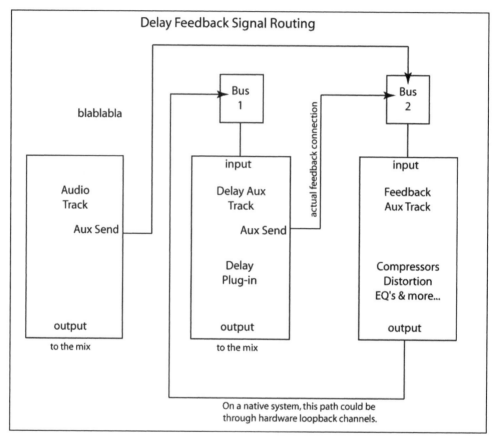

With a compressor inserted in the feedback Aux track, delays with significant feedback amounts will behave dynamically when a new signal comes through the delay. For example, say one note is picked on an electric guitar that is echoing through the delay/feedback chain. If the feedback amount is high enough, the echoes can go on for a long time, because the compressor is bringing up the signal as it decays, making it last longer and sound more grainy and warped in a cool way.

Striking another note on the guitar will send the compressor back into gain reduction and immediately turn down the long echoes of the first note, replacing them with the second. The compressor is doing this automatically. Whenever the guitar is playing, the feedback is low. When the guitar plays a sustained note, the feedback increases as the compressor lets go of the signal, bringing it up. This is called a *dynamic delay* and can be very useful on lead instruments and vocals when you don't want to hear the delay while they are playing or singing but, when they hold out on a note, you want the delay to open up and echo longer.

This is but one example of how you can use processing on a feedback signal to create interesting and sophisticated effects. Try putting a distortion modeler on the feedback signal. Try a pitch-shifter or an envelope generator. The possibilities are endless.

Flanging and Chorusing

Chorus and flanging sounds are created when the dry and modulated short delays are mixed together at roughly the same volume. The subtle pitch changes in the delayed signal blend with the dry signal and create the swirling, shimmering chorus effect. With shorter delay times (1–8ms), the comb filtering creates the more severe flanging sound.

Flanging

The *comb filtering* is a by-product of short delay times in a flanger. There is another type of filter processor called a *phaser*, which actually uses several notch filters to create a comb filter and then modulates the center frequencies of those filters to create the phaser sound. Flangers use delays and phasers use filters. They sound similar, but are not the same type of processor.

Flanging is a more severe effect and is usually reserved for special effects that only occur once during a mix—a pivotal moment in the production. Constant use of a flanger might be annoying in a typical music mix. Anything is possible, though.

A classic use of the flanger is when processing a whole mix leading up to a climactic point. The modulation is usually very slow, only going through one cycle of speeding up and slowing down. The point at which the delay is the smallest coincides with the climactic sound of the flanger and high point of the music.

Chorusing

Chorusing can create movement in a mix when the dry signal is panned to one side and the wet signal to the other side. The "rubbing" of the two signals in the stereo field creates a movement back and forth. It is also possible for a stereo chorus to have two discrete delay times that independently modulate to create a true stereo effect. The UAD Roland CE-1 plug-in has both operating modes: classic and dual.

A good mix trick is to set up two delays between 7 and 15ms that are modulating at slightly different speeds and depths, in essence, a stereo chorus. Pan each one hard left and right. They should be set up as send effects. Any signal that you have panned to the left and want to add some motion to, send it to the delay on the right. And any signal on the right you can send to the left delay to create motion. Each side has a different delay time and modulation, giving a wide stereo field of motion.

Remember to always check stereo effect in mono. Some signal level might be lost due to phase cancellations that occur in the summed mono mix.

Chorusing can be used to create pseudo-stereo sound from a mono source. Using a subtle modulated delay anywhere from 5–15ms panned opposite the dry signal will create a false stereo image. The image will usually lean towards the dry side simply because that sound will arrive earliest to the ear and our hearing tells us that the earliest sound indicates the location of the source. Pseudo-stereo helps maintain an even left-right balance on a mono sound without center panning and taking up space in the middle of the mix where other instruments might lie.

Chorusing works well with sustained sounds, making them flourish and giving them color. Crash cymbals can benefit from a chorus effect because it gives them more of a swirl. Background vocals can appear to have more voices when chorused. Sometimes just a small amount of chorusing provides the desired effect. Overuse of chorusing (or any effect) can have diminishing returns after a certain point.

Reverb Settings

The art of designing reverb and ambience sounds could fill another entire book. But there are some basic principles that can help you start the process and provide you with options for creating various reverb settings. First of all, there are various purposes for reverb.

Some purposes for adding reverb:

* Ambience that creates a physical space for an otherwise dead or dry sound to occupy. This also applies to film and post-production audio for dialogue replacement, among many other things.
* Reverb that adds sustain and depth to various tones or musical notes.
* Reverb that has a rhythmic shape to it that enhances the groove.
* Special effect reverb for dramatic endings or fade-outs.
* Reverb that glues together disparate elements in a mix, a common space for everything to exist in.
* Textured reverb that uses some sound source as a trigger, generating tones from the initial sound.

Once you determine what type of reverb you need, determining the settings is a bit easier. Ambience settings usually have smaller decay times, whereas sustaining reverb have longer decay times. The following section describes the various common reverb parameters. The various reverb types are a good starting point.

Room Shape/Algorithm

There are several basic reverb types or algorithms that form the basis for a reverb setting. Most reverb plug-ins have a select choice of type to start with. The algorithm has an effect on every other parameter of the reverb. As such, you begin by determining what reverb type is appropriate for the current situation. Each type has a particular decay shape that is identifiable. Each shape or type has its applications and will have a particular sound regardless of decay length.

✳ *Room*—Room reverbs focus more on early reflections and localization within a realistic acoustic space. Reverb times are anywhere from 0.3 seconds to 1.5 seconds. Longer decay times are possible, but enter into the realm of special effects, not realistic reverb. The early reflection pattern is dense, imitating the closeness of reflective surfaces in a room.

✳ *Hall*—Hall reverbs emulate larger acoustic spaces whereby the early reflection pattern is spaced out with more discrete reflections before the onset of reverb decay. Hall reverbs have more resonance to them, reflecting the larger dimensions of typical halls. Reverb times can vary but anywhere from 1 second to 4 or 5 seconds.

✳ *Plate*—The plate reverb is modeled after the mechanical device that uses a metal plate to generate reverb. The reflection pattern and reverb decay follow the sound a physical plate makes. Plate reverbs can vary in duration from less than a second to absurdly long decay times. A plate reverb is not very natural sounding, but it has a musical flavor that we are all familiar with from the many recordings made with plates.

✳ *Non-Linear*—Non-linear reverbs follow a very unnatural decay slope. Instead of steadily decreasing in level as the reverb decays, non-linear reverb can do just about anything. Gated reverb is the most common example of this. A gated reverb is made by placing a noise gate after a reverb plug-in. Adjusting the threshold so the gate shuts before the reverb has completely decayed creates this unique sound. The term non-linear refers to this type of decay profile. Reverb that starts soft and increases in level to a point is non-linear as well and is often called *reverse reverb*.

✳ MIX TIP: TRUE REVERSE REVERB

In the "old" days of analog, creating reverse reverb required some very mechanical manipulation of the actual tape itself. It required flipping the multi-track tape over on the machine and recording the reverb returns on a separate set of tracks and then flipping the tape back over for playback. The reverb decay would then occur before the sound that created it and it would be heard in reverse.

Creating true reverse reverb in the digital world is much simpler but still requires a bit of manual editing. To start, route the desired signal to an effect channel with a reverb plug-in inserted on it. Depending on the DAW software, there can be several methods of recording just the output of the reverb effect channel to an audio file. The idea is to create an audio file that contains just the reverb signal by itself, 100% wet. Once this is done, import the audio file to a new audio track in alignment with the original dry sound. Next, using offline processing, reverse the reverb sound file. You then have to move the reversed file so that it comes before the original dry sound. The reverb will "ramp up" before the sound, as shown in Figure 7.25, creating this unique effect.

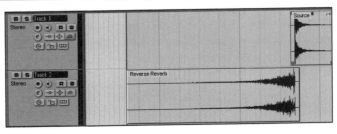

Figure 7.25
The finished reverse reverb edit showing the reverb signal (on Track 2) "ramping up" to the original dry signal on Track 1.

Reverb Time

The reverb time parameter, also known as decay or RT60, indicates how long the reverb sound will last before it falls 60dB from its initial level at onset. This value is indicative of how long we will perceive the reverb decay when it is by itself. Within a mix, less of the reverb tail is heard due to the masking effects of other elements in the mix, so the perceived length of the reverb decay might not equate to the decay value in this context.

Setting the reverb decay for musical elements is often tied to the tempo or rhythmic speed and variation. Reverb that is too long can tend to blur elements by just filling in the areas between individual sounds. Having a reasonable decay time that allows listeners to hear the individual sounds requires careful setting of this parameter.

Some plug-ins have decay times for both high and low frequencies as separate controls. Figure 7.26 shows the TC MegaReverb plug-in, which has decay times for three frequency areas: highs (0.50s), mids (1.20s), and lows (4.00s). Each frequency area is adjustable by moving the handles on the visual display or entering in crossover values for low and high crossover points. The two crossover points divide the spectrum into three areas.

Figure 7.26

TC's MegaReverb with three decay times for different frequency bands.

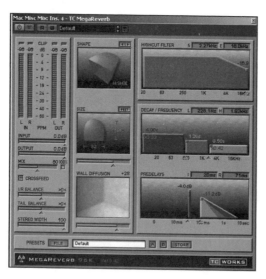

High-Frequency Damping

Sometimes, the plug-in will have a high frequency decay factor. This factor is used to adjust the decay time of high frequencies as a function of the overall decay time. For example, Figure 7.27 shows the frequency response curve of Waves TrueVerb plug-in. The high-frequency damping is set to 0.50×, starting at 2kHz. This roughly indicates that frequencies above 2kHz will decay up to twice as fast as lower frequencies. In other words, they will last half as long (0.50×) as the rest of the spectrum.

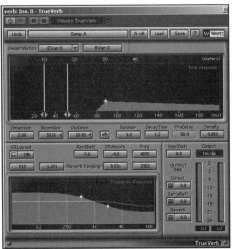

Figure 7.27

Waves TrueVerb plug-in with high-frequency damping enabled for 0.50x at 2kHz.

High-frequency damping is basically a low-pass filter on the output of the reverb decay. It is used to simulate the various materials that might be on the surfaces of the reverberant space. Materials such as carpet or ceiling tiles tend to naturally reduce the volume of high-frequency reflections in a space, due to the absorption coefficient of these materials. Increasing the amount of damping of the highs (lowering the frequency of the low-pass filter) creates the same sort of effect.

Steinberg's RoomWorks plug-in, shown in Figure 7.28, has two damping controls, one for high frequencies and one for low frequencies. Each damping control has a frequency and amount parameters. The frequency determines where the damping effect begins and the amount determines how

Figure 7.28

Steinberg's RoomWorks reverb plug-in with two sets of damping controls.

much reverberation loss there is at those frequencies. Notice that there are also input shelving filters that process the input signal prior to reverberation. Damping controls are different and affect the type of reverberation.

Diffusion

Diffusion is the measure of how dense the reverb decay is; how many discrete echoes make up the decay sound. This relates to the complexity of geometry in an acoustic space. For example, an empty room that is rectangular in shape and has a normal, flat ceiling, has a low diffusion factor. On the other hand, a room that had various angles in its walls, a sloping ceiling, and multiple pieces of furniture would have a much higher diffusion amount. Higher diffusion yields a smoother reverb decay, whereas less diffusion creates a more "echoey" sound that is not even or smooth.

Some people tend to equate higher diffusion with better reverb and, although it is true that it takes more processing power to create higher diffusion, it does not mean that it is better in every situation. Highly diffuse reverb can be less noticeable in denser mixes. For a more identifiable reverb character, experiment with lower diffusion settings to create quirkier sounding decays.

Pre-Delay

Pre-delay is the time between the initial sound and the arrival of the first reflection. This is the primary factor our hearing uses to determine the size of a particular space and the distance we are from the sound source. Sound travels at a relatively standard speed through the air and our hearing uses that factor in measuring the size of a space by the timing of each echo.

 MIX TIP: USING PRE-DELAY WITH VOCALS

On vocals with very long reverb times, it can become difficult to have an intimate clarity with the voice. By using longer pre-delays, the dry vocal can be separated from the reverb decay, providing more clarity and presence while preserving the resonance and depth of longer reverb. By itself, this technique can sound very unnatural, but in the context of an entire mix, it can create the right balance of intimacy and size.

Early Reflection Control

Early reflections are made up of the strongest echoes that arrive to the listener within the first 300ms or so of any reverb signal. These stronger echoes define the signature of any acoustic space and have the greatest effect on our perception of size and even the material makeup of a space. The timing and spectral balance of early reflections create a model of the acoustic space in the brain of the listener. Modifying the early reflections alters this model.

Modern reverb plug-ins such as UAD's DreamVerb offer complex ways of altering the early reflections. DreamVerb uses various shapes to define the pattern of early reflections. Figure 7.29 shows the reflection pattern of a standard rectangular room, or *shoebox*, as defined in DreamVerb. In Figure 7.30, the shape has been changed to a cylinder. DreamVerb allows the creation of complex geometry by blending two shapes together in various proportions to create the final early reflection pattern. For example, Figure 7.31 shows two shapes that are blended 70/30 to create a third reflection pattern.

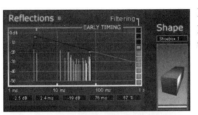

Figure 7.29

DreamVerb's early reflection pattern of a rectangular room.

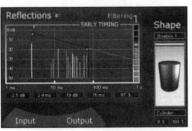

Figure 7.30

DreamVerb's early reflection pattern of a cylinder.

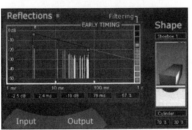

Figure 7.31

Two reflection patterns combined in a 70/30 proportion, creating a third unique pattern.

The length of the early reflection period is also adjustable in DreamVerb, along with its relative volume in relation to the diffuse reverb level. Sometimes, just using the early reflections of a reverb plug-in can create a great ambience effect, placing an otherwise dead sound into an acoustic space without adding a lot of reverb, just early reflections.

TC Electronics VSS3 Virtual Space Simulator uses many early reflection models to create stunningly realistic spaces especially useful to film and television post-production where it is often necessary to emulate various real-world acoustic spaces to match dialogue recorded on location with replacement tracks recorded in the studio. Figure 7.32 shows the early reflection page of the VSS3 plug-in interface. Although there is no graphic depiction of the echo pattern, the names of each early reflection model evoke an accurate image. Some of the models included in the VSS3 are:

* Forest
* Car park
* Phone booth
* Alley
* Street
* Airport
* Bathroom

Figure 7.32

TC Electronics VSS3 Virtual Space Simulator's early reflections edit page.

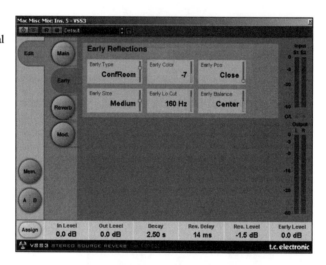

With this list, video and film mixing engineers have a head start in creating ambiences that match various on-camera locations. The early reflection pattern is the most important cue our hearing has to determine the space a sound occurs in. Once the ear has determined what sort of acoustic environment there is, the reverb decay can be adjusted to taste without disturbing the identity of the space too much.

Gated Reverb and Non-Linear Decay

Non-linear reverbs have decays that do not occur with a natural sounding slope. They tend to have an unnatural sound and are used for special effects. Figure 7.33 shows the TC NonLin2 plug-in that provides many options for this type of effect. With lists of models for both reverb type and "twist," a large number of variations are available. The NonLin2 has a variable envelope that you can use to tailor the shape of the reverb tail. Using the familiar attack, hold, and release parameters of a gate, the reverb decay can take on a surreal sound.

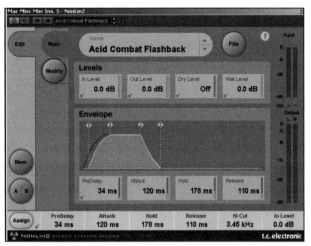

Figure 7.33
The TC NonLin2 Gate-style reverb plug-in with envelope controls.

The NonLin2 uses a reverb style that is modified by a "twist" function creating more dramatic effects. Figure 7.34 shows the list of reverb styles and twist types. Once the reverb has been generated, it is subjected to the settings of the envelope, resulting in non-linear reverb decay.

These types of effects are useful for making certain mix elements stand out and have a unique spotlight placed on them. Unlike normal reverbs, which are intended to sound natural and be perceived as normal, non-linear reverbs place larger-than-life emphasis on elements, allowing for a more dynamic mix.

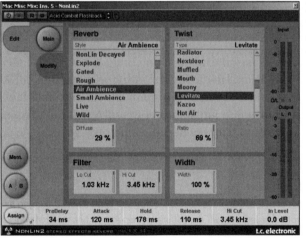

Figure 7.34
TC NonLin2 Modify page with lists of reverb styles and twist types.

> ❋ **MIX TIP: LEAD VOCAL AMBIENCE**
>
> A common technique in modern pop music is to create a most unreal ambience for lead vocals. This space places you very close to the vocal while also spreading out the image into wide stereo. Diction becomes clearer because the ambience extenuates the consonant sounds of words without the use of massive high-frequency EQ.
>
> Using a very short non-linear reverb with some sort of modulation can achieve this effect. The NonLin2 with the various twist types is a good example of a plug-in well suited for the job.

> ❋ **MIX TIP: SNARE DRUM EXTENSION**
>
> Another great use of non-linear reverb is the lengthening or extension of the snare sound of the snare drum. The actual metal windings found on the bottom of snare drums create the noise signature that defines the snare. Often these snares have limited resonance due to the damping of the drum in the course of recording. The damping is usually the result of resonances in the drum that are not compatible with the music being recorded. The result is a snare drum that sounds a bit cramped and tight. Adding the right kind of non-linear reverb to the snare can elongate the noise made by the snares and recreate the sound of a naturally tuned drum without added damping. Adjusting the length of the reverb with envelope controls gives you a very precise way of determining the perceived length of the snare resonance. This is a good way to get a big snare sound without samples or over-equalizing.

Pitch-Shifting

Pitch-shifting has several varied uses for both music and film post-production. Although severe pitch-shifting is sometimes used to create surreal effects and mangle sounds, subtle use of pitch-shifting can add dimension and character to vocals and other instruments. Used in conjunction with pitch-detection software, tuning of vocals and individual instruments is possible with plug-ins such as Auto-Tune. Chapter 9 deals with all aspects of pitch-correction plug-ins and techniques. With modern algorithms, it is even possible to create harmonies for vocals and instruments by merely pitch-shifting the original tracks.

Musical Intervals

Having an understanding of musical intervals is important when setting up a pitch-shifter. The most basic musical interval is the octave. The easiest way to describe an octave is that it is the same note, only higher in the scale. Octaves sound identical because they are multiples of each other in frequency. If a note has a frequency of 250Hz, an octave above that is twice the frequency or 500Hz. Doubling the frequency creates an octave. Subsequently, an octave lower is half the frequency, or 125Hz.

Each octave is divided into 12 equal pitches that make up the chromatic scale. Each twelfth of an octave is called a half-step or semi-tone. Two twelfths of an octave are called a whole-step or (whole) tone in musical terms. Musical scales are made up of various combinations of half-steps and whole-steps. Pitch-shifters often have musical parameters that allow adjustment of pitch in musical terms such as Nuendo's pitch-shift process shown in Figure 7.35.

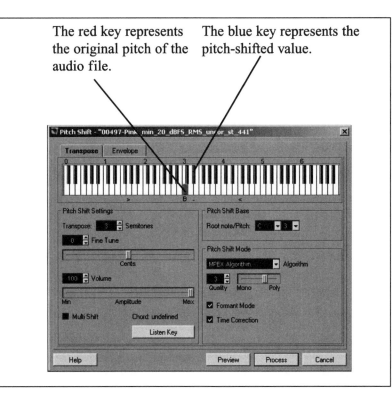

The red key represents the original pitch of the audio file.

The blue key represents the pitch-shifted value.

Figure 7.35
Nuendo's pitch-shift process with piano keyboard display.

The piano keyboard displayed is one method of musical control. The red key indicates the original pitch of the audio file. This value is relative and can be adjusted in the Pitch Shift Base section. Basically, the keyboard GUI is just another method of arriving at a pitch-shifting value. It does not make the pitch of any given sound equal to the note on the keyboard.

> ❋ **MIX TIP: A440**
>
> The musical note middle A has a frequency of 440Hz. You may notice that some guitar tuners allow the adjustment of this value to slightly different settings such as 441 or 442. Most often these settings are used with orchestral instruments that benefit from a slightly higher tuning. Knowing what musical values correspond to frequencies can be a secret weapon in studio recording and mixing. There are charts available that display musical values as they relate to audio frequencies. A table can be found at http://www.phy.mtu.edu/~suits/notefreqs.html that displays this information.

The blue key in Nuendo's Pitch Shift shows the relative value of the pitch-shifted audio. If the blue key is on the same note an octave higher, the audio will be pitch-shifted up one octave. Figure 7.35 shows the red key on C and the blue key on Eb. Because each key on the piano is equal to one half-step or semi-tone, Eb is three half-steps above C. Notice the pitch-shift settings reflect this by indicating the transpose amount is three semi-tones.

It is also possible to pitch-shift by very small amounts less than one half-step. Musically, each half-step is divided into 100 cents. The cents slider in Nuendo's Pitch Shift has a range of –200 to +200 cents or plus and minus a whole step. Using such fine adjustments gives you exact control over the pitch-shift ratio.

Pitch Ratios

Figure 7.36 shows the Pro Tools Pitch plug-in. In addition to the musical values, there is a ratio setting in the Pro Tools plug-in. Defining a ratio is another method of determining the pitch-shift amount. A pitch ratio of 1:2 equals shifting up one octave or doubling the frequency. Ratios can be helpful when the intended purpose of pitch-shifting is not musical.

Figure 7.36

The Pro Tools Pitch plug-in.

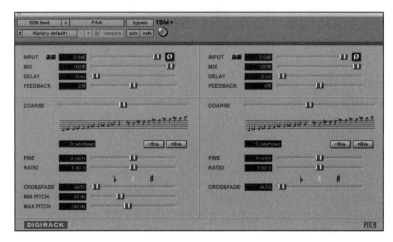

One example of a non-musical pitch-shift could occur with production audio recorded on a film shoot that has been transferred to video and as a result, has been speed adjusted to compensate for the 2:3 pulldown transfer process. Audio that is being added to these tracks might need to be shifted by a small amount to match the timber of the speed-adjusted audio. The telecine transfer process reduces the speed and pitch of audio by 0.1%. In terms of a ratio, this is 1:0.999. Using this ratio in a pitch-shifting plug-in will generate the correct pitch change to match telecine transferred audio.

❋ TELECINE 2:3 PULLDOWN

Transferring film to video requires a complex process called the 2:3 Pulldown. Film runs at 24 frames per second (fps), whereas NTSC video runs at 29.97fps. In order to reconcile these two frame rates, a small speed change is applied to both the picture and sound of −0.1%. For more information about this and many other audio or film and video post-production techniques and issues, refer to *Pro Tools for Film, Video, and Multimedia,* another book from Course Technology written by Ashley Shepherd (ISBN: 159200069X).

❋ ❋ ❋

Micro-Shift Chorusing

Using pitch-shifts of less than a half-step can create a chorusing effect useful in widening vocal tracks and adding color to background vocals. To create stereo pitch chorusing, signals are fed into two independent pitch-shifters that are panned hard left and right. One is set to a positive value of several cents (+3 cents) and the other is set to a negative value (–3 cents). The effect of having two slightly de-tuned signals panned out creates a rich chorusing texture without obvious modulation signatures that chorusing can have.

If you are using ratios to create this effect, try starting with one side set to 1:1.004 and the other side set to 1:0.996 and see how that sounds. In both cases, symmetrical pitch-shifts are used. You may find that using asymmetrical settings (+7 cents, –4 cents) sounds better. As always, your ears are the best measuring devices.

Octave Doubling and Harmonies

A very common musical use of pitch-shifting is to create an octave double of an instrument or vocal. Bass guitar or synth parts can benefit from creating a lower octave double to create a sub-bass signal to be mixed in with the original. This technique can enhance the low end of a bass part without the use of equalization. Take care not to damage speakers by using too much of a very low frequency bass signal.

Creating a lower or higher octave of vocal tracks is a bit trickier because the artifacts of pitch-shifting are more easily heard in the vocal range. Typically, lower octave shifts have less noticeable artifacts than upper octave ones. Subtle use of lower octave shifts with vocals can enhance the size of a vocal part, giving it more weight in the mix.

Melodic instruments and vocals can be pitch-shifted to create harmony parts. A thorough knowledge of music theory is very helpful in these cases. Musical scales are not uniform in their construction. Merely setting a pitch-shifter to one particular interval will not always yield a musical result as the melody moves through the scale. Careful one-by-one processing of notes is necessary to create a musically pleasing harmony result with a static pitch-shifter.

Dedicated pitch-manipulation software such as Celemony's Melodyne is better suited to creating complex musical harmonies than a simple pitch-shifter. These techniques are discussed in Chapter 9.

Sound Design

When creating new and imaginary sounds to augment cinematic productions, pitch-shifting is a commonly used tool. Pitch-shifting normal sounds in extreme amounts can generate new and unusual sonic textures that still retain some elements of the original sound, helping to tie it to reality. Sometimes it is necessary to change the pitch of a sound effect to blend more effectively with the music in a movie. If the drone of a car engine conflicts with a musical cue, the drone can be pitch-shifted to a more pleasing register.

Adding copies of a sound that have been pitch-shifted can increase the perceived size of an explosion, for example. Take the original explosion sound and create a copy that is one octave lower. Add this sound to the original for a larger-than-life effect. Other intervals can add density to effects.

In the movie *Backdraft*, many animal sounds were lowered in pitch and used to augment the sound of the fire. This gave the fire an element of life and personality. A bear growl lowered by an octave or more could add a sense of anger to the thrust of a plume of smoke and fire. Subtle use of similar elements can cause the viewer's subconscious to react without identifying the original sound source.

❄ MATRIX REVOLUTIONS 96KHZ PITCH-SHIFT

"For the large metal sounds of the machines that are in the real world, we recorded big metal bangs and hits at very high sample rates to capture ultrasonic frequencies. That way, we could pitch them down while still maintaining the whole harmonic structure." —Eric Lindemann, from an article in *Mix Magazine's* June 2003 issue (reprinted with permission).

Sound designers Eric Lindemann and Dane Davis used a Neumann digital Solution-D microphone to capture ultra-sonic material at 96kHz that would be pitch-shifted down in order to bring those upper harmonics into the audible range. Remember, when attempting to use this sort of technique, you need a microphone capable of capturing ultra-sonic frequencies. Most microphones roll off after 20kHz or lower.

A classic example of pitch-shifting sound design is using multiple pitch-shifts to create a robot voice from a dialogue track. Figure 7.37 shows the Waves UltraPitch plug-in set up to create a computer voice effect for dialogue. Adjusting the various intervals changes the sonic texture of the voice. Also, shifting the formants around adds another dimension to the effect.

Figure 7.37

Waves UltraPitch 3 set up to mimic a robotic voice sound.

Time Compression and Expansion

Time compression and expansion are closely related to pitch-shifting in the sense that they manipulate one aspect of time (speed) without affecting the other (pitch). Wave Mechanics Speed plug-in even combines the two processes in one interface, as seen in Figure 7.38.

Figure 7.38
Wave Mechanics Speed deals with pitch-shifting and time compression and expansion in one plug-in because both processes are related.

Timing versus Sound Quality

Because time compression and expansion deal with tempo and timing of audio files, signals are often analyzed for their rhythmic or timing characteristics. Various segments of the audio file are marked as having important timing info. The plug-in can use this information to determine where to apply more time stretching depending on the choices of the user.

When you're working with percussive audio such as drum loops, time stretching should not disturb the relative positions of each rhythmic transient or hit. The stretching should occur in the spaces in between these hits. Figure 7.39 shows a typical drum loop with markers at the prominent transients in the signal. These markers tell the software to keep their relationships intact as time stretching occurs.

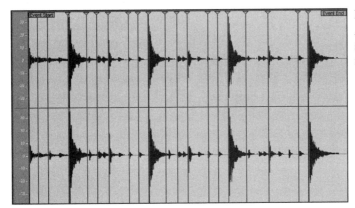

Figure 7.39
A typical drum loop in Nuendo's sample editor displaying hit points for use in time stretching.

This type of processing works great with rhythmic material that does not have much pitch content. With other sounds such as vocals, where pitch is terribly important, using hit markers will not bring about the best result. Most time stretching plug-ins have several algorithms to choose from in order to get the highest quality result for the material. Usually, these algorithms are a compromise between sound quality and rhythm. Figure 7.40 shows the Pro Tools Time Compression/Expansion plug-in with a slider that determines the emphasis on sound or rhythm.

Figure 7.40

Pro Tools Time Compression/Expansion plug-in with quality slider choosing sound or rhythm.

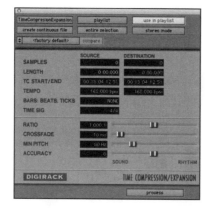

Calculating Ratios

As with pitch-shifting, time stretching is calculated with a ratio of the original length versus the new length. This can be expressed as two differing tempos: two lengths or a ratio by itself.

The most common use for time stretching in music production is matching of various samples and loops to different tempos. For example, if a song has a tempo of 120 bpm (beats per minute) and there is a drum loop that you want to include in the song but that drum loop is based on a tempo of 110 bpm, the loop will not play in time with the rest of the song. If you know the tempo of the drum loop, you simply divide the tempo of the drum loop (110 bpm) by the tempo of the song (120 bpm) and the result is the ratio of time stretching needed to make the loop play in time with the song. In this case, the ratio is 0.917:1.

Most time stretching plug-ins offer tools for easy calculation of these ratios. Figure 7.41 shows the Pro Tools Time Compression/Expansion plug-in using the same two tempos. Once the two tempos have been typed into the proper fields, a ratio is automatically created.

Figure 7.41

The Pro Tools Time Compression using two tempos to create a time-compression ratio.

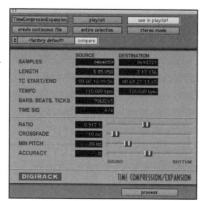

❋ ❋ ❋

The Pro Tools plug-in allows you to create time-stretching ratios using various timescales such as SMPTE frames, milliseconds, and bars and beats. You input two values for any of these timescales and Time Compression plug-in will calculate a ratio for time stretching.

As mentioned earlier, pitch-shifters and time stretching use small chunks of audio and vary their speed quickly in order to achieve the results. The crossfade parameter adjusts the size of the chunks in a way. If you are having difficulties getting good sound quality, try adjusting the crossfade up or down to get better results. It is dependent on the program material. Some combination of crossfade and accuracy settings will yield the best result.

Time Stretching and Tempo Mapping

Sometimes it is necessary to modify the tempo of a piece of music for musical reasons or to match the action onscreen in a film or video. If audio has already been recorded in a passage that needs to be altered, time stretching can be used to process audio to match the tempo changes. Often referred to as *tempo mapping time stretching,* or *warping,* this involves a connection between the timeline and tempo information in a DAW and a time stretching algorithm usually built in to the DAW, not a third-party plug-in.

Figure 7.42 shows a graphic representation of how this works in Nuendo. A drum loop has been time-warped to match the radical tempo changes seen in the lower tempo track window. Starting at 120 bpm, the drum loop is sped up to 173 bpm and then back down to 72 bpm using real-time time compression and expansion. The ratio is tied to the tempo track. You can see the lengths between beats visually change as the tempo changes.

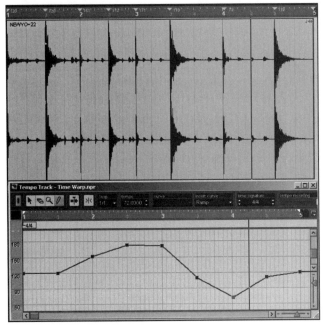

Figure 7.42

Nuendo's Time Warp feature demonstrated on a drum loop.

As a compositional tool, this type of feature is extremely helpful. For example, if you have completed a demo recording of a new song but want to try out a new tempo, it is not necessary to re-record all the audio tracks. For a quick reference, you can use a time-warping feature to change the tempo quickly to see if it is an improvement.

Another example involves scoring music to picture. Musical cues in film and television often align in time with visual actions on the screen. The tempo is very important in these situations. Being able to vary the tempo after recording can help you fine-tune the alignment of various musical moments with their counterparts onscreen.

The real-time processing is not as high quality as the offline processing due to CPU usage issues. Once you have arrived at a final tempo map, you can render the time-stretching settings to a file using higher quality processing algorithms.

Aligning Vocals

You can also use time stretching to align one audio file to another. A common use for this is aligning various takes of vocals to each other, both singing and dialogue. Tools such as VocAlign, shown in Figure 7.43, are capable of analyzing one audio file for timing and applying that timing analysis to another file. The rhythmic aspects of the reference audio are imposed upon another.

Figure 7.43

Synchro Arts VocAlign plug-in allows the timing of one audio file to be applied to another (www.synchroarts.com).

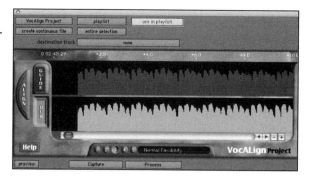

In music production, vocals are often doubled or even tripled to achieve a certain sound. Sometimes having each vocal in perfect time with one another is the desired sound. This can be very tricky to record naturally and demands a great deal of talent and control from the singer. Using a tool such as VocAlign, various discrepancies between takes can be ironed out, resulting in a very tight double track.

In audio post-production for film and video, there are many instances where the dialogue for a film is re-recorded in the studio. This can be due to environmental noise on the set, such as air handling noise, generators, or jet airplanes that render the production dialogue unusable. Sometimes, the voice quality of the actor or actress is just not ideal. Another person might re-record the lines with the desired tone and performance. This is called ADR or automated dialogue replacement.

When recording ADR, the talent will view their image on a screen or monitor and mimic themselves while recording in a controlled sound studio. The trouble is achieving "lip-sync" with the visual image. Some people are better at it than others. A tool such as VocAlign can make up the difference in performances that are not quite synched to the picture but have the emotional performance that is desired.

The engineer can analyze the original line from the production audio and apply that phrasing to the ADR recording. This works amazingly well, even with loosely synched ADR tracks.

Summary
The palette offered by time-domain processors is wide and varied. So many of today's production tricks are based in this type of processing. From simple delays and reverb to complex time stretching and re-tuning of vocals, time-domain processing is an incredibly valuable resource to any audio engineer.

8 } Convolution

One of the most interesting and potent developments in audio DSP is the use of impulse modeling convolution to recreate the reverb and ambience characteristics of real acoustic spaces. Traditionally, small room acoustics have been terribly difficult to recreate with digital algorithms. Devices such as the Quantec Room Simulator have offered expensive hardware solutions to this problem. Studios with great sounding recording rooms can simply play audio through speakers in the room and set up microphones to record the ambience of the chamber.

Obviously, recording sounds in a wonderful acoustic space such as a performance hall, recital chamber, or famous recording studio is ideal. But for those of us who do not have the expensive hardware boxes, access to large concert halls, or professionally designed recording rooms, convolution of impulse responses has become a wonderful substitute for these needs. Additionally, convolution can be used to imitate other things besides acoustic spaces.

Plug-ins such as Altiverb for Pro Tools and SIR for the VST world have made impulse convolution available to just about everyone. This availability has led to many users creating their own impulse files for these plug-ins. Libraries of impulse files are available online for anyone interested in using and sharing them. There are whole networks of users based around this type of processing. Suggested locations for this information is presented later in this chapter.

Convolution Basics

Convolution involves two stages. The first stage is capturing the impulse response of an acoustic space or other audio system. The second stage involves using that impulse file to process another audio signal. The result of the second process theoretically creates an audio signal that sounds as if it were heard in the space where the impulse file was generated. The convolution of the input signal with the impulse file generates the reverb signal.

This process can be applied to other situations besides room acoustics. Theoretically, any audio system can be analyzed using an impulse and the resulting impulse-response file can be used in a convolving plug-in to recreate the sound of audio passing through that system. For example, instead of an acoustic space, a guitar amplifier, a tape machine, speaker phone, or a classic digital reverb can be the subject of impulse modeling. In essence, any audio system, acoustic or electrical, can be the subject of impulse modeling.

This sounds almost too good to be true. You can simply impulse-model every piece of classic recording equipment, all the great acoustic spaces, each classic guitar amplifier, and whatever else you can think of and then have all of these sounds available at any time with just a plug-in.

In reality, it is too good to be true. Although impulse modeling is absolutely brilliant for modeling acoustic spaces and other static audio systems, it provides only one snapshot of how any audio system behaves. In other words, an impulse file is only one view of how an audio system reacts.

For example, a guitar amplifier reacts differently to sounds at lower input volumes than at higher input volumes. To accurately model an amplifier, you would have to take an impulse file at every possible input level to model every possible output sound. This is just for one set of control settings on the amplifier. You would have to create a new set of impulse files for every setting the amplifier was capable of. This is simply not practical. Even real acoustic spaces have a much more dynamic response to sound than one impulse file can capture.

Convolution and impulse modeling are capable of capturing one particular set of circumstance with uncanny realism. However, the realities of processing power and impulse creation limit convolution to capturing a static state of any audio system be it acoustic, electrical, or even imaginary.

The concept of impulse modeling states that any audio system, when stimulated by an impulse, will have a spectral and time-based response to that impulse that can be captured by simple recording. The convolving algorithms can then use the captured impulse response to process other audio signals to sound like they were run through the modeled audio system.

Impulses

An impulse is simply a very short spike of audio, a transient by itself. An ideal impulse contains information at all frequencies at an equal energy level. Thus, when exciting a room with an impulse, you have effectively sent every frequency into the space at an equal volume. What happens as this signal bounces off the surfaces within the room and eventually arrives at a listening position becomes the impulse response.

Digital Ideal Impulse

Figure 8.1 shows the waveform of an ideal impulse. It is one sample in duration and goes from nothing (–infinity) to maximum level (0dBFS) and back in that span of one sample. That is the quickest possible impulse that can be made digitally. Playing this signal back through a high-quality playback system into a room will excite the acoustics of that room evenly across all frequencies.

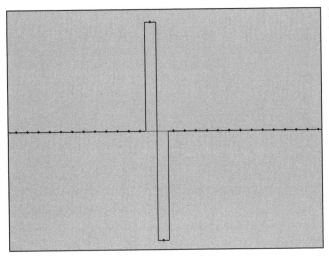

Figure 8.1
The waveform of an ideal impulse created digitally.

The problem with digital spike impulses is that they are so transient that limitations in the slew rate, or transient response, of most playback systems is incapable of reproducing this signal at the needed volume without distortion. The digital spike impulse is best used to generate impulse responses from other digital equipment such as hardware reverb units or even other plug-ins.

Starter Pistol Impulse

It can often be difficult to get enough volume from an ideal impulse such as the digital spike. A common technique is to use the sound of a starter pistol to excite the room's acoustics. The starter pistol generates a great deal of volume that can help create impulse responses with better signal-to-noise ratios.

❋ **STARTER PISTOLS**

A starter pistol is a gun that uses blank cartridges for ammunition, *not real bullets*! You have seen them used at track meets and the Olympics as methods of starting a race. Typically, a starter pistol will use ammunition that is the same size at a .22 caliber cartridge but without the projectile, called a blank. The barrel of a starter pistol is also sealed. Use hearing protection when working with starter pistols, as they generate up to 125dB SPL!

Firing a starter pistol from the source location (such as the stage in an auditorium) generates an impulse that will excite the acoustic space. However, the sound of a starter pistol is not even across the entire audio spectrum. It is weighted higher in the midrange, having less energy in the lowest and highest octaves. Impulses generated with starter pistols typically use some sort of post processing to compensate for the lack of extended response before being used for convolution. Audioease's

Altiverb has an impulse pre-processor that contains compensation EQ curves for the Flobert 6mm starter pistol and several other playback devices, as shown in Figure 8.2.

Figure 8.2

The Audioease IR Pre-processor compensates for uneven impulse spectrums such as a starter pistol's.

Swept Sine Wave Impulse

Another method for obtaining an impulse response is through the use of a swept sine wave tone. Starting at very low frequencies such as 5Hz, a sine wave is slowly increased in frequency all the way across the entire frequency spectrum, stopping up at 24kHz. The idea is to spread the energy of an impulse out over time by exciting every frequency one at a time with the sine wave. This method also provides a better signal-to-noise ratio in the resulting impulse response (IR).

Both Altiverb and Waves IR-1 can use this technique for obtaining IRs. It is a more time-consuming approach and can be affected by more environmental factors such as traffic and air-handling noise. Depending on the size of the room, Audioease recommends the use of longer swept files in spaces that have a longer reverb time to maximize the resolution for each frequency band.

IRs created with a swept sine wave technique must be processed before being used as IR files. Both Audioease and Waves have software that will perform this task and prepare the recordings for use in the convolver.

Recording Impulse-Response Files

One of the great things about the impulse modeling plug-ins is that anyone can create his/her own IR files from unique places that are familiar to them. For example, a church or concert hall in your area that always gives you a special feeling when you hear music there is a good candidate for IR modeling. If you can gain undisturbed access to the space for a few hours, you can capture the essence of the space in the form of a plug-in.

In order to record your own IRs, you need portable equipment:

* ✳ A multi-track recording system capable of recording at least two channels at a time. A DAW running on a laptop computer is the perfect tool for this, because it also allows you to play back the impulse from the same system, unless you are using a starter pistol.
* ✳ Two or four microphones that have a very flat response, preferably omni-directional or cardiod (heart-shaped) pickup patterns. With four microphones, you can create four-channel IRs that you can use in surround mixing. Also, each pair makes a separate stereo IR at the same time.
* ✳ Microphone preamps for each microphone that are as transparent as possible. The more accurate the recording, the more natural the resulting reverb is.
* ✳ A playback system for swept sine wave, impulse, or pink noise signals. There are many possibilities for a playback source, from large active studio monitors to consumer "boom boxes." Each system has its benefits and drawbacks. The larger systems have better overall frequency response but are hard to transport. Smaller playback systems have poorer frequency response but are easy to handle and can even be battery powered in remote locations such as a desert canyon.
* ✳ A Flobert or other brand of starter pistol with ammunition. Don't forget hearing protection!!!
* ✳ A space to record in. Hopefully, you can have access to the space for several hours to get as many recordings as possible. Remember that environmental noise outside of your control can ruin some recordings. Visit the space prior to recording to determine when the best time of the day or week is to record.
* ✳ Miscellaneous supplies for documenting the setup and marking positions for speakers and microphones, such as a tape measure, marking tape, notepad, and pencils. A digital camera is nice for capturing images of the space to share with other users and as reference for how the IR was created. Bring all the necessary audio cables, along with extras in case of failure. Don't forget the mic stands!

Recording Setup

First, determine where the sound sources are located in this space. In an auditorium, the sources are conventionally on the stage. In other locations, such as an outdoor plaza or living room, this might not be so obvious. Once you have determined both a left and right location, mark them with tape. Also mark a center location for mono sources in between the left and right locations.

In capturing IRs, it is necessary to record several versions of the impulse from each source location. Later, you can use various combinations of these files to create mono, stereo, and mono-to-stereo versions of the IR.

With a speaker placed in the center position and playing source material, walk around the space listening for sweet spots that capture the essence of the room. These spots can all be possible locations for microphones. The microphones should be placed symmetrically in relation to the sound sources positions. You can use a tape measure to make sure each pair of microphones are the same distance from the center sound source location to preserve the stereo image. Figure 8.3 shows a typical IR recording setup in an auditorium.

Figure 8.3

An IR recording setup in an auditorium. The microphones are symmetrical to the center sound source.

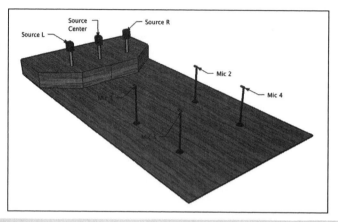

For each microphone setup, three recordings will be made of all four microphones; one for the center source location, another for the left location, and a third for the right location. These files are then used to create several actual IR files. Note that it is not necessary to have three speakers because only one location is recorded at a time. You can use a single speaker simply by moving it from one source location to another.

The examples here use four microphones. These four channels can be used to create a surround sound reverb using two stereo plug-ins, one for the front left and right and another for the surround left and right channels. The Waves IR-360 allows surround processing of impulse files in one plug-in, but it is still possible to do the same thing with multiple stereo plug-ins.

It is also possible to create multiple stereo IR files with just two microphones. Once you have recorded IRs in one position, move the microphones to another position and record new IRs. They can still function as the rear channels of a surround setup later on. In addition, the new pair can function as another stereo IR. Using two microphones in three positions yields three stereo IR files, plus three unique four-channel IR files.

Recording IR Files

In order to manage all the files generated during an IR session, you must understand how they will be used. Considering stereo reverbs only, there are four types of convolution for mono and stereo sources:

❄ Mono source to mono convolving output

❄ Mono source to stereo output

❄ Stereo source to stereo output using efficient processing

❄ Stereo source to stereo output using full resolution processing

The first convolving scenario (mono to mono) requires only one mono IR file and therefore one convolution process. Any one of the IR files can be used. Each one will sound somewhat different but will work just fine for mono convolution.

The mono to stereo type uses two convolution processes, one for the left output and one for the right output. The two IR files should be from a pair of mics that are equidistant from the center source and recorded with an impulse from the center source position. This will provide a true mono to stereo convolution.

You can process a stereo input signal in two ways. The first method is more processor efficient and still provides dramatic results. Using two convolutions, you can send input signals to each convolution process in variable amounts using a pan control. The two IR files can be from the center source position or one file can be from the left position and the other file can be from the right position as seen in Figure 8.4.

Remember that each sound source is captured in all microphones so that a true stereo input signal must have both channels fed to the left and right respective source locations. Because each source location has two IR files, one for left and one for right, a true stereo input to stereo output requires four convolutions; a left/right pair for the left source and a left/right pair for the right source. See Figure 8.4.

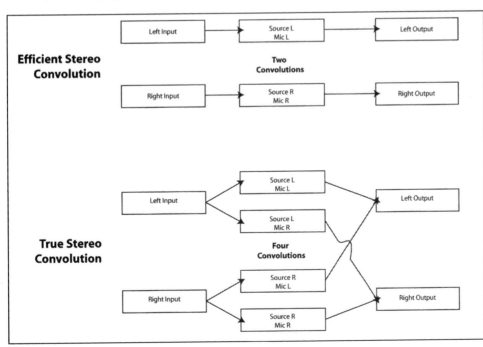

Figure 8.4
Signal path of a true stereo in to stereo out convolution process.

❄ ❄ ❄

As you can see, as the number of channels and sources increases, the amount of DSP explodes. A discrete 5.1 surround input to 5.1 surround output convolution requires 25 convolutions if you disregard the .1 LFE channel. This scenario is impractical in most situations. What is more common is the use of four channels of convolution for left, right, left surround, and right surround. This keeps the DSP load under control while providing a spacious, enveloped reverberant field.

File Management

Keeping track of each file and its intended purpose is very important when creating IRs. When working on location under time pressures, you can easily make mistakes if a system is not in place for naming of IR files. Audioease has some excellent tutorials on creating IRs, including a naming scheme that makes logical sense and is easy to implement. For a four-microphone configuration with left, center, and right source locations, the following list shows the name for each IR file:

First source location: Left:

1. Church_setupA_pos1_L-1.wav

    (Venue_speaker configuration_mic configuration_source location-mic number.file type)
2. Church_setupA_pos1_L-2.wav
3. Church_setupA_pos1_L-3.wav
4. Church_setupA_pos1_L-4.wav

Move the speaker to the center location.

Second source location: Center:

1. Church_setupA_pos1_C-1.wav
2. Church_setupA_pos1_C-2.wav
3. Church_setupA_pos1_C-3.wav
4. Church_setupA_pos1_C-4.wav

Move the speaker to the right location.

Third source location: Right:

1. Church_setupA_pos1_R-1.wav
2. Church_setupA_pos1_R-2.wav
3. Church_setupA_pos1_R-3.wav
4. Church_setupA_pos1_R-4.wav

Using the setup from Figure 8.3, there will be 12 IR files recorded. If you change the microphone positions, the file naming would change as well.

Church_setupA_pos2_L-1.wav

If you change the setup of the source speakers, the new files follow the change. Another speaker setup can simply involve placing the sources behind the listener for surround IRs. Usually, only two source locations are necessary for left surround and right surround. Center surround is used in some cinematic speaker setups, but might be overkill for IRs.

Church_setupB_pos1_L-1.wav

Using some sort of logical naming scheme helps you to make sense of all the files later in post-production. Also, take photographs and notes as you work to assist in keeping track of positions and also to document the process for others interested in the IR samples.

IR Resources and Community

Due to the unique nature of every acoustic space, creators of IRs sometimes share these files freely over the Internet in a community that supports one another in these endeavors. You can find loads of IR files and share your own files at these and other Web sites.

❋ www.noisevault.com—This Web site is a collection of IR files, primarily for the free VST plug-in SIR and Voxengo's Pristine Space. However, you can also use these files with other impulse modeling plug-ins after preprocessing them with the specific software, such as Altiverb's Preprocessor.

❋ http://www.voxengo.com/impulses/—Voxengo makes the Pristine Space convolution plug-in and the Impulse Modeler software that allows you to artificially create your own imaginary acoustic spaces and then calculate IR files from those designs. This Web site contains files made via Impulse Modeler.

❋ http://audioease.com/IR/index.html—Registered users of Audioease's Altiverb have access to a number of free IR files on its site. Altiverb is a very popular plug-in for Apple computers that has a long history in collecting quality IRs.

❋ http://www.echochamber.ch/—The Web site of a German studio that has a nice collection of IRs. The site is written in German, but it is possible to navigate without much trouble.

IRs of Recording Gear

It is much simpler to gather impulse responses from recording gear, such as digital reverbs, plate reverbs, equalizers, and other electronic processors. Even guitar amplifiers and stomp boxes are candidates for impulse modeling. Just about anything you can run audio through can be impulse modeled.

The point to remember is that the impulse is a description of only one state of that audio system. It can be a great tool for creating interesting sounds, but does not replace the item being modeled. For example, a digital reverb can be sampled to create an IRs file but only for the current settings of the unit. Every subtle adjustment of a reverb parameter would require re-sampling the IR file.

With this in mind, just about everything gets sampled for IR files these days, from guitar amps and speaker phones, to impulses traveling through structural guy wires and even swimming pools. The possibilities are endless.

Using the same techniques for room sampling, you can create IRs for other audio equipment or anything. All you need is some sort of impulse signal generator and a method for recording the result. A guitar effect pedal or "stomp box" can easily be sampled by running the same impulse tone, whether an actual impulse or swept sine wave, into the pedal and recording the output in the same fashion as sampling an acoustic space.

> ❈ **THAT ANALOG TAPE SOUND**
>
> It is also possible to sample the sound of recoding on analog tape. The process is the same except the tape machine must be in record and the output of the playback head must be recorded as the impulse file. In this fashion, you can obtain some of the attributes of analog tape recording though convolution. However, the effect that tape has on transients will not be the same because this effect is dynamic in nature, whereas the impulse response is static.

Understanding Convolution Plug-ins

What does a convolution plug-in do with all these IR files? Simply put, the plug-in multiplies each input sample by every sample in each IR file. The result should theoretically be the input sound as heard through the system that created the impulse file. The impulse file carries the signature of the room it was recorded in or the piece of gear that it was sampled from.

This requires quite a bit of processing power. For example, if a stereo impulse file of an auditorium is one second long at 44.1kHz, that makes 88,200 samples in each impulse file. Each input sample must be multiplied 176,400 times before the result is complete. That's a lot of math. The latency of a plug-in such as this would be absurdly long given today's computer technology.

Fortunately, DSP designers have found ways to improve the efficiency of this operation and process samples in chunks that allow results to be heard quickly in order to minimize the latency of convolution. Still, convolution plug-ins use a great deal of DSP.

SIR

The SIR plug-in, created by Christian Knufinke, is a free VST convolution plug-in. Despite its being free, SIR is a very capable plug-in that processes IRs made with simple impulse signals, such as the starter pistol. SIR also includes several parameters for modifying the response of the IR. Figure 8.5 shows the SIR interface with several parameters affecting the length of the resulting signals along with envelope control and a simple equalizer for contouring the output.

Figure 8.5
The SIR convolution plug-in is free and runs with any VST-capable host.

Loading Impulse Files

Before you can begin to use SIR, you must first load an impulse file. Use the Open File button on the upper-right side of the plug-in window to locate and load an impulse file. You can use mono or stereo WAV files. Once you load the file, the waveform display will show a graphic representation of the impulse response. As you make adjustments to the plug-in, this waveform display updates to reflect the changes.

 GUI TIP: SIR IMPULSE FILE MANAGEMENT

When you load an impulse file into SIR, any other files in the same directory will show up in a list in SIR, as seen in Figure 8.5. Simply clicking on another file name will load it into the plug-in. Related impulses can be stored in separate folders so that when one is loaded, all the related impulses can be accessed from this list.

Pre-Delay

The Pre-delay setting does the same thing most pre-delays do, determine the amount of time before the onset of reverb occurs. In this case, the convolution process will be delayed by this amount.

Attack

The Attack controls are made up of a percentage and time factors. These are used to contour the onset of the convoluted signal. Using a time greater than 0ms and a percentage less than 100% will create a sloped volume envelope at the start of the impulse, modifying how the convolution will occur at the beginning, as seen in Figure 8.6. This can be helpful for taming harsh early reflections in the impulse or for a smoother reverb effect.

Figure 8.6
SIR with an attack envelope.

Altering the attack of an impulse will dramatically change the sound because the early reflections are going to be more affected than the reverb tail. Early reflections define most of the acoustic space our hearing perceives in a room.

Envelope

The Envelope parameter is essentially a decay factor. The smaller the percentage, the quicker the impulse will decay. This is one way of shortening the reverb time. The pattern of early reflections will not be disturbed, as seen in Figure 8.7.

Figure 8.7
The SIR Envelope shown at 50%.

Length

The Length parameter determines how much of the impulse file is used for convolution. In many cases, the very end of the diffuse reverb tail is so low in level that it will not be perceived within the context of a whole mix. If this is the case, the length of the impulse can be shortened to conserve CPU resources and also clear up the noise floor of a mix. The long reverb tail might not be adding anything creatively to the mix but can easily cloud things by being present at low levels.

Use the Length control to trim off the insignificant portions of the impulse file, as shown in Figure 8.8. Your ears will determine whether the reverb sound is adversely affected by the change in length. You can also use some amount of Envelope to smooth the shorter reverb tail a bit.

Figure 8.8
SIR's Length control is used here to trim off low-level portions of a room impulse.

Extremely short settings of the Length control will create a gated reverb effect simply by prematurely cutting off the reverb tail. Make a gated reverb out of any sampled acoustic space using the Length control.

Stretch

The Stretch parameter applies a time-stretching algorithm to the impulse file. This is a realistic way to adjust the reverb time of an impulse file. The pattern of early reflections proportionately change along with the reverb tail to present a shorter or longer reverb that retains a realistic perspective.

If you like the character of a particular impulse file but desire a different reverb length, try using the Stretch parameter first. This will retain as much of the original character of the impulse files, just shorter or longer.

Stereo In/IR

These two sliders control the stereo width of the input signal (In) and the width of the processed impulse file (IR). The default setting for the input is 0%, making SIR a mono to stereo plug-in when using a stereo impulse file.

Setting the input to 100% stereo will process signals in proportion through each channel of the impulse file. In other words, a signal entering the right channel input of SIR will only be processed by the right channel of the impulse file. This could work just fine if you are using one stereo impulse to process a stereo input. However, a true stereo impulse processing requires four convolutions, a stereo pair for the left source and another stereo pair for the right source. If you are using one instance of SIR for the left pair of convolutions, the input should be set to 0% so that all left-side input signals will be processed by both IRs. You would need two instances of SIR, each running a stereo impulse, to generate a true stereo convolution reverb signal from a stereo source. Refer to Figure 8.4 for a visual representation of this concept.

Filter Section

The filter section of SIR adjusts the spectrum of the impulse file. It is similar to an equalizer on the reverb output, but this is processing the impulse file before audio is convolved. This is unlike the EQ on a reverb, which processes the wet signal. It provides a slightly different result. Figure 8.9 shows some possible filter settings.

Quite often, the low-frequency response of larger rooms can be a bit boomy. The lower frequencies of the impulse file can be rolled off using these filters. Figure 8.9 shows the lowest three octaves being gradually rolled off to avoid this boomy sound.

Figure 8.9
The filter section of SIR.

Reverse

Just to the right of the impulse waveform display is a Reverse button. This reverses the impulse file to create some very interesting effects. When a room impulse is reversed, a non-linear reverb decay is created. To control this and make creative use of the effect, use the Length control to shorten the reverb tail (which has now become the beginning) in order to align the onset of reverb. Using this control, you can generate and control some very interesting rhythmic effects.

✳ **DYNAMIC CPU CONSUMPTION**

One of the options found in SIR's setup allows for dynamic CPU consumption. This helps free up CPU resources when SIR is not processing audio. Because convolution is a very processor-intensive routine, this option can be very handy for native workstations.

Waves IR

The Waves IR series of plug-ins includes a full featured version (IR-1), a light version with fewer controls (IR-L), and a surround capable version (IR 360, only for TDM systems). Each plug-in has a full resolution version and an efficient version that uses fewer convolutions to achieve the stereo output. The full versions use four convolutions for a true stereo processor. The efficient versions use only two convolutions with cross-feeding of input signals to generate a stereo result.

The unique processing that Waves brings to convolution is in the analysis of the impulse file. The IR-1 differentiates between the "recorded direct signal," early reflections, and the diffuse reverb.

❋ RECORDED DIRECT SOUND

When creating impulse files, the first sound to hit the microphones is the original sound after having traveled through the air in the room. This is called the *recorded direct sound* ("Direct" in the IR-1), because it is not a reflection and therefore should not be considered part of the reverb. However, this sound is being colored by the air in the room and the microphones used to record the impulse. It will sound somewhat different than the actual unprocessed signal coming into the plug-in. For this reason, Waves deals with the recorded direct signal separately from the dry, unprocessed signal coming into the IR-1.

Reverb Component Control

The IR-1 can control the level and timing of the recorded direct signal, early reflections, and reverb tail independently. This gives you control over the basic components of a sampled acoustic space. Figure 8.10 shows the complete IR-1 interface with reverb component pre-delay, level, and mute controls in the lower-right area. Each component can have its own pre-delay to adjust the timing and level control for balancing the various aspects of the room sound. Also, each component has its own mute switch.

Figure 8.10

The Waves IR-1 convolution plug-in.

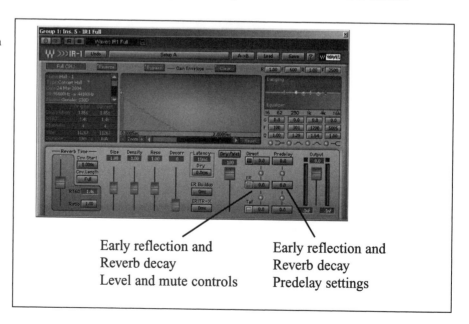

Early reflection and
Reverb decay
Level and mute controls

Early reflection and
Reverb decay
Predelay settings

Try listening to just one component of the impulse file at a time by using the mute switches. This will shed light on what each component really sounds like and how they react together to form the complete reverb sound. Make sure that you are only hearing the output of the plug-in and the balance control is set to 100% Wet. This will avoid confusion between the dry unprocessed signal and the recorded direct signal.

Wet/Dry Balance

The Dry/Wet balance controls the ratio of dry, unprocessed signal to convolved signal. The convolved signal might contain the recorded direct signal, depending on the plug-in settings. If you are using IR-1 as a send effect, the dry, unprocessed signal and the recorded direct signal can interfere with one another. It is advisable to have the unprocessed signal or the recorded direct signal in the mix, but not both.

Size

The Size parameter functions in the same manner as the Stretch function in SIR. Increasing this ratio lengthens the time between reflections, giving the impression of a larger space. Decreasing the size shortens the time between reflections and give the impression of a smaller space. For realistic reverb time changes, the Size parameter provides the most believable decay sound.

Density

The Density control in the IR-1 is a unique control among convolution plug-ins. This parameter is comparable to the diffusion parameter of a digital reverb. It determines how often reflections occur in the diffuse reverb tail.

In spaces with many varied surfaces and contours, there are many more small reflections that occur, creating higher diffusion. As surfaces become more uniform with fewer angles and contours, diffusion is lowered. The sound of lower diffusion can be described as *grainy* sounding. Higher diffusion sounds smoother and sometimes darker as each reflections obscures the next. Density has the same effect on impulse files, changing their character from grainy to smooth.

Resonance

The Resonance parameter adjusts the length of predominant resonances already present in the impulse file. Larger acoustic spaces have various frequencies that sustain longer than others in the reverb decay. These resonances are dependent on dimensions and the material makeup of the space. The resonance control can elongate or shorten these resonant tones in the reverb decay.

Adjusting the size can tune these resonances up or down in frequency. This is "tuning" the reverb in the literal sense. Extremely long resonance settings (above 3.00) yield some interesting results depending on the source material. Artificial sounding tones are ghosted out of the reverb decay. This can be very useful in sound-design applications where synthesis of unique sounds is necessary.

Decorrelation

Decorrelation affects the stereo width of the impulse convolution. If the left and right channels become more correlated, the reverb tends to sound "mono-ish." As the signals become decorrelated, the stereo image widens and becomes more spacious. You can use this control to take a mono impulse file and create a stereo output using a decorrelation setting of 100.

Convolution Start

The Convolution Start setting determines which sample of the impulse file is the first to be used for convolution. You can choose to eliminate the first portions of the impulse by up to one second in order to avoid processing unwanted early reflections and the recorded direct signal. A small white line appears in the waveform display, indicating the starting point of convolution, as seen in Figure 8.11.

In this case, the unwanted data at the beginning is eliminated along with the recorded direct signal and most of the early reflection period. The waveform display shades the various regions of the impulse file to represent how it has been analyzed by the IR-1.

Figure 8.11

The white line shows the convolution starting point within the impulse file. Once you set the starting point, the IR-1 will recalculate the waveform view. This impulse contains some erroneous data at the beginning that will be avoided by starting the convolution at the new point.

❄ GUI TIP: IR-1 WAVEFORM DISPLAY

The IR-1's waveform display has three shaded areas that represent the division of the dry recorded sound, the early reflection period, and the diffuse reverb decay as analyzed by the IR-1. When adjusting parameters that affect the different components, watch the different shaded areas to see the result. Try using the component mute buttons to see how the impulse file changes. Turning off the recorded dry sound (Direct) will result in a recalculation of the waveform where the darkest shaded area will be removed. Use the zoom controls at the bottom of the waveform display to inspect the early portion of the impulse file more closely. The darkest area represents the recorded direct signal. The medium shade level defines the early reflection period. The rest of the display is considered the diffuse reverb decay.

Convolution Length

The convolution length is the same as SIR's length control. It determines how long the convolution lasts. Usually, there are portions of the impulse file at the end that are not contributing much information to the overall signal and can be ignored. Reverb decays below the overall noise floor will not be heard as well in the mix and the processing power needed to convolve these samples is not necessary.

Bear in mind, however, that when working with much more dynamic and sensitive material such as classical recordings, the information contained in the end portions of impulse files could be very important to the sound, especially in quiet passages. For these purposes, using the complete impulse file is appropriate.

RT60 Ratio

The RT60 of any reverb is defined as the time it takes for the decay to go down 60dB from the initial level. This term reflects how our hearing perceives the reverb decay. Below –60dB, not much information is present to affect our perception. The RT60 is a convenient way to define the reverb time standard.

The IR-1 calculates the RT60 of any impulse loaded into it. Then, using the reverb time adjustment, the RT60 value can be changed. This will lengthen the impulse response so that the desired RT60 value is achieved. This is similar to the size parameter, but uses the RT60 value for calculation instead of a ratio of size. More drastic changes are possible with the RT60 control than with the size parameter.

ER Buildup

The ER Buildup control determines how the early reflections arrive at the listener. Increasing the ER Buildup time pushes the initial energy of the early reflections out over a larger span of time. It is not the same as delaying the early reflections. It is more like using an envelope on the early reflection pattern. Over the same period of time, the energy of early reflections will be more spread out instead of being concentrated at the beginning. This difference is best heard while listening to both the early reflections and reverb tail together. Longer ER Buildup times can give the impression that the listener is further from the source without lengthening the reverb or reflection times.

ER/TR-X

The IR-1 performs an analysis of the impulse file when it is first loaded. This analysis determines which portions of the impulse are early reflections or part of the reverb decay. The point at which the early reflections become the reverb decay is the *separation point* (shown as the ER/TR-X in IR-1). You can adjust this point with the ER/TR-X parameter.

The separation point can be adjusted +/–100ms. If you feel that the IR-1's analysis of the impulse did not isolate all of the early reflections and you would like to modify their behavior, lengthening the ER/TR-X value will include more of the impulse as part of the early reflection period. Figure 8.12 shows the IR-1's waveform display with the various reverb components labeled.

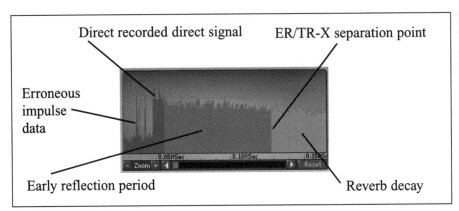

Figure 8.12
The IR-1 reverb components and key points labeled in the waveform display.

Damping

The IR-1 has true damping controls. Unlike EQ on the output of the reverb, damping controls affect the spectrum of reverberation dynamically over time. In most normal acoustic spaces, the high frequencies tend to decay quicker than low frequencies. This is mostly due to the fact that it does not take much to weaken the strength of high frequency reflections because they have relatively low acoustic energy. Many common construction materials have some amount of high-frequency absorption qualities.

The result of damping is that each progressive reflection has less and less high-frequency energy. It is a dynamic process that happens over time. An EQ on the output of a reverb statically affects the spectrum, turning the high end down by one set amount.

The IR-1 has two separate damping controls; one for highs and one for lows. Each damping control has a frequency and ratio control. The frequency determines the turnover frequency that damping begins, similar to a shelving filter. Figure 8.13 shows the damping filters adjusted to damp both lows at 0.75x and highs at 0.5x.

Figure 8.13

The IR-1 damping filters dynamically affect the spectrum of reverb over time. The low ratio is 0.75 starting at 200Hz and below, whereas the high ratio is 0.50 starting at 2.5kHz.

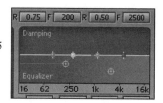

The ratio determines the RT60 value for the frequencies defined by the filter setting. If the highs are set for a ratio of 0.50 starting at 2.5kHz, frequencies above 5.2kHz will decay twice as fast as the rest of the spectrum. It is also possible to have ratios larger than 1:1. This will cause the frequencies to decay slower, lasting longer than the overall RT60.

Filters

The IR-1 does not stop with damping. There is also a four-band equalizer with two shelving bands and two parametric mid-bands. This equalizer only affects the wet processed signal.

Gain Envelope

A reverb's level has a natural linear decay over time; however, to get a more artificial or nonlinear reverb decay, you can use the gain envelope. Use the yellow line found in the waveform display to create the gain envelope and alter the decay pattern of the impulse.

Double-clicking on the line creates a new point, which you can then move around to create a gain change at that point in the impulse. When you edit a point, crosshairs pop up and display the time and gain settings for it. Figure 8.14 shows a very non-linear gain curve applied to an otherwise normal impulse.

Figure 8.14
A non-linear gain curve in IR-1.

The gain curve can be used to create non-linear reverb from normal impulses such as a gated reverb. It is also helpful when the convolution size has been shortened to the point where the impulse cutoff is audible. The gain curve can smooth out the tail of a shortened impulse.

> ❋ **GUI TIP: RECALCULATION TIME**
>
> Every time you adjust a parameter on the IR-1, the impulse is recalculated. When creating gain envelopes, it might be necessary to make many quick adjustments, adding points and moving them around to achieve the desired gain slope. Bypass the gain envelope temporarily while adding multiple points quickly to avoid multiple recalculations of the impulse file, saving a bit of time.

Loading Impulse Files

You can load impulse files from the Waves library that comes with IR-1 or you can load any other WAV file of an impulse. To do so, use the Load button at the top of IR-1. There, you will find two options for importing external files:

- ❋ Import Impulse Response from File
- ❋ Import Sweep Response from File

You can then import any file you choose to be the impulse file. Besides normal impulse files, try other files. Anything is possible. One sound convolved with another always leads to interesting, if not useful results—a sound designer's paradise.

Altiverb

Audioease created a loyal user base when it released Altiverb in 2002 for the Macintosh platform in TDM, RTAS, and MAS formats. Altiverb was one of the first native convolution plug-ins available. For most users, hearing the sound of an IR reverb was stunning compared to the normal assortment of digital plug-in reverbs. Plug-in reverbs had not yet lived up to the promise of sound rivaling the classic hardware boxes such as the Lexicon 480L, Quantec QRS, or Sony DRE-2000.

Plus, Altiverb made it possible for users to create their own IR files and thus created a community where IR samples could be shared and the techniques for creating them became well known. Even though Altiverb is only available on Apple computers, the user base is loyal and active in the creation of IRs and the sharing of this data. Visit the Altiverb forum for more information:

http://www.audioease.com/cgi-bin/forum/YaBB.cgi?catselect=Support_Help

The Altiverb interface is relatively simple. Figure 8.15 shows Altiverb with one of the standard impulse files that you can download from the Web site. The visual display of Altiverb is wonderful with a full spectral waterfall display of the reverb time and actual photos of the acoustic space that was sampled for the impulse.

Figure 8.15

Altiverb's GUI with photo of actual space that the impulse was recorded in.

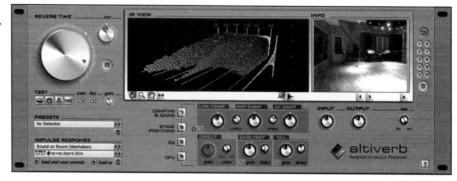

Reverb Time

The overall reverb time has the largest displayed control in the interface. When it is adjusted, the visual display will update to show the new waterfall image. Reverb time basically applies a volume curve to the impulse, turning up the end of the file to increase the reverb time and turning it down to shorten it. Audioease warns that lengthening the reverb time too much can emphasize the noise floor and any errors in the impulse file itself.

The Size control affects reverb time as well. However, this adjustment works more like SIR's stretch parameter, shifting room resonances and early reflections to more realistically achieve a smaller or larger space.

The R button reverses the impulse, creating reverse reverb.

Damping

Damping controls have more features than IR-1, with three bands of damping control. Each band is adjustable by setting the crossover points between bands. In order to access the damping controls, you must click the Damping and Gains button. Figure 8.15 shows the damping controls along with the levels of early reflection and reverb tail.

Component Levels

Altiverb has similar controls for the various components of the reverb signal. The recorded direct sound is controlled by the direct color and gain. Adjusting the color to "flat" will remove the recorded direct sound so as not to color the unprocessed signal. Setting the color to "IR" allows the recorded direct signal to be present, coloring any unprocessed signal that it is mixed with. Using the "IR" setting is more appropriate when the entire signal will pass through Altiverb and nowhere else.

The early reflection gain and delay alter the volume and time position of some of the early reflections as analyzed by the Altiverb preprocessor. The gain and delay controls for the reverb tail do the same thing for the diffuse reverb decay.

Stage Positions

Altiverb has a unique control that adjusts the distance and spacing of the sources (speakers) in the impulse. You can move the speakers farther back on the stage and space them farther apart, as seen in Figure 8.16, changing the character of the direct signal. When the stage position is active, the direct gain control is disabled because the stage position affects the timing and volume of the direct signal itself.

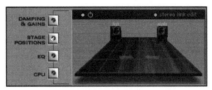

Figure 8.16

Altiverb's unique speaker stage position control.

EQ

This equalizer is placed after convolution and modifies the wet signal only. Some equalizers such as Voxengo's Pristine Space alter the impulse response itself, not just the wet signal after convolution. The equalizer includes two shelving and two parametric filters, as seen in Figure 8.17.

Figure 8.17

The equalizer in Altiverb affects only the wet signal.

Altiverb includes a basic input and output gain with a wet/dry balance control. The simplicity of the overall interface disguises the intricate and powerful DSP algorithms hiding inside. The graphic displays and inclusion of actual photos make the plug-in experience more interesting and enjoyable. Being able to actually see the room that Altiverb is simulating seems to make adjustments easier. You can see the space you are hearing. Of course, the sound quality is excellent due in no small part to the vast library of quality impulse files that have been created for Altiverb.

❋ **MIX TIP: TAKE PICTURES**

If possible, always document original IR recordings that you make with photographs. These resources can make it possible to share the techniques you used with others and also document the look of the physical space for later examination and understanding.

A digital camera is a very useful tool in the studio or on location. Documentation of microphones setups and positions can come in handy if at some point in time you need to recreate the situation for another recording. When using outboard equipment during a session, a photograph of the settings can be more useful than any written notation of those setting on paper. With DAW's, all audio media is stored digitally. You can save digital photos along with session data in archives to be used later.

Voxengo's Pristine Space

Voxengo has a very powerful eight-channel convolution plug-in. Pristine Space is designed as a "purist" convolver with very little synthesis of impulses components such as the IR-1. What is impressive about Pristine Space is the free routing ability of its internal structure and multi-channel ability. Using the internal matrix, a signal can be convolved by one impulse and then again by another. This serial convolution is possible with multiple instances of other convolution plug-ins, but with Pristine Space, it all can be done in one plug-in.

With independent convolution "slots," true stereo in to stereo out convolution is possible by loading mono or stereo impulses into each slot and routing inputs and outputs accordingly. Other convolution plug-ins require pre-processed files to create true stereo convolution. Pristine Space is more open in its design, allowing more control and flexibility. The amount of parameters involved in this can be daunting. Once you get the hang of it, Pristine Space affords some unique processing opportunities.

Impulse Slots

Pristine Space has eight impulse slots. Each slot is capable of loading a mono, stereo, or multi-channel impulse file that can be used for convolution.

* ❋ Using two stereo slots, four channels of convolution can create a true stereo to stereo reverb.
* ❋ With mono files, four slots, each with one mono impulse files, can do the same thing.
* ❋ One multi-channel file can create a mono input to surround output reverb.
* ❋ A true surround input to surround output requires five slots, each loaded with a five-channel impulse file or 25 channels of convolution.

Now that would be a lot of DSP! Unfortunately, Pristine Space only has eight convolving channels, but you can use multiple instances of the plug-in to create a monster of convolution processors.

In practice, most users will only need to create a true stereo to stereo convolution at the most. The stunning realism that a four-channel convolution can create is amazing. Plus, four-channel convolution keeps the reverb very de-correlated and diffuse. This results in a more natural sound. A mono to stereo two-channel convolution works if sources are only going to be panned in the center. This will save DSP resources that are not necessary.

> ❋ **WATCH THE INTERFACE CAREFULLY**
>
> Each slot is color-coded in order to help you differentiate which impulse file you are currently working with in the GUI. This interface can get confusing quickly, so pay attention as you edit various parameters to make sure you are working on the correct file or slot.

Loading impulse files works in much the same manner as with SIR. Once you've loaded a file from a directory, all other files in the directory become available in a menu shown in Figure 8.18. By first selecting the appropriate slot, you can use the File button to locate any impulse file in WAV format.

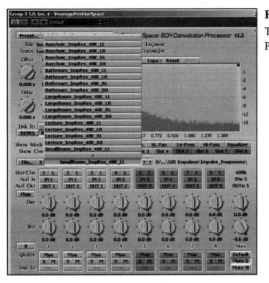

Figure 8.18

The file-loading menu of Pristine Space.

Convolution Channels

Once you've loaded the impulse files into Pristine Space, you must configure the convolution channels. Each convolution channel can process one channel of any impulse from any slot. In other words, if you have a stereo impulse in slot one, you must use two convolution channels to process both channels (L and R) of the impulse. If you had two four-channel impulses in slots one and two, you would need all eight convolution channels to completely process the impulse.

You determine which impulse the channel will process by selecting the appropriate slot and impulse channel from the top of each convolution channel. Figure 8.19 shows a convolution channel set to process the right side of the stereo impulse in slot 3.

Figure 8.19

The convolution channel setup in Pristine Space.

Audio Inputs

Each convolution channel has a choice of audio inputs for signals to process. You must first define how many inputs and outputs the plug-in will create to and from the host application. This is set in the "help area" found by pressing the small question mark at the top-right side of the GUI. Doing so replaces the upper portion of the screen with several options. Figure 8.20 shows the list of options, including Set Inputs and Set Outputs. Using these two options, you can set Pristine Space to have up to eight inputs and outputs. For surround work, typically four inputs and outputs suffices for creating enveloping reverb.

Figure 8.20

Options available in Pristine Space.

> ## ❋ GUI TIP: SLOTS VERSUS CONVOLUTION CHANNELS
>
> Voxengo's terms can lead to some confusion. A slot can contain an impulse file that has more than one channel (a stereo file has two channels). A convolution channel can process only one of the slot channels. So, for a slot containing a stereo impulse file, you need to use two convolution channels in Pristine Space to processes the impulse. The first convolution channel needs to be set to Slot X, channel L and the second convolution channel should be set to Slot X, channel R. Figure 8.21 shows how this looks in the GUI.

Figure 8.21

Convolution channels in Pristine Space set to process the left and right channels of an impulse file loaded in slot 1.

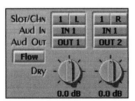

One unique feature of the audio input selection in the convolution channels is the ability to select the output of another convolution channel as the source. This allows for serial convolution where the audio is processed by one impulse (a guitar amplifier perhaps) and then by a second impulse file (such as a room ambience file). In this fashion, a complex convolution process can be created in one flexible plug-in.

Figure 8.22 shows the input list of one channel in Pristine Space with the option to use one of five plug-in inputs and also the output of four convolution processors. The only limitation to this is that only convolution channels with lower numbers are available as inputs. Also, host applications cannot compensate for the additional plug-in delays caused by serial convolution. Each convolution process takes a certain amount of time. To serially process another impulse takes the same amount of time again, doubling the total latency of the process.

Figure 8.22

The input choices for a convolution channel in Pristine Space.

Audio Outputs

You can route each convolution channel to any of the available output channels defined for the plug-in. The output channels are limited also by the channel configuration of the host mixer in which the plug-in is inserted. For example, if you have a stereo Group Channel in Nuendo, Pristine Space should have two inputs and two outputs defined, because that is all that will be available from the host application.

Impulse Timing

Each impulse slot has several timing controls similar to SIR and IR-1 found to the left of the wave-form display. The Offset controls the impulse start time, thus allowing you to trim unwanted portions of the impulse such as the recorded direct sound or a portion of the early reflections.

The Length controls how much of the total impulse file is convolved. If there is low-level impulse data that is not adding to the sound, trimming the length will eliminate this. Also, the classic gated reverb can be created by using a much shorter length, cutting of the impulse prematurely.

The Delay is differentiated from the Offset control in that it delays the start of convolution not the start of the impulse file. This is identical to a pre-delay in a conventional reverb algorithm.

Envelopes

Each impulse file has six non-destructive editing controls that affect the convolution.

* Volume
* Stereo Width
* Stereo Pan
* Low-Pass Filter
* High-Pass Filter
* Equalizer

In order to work with each envelope, it first must be activated by pressing the Env Enable button for the appropriate parameter. Next, the waveform display has the envelope line imposed over the impulse display for easier editing. The buttons at the top-left side of the waveform display change the envelope line between volume (V), stereo spread (S), stereo pan (P), low-pass (L), high-pass (H), and equalizer (E). In order to edit a particular envelope, you must press the appropriate button. Each envelope displays a different scale on the right side of the waveform display, as seen in Figure 8.23.

Additionally, the envelope itself must be enabled for that slot. The enable buttons are found below the waveform display, just above the slot selectors. The envelope settings have no effect if it is not enabled.

Figure 8.23

The high-pass envelope display shows the frequency scale at the right, with various points altering the impulse response over time.

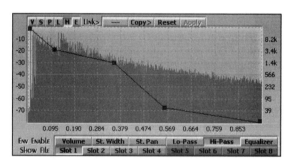

The volume envelope works in the same fashion as the Waves IR-1, with an envelope display of volume over time. You can add control points by double-clicking on the line and moving the point to the desired position. You can also use the volume envelope to smooth out the tail of reverb or create non-linear decays.

What is unique to Pristine Space is that the envelope concept is applied to many other parameters. For instance, you can adjust the high-pass to change over time, as seen in Figure 8.23. As the reverb begins, lows are removed. Over time, the reverb will bring the lows back in as the envelope curve suggests. This creates a unique effect.

The equalizer is a static filter that is applied to the impulse, altering the spectrum of convolution output. This is almost equal to placing an equalizer on the output of the reverb. However, the equalization is applied to the impulse file, not the audio coming out of the convolution process. It is a similar result but there are subtle differences. Try it out and listen to what your ears tell you.

The possibilities this offers are many. The combination of serial convolution along with time-based envelope processing make Pristine Space an in-depth plug-in with many unique sounds awaiting discovery. Sound designers will find this plug-in very useful for creating new imaginary sonic textures that are still tied to reality through complex convolving of natural sounds.

Mastering Convolution Techniques

The most obvious use of convolution is for room ambience and reverb. However, you can create impulses from just about anything. Even using normal audio files as impulses can yield amazing results. The possibilities of convolution are still being explored. Maybe convolving your voice with the sound of a bulldozer will raise the hairs on the back of your neck. There are no rules.

Reverb

This whole chapter used examples of reverb, because this is what impulse modeling was first developed for. The uncanny ability of impulse modeling to capture the essence of an acoustic space is amazing. The ear hears a sense of reality in the sound of ambience and space using convolution reverb.

Convolution is especially good at replicating small spaces and intimate ambience with great realism. This has classically been the problem with many digital reverbs. Long sustained reverb seems to be no problem for a quality digital reverb. However, when the RT60 gets down to around a second or less, most digital reverbs begin to sound unnatural. If you desire natural ambience under one second, you must consider convolution.

When using true four-channel stereo convolution, longer reverbs can also benefit from impulse modeling. The interaction of four convolution processors yields a richer, more colorful decay. Of course, this all depends on the quality of the impulse recording itself.

The capability to create your own reverb processing by sampling various acoustic spaces is probably the most attractive aspect of convolution. Preparing a portable impulse recording setup can prove to be a wise investment if you are looking to create ambience that has an original character to it. No two acoustic spaces sound the same.

ADR Dialogue Ambience Matching

One of the most difficult jobs in audio for film and video post-production is dialogue replacement. Often, filming sets are filled with equipment and environmental noise that render production audio unusable. When this occurs, dialogue is re-recorded in the studio using ADR techniques. Once recorded, it is the dialogue mixer's job to make it sound as if the original and re-recorded dialogue emanate from the same acoustic space.

Dialogue recorded in the studio will most likely have little to no ambience on it by design. Creating a digital reverb to realistically match various onscreen spaces can be time consuming at best and often unsatisfying. Impulse modeling of the actual location of filming with microphones that were used on the shoot can make this task more of a pleasure than pain.

Hopefully, the production sound mixer has the time and ability to record quality impulse files during filming while the crew is on break or at some other opportunity. Often, the case is that filming schedules are too grueling to take time out after every shot to grab another audio impulse while 20-50 cast and crewmembers are sitting around getting paid. A quick little trick can be used to create impulses for this without the need for on-location impulse recording.

Figure 8.24 shows the film slate device, or *clacker,* as it is affectionately known. This device has been used to synchronize film with the audio that was recorded along with it. Audio is not recorded directly to the film during production. It must be captured by a separate recorder and then married back to the visual image later during transfer.

Figure 8.24

The film slate or "clacker" used to synchronize film and sound.

Before modern synchronization techniques were available using SMPTE timecode, the simple clacker system was used. Before each take, the slate was held up in front of the camera with the identification of which scene was being currently filmed and then the arms were slapped together creating a loud "clack" sound that would be seen on film and heard in the recording. The two could then be lined up later to achieve synchronization.

The practice of using the clacker continues today as a backup system because modern timecode use can be quicker and easier to use. The interesting thing is that the clacker's sound is very similar to an acoustic impulse. By using the sound of the clacker as an impulse file, a convolution plug-in can create ambience that closely mimics the sound of the actual room.

In a sense, an impulse file is created before every take of every scene in a whole movie. Granted, many of these recordings have contaminating noise from various elements on the set and might also contain distortion from overloading of mic preamps set to levels appropriate for soft dialogue. Certainly out of many takes, several "clacks" can be found that will work just fine as impulse files. Advise production sound mixers, if they are not already aware of this, to make sure that "clacks" are recorded in a high-quality fashion for just this purpose.

Gear Modeling

Another use for convolution is the modeling of audio devices other than digital reverbs. Any device that can pass audio can be sampled for convolution. Typical sources for this type of modeling include guitar amplifiers, speaker phones, and even analog tape recorders. Tube microphone amplifiers often have a desirable sonic characteristic that can be sampled as well.

What does not work well using convolution techniques are processors that have a dynamic response to signals, such as compressors. The impulse only captures a static instance of how an audio system responds. If the whole point of the audio system is to change that response as the level changes (compressors and gates) or as time passes (flangers and chorusing), the convolution technique does not work.

Sampling a flanger for instance, only yields a static comb filter and not a sweeping filter that moves over time. Sampling a compressor only yields one amount of gain reduction that would have the same effect no matter what the input level was. This might be interesting, but it would not mimic the response of the compressor. It would be something new entirely.

Crazy Stuff

Because convolution plug-ins do not care what the impulse file being convolved is, it is possible to convolve audio through files that are not impulses at all. In fact, the impulse file might not even be a true audio recording, but an imaginary construct made in software.

Impulse Creation: Voxengo's Impulse Modeler

Voxengo has a piece of software that allows you to actually build an acoustic space virtually for the sole purpose of creating an impulse. In the comfort of your chair, you can build and sample acoustic spaces of any size and composition without leaving the studio. Figure 8.25 shows a model that was created in Impulse Modeler.

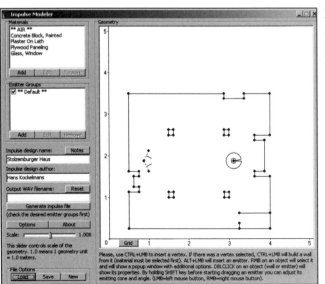

Figure 8.25

An acoustic space modeled by Hans Kockelmans in Voxengo's Impulse Modeler.

After defining various materials in terms of their sonic characteristics, a floor plan is created using those materials. Various sound sources and "receptors" (virtual microphones) are placed within the space. All of this is taken into account when the impulse files are created mathematically. The saved WAV files can then be loaded into a convolution plug-in to see what they sound like.

Impulse Substitution

If you are looking for something out of the ordinary, try using audio files other than true impulses as convolution sources. This can lead to very interesting results or utterly useless sounds. It all depends on the impulse and the source material. Do not be afraid to try anything.

When creating an impulse that is not necessarily for room ambience, there are no rules. Try using a small portable recorder and a homemade "clacker" to gather impulses just about anywhere. High-quality microphones and recording devices with expensive and bulky playback systems do not always mean interesting results. Sometimes a simple handheld recorder and an odd sound in a remote place is the most interesting impulse you can find. The possibilities are endlessly fascinating. Experiment to see what works for you.

Summary

Convolution is one of the most exciting developments in DSP, offering new and unlimited ways of processing audio in unique ways. Plus, it empowers individual users in creating their own processes by recording impulses of anything they can think of. When you find that incredible drum room but it happens to be the local hardware store, you can now go in and sample the room and take it with you without bothering anyone or transporting an entire recording setup to use the space repeatedly. Convolution lets you take it with you.

9 Pitch Correction and Adjustment

Using time-stretching and pitch-shifting DSP, it is possible to change the pitch of vocals and instruments without drastically affecting the sound quality and naturalness of the recording in most cases. This development has affected modern music production in both positive and negative ways.

On the plus side, you can now salvage wonderful performances that have several pitch flaws with the judicious use of pitch correction plug-ins. Instead of punching in and re-recording sections that have bad pitch or tuning, you can maintain the integrity of the performance by correcting for small pitch variations. This can improve the speed and efficiency of production schedules, especially with live recordings.

You can also use pitch correction plug-ins to generate new melodic variations of recorded material. If you want to create a harmony track for a lead vocal, you can use a tuning plug-in to change a copy of the lead vocal to create harmonies. In some cases, this might sound just fine. In others, you can use it as a composition tool to try out things before actually recording them.

Antares Auto-Tune was made famous by the song "Believe" recorded by Cher. In that production, Auto-Tune was used in automatic mode with severe settings to create a unique vocal effect using strict pitch correction. Her voice was transformed into an artificial-sounding tone. From that point on, anything was fair game for tuning.

Abuse of pitch correction has run rampant through the music production community. It has made it possible to use recordings of mediocre performances to create master recordings for the radio and retail sale. In many ways, pitch correction has done for singers what the drum machine did for drummers; just about replaced them. It seems there is no excuse these days for anything to be remotely out of tune. Production tastes change in cycles and this too shall pass.

Regardless of the negatives, there are many uses for pitch correction that can enhance productions and preserve performance qualities. There are now many choices for tools used to correct pitch.

245
❅ ❅ ❅

Using Antares Auto-Tune to Correct Pitch

Antares Auto-Tune is considered the original pitch-correction plug-in. Designed for Pro Tools and released in 1997, Auto-Tune became an instant success. Producers and engineers spent so much time in the studio trying to perfect vocal tuning that, when this tool became available, they snapped it up. It offered a quick and dependable tool for pitch correction of any solo voice or instrument.

Auto-Tune has two modes of operation. The first is an automatic mode that detects pitch and corrects based on a user-defined fixed musical scale. The second mode is manual. In this mode, you can view the detected pitch envelope and move, reshape, or redraw the pitch envelope for complete control.

Automatic Operation

In automatic mode, shown in Figure 9.1, Auto-Tune can detect the pitch of incoming notes, reference them against a predetermined musical scale, and adjust each note to match those in the scale. Additionally, various "target" notes can have special settings just for those notes.

You can use an external MIDI keyboard to determine the musical notes and scales—done in real-time or as a custom scale preset. The real-time operation allows you to play the melody of the processed signal with a MIDI keyboard. The scale can be the same for all octaves or different in each octave. There are also various ethnic tunings and microtonal scales that you can use.

Figure 9.1

Auto-Tune 4 in automatic mode.

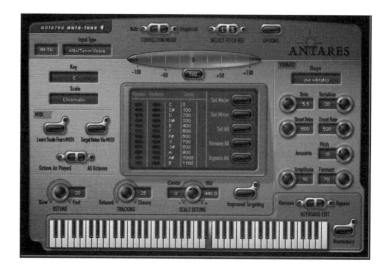

Key and Scale

The most important settings in automatic mode are the key base and scale type. The key determines the first note of the selected scale. Keys change in music and so the key might have to change in Auto-Tune in order to correctly adjust the pitch in various sections of a song or musical piece. For this, you can use automation of the key parameter to change keys at various points during the song.

Once you determine and set a key, the next step is figuring out what scale to use. A musical scale is the series of notes that connect one octave to another. In western music, there are 12 basic divisions between each octave. This is known as the 12 semi-tone chromatic scale. The 12 divisions, called half-steps or semi-tones, are most often divided into groups of seven that make up one musical scale. The major and minor scales are seven notes per octave, with the eighth note (hence the term *octave*) representing the starting point of the same scale, one octave higher. Each scale uses a combination of pitches from the 12-tone western octave divisions. Each octave division has a letter name for it.

❋ C

❋ C# or Db (pronounced C sharp or D flat)

❋ D

❋ D# or Eb

❋ E

❋ F (E# does not exist)

❋ F# or Gb

❋ G

❋ G# or Ab

❋ A

❋ A# or Bb

❋ B

❋ C upper octave (B# does not exist)

In Auto-Tune, when all 12 divisions are part of the tuning scale, it is called *chromatic*. For most western music, every note in every melody will fall on or around one of these 12 tones. If only small pitch variations are encountered in the performance, use of the chromatic scale can work just fine.

The two main musical scales are major and minor. They are derivatives of each other but have different tonal centers. For example, a C major scale contains the same notes as an A minor scale. The difference is the tonal center for the same group of pitches, A or C. Just about every other scale in Western music is based on the major or minor scale.

There are many more options for scales in Auto-Tune, including *microtonal* scales that use more than 12 divisions in the octave, as seen in Figure 9.2. These are useful if you are doing experimental and certain ethnic music, but can also prove interesting if you are looking for a new effect or want to create sound design elements.

Figure 9.2

The list of scales in Auto-Tune.

You must have the key and scale set properly in automatic mode for Auto-Tune to function correctly. The writers of the music can give you this information, or you can get it from using a simple piano or guitar set the key and scale first.

Custom Scales

It is also possible to create your own custom scale to use in Auto-Tune. The center display shows all 12 notes in the octave and their status as far as pitch correction goes. The keyboard displays the same information over all relevant octaves. To start, choose Chromatic from the Scale menu. This will display all 12 tones of the octave.

There are two columns in the center display; Bypass and Remove. *Bypassing* a note instructs Auto-Tune to ignore pitches that are close to the bypassed note. In other words, any pitch that is relatively close to a bypassed note will not be processed by Auto-Tune. This is useful when a performance has subtle "pitch gestures" around that note. Many blues scales and riffs use pitches that do not fall exactly on one of the 12 tones. Bypassing these notes will leave them untouched, preserving the "blue notes" of the performance.

Removing a note (the second column) instructs Auto-Tune to adjust pitches to notes around the removed note. In other words, if C# is removed and a pitch comes into Auto-Tune around C#, it is altered to be C or D, the next closest notes in the chromatic scale. This allows you to force a melody to fit within a particular set of notes regardless of the original performance.

Figure 9.3 shows Auto-Tune set to process melodies with a blues scale in the key of C. There are several ways to do this depending on the type of blues being performed. This is but one example. The notes F and F# have been bypassed, allowing blue note pitch gestures to occur there without Auto-Tune's influence. Several other notes have been removed so that pitches are forced to fall into the remaining notes.

Notice that the keyboard displays the same state as the center display but over all the octaves. It is possible to define different note combinations in each octave using the keyboard display. In an upper octave, there might only be certain notes that you need to tune and you can bypass the rest. There might be one note in particular that has tuning issues, perhaps the highest note in the vocalist's range. In this case, you can bypass all the other notes so that only the note in question is processed by Auto-Tune.

Clicking on individual notes in the keyboard display will change the status to either be bypassed or removed, depending on the keyboard edit mode, as shown in Figure 9.3.

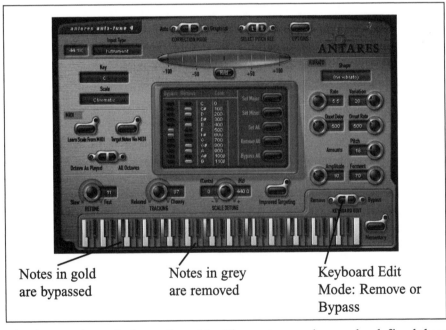

Figure 9.3

Auto-Tune set to process a blues scale in the key of C, avoiding some "blue notes" where pitch gestures might fall in between tones.

Notes in gold are bypassed

Notes in grey are removed

Keyboard Edit Mode: Remove or Bypass

The Automatic mode is configurable. The custom scales can be defined through the use of an external MIDI keyboard. Auto-Tune can accept MIDI information relayed by the host application to define notes in the scale. It is also possible to "play" Auto-Tune live or with a recorded MIDI track to program each target note as part of the performance in real-time.

This "playing" of Auto-Tune can get almost absurd for real vocal pitch correction, but it provides a unique tool for sound design and some bizarre effects.

> ### ❈ MIX TIP: AUTO-TUNE DRONE
>
> Using the custom scale options, you can create a very select amount of notes in one octave (perhaps a chord) and process vocals or solo instruments with this very limited note choice. Antares suggests that this "drone tone" can be sent to a reverb processor to create a ghosting drone sound as a backdrop for the music. Using strict settings in creative ways can be the basis for many interesting musical effects.

Input Type

Most pitch-correction plug-ins use several algorithms to detect the pitch of incoming signals. These algorithms are sensitive to the harmonic content of the sound itself. Different sources require optimized algorithms for dependable pitch detection. Auto-Tune is no exception.

At the top-left side of the plug-in's GUI, there is the Input Type. There are several choices.

* ❈ *Soprano Voice*—This type is primarily for female vocals or male voices with very high ranges.

* ❈ *Alto/Tenor Voice*—This type works well with most male voices and lower female voices.

* ❈ *Low Male Voice*—Need I say more?

* ❈ *Instrument*—This algorithm should be used for non-vocal sources such as solo flute. Voices present particular detection issues that most other instruments do not.

* ❈ *Bass Instrument*—With very low frequency instruments, such as bass guitar, the detection algorithm avoids certain frequency ranges. The lower range of pitch is extended by an octave to include the very lowest notes that we can hear. Use this type only when working with very low instruments. Otherwise, odd detection of pitch occurs in mid-ranges.

Retune Speed

After you have defined all the scale notes, the Retune control needs to be set according to the program material. The Retune speed determines how fast pitch correction is applied to incoming audio. The parameter is measured in milliseconds and ranges from 0 to 400ms. The fastest setting (0ms) produces the infamous "Cher" effect heard on "Believe." The effect is the sound of notes instantly changing pitch without any natural slide that is inherent in the human voice. This quick changing pitch sounds somewhat robotic and mechanical in nature.

Depending on the melody and tempo of the music, the Retune speed needs to be adjusted to provide the most natural-sounding correction possible. Too slow will make things sound lazy and not precise. Too fast and the "Cher" effect kicks in. Once again, your ears are your guide.

Tracking

The tracking control in Auto-Tune determines how the plug-in decides when a sound becomes an identifiable pitch. Auto-Tune can be "choosey" or "relaxed." Relaxed tracking provides a more severe processing, whereas choosey tracking affects less of the melody. This control can be used if Auto-Tune starts to affect elements in the sound that might not be part of the melody, including raspy breaths and sounds. If Auto-Tune is having a tough time recognizing notes and adjusting them, set this to more "relaxed" and see if that helps. Notes that might not have triggered detection in a choosier setting will be recognized as a note more often with a relaxed setting.

Vibrato

After you have "Auto-Tuned" your note, you can remove some of the natural vibrato, because it involves some pitch variation over time. Auto-Tune has controls to replace some amount of vibrato if it is desired. The waveform and speed are definable along with an amount of randomness to humanize the sound. There are various delay amounts to control how the onset of vibrato is managed. The Auto-Tune manual has comprehensive instructions on these controls.

Manual Operation

In graphical mode, you can see the individual pitch envelopes displayed in an editor and alter each one until it sounds right to your ears. This method is much more precise and offers a way to minimize the sound of pitch correction. It is possible to retain more of the original pitch envelope while tuning the melody. Graphical mode requires editing of individual notes and as such, takes more time. The results are more natural and offer more control over the process. In order to enter graphical mode, select Graphical from the Correction Mode option, as shown in Figure 9.4.

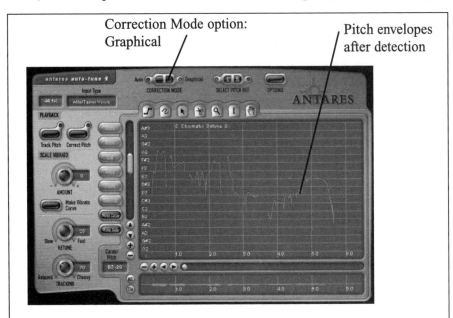

Correction Mode option: Graphical

Pitch envelopes after detection

Figure 9.4
Auto-Tune's graphical mode displaying the pitch envelopes of analyzed notes.

In order for graphical mode to function, the melody must first be analyzed. The Track Pitch button is used for this. When Track Pitch is active, audio going through Auto-Tune is analyzed and you can view a display of the resulting pitch envelopes in the central editor area, as seen in Figure 9.4. Pitch envelopes are a display of the pitch variation over time. The pitch is displayed vertically and time moves horizontally.

Creating Pitch Envelopes

After you have analyzed the melody, there are several options to begin editing. The display shows the detected pitch for incoming audio. So far, no pitch correction has occurred. There are two choices to create pitch correction curves for the analyzed audio.

* *Make Curve*—This option generates a pitch-correction curve that exactly matches the analyzed curve. In other words, no pitch change occurs with this but it does allow you to edit those curves by hand.

* *Make Auto*—This option creates pitch-correction curves based on the settings of key and scale in the Automatic mode window. This will show what Auto-Tune would have done using Automatic mode. Once again, you can now edit these curves by hand.

It is also possible to draw in pitch envelopes by hand using the Line tool or the Curve tool. Figure 9.5 shows what is possible with each tool.

Figure 9.5

Pitch Envelopes drawn by hand with the Line tool on the left and the Curve tool on the right.

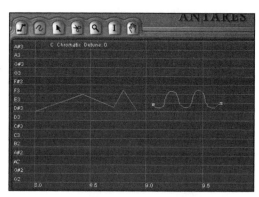

Editing Pitch Envelopes

After you have created your pitch envelopes, you can edit them to provide precise control of pitch correction. There are two major tools used for this.

* *The Arrow tool*—This tool moves pitch envelopes or their endpoints around.

* *The Scissors tool*—This tool can separate one pitch envelope into two, providing more precision.

Using the Arrow tool, you can move a pitch envelope to alter the overall pitch center without disturbing the shape, as seen in Figure 9.6. Control+clicking on the envelope will constrain the movement to the horizontal or vertical axis.

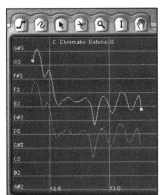

Figure 9.6
Moving a pitch envelope by Control+clicking on it with the Arrow tool constrains the movement to the vertical axis.

By clicking on an endpoint of the envelope, you can raise or lower the beginning or end of a note, as seen in Figure 9.7. This can be very useful when the singer has fallen flat at the end of a sustained note.

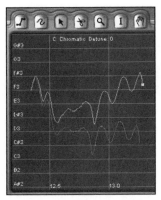

Figure 9.7
The endpoint of the pitch envelope has been raised to lift the pitch at the end of a note.

By using these tools, you can manipulate the original pitch envelope to correct various pitch errors, thus retaining as much of the original performance and sound as possible. If you are trying to create natural sounding pitch correction, you do want to maintain as much of the original pitch envelope as possible.

It might become necessary to actually draw in a new pitch envelope if editing does not provide satisfactory results. Also, using the "Make Auto" function creates pitch envelopes that have already been adjusted according to the settings in automatic mode. This can provide a starting point for further editing.

Graphical editing is much more of a time-consuming process, but can provide a better result that is tailored to the performance instead of a "band-aid" type of approach you sometimes get using automatic mode. It depends on how much time you have and what the desired results are.

Using Waves Tune to Correct Pitch

Waves has now contributed their knowledge of DSP in the pitch-correction department with the release of Tune, a fully integrated pitch-correction plug-in for TDM, RTAS, and VST. Tune has many of the same parameters as Auto-Tune but functions only in a graphical mode. However, the graphical mode has many automatic functions that let it perform in a similar fashion to Auto-Tune's automatic mode.

One main difference in operation between Tune and Auto-Tune is that Tune needs to analyze incoming audio prior to correcting any pitch errors. Conveniently, there is no need to analyze a complete track before correcting pitch, so it can work on individual sections immediately.

Melodic Analysis

When Tune is first inserted on an audio track, the interface shows up empty because no audio has been analyzed yet. As soon as the DAW enters play, Tune is synchronized to the DAW timeline using a Rewire connection to the plug-in. Once audio is sensed, Tune begins to analyze the pitches within the recording, as seen in Figure 9.8. Tune can analyze up to 10 minutes of audio data at a time.

Figure 9.8

Waves Tune analyzing incoming audio.

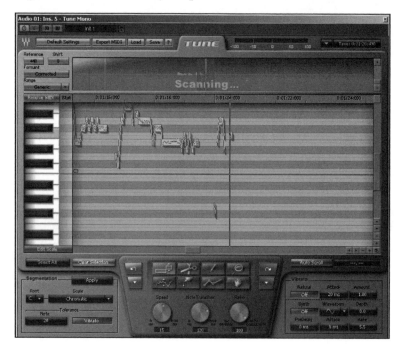

Note Separation

Tune divides the pitch envelope into notes. How this occurs depends on several settings found in the Segmentation area of the GUI.

* *Root*—The root note of the scale being used to define the notes.

* *Scale*—Tune provides many scale types, including altered Eastern scales with microtonal variations.

❊ *Note Tolerance*—The amount of pitch variation that Tune will allow and still define as one note. Try selecting several closely tied notes and adjusting this setting to see how it affects the note separations. Figure 9.9 shows a group of notes first with a Note Tolerance of 0 and second with a Note Tolerance of 70.

❊ *Vibrato Segmentation button*—When a singer adds vibrato to a note, it can be incorrectly analyzed as several notes going back and forth, as seen in the first example in Figure 9.9. For selected notes, Tune will analyze for vibrato and create a special note separation highlighted in red as a vibrato note, as seen in the second example in Figure 9.10.

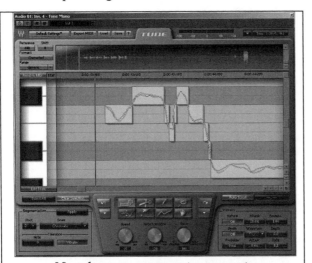

No tolerance, many note segments

Figure 9.9

One pitch envelope in Tune with a Tolerance of 0 and next with a Tolerance of 70.

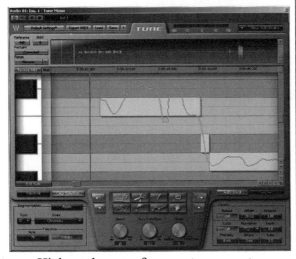

Higher tolerance, fewer note segments

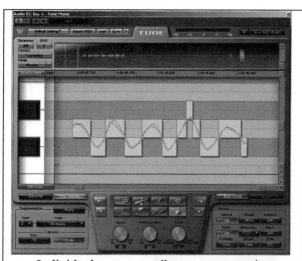

Individual notes: no vibrato segmentation

Vibrato segmentation marked in shaded area
(tinted red in actual GUI)

Figure 9.10
A series of notes without vibrato tolerance
and then with it.

Segmentation parameters can be applied at any time after analysis. Having good segmentation can help the overall tuning process go smoothly and quickly. You should get the segmentation of a musical phrase properly set before trying to apply pitch correction.

If the Segmentation settings still do not yield the desired note separations, both the Note tool and Slice tool offer ways to manually change and add new note separations. When the Note tool is rolled over a boundary between two notes, it changes into a separation tool. Click and drag the note separation point with this tool to change where Tune defines the next note. If you need to add another note separation, click the point you want to separate with the Slice tool to create two new notes from one original.

The combination of the Segmentation controls, the Note tool, and the Slice tool give you complete control over how Tune defines each note in a melody. The operations are fast and intuitive, making Tune a very friendly plug-in to use.

Pitch Correction

After you have analyzed the audio in a section, you can begin editing the pitch envelopes. Tune always applies a default pitch correction right after analyzing audio. You can alter the automatic correction that Tune applies by selecting various notes and changing the three settings found at the bottom of the interface.

❋ *Speed*—This controls how fast Tune adjusts the pitch of a certain note. It controls the "attack" of the pitch change. Slower values (in ms) leave the beginning of notes intact, whereas faster values quickly change the pitch to the corrected value.

❋ *Note Transition*—Note transition speed is the time it takes for the corrected pitch curve to move from one note segment to the next. Low values make quicker transitions and can start to sound quantized and robotic. Higher values slow the transition down for a more natural sound.

❋ *Ratio*—The ratio determines how far a pitch is moved from its original value to the corrected value. This is a sort of "strength" parameter that determines how much of pitch correction is applied.

The Select All button, found to the lower-left side of the GUI, allows you the change the automatic settings for all analyzed notes at the same time. This can be useful if the automatic adjustment that Tune applies does not work in general for the material you are working on. This is a good starting point for further editing, a global setting for all analyzed notes. Once an overall setting has been made for the track, fine-tuning can begin.

In order to alter the automatic pitch correction for one or more notes at a time, do the following:

1. Using the note selection tool, click on one note or click and drag around a series of notes to select them. You can Shift+click on various notes to select multiple noncontiguous notes for editing. The Select All button will select all analyzed notes in the current Tune timeline.

2. After you have selected one or more notes, the three rotary controls at the bottom will affect how the pitch correction is applied to those notes. Keep in mind that you can change the three correction parameters for just one note at a time. Each note can have a unique set of correction parameters.

To start out, adjust the correction settings for all the analyzed notes to a reasonable level of correction. In some cases, this might be no correction, using a 0% ratio to start with. As you notice problem areas, you can get more specific by adjusting the settings for individual notes. Use the magnifying glass (Zoom tool) to zero in on problem notes to see the pitch envelopes in more detail. The original pitch curves are displayed in yellow, whereas the corrected curves are shown in green. As you change the settings for various notes, you can see how the corrected pitch curves are being altered.

Manual Editing

Sometimes it is necessary to actually draw in pitch envelopes by hand to achieve a certain effect or manipulate a performance further. Tune provides tools to manually edit pitch envelopes and draw in your own.

The simplest form of manual editing uses the Curve tool shown in Figure 9.11. The Curve tool can be used to move the pitch curve up and down freely to adjust the overall pitch center of a note. It can also move the beginning or end of a pitch envelope to change the "angle" of the note or its rotation, as seen in Figure 9.11.

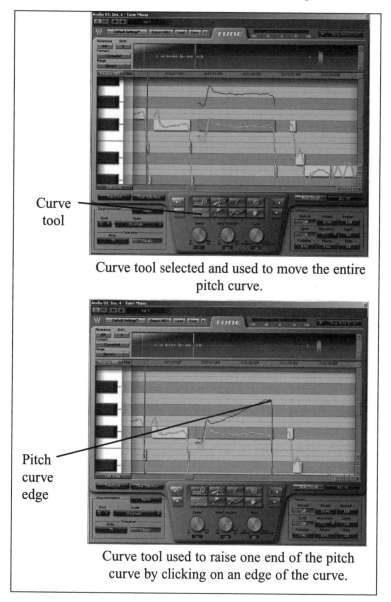

Curve tool

Curve tool selected and used to move the entire pitch curve.

Pitch curve edge

Curve tool used to raise one end of the pitch curve by clicking on an edge of the curve.

Figure 9.11

Using the Curve tool, you can move the entire pitch curve by clicking anywhere within the edges of the curve and dragging up or down. To move just one end of the pitch curve, click with the Curve tool at either edge of the curve and drag up or down. The cursor icon changes when you are over an edge.

The Curve tool allows you to retain the subtleties of the original performance while having more control over the corrected pitch curve. When more severe correction is required, you can use the drawing tools to create completely new pitch curves by hand.

Figure 9.12 shows the Line tool being used to create a pitch curve made up of connected dots made with the mouse. The Pencil tool allows freehand drawing of pitch curves for subtle control and fine-tuning.

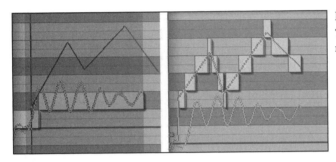

Figure 9.12

The Line tool is creating an entirely new pitch curve from scratch.

Undo!

Because the Tune plug-in functions almost as a separate audio application with its own timeline and editing, the normal undo functions of the host DAW will not apply to the functions of Tune. Fortunately, Waves has provided complete undo/redo functionality built into Tune. The Undo button and pop-up menu is found to the left of the tool selection palette and provides up to 32 levels of undo. You can use the pop-up menu to skip back to any of the undo steps by choosing that step from the list, as shown in Figure 9.13.

Figure 9.13

The Undo pop-up menu showing the 32 levels of undo. Selecting one of these steps will return Tune to that state.

The Redo button and its pop-up menu are found to the right of the tool selection palette. The redo button and pop-up menu are grayed out until an undo step has been used. Then the Redo option becomes active.

Tune offers a very quick and intuitive interface for pitch correction. The analysis tools and note separation capabilities help accurately detect melodies, which certainly makes editing easier. The visual display is clear and very stable, allowing you to work quickly. The integration with the host DAW is well implemented. The capability to constantly change parameters of each note non-destructively makes Tune a very convenient way of correcting pitch on individual tracks.

Using Melodyne to Correct and Alter Pitch

Melodyne is a comprehensive pitch- and time-editing environment. It can function as a plug-in (Uno) or as a standalone application (Cre8 and Studio Edition). Either way, audio going through Melodyne can have its pitch, formant, length, and timing altered with the tools it provides.

Melodyne does not have as many automatic functions as Antares Auto-Tune or Waves Tune, but it does have more tools for manual adjustment of the pitch and timing of each note in a melody. Using these tools, it is possible to create entirely new performances from an original melody, including harmonies, double tracks, and even whole multi-part arrangements out of just one melodic performance.

Detection of Melody

Melodyne has a sophisticated set of functions to analyze audio for melodic content. There are 42 presets for various instruments and detection settings. Because Melodyne is also a rhythmic performance editor, these presets include controls for rhythmic as well as tonal factors. Melodyne has two basic presets. If each audio file has a decent amount of isolation, the two basic presets should work well in most cases.

* *Pitched, Melodic*—This setting should be used for all pitch correction tasks, because it will define melodic notes for the audio file.

* *Unpitched, Percussive*—This setting is for audio files that are primarily drums or other non-melodic instruments. Melodyne can edit the timing and duration of elements in percussive tracks.

After you choose a preset, there are more detailed parameters that can be fine-tuned to optimize the melodic detection. Opening the detection parameters tab reveals all the controls for pitch and rhythmic detection, as seen in Figure 9.14. The presets work well in most situations. However, it is possible to adjust these settings to refine the detection process.

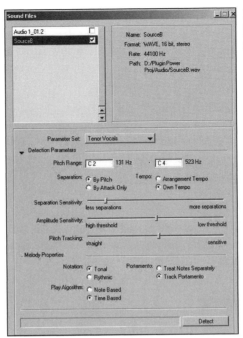

Figure 9.14
Melodyne's Detect Melody options displaying the advanced parameters.

It is possible to detect the melodies on several audio files at once using a batch process in the Studio Edition. Place a check mark next to each file that you want Melodyne to analyze. Each file can have its own set of detection parameters. Once Melodyne detects the melody, the check mark and settings are grayed out. Additionally, if you feel the detection process was not accurate, double-clicking on the grayed out check mark allows you to change settings and re-detect the melody.

Once a melody has been detected, the waveform display changes dramatically. Figure 9.15 shows one audio file that has not had the melody detected and the other showing melodic content as the waveform is shifted all around in accordance with the melodic detection.

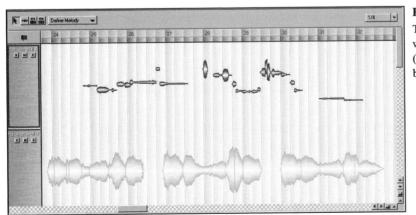

Figure 9.15
Two tracks in Melodyne, one without melodic detection (bottom) and one that has been analyzed (top).

You can edit the melodic definition that Melodyne comes up with if you feel that some notes were incorrectly identified. Emotional vocal performances often have elements that can be hard for any pitch-detection algorithm to correctly identify, so some editing of the melodic definition might be necessary. The Define Melody button has the option to edit this definition.

Editing Pitch in Melodyne

Once you have properly defined the melody, it is possible to change the pitch of each note in many ways within the melody editor. Double-clicking on a waveform in Melodyne Studio Edition opens the melody editor, as seen in Figure 9.16. This is where all the pitch-correction tasks occur. All pitch correction in Melodyne is manual.

❄ **MELODYNE UNO**

Melodyne's Uno is a single channel version of the pitch-correction software that runs along with the host application as a Rewire device. Uno is limited to one channel at a time but has the same editing features as the Studio Edition. The only window in Uno is the melody editor itself.

Figure 9.16

Melodyne's melody editor displaying the pitch curves. Editing tools appear in the upper-right corner.

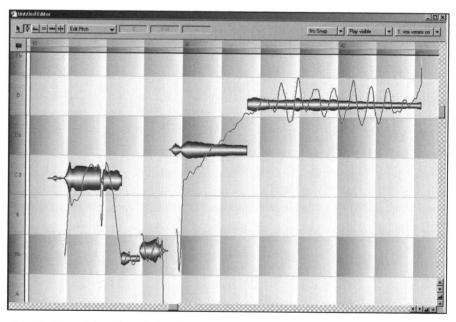

Melodyne has a variety of tools for editing the pitch of a given note. You can move the entire pitch envelope to alter the pitch center. If the performance of the note was good but the whole thing was a bit flat or sharp, the Change Pitch tool works quite well.

❊ **GUI TIP: MELODYNE'S EDITING TOOLS**
You can access Melodyne's editing tools in two ways. The first is in the upper-right corner of the melody editor, as shown in Figure 9.16. The second method is using the contextual menu of the cursor. Right-click (PC) or Control+click (Mac) anywhere in the melody editor and the editing tool selection will appear underneath the cursor.

Using the Pitch Alignment tool, you can decrease the variation in the note partially or all the way to a flat line. Figure 9.17 illustrates how the Pitch Alignment tool works, using an intense vibrato as the source of the pitch variation. The original note wavered quite a bit. Using the Pitch Alignment tool to reduce the variation leads to the second Figure 9.17. It can then be made into a flat line, indicating no variation, similar to using the Line tool in Auto-Tune. Moving the control further will invert the variations.

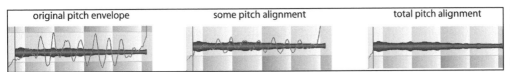

| original pitch envelope | some pitch alignment | total pitch alignment |

Figure 9.17
Using the Pitch Alignment tool in Melodyne.

The Wide Pitch Alignment tool is unique. It somehow rotates the pitch envelope around the center. It straightens the variations without removing or lessening them. Figure 9.18 shows the results of the Wide Pitch Alignment tool in centering the pitch envelope and then reversing its slope. This tool is incredibly useful and musical. Many typical pitch errors made by singers can be resolved with this tool without any adverse effects. It is a wonderful way to preserve the original pitch variations and gestures while also fixing pitch errors.

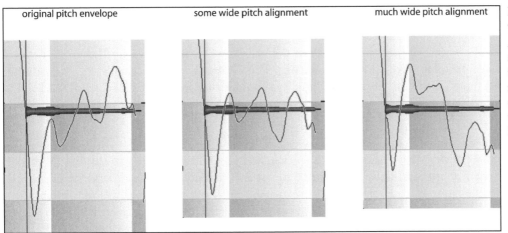

| original pitch envelope | some wide pitch alignment | much wide pitch alignment |

Figure 9.18
The Wide Pitch Alignment tool alters the variations in pitch relative to the center note without reducing them.

If a fair amount of pitch changing is going on, you might need to edit the transitions between the notes. When the Transition Change tool is selected, blue transition lines appear between notes. The tool can cause the transitions to become quicker and more severe or smoother and more drawn out, as seen in Figure 9.19. This is similar to the Retune speed option in Auto-Tune or the transition time in Waves Tune, and can be adjusted for every note in a melody.

Figure 9.19

The Transition Change control affects how fast pitches change from one to the other.

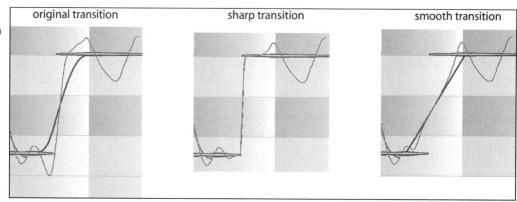

Formant Editing

The next set of tools deals with formants of each notes. Changing the formant of notes will alter the harmonic content of each note, altering the personality of the voice. For creating realistic harmony tracks that sound like another person, altering formants can achieve this effect. Used in extremes, formant altering can be a tool for sound design. In fact, most every control in Melodyne can be set to absurd values and still retain good sound quality. This makes for a great sound design tool.

You can alter the actual formant of individual notes using the Change Formant Position. You can alter the formant shifting style using the Change Formant Shift Style tool. You can adjust the transition between the formants in a similar fashion to note transitions with the Formant Transition tool.

Amplitude Editing

Each note can have its volume edited in a similar way. The Change Amplitude tool alters the volume of each individual note. Also, the Amplitude Transition tool helps smooth out varied amplitude levels between notes.

Note Timing Editing

Melodyne includes a group of very powerful tools designed to alter the timing and length of notes. What is unique about these essentially time-stretching tools is that all the notes around the edited one alter their relationship to match the edits. For example, Figure 9.20 shows a note in original position and then after moving the beginning of the note with the Move Notes tool. The note to the left adjusts its end position to match the move. Also, the note itself is not merely moved, but the beginning is stretched as well.

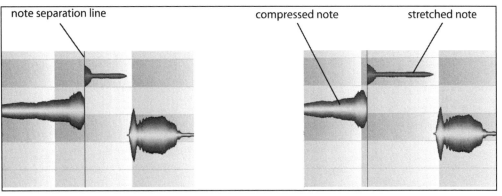

note separation line   compressed note   stretched note

Figure 9.20
Melodyne's Move Note tool used to alter the start time of a note. Adjacent notes alter themselves relative to the edited note. In essence, the note separation tool edits two notes at a time.

❄ **MIX TIP: MELODYNE FIXES VOCAL DOUBLES**

Use Melodyne's Move tools to align various vocal takes together for that "polished" sound. Attacks and releases of consonants can be highly controlled with these tools. Also, with the standalone application, multiple tracks can be superimposed upon one another in order to see these pitch and timing errors easily. Vocal editing has never been so quick and easy as with this tool set.

You can use the Stretch Note tool to move the beginning or end of a note and adjacent notes will follow. This works exactly like the note separation tool except you can move the beginning or the end of the selected note.

The other interesting and unique tool in the position group is the Change Initial Speed or Altering Attack tool. When it's selected, blue lines appear in between each note, as shown in Figure 9.21. Clicking on the blue line and dragging up causes the note to become more legato, or have a smoother attack. Conversely, dragging down on the blue line makes the note more staccato, or sharp in attack.

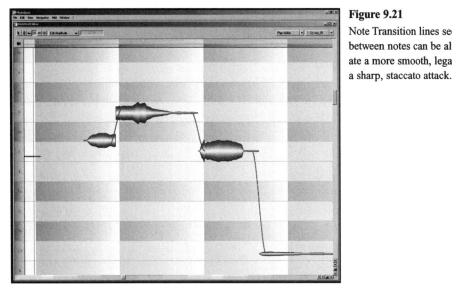

Figure 9.21
Note Transition lines seen in between notes can be altered to create a more smooth, legato attack or a sharp, staccato attack.

Note Separation

You can change the division between notes with the Separation tool. When it is selected, vertical lines appear between notes, as seen in Figure 9.22. You can move these lines to change the point that one note becomes another. Also, double-clicking within one note divides that note into two editable notes. Double-clicking on a note separation line fuses the two adjacent notes together.

Figure 9.22

Note-separation editing in Melodyne.

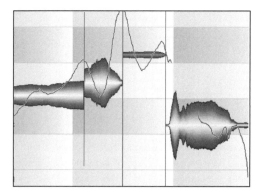

Melodyne provides a very sophisticated tool set that makes manipulation of pitch and timing almost effortless. This allows for a very high degree of control and creative possibilities with everything, especially with vocals. Melodyne is a complex application and this section by no means covers the topic in detail. There are other tools and techniques that can be used in this powerful DSP application.

Subtle Performance Enhancement

With tools such as Auto-Tune, Waves Tune, and Melodyne, it might seem as if the issues of pitch and tuning are a thing of the past. And for some applications, they are. Subtle pitch variances in an otherwise wonderful performance can easily be tackled by any one of these plug-ins.

One of the key issues in subtle performance enhancement is to process as little of the audio as possible. These plug-ins sound wonderful considering what type of processing they are doing. However, they do change the sound in noticeable ways. It is best to just process those problem areas where pitch issues can be heard.

It can be convenient to simply slap on the plug-in and process the whole track. One technique that can help is to process the whole track for improved pitch. Then, place that processed audio on an adjacent track in the DAW and mute it. When one of the problem phrases is encountered, simply edit a section of the processed track into the original to improve just that phrase or section. In this manner, you avoid degrading the sound when no pitch correction is needed. Sometimes, less really is more.

If you want to avoid the telltale artifacts of auto-tuning, always try to use as much of the original pitch envelope as possible. Try moving the entire envelope first and then if further correction is needed, rotate or reshape the envelope. Only as a last resort should you draw in a straight line or use a Line tool. The human voice does not generate a "straight line" pitch naturally. Unless you are going for the effect, the straight-line approach will generate an unnatural vocal tonality.

Performance Creation from Scratch

One step beyond pitch correction is creating pitch from original performances. The power of pitch-correction DSP allows the manipulation of notes to create harmonies or completely new performances and melodies from original recordings. Taken to extremes, this type of DSP can generate some really interesting sound design elements out of otherwise normal recordings.

Simple Harmony Track

All of these plug-ins are capable of creating simple harmony tracks from an original performance. They vary as to how convenient the process will be, but it can be done. A simple technique is to copy the original vocal to a new track and insert a pitch-correction plug-in on it. Then, line-by-line, you can manually set the pitch of the second track to create simple two-part harmonies. This requires some basic music theory knowledge, as discussed earlier.

Multiple Harmonies

Melodyne Studio Edition has more advanced capabilities in this regard. The Studio Edition is a standalone application that supports multiple tracks of melodic material that you can edit independently. Importing a reference mix of instruments along with multiple copies of a lead vocal track provides an opportunity for you to create harmonies.

The unique aspect of Melodyne in this regard is its capability to open multiple melodic tracks superimposed upon one another. This allows unprecedented visual editing of multiple harmonies at once in a single editing window, as seen in Figure 9.23. This allows you to switch back and forth between the multiple tracks instantly for quick creation of harmonies.

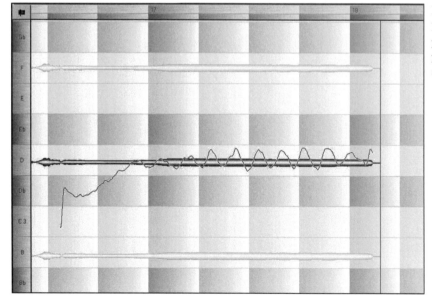

Figure 9.23

Melodyne Studio Edition pitch-editing window displaying multiple melodies simultaneously.

Sound Design Applications

Now, on to the fun stuff. Pitch-correction DSP can do all sorts of mangling and torturous reshaping of audio best suited for sound design applications. The capability to separate the formant from the pitch and use extreme settings for each can result in striking new audio textures from rather normal source material.

For the most part, only tonal sounds that actually have a definite pitch work well in this application. However, drum loops can be an interesting subject for pitch alteration. Melodyne is capable of editing the timing of audio files along with the pitch. The groove of a loop can easily be altered with the length and separation tools in Melodyne. Drum loops can actually be "tuned" by individual drums using the pitch tools. You can use these tools also to conform a drum loop to another tempo or to align several drum loops together. Then, you can tune the pitches of each drum to one another, creating a whole new sound.

Summary

In searching for the perfect performance, all sorts of tools that use digital technology to edit. or even create, musical performances have popped up. The area of pitch correction is no exception. These powerful tools have changed the ways that some music is now created. Production techniques have come to rely on this type of DSP to achieve desired results. In some cases, the processing itself has come to define a unique sound (think Cher). In other cases, the use of pitch correction is not noticeable to anyone but the creators.

For some, "auto-tuning" is a crutch they must rely on. For many, it is a time- and money-saver for limited budgets and tight schedules. Still others use these plug-ins as creative tools, generating sounds that are otherwise impossible. At the end of the day, it is just amazing that these types of tools even exist! Enjoy.

10 } Restoration

Too often, great recordings are marred by external problems and noises. Poor signal-to-noise ratios generated during recording or uncontrollable background noise can contribute to the demise of a wonderful recording. Even simple mishaps such as dropping keys, a passing airliner, or a cough from an audience member can detract from the quality of recordings. From music recording, film and video post-production, to vinyl disc remastering and even forensic audio processing, noise, clicks, hum, rumble, and other unintended artifacts wreak havoc for audio engineers on a daily basis.

There are many plug-in DSP tools now available for the purpose of removing unwanted noise from recordings without damaging the original signal. They include de-hissers, de-clickers, hum reducers, incidental noise removal, and broadband noise-reduction plug-ins. Companies such as Cedar, Waves, Bias, and Algorithmix offer powerful tools that can help you restore your recordings to their best possible form.

The simplest form of noise reduction is the gate. It simply turns off the signal when it travels below a set threshold. This is a very crude method of noise removal that is often very noticeable on isolated tracks and does not always retain the utmost detail while removing noise. It is either on or off. An expander can do slightly better, with a smoother ratio that is not as noticeable. Gates and expanders can only identify noise by the level it generates. The closer that level gets to the level of recorded sound, the more difficult this process becomes. Noise that occurs at the same time as a recorded sound cannot be removed by a gate. You have to employ more sophisticated means at that point.

The issues involved in restoration consist of identifying noise artifacts and then eliminating them. To that end, there are several kinds of noise-removal tools that are based on the type of noise they remove. Most restoration tasks involve several steps with different plug-ins to get rid of various types of noise. Typically, audio noise can be classified into four categories:

❋ *Steady state tones:* Steady state tones are background sounds that remain the same or almost the same for long periods of time. Examples include electrical hum, HVAC fans, generators (and other stationary engines), and computer fan noise.

* *Clicks and pops:* This category is made up of all sorts of mechanical, electrical, and electronic errors that cause very short bursts of sound. The causes of this type of noise can be anything from the clipping of a digital converter to a loose connection in a microphone cable. Sometimes, lower-level clicks (commonly called "crackles") are dealt with as a separate form of noise with different processors such as Waves X-Crackle.

* *Broadband noise:* This category covers all sorts of noise that are typically constant and exist all over the frequency spectrum. Common noise from audio circuits, hiss from tape machines, and air-handling noise all qualify as examples of broadband noise.

* *Incidental noises:* This category is the grab bag for any other sound that only occurs once, such as a cell phone ringing in an audience, a squeaky chair, or keys dropping on the floor. These items are single occurrences, but still qualify as noise if they are not intended as part of the recording.

With all four categories of noise and four types of processors used to remove them, you must make a plan in order to proceed and be effective with restoration. Typically, the order in which you remove noise follows the previous categories: hum and steady state tones are removed first, followed by clicks and pops, and then broadband noise, and finally incidental sounds.

The last category of incidental sounds can sometimes fall under clicks and pops if the sound is a very short and loud burst. Often times, these incidental sounds become more audible as the other noises in a signal are removed. Once they have been exposed, it is easier to identify and remove them.

To start the process, the chapter examines hum removal tools first.

Removing Hum from a Recording

Hum from electric motors, power lines, and other electric sources is probably the simplest form of noise common to audio recordings. It is simple because it is easy to identify. It is a constant tone typically based on known frequencies of the electric supply system. However, because it is constant, it can be a bit tricky to remove without removing some of the recorded sound as well.

50Hz and 60Hz Hum

First off, what is the frequency of the hum? There are two choices if the source of hum is from electrical supplies:

* 50Hz—The carrier frequency of the European electric system as well as most of Asia, Africa, and parts of South America.

* 60Hz—The carrier frequency of the American electric systems used in North America and most of South America, as well as a couple other very small places in Asia.

In reality, there can be more choices due to factors such as film transfers, variation in the actual frequency of the local power plant, variations in the speed of a tape recorder used on location, and many others. 50Hz and 60Hz are starting points. Fine-tuning is always necessary.

Hum Harmonics

In addition to the basic frequency of the hum, there can be (and usually are) additional frequencies generated that follow a harmonic pattern based on the prime hum frequency. This is where hum removal becomes even more difficult, as these harmonics enter into the speech ranges where it is more noticeable. If hum were only 50Hz or 60Hz, it would be a breeze to remove from sources that do not contain a great deal of the lower octaves. You simply create a very narrow filter (a notch filter) centered at 50Hz or 60Hz and turn the gain down until the hum is sufficiently removed. The harmonics in most cases will remain and continue to generate the perception that the hum has not been removed.

Harmonic filtering such as the one found in Elemental Audio's Eqium, shown in Figure 10.1, can tackle many of the issues of hum harmonics. The capability to use very narrow bandwidths prevents undue removal of the desired sound. Also, as the harmonics increase in frequency, they often do not have as much volume and might not need as much gain reduction. Possibly, one harmonic in particular might be stronger than the rest.

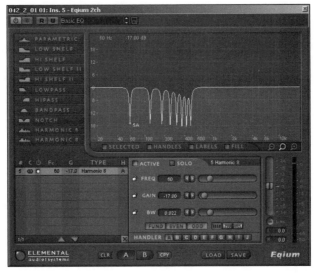

Figure 10.1

Elemental Audio's Eqium using a harmonic filter with narrow bandwidth to remove 60-cycle hum and its harmonics.

When you need individual control over harmonics, Waves X-Hum provides linked odd or even harmonics and individual gain control over each harmonic, if necessary. Also, because X-Hum is designed to deal with hum noise directly, the filters are steeper and have up to 60dB of reduction for the most severe hum interference. Figure 10.2 shows X-Hum set to reduce various harmonics of a 50-cycle hum at different amounts.

Figure 10.2

Waves X-Hum set to remove various harmonics of a 50-cycle hum at different amounts.

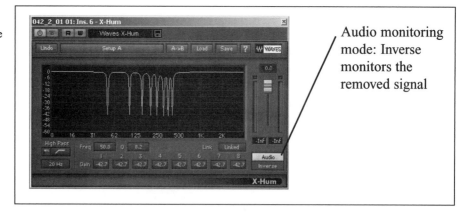

Audio monitoring mode: Inverse monitors the removed signal

The bandwidths of these filters are very narrow to avoid removing anything aside from the hum itself. It is possible to widen the filters if necessary. If the filters are becoming too wide in order to remove the hum, there could quite possibly be other broadband noise in the signal as well.

X-Hum provides a feature that allows you to hear what portion of the signal is being removed. Using the difference button, you can preview the sound that is being filtered out by the notch filters. It is always a good idea to check this to make sure you are not removing any part of the desired signal.

Once you've reached an effective setting, it might be a good idea to actually process the file with the plug-in and create a new audio file without the hum. In this manner, you can render each step of the restoration process to a file in order to retain the most flexibility for changing settings later. Also, restoration plug-ins can use quite a bit of DSP and latency, so processing eliminates these factors once you reach a setting. Creating new copies of the audio file allows you to always return to the source material if you want to make changes.

If you are working strictly on a single audio file in a forensic situation, running all of the restoration processes at once in real-time is more feasible. Latency issues would not present any difficulty and the entire CPU would be available for DSP resources.

De-Clicking and De-Crackling

The next stage of restoration is usually de-clicking and de-crackling. These types of disturbances are very short in duration and can overtake the signal, such as a pop on a vinyl record, or can be at low levels, like the crackling of a well worn record. You can deal with these small spikes in level by using one of the de-clicking or de-crackling plug-ins.

To Click or To Crackle

The first thing to determine is what sort of noise you are dealing with. Is it a click or a series of crackles? Clicks are usually more pronounced, and generally speaking, occur less often than crackles, such as a skip or scratch on a vinyl record. Crackling is a pervasive issue that is made up of many small clicks or pops (usually only several samples long) at lower levels.

Each developer has tools that deal with both types of phenomena in different ways. Waves has both a click removal and crackle removal plug-in. Cedar has a DeClip process primarily designed to reduce the audibility of audio that has exceeded the analog or digital maximum level and caused clipped samples in the waveform. Algorithmix has ScratchFree processing, which addresses most of the clicking and crackling issues in one process, including algorithms for overloads.

Waves X-Click and X-Crackle

The Waves restoration bundle provides an entire suite of plug-ins for restoration. Each one is tailored to a specific type of noise. Waves X-Click and X-Crackle plug-ins have the tools necessary to deal with these types of noises.

X-Click

X-Click has a very simple interface including the two parameters, Threshold and Shape, and a waveform display that shows the detection and reduction of clicks found in the signal. Figure 10.3 shows X-Click in operation with various clicks displayed in the waveform area. These were severe record scratches that required a great deal of de-clicking.

Figure 10.3

Waves X-Click working on clicks shown in the waveform display as vertical lines.

The Threshold parameter controls the level of clicks to be removed. The higher the threshold, the more clicks that are affected. The Shape parameter determines how long the clicks are that are removed. Higher shape settings remove longer clicks in the signal, such as record pops. Once again, using the Waves Difference button allows you to listen to just the audio signal being removed in order to tweak the settings for maximum benefit. Or, if you want to keep only the noise for a sound effect, you can process the sound in Difference mode to reject the original content and keep the clicks and pops.

X-Crackle

For smaller and more pervasive types of clicks and pops, X-Crackle can be a better tool. X-Crackle has a very simple interface similar to X-Click. The Threshold parameter determines the level of crackles that will be removed. Higher thresholds affect more of the audio signal. The Reduction parameter determines how much gain reduction is applied to each crackle.

Figure 10.4 shows X-Crackle processing audio. The upper portion of the waveform display shows the input signal. The lower portion shows the crackles that are being analyzed and removed in both time and spectral displays. The vertical axis shows frequency, whereas the horizontal axis is the timeline. You can see the spectral makeup of the crackling detected in the signal. X-Crackle also includes the Difference monitoring capacity to analyze the removed signal material.

Figure 10.4

Waves X-Crackle working on audio shown in the upper display, whereas removed crackles are shown in the lower display.

Cedar DeClip

Cedar Audio has been a well-respected name in audio restoration for many years. In the audio post-production and film-mixing worlds, its hardware processors are standard equipment for most dubbing mixers. They have provided some of their tools in plug-in format for Pro Tools. The DeClip Audiosuite plug-in is one example of such tools that you can use to remove clicks from audio.

Although it is primarily designed for restoration of the waveform around an area that has been clipped, this plug-in can be effective at removing clicks as well. DeClip functions exclusively as an offline process in the Audiosuite format.

Algorithmix ScratchFree

Algorithmix is a German company founded in 1997 that has spent a great deal of time creating DSP algorithms that have been used in other products, including digital mixing consoles, rack-mount outboard processing, virtual instruments, and even technology used by other plug-in developers. They also have developed a line of professional audio DSP plug-ins, including ScratchFree.

INSIDER TRADING: SHARED TECHNOLOGY

In this very small world of audio DSP developers, it is interesting to note that the Algorithmix technology is used in the Waves Restoration plug-ins mentioned in this chapter. Although this does not mean that the Algorithmix and Waves plug-ins are identical, they do share some basic technology that helps achieve the amazing results that both products are capable of.

ScratchFree is available as a DirectX or VST plug-in. It is designed as both a DeClicker and a DeCrackler with two separate sets of controls.

ScratchFree's DeClicker

The DeClicker portion of ScratchFree, shown in Figure 10.5, has five separate profiles depending on the type of clicks being removed. The Clip profile is similar to Cedar's DeClip process in removing distortion caused by overloading of audio equipment or digital signals. The Threshold control in ScratchFree determines how much DeClicking is applied. There are also three interpolation choices for how ScratchFree fills the space left by the click. You can use the interpolation choices by themselves or in combination with one another to obtain the smoothest filling of the gaps.

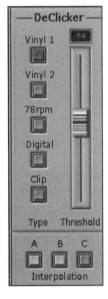

Figure 10.5
The DeClicker portion of the ScratchFree GUI.

❊ A—This algorithm is best used for vinyl record restoration.

❊ B—Designed for digital spikes.

❊ C—Especially made for clicks found on old 78 rpm records.

❊ **INTERPOLATION**

Interpolation is the mathematical process of creating missing data. Restoration processes depend on good-quality interpolation algorithms to replace sections of audio that have been removed, such as a click. Interpolation in this situation uses data from the surrounding signal to generate new audio data that will take the place of the removed click. That is how the resulting audio sounds smooth and undisturbed.

ScratchFree's DeCrackler

The DeCrackler portion of ScratchFree has two basic parameters: Detect and Remove. The Detect setting determines what frequency range is analyzed when looking for crackles. The Remove parameter sets how many crackles are removed.

The DeCrackler has its own set of the same three interpolation algorithms as the DeClicker. The Expert parameter called Smooth has the most effect on how the DeCrackler works.

ScratchFree's Expert Parameters

There are three expert parameters that help minimize the audibility of artifacts created by extreme amounts of de-clicking and de-crackling.

* The Width setting determines the size of clicks that are removed. For very loud record pops, a higher setting will remove the longer click. Very short clicks such as digital "snaps" caused by improper clocking setups benefit from a smaller width setting.

* The Smooth control adjusts the brilliance of the processed signal to compensate for any high-frequency detail that might be lost in the DeCrackle process. Leave it at the default setting unless you are noticing a very dull sound as a result of too much DeCrackling.

* The DePlop parameter sets the detection range for plops or low-frequency bumps that can result from the removal of a click exposing a low-frequency anomaly. This can help smooth out rumbly sounds without the use of an EQ.

> **GUI TIP: THE DIFFERENCE**
>
> Always use the Differ (or Difference) monitoring function, found in the lower-right corner of the interface, to hear what the plug-in is actually removing from the signal. If you hear any program material, such as the music itself, the processing is possibly too severe. The plug-in should not remove any of the original material that is being restored. Often, listening to the audio "junk" that is being removed makes adjusting the plug-in easier.

Figure 10.6 shows ScratchFree's spectrogram display of typical vinyl record noise running in a loop. The section to the left shows the original audio signal with noise, a repeating record pop and various crackles. The center section shows the same audio with the DeCrackle function engaged. Notice all the higher frequency disturbances have all been removed. What's left are the record pops resulting from a scratch on the surface of the vinyl. The third section shows the pops removed by the DeClick function. ScratchFree is a very effective plug-in for removing clicks and crackles.

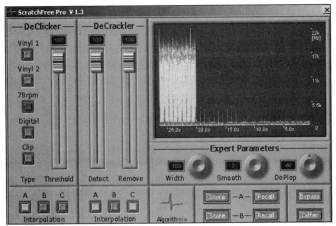

Figure 10.6
Algorithmix ScratchFree in operation showing the original signal, the crackles removed, and finally the record pop removed.

Now that you have removed the hum, clicks, and crackles, you are ready to check for general hiss and other broadband noises.

Reducing Broadband Noise

Hiss and the general background noise of audio electronics and diffuse location ambience are commonly termed *broadband noise*. This type of noise occurs at all frequencies (broadband) and normally does not have a time window. It is there all the time, practically speaking.

Plug-ins that are adept at removing this kind of noise must be able to discern between the portions of the audio signal that are not important and can be discarded and the signals that need to be preserved. To do this, there are basically two processing techniques:

❋ *Noise profile identification*—This technique involves analyzing a portion of the signal that only contains the noise to be removed. The spectral response is measured, providing a sonic fingerprint of the noise. The plug-in can then use this information to reduce the noise in various bands when it fits within the analyzed profile.

❋ *Adaptive noise filtering*—This technique analyzes the audio on the fly and adapts the noise profile as the signal changes.

The Multi-Band Expander

In both of the processing techniques described previously, the resulting noise profile is used to selectively turn down various frequency bands when they fit under the noise profile. In other words, for a given frequency band, if the current level of that band is at or below the noise profile level, the band will be turned down, thereby reducing the level of noise in that band.

Depending on the resolution of the plug-in process, there can be many individual frequency bands that are functioning this way at the same time. Think of it as a giant multi-band expander/gate, where the threshold for each band is set to the level of the noise profile. As energy in the band passes below the threshold of the noise profile, the expander turns that band down, reducing the noise level. When this is done with many individual frequency bands, dramatic results are possible.

Waves X-Noise

The Waves X-Noise plug-in uses the Noise Profile Identification technique. A section of audio that only contains the noise you are trying to remove must be analyzed to generate a noise profile. Once X-Noise "learns" the noise profile, you can adjust several other controls to determine how X-Noise processes audio. Here is a step-by-step method for using X-Noise in a typical noise-removal process:

1. Locate a portion of the audio file that contains just the noise you are trying to remove. It can be a relatively small section, but must at least be a second or so long in order for X-Noise to analyze the noise profile.

2. Press the Noise Profile button to launch X-Noise into learning mode and play the section of audio. The display in X-Noise will show the spectral composition of the signal coming into the plug-in. Figure 10.7 shows X-Noise as it is "learning" the noise profile of this section of audio. Before the section is over, press the Noise Profile button again to stop the learning process.

Figure 10.7

Waves X-Noise learning the noise profile of a section of audio.

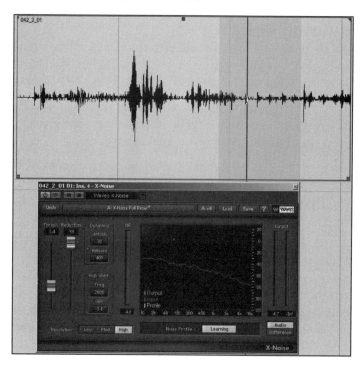

❋ GUI TIP: X-NOISE 34 RESOLUTION

There are three choices for the resolution of audio analysis in X-Noise: Low, Med, and High. This resolution determines how many frequency bands are used to analyze and process the audio signal. The High setting consumes the most CPU resources but also provides the greatest resolution in the frequency domain. However, it does not provide the best response in the time domain. If you experience smeared transients while using X-Noise, reduce the resolution setting to Med or Low. Waves recommends that you use the same resolution for noise profile analysis and processing. But, it is possible to analyze with one setting and process with another.

---

3. Once X-Noise has learned the noise profile, it will be displayed by a white line, as seen in Figure 10.8. Now play back a section of audio containing the desired program material and listen.

4. The most important setting is the threshold. The higher the threshold, the more signal is removed. Lowering the threshold allows more signal to remain. This works just like a gate or downward expander. The difference is that you are adjusting the threshold of many different expanders, one for each frequency band. Visually, the profile line will move up or down in the display as you adjust the threshold. Figure 10.8 shows X-Noise in operation. The input curve is exceeding the noise profile line starting around 400Hz. This means that X-Noise will not affect those frequency bands . Above 4kHz and below 100Hz, the signal is below the noise profile line and X-Noise will reduce the volume of those frequency bands, reducing any noise they are contributing. Notice that, in those areas where the input level is below the noise profile, the output curve has been reduced.

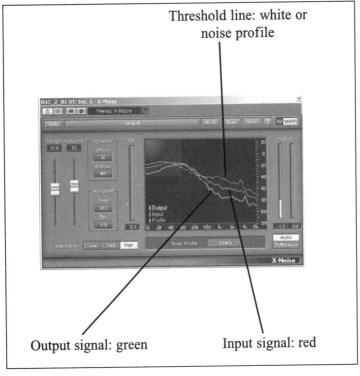

Threshold line: white or noise profile

Output signal: green

Input signal: red

Figure 10.8
X-Noise in operation during a section of dialogue. Note the input, output, and profile curves.

5. The Reduction setting is similar to the ratio of an expander. The higher the reduction number, the more dB loss for frequency bands falling under the noise profile level. Set it to 0% for the most mild noise reduction and 100% for maximum reduction. The Threshold and Reduction controls work together to achieve the desired results.

6. Once X-Noise is reducing a fair amount of the noise, you might notice some time domain effects that can sound like garbling or a dulling of the sound. One possible solution for this is to adjust the attack and release times for X-Noise. These parameters work just like any other dynamics processor, determining how fast gain-reduction occurs once signals have passed below the threshold point. Shortening them should bring back some life and brightness to sounds, whereas lengthening them can smooth out the X-Noise processing.

7. Many noise artifacts occur in the higher frequency areas where critical speech bands are found. Sometimes, using the analyzed noise profile will work for a majority of frequencies but can obscure certain vocal ranges and affect intelligibility of the output. X-Noise provides a means to adjust for this bias towards high frequencies with a shelving control. This filter only affects the actual noise profile itself, not the incoming audio. If you are having intelligibility issues, try adjusting the shelving control. Figure 10.9 shows the same noise profile with frequencies above 2kHz reduced so that there is a lower threshold for those frequencies, allowing them to come through more readily.

Figure 10.9

The X-Noise profile modified by the shelving control to allow more high-frequency content to remain.

8. Finally, use the Difference monitoring function (the Difference button in the lower-left side of the interface) to hear what is actually being removed. This is always a very effective way of finding out whether you are removing too much from the signal.

You can save both the noise profile and the plug-in settings as presets to be used again. Presets are good for offline processing. X-Noise uses quite a bit of CPU to process high-resolution noise profiles. It also has a high latency of 5120 samples, which can affect timing in hosts that do not support plug-in delay compensation.

In both cases, it is beneficial (once you've made proper noise-reduction settings in real-time) to process the files offline in order to conserve CPU resources and latency management. Once you have created a noise profile and made the adjustments to all the settings, save this as a preset. When you call up the X-Noise offline process, simply load this preset and process all the files recorded with the same noise print.

> ❋ **MIX TIP: CREATE NEW COPIES**
>
> Always create new copies of the audio files when you're using offline processing to ensure that you can undo or redo the processes with different settings later. Some applications, such as Nuendo, offer an offline process history with undo capabilities that take care of this issue for you. It is always better to be safe than sorry. After all, hard drives have become more affordable, whereas your time has not.

Algorithmix NoiseFree

Algorithmix NoiseFree is a broadband noise reducer that functions in much the same manner as Waves X-Noise. Perhaps this is due to the fact that they share common technology created by Algorithmix. However, NoiseFree can also function as an adaptive noise filtering plug-in, gathering the noise profile and adapting it as the noise floor changes.

Noise Profile Generation

For the most part, the capturing of noise profiles works in same way as in X-Noise. Additionally, you can choose to learn the noise profile from the actual program material, as shown in Figure 10.10. The learn option has two choices: From Noise and From Signal. It is not necessary to find a portion of the signal that only contains noise. This can be a time-saving method. It's also helpful when no section can be found containing noise by itself, as in forensic-restoration situations.

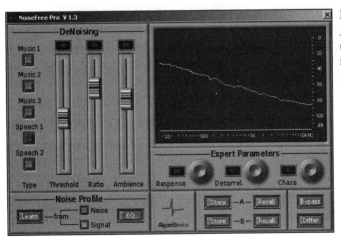

Figure 10.10

Algorithmix NoiseFree can learn the noise profile from just the noise or from the entire signal.

Whereas X-Noise has the ability to adjust the high-frequency tilt of the noise profile to improve intelligibility, NoiseFree has five bands of parametric EQ that can be used to modify the noise profile in many ways. Figure 10.11 shows the Noise Profile EQ window in NoiseFree with several active bands modifying the noise profile. You can use this EQ to generate custom noise profiles from scratch using a white noise template. You can then save each noise profile for comparison and future use.

Figure 10.11

You can use the Noise Profile EQ in NoiseFree to modify captured profiles or create new ones using a white noise template.

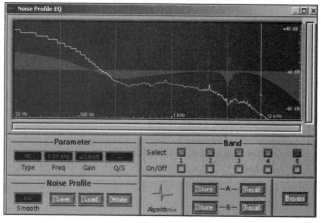

There is a special smoothing control used to even out specific peaks and dips in the noise profile if necessary. Figure 10.12 shows the same noise profile smoothed out.

Figure 10.12

The same noise profile after smoothing.

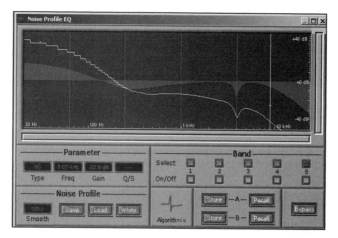

Processing Modes

NoiseFree has five processing modes, depending on the type of program material you are working with.

❊ *Music 1*—Designed for classical music that does not contain many hard transients.

❊ *Music 2*—Designed for average music with a combination of smooth and transient material.

❊ *Music 3*—Designed for percussive music that contains many fast transients.

❊ *Speech 1*—Designed for forensic speech recovery primarily concerned with intelligibility.

❊ *Speech 2*—Designed for dialogue that needs removal of reverberation in conjunction with the Chase control, which adaptively alters the noise profile.

De-Noising Parameters

NoiseFree has the basic two controls that X-Noise has: Threshold and Ratio (what X-Noise calls Reduction). These two parameters define how much noise reduction is happening. The Ambience slider is unique. It controls how an intelligent algorithm preserves low-level harmonics and detail so heavily processed audio does not lose liveliness and ambience. Use the Ambience slider carefully, because too much can yield distortion and more noise.

The expert parameters affect how artifacts of de-noising are dealt with and minimized:

❊ The Response factor determines the dynamic speed at which the process runs. Increasing the response can smooth out artifacts, whereas shortening the response retains more transient information at the cost of potentially more artifacts.

❊ The Decorrelation parameter is designed to recover small transient details in music recordings, reducing artifacts even more. This setting works in tandem with the Response, Threshold, Ratio, and Ambience settings. Adjusting one might require adjusting any combination of the others in order to achieve the best results.

❊ Chase works with the noise profile to adapt the profile to continuous changes in the noise floor, including reverberant noise in dialogue using the Speech 2 mode. As Chase increases, the speed at which the noise profile changes becomes faster, adapting more quickly to changes in the environment. This works quite well for cleaning up production dialogue in films.

A/B Comparisons

NoiseFree can store two presets within the GUI at one time for easy A/B comparisons to be made between two sets of settings and noise profile. This is a very good way of double-checking to see that you are getting the best possible results. The capability to swap noise profiles quickly allows you to see which one works the best. Algorithmix recommends capturing several noise profiles when working on heavily damaged material so that the optimal one can be used for various sections of the material.

NoiseFree is a very powerful plug-in, with settings that go beyond casual usage into professional forensics and vinyl-restoration tasks. There are additional Advanced Options to further refine the noise-reduction process that should only be addressed after a mastery of the basic controls discussed here. One thing is for sure; NoiseFree is quite powerful and effective when you use the proper settings and explore all the parameters. Some material that could easily be considered useless can be radically improved by the use of NoiseFree.

Removing Incidental Noises

The most difficult types of noises to remove are those that only occur once or are not pervasive in the signal. Noises such as ringing cell phones or dropped keys in a live performance, or foot scuffs and squeaky chairs in studio recordings, prove the most difficult to get rid of in a pleasant fashion.

In some situations where the incidental noise occurs by itself and not during desired material, you can replace the noise or interpolate it with surrounding data, or simply edit it out. This becomes most difficult when the offensive sound occurs at the same time as other desired sounds, such as dialogue. Interpolating data in this situation gets much trickier. Fortunately, the designers at Cedar and Algorithmix have spent an enormous amount of time figuring out how to do just this.

Algorithmix reNOVAtor

Algorithmix reNOVAtor is a unique sound-restoration plug-in. It uses a visual method for processing. The plug-in requires a special connection between the host editor and DSP engine and, as such, is only integrated into a few host DAWs. Fortunately, it can function as a stand-alone application with its own audio editor, AlgoEdit. The AlgoEdit application loads audio files and plays them back while reNOVAtor processes the audio signal.

Once you load a file into AlgoEdit, you can press the reNOVAtor button to call up the reNOVAtor interface. This interface will immediately analyze the audio file and create a color spectrogram that represents the audio in three dimensions. The X-axis shows time, the Y-axis represents frequency, and the color depth shows amplitude at those frequencies, as illustrated in Figure 10.13.

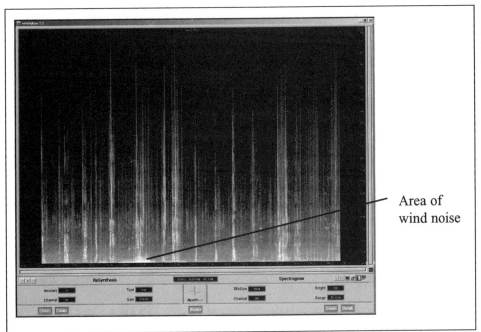

Figure 10.13
Algorithmix reNOVAtor's spectrogram display of an audio file. This recording is feature film dialogue recorded outside and containing wind noise, which you can see at the bottom of the display in white.

Area of wind noise

This view offers a very intuitive interface for identifying and isolating disturbing noises for processing. The display uses color to indicate intensity. Starting with black for silence, the scale follows the natural color progression of the rainbow:

- ❋ Reds for low-level energy
- ❋ Yellow for low-medium energy
- ❋ Green for mid-level energy
- ❋ Blue for high-energy
- ❋ White for maximum energy

There are two other color schemes. One reverses the color order, using blue for low-level and red for high-level and again white for maximum energy. The third color scheme is a black and white or grayscale scheme, whereby black is low and white is high. Once you know what scheme is being used, identifying sounds by time and frequency spectrum becomes quite easy and intuitive.

Using the mouse, you can frame a portion of the spectrum and right-click to choose options, including zooming in to have a closer look. Surgical precision is possible using the zoom functions. Figure 10.14 shows a very small portion of the spectrum that is the sound of a birdcall in the distance. The same area is shown again on the bottom in Figure 10.14 after processing with reNOVAtor. The birdcall is gone, replaced by interpolated audio from the surrounding areas.

Figure 10.14

A bird call in the spectrum on the top. After processing, the same area seen on the bottom containing interpolated data to replace the birdcall.

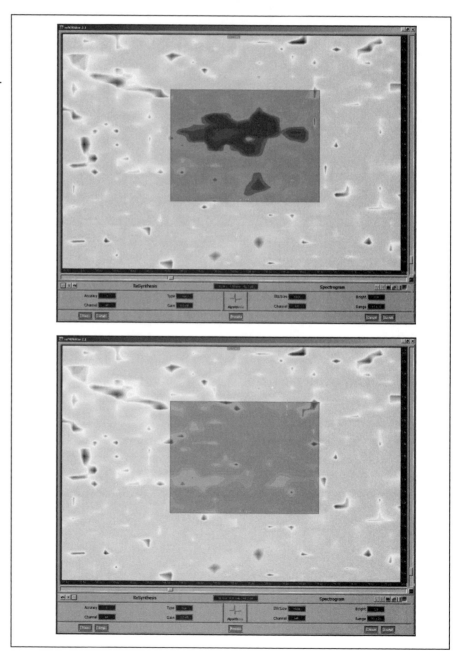

The same framing technique determines just which portion of the spectrum over time will be processed. In this way, only select portions of the audio file are processed, leaving the rest untouched. In its simplest form, you can use the reNOVAtor this way without additional settings to achieve amazing results. Just select an area where the incidental sound occurs in time and frequency and click the Process button.

Data Interpolation (ReSynthesis)

This is just the beginning with reNOVAtor. Once you've used reNOVAtor to remove a portion of the spectrum, it replaces it with data resynthesis interpolated from surrounding audio. Figure 10.15 shows the parameters that affect how data is interpolated.

Figure 10.15

The ReSynthesis parameters of reNOVAtor affect data interpolation.

These parameters affect how interpolated audio is generated once the disturbance has been removed. The first option is the ReSynthesis type. There are eight types available, which determine what area around the processed portion is used for interpolating new data. Depending on the type of disturbance, certain interpolation types are more effective in each situation.

There are eight ReSynthesis types:

❈ *Horizontal (hor)*—Uses data to the left or right of the processed area to create interpolated data.

❈ *Vertical (vert)*—Uses data above or below the processed region for interpolation.

❈ *Left*—Only uses data to the left. If a disturbance is next to other important program material or transient information, interpolation should be taken from only one side.

❈ *Right*—Only uses data to the right.

❈ *Top*—Only uses data above the processed region.

❈ *Bottom*—Only uses data from below the processed region.

❈ *Two Dimensional (2-dim)*—Uses data from all around the processed region to reconstruct new data for the hole left by the disturbance. This is designed for replacing island-type of sounds, such as the birdcall.

❈ *Gain*—When using the simple gain type, the selected region is turned down by whatever the gain setting is under the ReSynthesis parameters.

The Accuracy option determines the time-domain precision used for interpolation. The higher the precision, the shorter the chunks of time used for interpolation and therefore the higher the resolution. Higher time domain resolution is not always the better option for good noise removal.

For smaller disturbances such as clicks and pops, a higher Accuracy setting works best. This also works in tandem with vertical interpolation, using data in the same time slice as the click. For longer sounds such as tones and buzzes, a lower accuracy works best in conjunction with horizontal interpolation, taking data from either side of the tone.

The Channel option determines which channels of the stereo audio file are processed and interpolated. You can choose to process all, which is the default.

The Gain setting only applies when the Type is set to gain. The selected area has this gain amount applied to it in a simple fashion. No interpolation is performed.

Spectrogram Controls

The 3D display of audio in reNOVAtor is known as a *spectrogram*. It analyzes blocks of audio to generate the color display. There are several parameters that affect this display, as shown in Figure 10.16.

Figure 10.16

The Spectrogram controls in reNOVAtor.

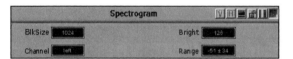

* *BlkSize (Block Size)*—This parameter influences how audio is processed by reNOVAtor. A small block size allows the spectrogram to be very accurate in the time domain but less so in the frequency domain. As the block size increases, the accuracy moves from the time to the frequency domains. Disturbances that are relatively short in duration benefit from shorter block sizes. Larger block sizes are more appropriate for isolated tones that have a longer duration but are more specific in terms of frequency. Changing the block size requires a complete recalculation of the spectrogram. Therefore, if you have a large file loaded, changing this can take a moment or two.

* *Channel*—The channel setting determines which channel is displayed in the spectrogram, left, right, or both (l+r).

* *Bright*—This is a cosmetic option only that determines the brightness of the selected region in the spectrogram. The default is slightly dimmer than the surrounding areas.

* *Range*—This control is slightly less intuitive at first glance. It determines the range of level that is displayed by the color spectrum of the spectrogram. In other words, you can control which parts of the dynamic range are visible as color. The left number is the center point of the display range. The right value, including the +/–, is the range around that center value. For a setting of –51 +/–34, the spectrogram displays a range of –85dB to –17dB. Anything below –85dB is black and anything above –17dB is white. This control really helps zero in on just the types of noises you want to isolate. When you click on this value, moving the mouse up or down changes the left (range center). Moving the mouse left or right alters the right (display range) value.

Examples

To illustrate how effective this tool is, here are a couple of examples of various noises that have been removed using reNOVAtor.

❋ *Footstep*—In Figure 10.17, the footstep spectrogram appears on the top. Using horizontal interpolation, the sound was replaced by similar data to the left, right resulting in the image on the bottom. The sound is very natural, containing ambience from the outdoor scene that this audio recording came from.

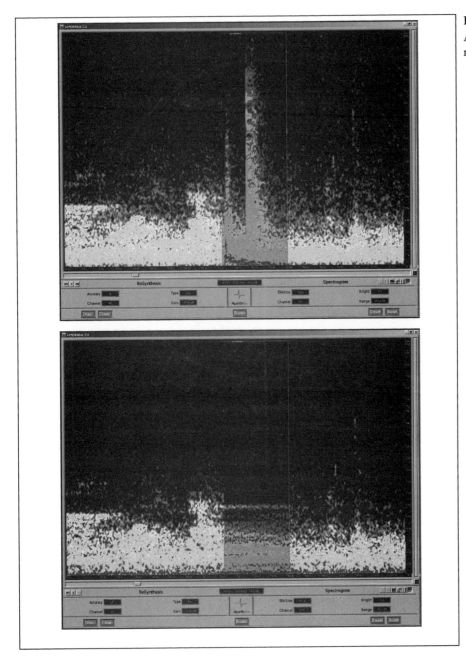

Figure 10.17

An outdoor footstep as removed by reNOVAtor.

✳ *Breath*—In this same scene, there was a breath just before a line of dialogue that was not appropriate. In Figure 10.18, left interpolation was used so that data from the dialogue line to the right would not be used to create replacement audio for the breath.

Figure 10.18

A breath removed just before a dialogue line in reNOVAtor.

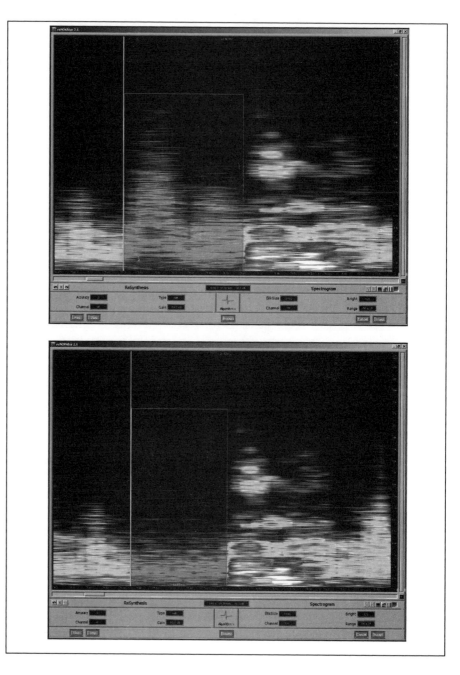

There are even more advanced options with reNOVAtor for expert operation, including harmonic identification and selective gain isolation. For those in need of sophisticated noise removal, reNOVAtor is an excellent tool. Algorithmix also offers easyNOVA, which has many of the same features at a much more affordable price.

Bias SoundSoap

Bias, the makers of the popular 2-track editor Peak, also created two versions of their restoration processing plug-in, SoundSoap. Each version uses similar processing algorithms but have different amounts of control and precision. SoundSoap 2 is the smaller, more affordable and less sophisticated plug-in, whereas SoundSoap Pro has complete features and controls.

SoundSoap 2

SoundSoap 2 offers a simple interface that contains all three basic types of noise removal—de-clicking, hum removal, and broadband noise reduction—as shown in Figure 10.19. The display and controls are simple in order to provide novice users with an effective tool that does not require extensive knowledge to operate.

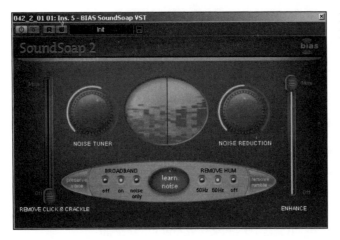

Figure 10.19
Bias's SoundSoap 2's simple GUI

SoundSoap 2 has a noise-curve learning function and noise tuner to zero in on areas of broadband noise. There is a vocal optimization algorithm used for retaining as much intelligibility as possible. The hum removal has both a 50Hz and 60Hz filter.

There is also a special enhance control that attempts to retain more clarity when heavy amounts of noise reduction are being used. Overall, the interface is intuitive and the results are decent. SoundSoap 2 is a consumer-level product that is simple and quick to use but lacks the in-depth controls that professional audio restoration requires.

SoundSoap Pro

SoundSoap Pro is an extended version of SoundSoap 2, with more controls and a better visual display. Each type of noise processing has its own GUI screen within SoundSoap Pro. Each screen is accessible via tabs found at the bottom of the interface, as shown in Figure 10.20.

There are four tabs in SoundSoap Pro, each for a different type of noise reduction:

* Hum & Rumble
* Click & Crackle
* Broadband
* Noise Gate

Figure 10.20

SoundSoap Pro's Hum & Rumble tab.

The first tab deals with hum and rumble removal. There are controls for frequency, Q, gain reduction, and harmonic content of hum, along with a low-frequency filter designed to remove rumble.

The second tab has controls for click and crackle removal. There is a click meter to indicate the presence of clicks and then two simple sliders for click and crackle thresholds.

The Broadband tab, shown in Figure 10.21, has the most complex GUI. There are several bands of noise reduction, each with a threshold and reduction control. These controls default to being grouped together but you can unlock them and adjust them individually. You can analyze the noise profiles to initially set the thresholds of each band. There are also Attack and Release controls for the expander action, with special tilt parameters that adjust the attack and release times between low- and high-frequency bands.

Figure 10.21
SoundSoap Pro's Broadband tab.

The Noise Gate tab has a simple gate with the standard parameters.

SoundSoap Pro offers users a quick and effective noise-reduction tool that is packaged in one easy-to-use plug-in interface. You can deal with all types of noise without having to switch between different plug-ins. You can hear the results of your entire restoration process in one step.

Summary

The area of audio restoration has seen many improvements, as demonstrated by the tools shown in this chapter. Psychoacoustic research opened up the possibilities for this type of processing dramatically as people have learned more about how human hearing perceives sound. Digital technology has allowed people to process audio outside the restrictions of the time domain for even more dramatic results in this regard.

11 } Surround Sound

Even though surround sound is really a speaker configuration and not part of the signal-processing chain, there are plug-ins that deal specifically with the issues that surround mixing creates. Concerning the speaker configuration, there are issues relating to calibration, speaker position, and bass management that can be handled by plug-in DSP. The ability to audition multi-channel mixes downmixed to stereo or even mono also falls into the plug-in department. DAWs such as Nuendo, which are designed to primarily deal with surround sound, also have key features centered on surround processing.

In addition, the various delivery formats of surround sound require encoding and decoding steps that can be performed by DSP. Dolby Laboratories is the leader in development and certification of many multi-channel audio delivery and playback systems. Its standards are used throughout the industry. For any information relating to surround sound, visit www.dolby.com for extensive articles and resources.

Surround Sound Primer

In order to understand how some of these plug-in are used in a surround environment, there are some basic principles that you should understand. Although there are many surround sound configurations, for the purposes of this book, the 5.1 standard provides the best example.

Speaker Configurations

5.1 surround is the most common form of surround mixing being done today. It's used in theatrical presentation, DVD releases, in HDTV broadcasts, and even game consoles, making it the most highly used configuration for surround sound. The basic equilateral triangle that is used for stereo mixing forms the basis for the 5.1 surround setup. Four additional speakers are added to the stereo pair: center, subwoofer, left surround, and right surround.

The Center Channel

The center channel is primarily used for dialogue. Its proximity to the center of the screen makes it the most appropriate location for dialogue. Also, people in the audience who might not be sitting towards the center of the room can still perceive sound coming from the center channel as being very closely tied to the center image onscreen. Be sure to place the center channel so that it is aligned with the center of the screen, as shown in Figure 11.1.

Figure 11.1

The center channel speaker should be aligned with the exact center of the viewing screen. If possible, all three speakers should be on the same horizontal plane, that is, level with each other.

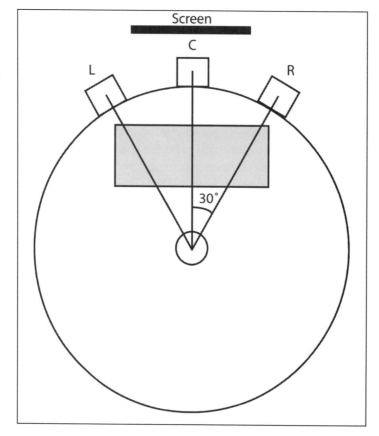

Sometimes, for practical considerations, the three front speakers cannot be on the same horizontal plane. In order to accommodate a convenient screen location, the center speaker will often be lowered so as not to be in front of the screen. When this is necessary, you must endeavor to keep the tweeters of all three speakers as aligned as possible. Figures 11.2 and 11.3 show two common alternatives for center channel placement when accommodating a large viewing screen.

Stereo creates a phantom center image by having equal volumes of a signal in both the left and right speakers (panned in the middle). In a large viewing room, audience members located off to one side of the room will perceive a shift in that phantom center image that will disassociate the dialogue from the images onscreen. The center channel speaker eliminates this problem. Only in very limited circumstances will you hear dialogue elements in either the left or the right speakers. These cases are primarily instances when a character enters from the extreme left or right of the film frame while talking.

Place the center channel speaker equidistant from the listener, the same as the two left and right speakers. This places the front three speakers on an arc in front of the listener, as shown in Figure 11.2.

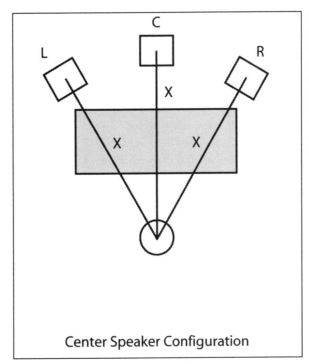

Figure 11.2

Placement of the center channel speaker. Notice that the distance from each speaker to the listener (X) is the same, placing all speakers on an arc in front of the mix position. This keeps all signals phase-coherent or arriving at the same time.

Center Speaker Configuration

❊ **MIX TIP: LARGE MIXING ROOM ISSUES**

In very large mixing rooms used for feature film mixing, the speakers are placed in a straight line at the screen. This correlates to the positioning of speakers in commercial theaters. Rooms with large dimensions that result in a distance of 18 feet or more from the mix position to the screen and the front speakers should use the theatrical positioning method for film mixing. In this scenario, sound from the center speaker arrives around 1ms earlier than the other speakers. This has the benefit of giving dialogue a time-based boost in clarity. Panning sounds between all three front speakers can result in unpredictable results in different theaters. It's better to use a more discrete approach to film mixing.

Smaller studios should follow the arc method for positioning, even when mixing for film. This book deals with the smaller mixing rooms that use the arc method.

Be sure to keep each speaker equidistant from the mix position. This keeps signals *phase-coherent* (they all arrive at the same time) from all speakers, allowing accurate level and pan information to reach the listener. If the center channel was to be placed forward of this position to accommodate a monitor or viewing screen, signals coming from it would arrive at your ears earlier than signals emanating from either the left or right speakers. When this happens, signals in the center channel are perceived as louder and closer to the listener. You have to adjust levels of the signals lower than they should be to compensate for this inaccurate perception. Phase coherence between all speakers in a surround sound setup is critical for accurate monitoring.

The viewing screen often becomes an obstacle for placement of a center channel speaker. There are several options that will for accurate monitoring while still giving space for a sizable viewing screen. You can tilt the center channel speaker on its side 90 degrees in order to lower it and move it out of the way, as illustrated in Figure 11.3. You can also invert the center channel speaker and place it over the viewing screen in some situations. When you use this placement, be sure to make every attempt to align the high-frequency drivers in each speaker in the same horizontal plane, as shown in Figure 11.4. This allows for a more seamless soundstage. Figure 11.5 shows the optimal position for the center channel speaker in the same horizontal plane as both left and right speakers.

Figure 11.3

Here, the center channel speaker has been placed on its side in order to lower it to accommodate the viewing screen. If possible, the left and right speakers should be lowered somewhat to maintain alignment with the high-frequency driver of the center channel speaker.

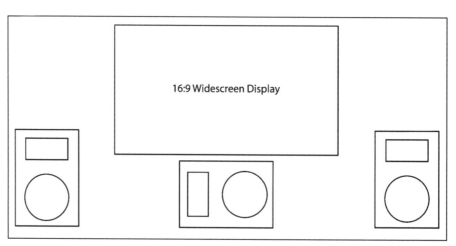

16:9 Widescreen Display

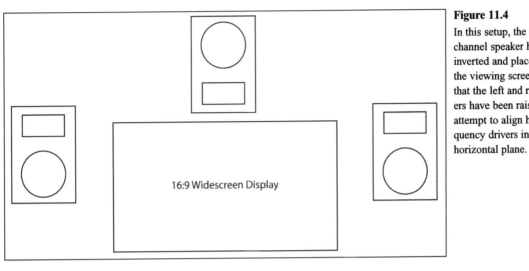

Figure 11.4
In this setup, the center channel speaker has been inverted and placed above the viewing screen. Notice that the left and right speakers have been raised in an attempt to align high-frequency drivers in the same horizontal plane.

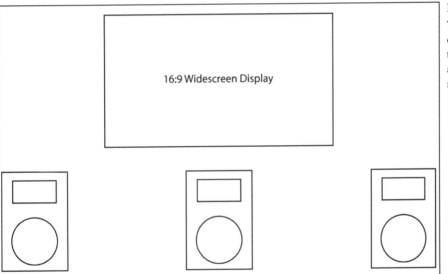

Figure 11.5
The optimal position for the center channel speaker is in the same horizontal plane as both the left and right speakers.

❋ PERFORATED SCREENS

It is possible to use a perforated screen and place all three speakers behind it. This requires a projection system and also has an effect on frequency response of the speakers, reducing higher frequencies. Commercial theaters use perforated screens with the speaker placed behind them. Additionally, the speakers are in a straight line and not in an equidistant arc. For film mixing, this can be a better setup. For music mixing, it is a poor compromise.

Surround Speakers

Surround speakers are intended to provide an immersive experience by creating a 360-degree sound field within which the listeners are placed. In order to provide such an encompassing sound field, these speakers must be placed behind the listeners. ITU-R specifications outline the position as 110 degrees off axis from the center channel speaker position and equidistant from the listener. Figure 11.6 shows the complete ITU-R surround configuration.

> ## ❄ DOLBY SURROUND VERSUS DOLBY DIGITAL OR 5.1
>
> The Dolby Laboratories reference material (found at www.dolby.com) suggests that surround speakers not be aimed directly at the listening position but rather at a point that is approximately two feet above that position and mounted higher than the front speakers if you're mixing material that is to be encoded in the Dolby Surround protocol. Dolby Surround differs from Dolby Digital and 5.1 in that there is only one surround channel. When you're mixing a Dolby Digital or 5.1 surround with two surround channels, Dolby's recommendations follow the ITU-R specifications.

Figure 11.6

The ITU-R specifications for 5.1 mixing environments. The geometry of placement of a 5.1 surround configuration has been specified in this setup.

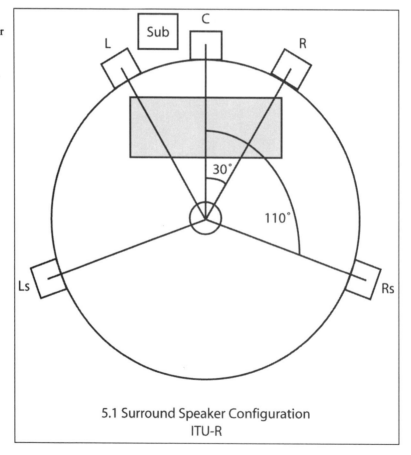

5.1 Surround Speaker Configuration
ITU-R

Recently, the position of the surround speakers has come into question by a number of experienced engineers working in 5.1. The new recommendations suggest that the surround speakers can be placed anywhere from 110 degrees all the way to 150 degrees away from center and be effective. The new optimal angle is 135 degrees. Figure 11.7 shows a 5.1 setup with these new guidelines.

These recommendations are focused on music mixing in 5.1 and reflect the need for more rear localization of sounds. The ITU-R speaker placement is better for film mixing where diffuse envelopment is required. The 135-degree angle represents an optimum compromise between the two. However, the rear speakers can be moved depending on the type of material you are mixing.

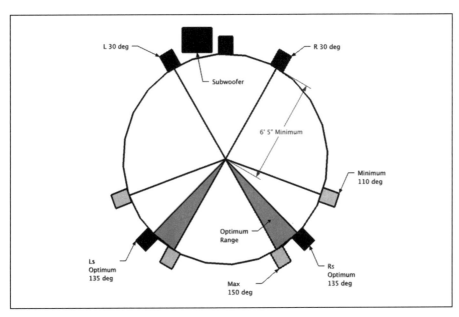

Figure 11.7
Current surround sound speaker placement recommendations for better rear localization needed in music mixing.

Subwoofer and Low-Frequency Effects (LFE) Channel

The subwoofer is perhaps the most difficult speaker to place properly in a mixing room. Because low-frequency information is not very directional in nature, the position of the subwoofer does not necessarily have to be in the center of the front speaker array. In fact, symmetrical placement of the subwoofer can cause poor room mode response. You should place the subwoofer based on the acoustics of the room in order to provide accurate frequency response from the subwoofer. The recommendation to place the subwoofer somewhere between the left and right front speakers, but not directly under the center channel.

Figure 11.7 shows the typical placement of the subwoofer—it's just off center and behind the front speaker array. A practical technique for placing the subwoofer is to initially place it at the mix position. Then, while you're playing program material that has a significant amount of low-frequency information, walk around the room until you find the most pleasant and accurate low-frequency sound. Place the subwoofer there. You'll get more accurate results if you do this using pink noise and a Real-Time Analyzer (RTA), such as Elemental Audio's Inspector plug-in.

Now, when you're sitting at the mix position, you should hear the same type of response. Subwoofers excite the low-frequency room modes. Unless acoustic treatment has been applied professionally, there will always be some anomalies in the low-end response of any small mixing room. Placing the subwoofer a great distance away from the other speakers can cause some phase problems with signals that are sent to both the LFE channel and another speaker in the array. Even changes in subwoofer placement of a foot or so can dramatically affect the response of the system. Try lots of positions until you find one that is most acoustically satisfying.

BASS MANAGEMENT AND SUBWOOFER POSITION

Before you determine the position of your subwoofer, refer to the bass management section later in this chapter. Bass management can affect the relative level between the subwoofer and the other speakers. Your system needs to be properly set up before you can accurately determine the bass response of your subwoofer's position.

Surround Panning

Stereo panning is quite simple, involving only two channels. Surround panning becomes exponentially more complex in both technical and creative terms. Balancing a signal within five or even seven various output channels creates unique issues. Creatively deciding what to do with all of this can be overwhelming.

The Joystick Control

The typical surround panner appears as a sort of joystick that roughly indicates the position of the source within the surround sound field. Figure 11.8 shows the Nuendo surround panner with a position behind and to the right of the listener. This is only a rough approximation of the perceived localization of the sound. The panner determines the proportion of signal level in each speaker that should yield this perception.

In a normal surround panner, when a signal is positioned entirely to one speaker location, only that speaker channel has any signal level being fed to it. The source should be perceived as emanating from that speaker only, as shown in Figure 11.9. There are, however, many other ways to localize sources. Also, sources do not have to be in one speaker at a time.

Figure 11.8
The Nuendo surround panner positioning a source behind and to the right of the listener.

Figure 11.9
A source placed discretely in one speaker channel.

Divergence

In addition to this joystick control, there are a couple of other settings that affect the positioning of the sound. These extra settings affect what is known as *divergence* in the surround field. With maximum divergence, sources have more localization between speakers. With less divergence, the source is heard through more speaker channels and have less discrete localization.

For instance, in film sound, dialogue is most often placed in the front center of the overall sound field through the center channel only. The center channel in a 5.1 setup for film is primarily dedicated to dialogue. However, the use of the left and right channel speakers can also place a sound virtually in the center position by having equal amounts in each channel, often referred to as the *phantom* center image. A sound that is panned to the front center of a surround speaker array can be in all three front speakers and still be heard as coming from the center. The less divergence there is, the more sound there is coming from other speakers. Figure 11.10 shows a signal panned to the center with no divergence between all speakers.

Figure 11.10

A source panned to the center with no divergence. Nuendo indicates full divergence as 0% and no divergence as 100%.

❄ **MIX TIP: CENTER PERCENTAGE VERSUS DIVERGENCE**

With the center channel, divergence controls are often called center percentage. When a source is panned to the center, the center percentage determines how much of the image is created by the center channel and how much is created by the phantom image of the left and right speakers.

A sound coming directly from one speaker and no others has 100% divergence, whereas a sound that is emanating from all speakers equally has 0% divergence. What divergence adds is a sense of width to the sound. Even though the sound is still coming from one direction, there is a sense of envelopment with a less divergence. You control divergence depending on the DAW and the plug-in.

Phantom Center versus Center Channel

One important type of divergence control affects how the center image is constructed. A source can be localized in the center in two ways:

❄ Equal volume in both the left and right speakers (phantom center)

❄ Volume in the center channel only

The proportion of phantom center image and center channel is a critical form of divergence. There are different issues for film mixing and music mixing in surround and one of those key issues involves the use of the center channel.

❄ For film mixing, the center channel is critical and used for a majority of sound, including dialogue and foley. The rest of the speaker channels are used mostly for music and effects. The idea is that the center channel ties the viewer to the screen. Events onscreen should primarily come from the center channel. The other channels provide envelopment for the viewer, but can be distracting when overused.

❄ In music mixing for surround, simply placing the lead vocal or instrument in the center channel has mixed outcomes. On one hand, it does provide a very solid anchor for prominent instruments and voices within a song. On the other hand, if certain signals are present in only the center channel, various configurations of home listening systems can widely affect the musical balance. The center channel in music is often used for reinforcement of the center image and not discrete signals.

The LFE Channel and Bass Management

The LFE channel in a 5.1 surround system (that's the .1) is dedicated to the low-frequency effects channel. In theaters and home playback systems, this channel is lo-pass filtered at 120Hz and played back +10dB louder than the other five channels. The reason for this gain is to provide headroom and punch for high-energy low-frequency effects, such as earthquake sounds and spaceship engines.

Many re-recording mixers (the folks who mix movies) refer to it as the "boom" or "rumble" channel. It is intended to provide more of an extended sensory experience rather than adding detailed low end to a mix. It is used sparingly in most situations in order to maintain the shock value that subwoofers can have on an audience.

For music mixing, the LFE channel is problematic in the sense that the choice to use it depends on the mix engineer and the final consumer playback system. There is really no standard practice for using the LFE in music mixing. The most obvious choice is the kick drum and bass parts in popular music. However, many consumer playback systems use the subwoofer for the LFE channel and low-frequency augmentation of the rest of the speakers in the system. This is called *bass management*.

Typical home theater systems use a set of smaller full-range speakers for the left, center, right, left surround, and right surround channels. These smaller speakers reproduce the sounds of dialogue and most effect sounds without difficulty, but when it comes to very loud low-frequency sounds (such as those often found in action films and sci-fi films, as well as full-range pop and orchestral music), they simply are not big enough for the task.

Figure 11.11

A typical home theater system with small satellite speakers and subwoofer. The system uses bass management to get full-range response from each speaker channel.

Bass-management systems are employed to direct much of the low-frequency information coming from the five main channels into the dedicated subwoofer. Because most directional cues human hearing uses are based in the middle and higher frequencies, having the low-frequency content of all five channels coming out of one subwoofer does not affect the imaging of the rest of the speakers. Sound becomes less directional to the human ear at lower frequencies. At some point, perhaps around 100Hz and below, it is not possible to localize sounds. So, having all the low frequencies from all five channels coming through the subwoofer does not disrupt the panorama of sound.

Surround panners have a dedicated control for the LFE channel, as seen in Figure 11.12. This give you maximum control over which signals are sent to the dedicated LFE subwoofer in theater systems. Remember that, with consumer systems, it is not necessary to send every low-frequency sound to the LFE in order to get full frequency response because bass management will usually be employed to extend the low-end response of smaller systems.

Figure 11.12
The LFE control in this surround panner has been turned up. This is in addition to the source already panned within the five speaker array.

Understanding Surround Panners

Surround panning is more complex than simple stereo and requires a more sophisticated interface to operate. DAW designers and plug-in developers have created various versions of the surround panner that usually involve a "joystick" type of control to position sources within the two-dimensional sound field. Divergence offers more choices than simple joystick placement and comes into play in each type of panner. Also, more sophisticated DSP can be implemented to create room reflections that aid in depth perception in the surround field. Each panner has benefits in various applications. The panners used in Nuendo, Pro Tools, and Waves all have unique features that are representative of typical surround panner operation.

Nuendo's Surround Panning

Having been designed from the ground up as a surround sound DAW, Nuendo has a very simple, yet powerful surround-panning tool. The surround panner has three modes: standard, position, and angle. Each mode offers another way to adjust the source localization. The standard and position modes function in a manner suited to cinema mixing, whereby the front three speakers are not equidistant from the mix position. This allows you to move the sources between the speakers without level reduction.

In angle mode, the speakers are all the same distance from the listener. Moving a source between them requires level reduction to be smooth and even. This mode applies more to smaller mixing rooms that are tailored to home theater and music mixing rather than full-scale theatrical film mixing. The panners themselves can be used in either situation but operate based on the idea of speaker placement.

Standard Panner

Nuendo's standard surround panner, shown in Figure 11.13, has a standard joystick control along with several divergence settings and a dedicated LFE level. The display shows the position of the source along with readouts of the gain applied to each speaker channel. This level is also represented by energy rays in blue coming from each speaker proportional to the gain of each channel. The dotted box is a visual indication of divergence settings.

The Center percentage determines the balance between phantom center and the actual center channel that's used for signals panned to the front center position. In Figure 11.13, the Center percentage is 100%, so signals panned to the center are only be heard in the center channel, not the left-right pair. As the percentage is turned down, more signal is fed to the left-right pair to create a phantom center image.

Figure 11.13
The Nuendo standard surround panner.

Front divergence determines how far a sound can be panned to the left or right. In Nuendo, as the divergence percentage increases, signals panned to one side or the other are heard more in both speakers. At 100%, left or right panning has no effect. The source remains in the phantom center.

The Rear divergence has a similar effect. As the percentage increases, signals panned to the rear begin to emanate from both rear speakers. At 100%, signals panned to the rear are heard equally in both rear speakers.

The F/R divergence controls the spread of signals between the front and rear speaker pairs. As the control is increased, there is less difference between signals panned to the front and to the rear. At 100%, signals are equally fed to both front and rear pairs.

The Mono/Stereo options determine how stereo pairs are dealt with. There are four possible modes.

* *Mono*—The left and right signals are panned to the same location; in essence, this mixes the signals together and moves them as a signal source.

* *Y-Mirror*—The left and right signals are panned symmetrically around the Y-axis, as shown in Figure 11.14. One signal is on the left side and the other is on the right side. This mode is used to place a stereo signal in proper position within a surround configuration.

Figure 11.14

The Nuendo surround panner in Y-Mirror stereo mode.

* *X-Mirror*—The left and right signals are panned symmetrically around the X-axis; one signal to the front pair and the other to the rear pair.

* *XY-Mirror*—The left and right signals are equidistant from the midpoint of the panner in opposite directions. Figure 11.15 shows the XY-Mirror mode with the left channel to the front and left and the right channel opposite (to the rear and right).

Figure 11.15
The Nuendo surround panner in XY-Mirror mode.

Position Panner

The Position Panner deals with localization slightly differently than the standard mode. The source has a discrete position and a radiation pattern determined by the attenuation control.

In order to control divergence, the attenuate and normalize controls work together to create localization of sources. With less attenuation, sources appear in more speakers, which spreads the sound around all channels. With more attenuation, the source is positioned more discretely in one place.

The concentric circles shown in Figure 11.16 display how the source's volume spreads over the sound field. Each line represents a drop of 3dB in the perceived level as you move away from the source. The attenuation control widens or shortens these circles.

Figure 11.16
Nuendo's position panner with attenuation control.

Normalization controls the overall loudness in all speakers. With Normalization set to 1.0, the combined volume of all the speakers is 0dB. Turning the Normalization down allows the total of all speaker channels to exceed 0dB.

Angle

The Angle mode assumes that all speakers are equidistant from the listener and adjusts various speaker levels accordingly. The same Attenuation and Normalize controls work here as well. The graphic display, shown in Figure 11.17, shows a circle with the various speakers and an arc depicting the source and its overall width.

Figure 11.17

The Nuendo angle panner with arc display of divergence.

The Angle panner is designed for small room mixing whereby the speakers are arranged in ITU-R standard and at the same distance from the mix position. Level attenuation must happen when panning sources across the front speakers.

Pro Tools Surround Panning

The Pro Tools surround panner shown in Figure 11.18 has the same basic controls as Nuendo but uses three modes of operation.

Figure 11.18

The Pro Tools surround panner.

- ✳ *X/Y*—In this mode, the Pro Tools panner acts much like the Nuendo panner in standard mode. You can move the sound source freely throughout the entire sound field.

- ✳ *Divergence Editing*—In this mode, you can graphically edit and automate the divergence settings.

- ✳ *3 Knob*—In this mode, you can perform discrete panning from diagonally opposed positions without bleeding into other channels. In other words, you can pan a signal from the rear right speaker to the front left without bleeding into the other channels as the signal moves through the center. The sound is heard only in those two channels at any time. This mode allows the angle of this trajectory to be modified.

There is also the unique Auto-Glide function that allows a timed movement between two pan locations. The glide time is set as a preference and then when in glide mode, clicking anywhere in the surround field causes the pan position to "glide" to that spot in the given amount of glide time. This can help create smooth panning moves across the sound field. Auto-Glide moves can be retained in automation.

Waves S360 Panner and Imager
Waves created a pair of surround panning tools that have some unique functionality that ties in with the other plug-ins in their Surround series. The S360 has two versions.

- ✳ *S360 Panner*—This panner is set up for ITU-R standards. It uses a center percentage control to deal with center versus phantom image ratios. The Rotation control determines where in degrees the source emanates from. You can position sources with pairs of speakers or three channels if needed. Width controls the amount of divergence among all the speakers.

- ✳ *S360 Imager*—The Imager, shown in Figure 11.19, has the same controls as the panner, with the addition of early reflection controls to help create the illusion of distance in the surround field. The source can be pulled closer or farther from the listening position, which affects the level and makeup of the early reflections.

Figure 11.19

The Waves S360 Imager with early reflection controls.

Each speaker in the panner can be soloed to isolate signals in that speaker and also to avoid certain speaker channels by soloing all but one speaker. For example, the musical score in a film usually is not heard in the center channel. On the surround panner for the music stem, all channels except the center can be soloed to avoid routing music to the center channel.

Creating the Surround Mix Environment

Adding four speakers to your studio makes things a bit more complicated. The inclusion of a subwoofer and various forms of bass management add to this complexity. Mixing material destined for the theater, DVD, or television broadcast requires the use of various standards to ensure compatibility with other material in the medium. All of these factors add up to the need for precise setup and calibration of your surround speaker system.

Armed with several tools, including some plug-ins, you can accurately set up and tune your speaker system to provide excellent results for mixing in surround. The basic tools you need are an SPL meter (the Radio Shack one works just fine), a signal tone generator capable of creating high-quality pink noise, and a routing matrix or plug-in that has discrete controls for each channel of your speaker system. The Waves 360 Manager is a good example of this. You must be able to control the level, phase, and timing of each channel in order to create an accurate surround system.

Speaker Calibration

When mixing for film or television, the level at which you monitor can drastically affect the outcome of your mix. Theaters have calibrated playback systems that are designed to reproduce a wide frequency range. The levels you generate during your mix session should be faithfully reproduced in theaters due to this calibration. If your mixing system is not calibrated to the same reference points, there is no way of telling how it will reproduce in the theater. Similarly, television requires a slightly different reference point due the nature of home viewing. Listening levels in the home are lower than those in the theater. As such, you should calibrate your mixing system to this lower volume in order to create a mix that will translate well into the home listening environment.

Calibration of the playback system involves pink noise that can be generated by the Signal Generator plug-in in Pro Tools or the TestGenerator plug-in in Nuendo. You can also use a prerecorded signal tone. You need an SPL meter such as the one pictured in Figure 11.20.

A pink noise signal is generated at −20dBFS, which represents the reference operating level of your system and the standard digital reference level in the industry. You calibrate this signal to a specific volume in the mix room so that it will correlate to the same volume when the material is reproduced later. The SPL meter measures the acoustic output of each speaker channel in order adjust the gain stage in the monitor chain to the correct volume in the room.

There have been some issues with the way that Digidesign's *Signal Generator* plug-in creates pink noise. The accuracy has been called into question. The key to proper calibration of your studio starts with proper test tones. A highly respected collection of test tones developed by Tomlinson Holman (creator of the THX system), including a tutorial for its use, is available for a modest investment. Also, Bob Katz has a true stereo pink noise signal in WAV format available from his Web site at: www.digido.com in the Downloads section. You can accomplish most basic calibrations using just the Radio Shack SPL meter. An octave band real-time analyzer (RTA) is preferable, especially for low-frequency calibration, but is not necessary in all situations.

Figure 11.20

The Radio Shack SPL meter. This commonly found and relatively inexpensive SPL meter can be used to accurately calibrate your surround speaker system. This one is setup for C weighting, with a slow response. Any recording studio should own one.

Film Style Mixing

Film style mixing requires a slightly different calibration than when you're mixing for television or home theater applications. All calibration tests use the pink noise signal at –20dBFS. Here are the steps:

1. Create the test signal by using a signal generator such as the one in Pro Tools shown in Figure 11.21. Create a tone that is 5–10 seconds long that you can loop for continuous playback. Or, you can use test tones from a reference CD such as Tomlinson Holman's TMH Digital Audio Test and Measurement Disc Series (available from www.HollywoodEdge.com) or Bob Katz's pink noise file (at www.digido.com).

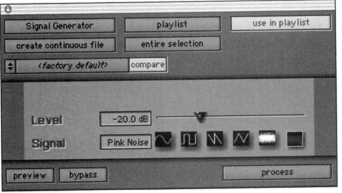

Figure 11.21

Pro Tools's Signal Generator setup to create a pink noise signal at –20dBFS. Make this signal 5–10 seconds long in order to loop it for continuous playback.

2. Route that track to the first speaker channel you want to calibrate. In this example, you start with the center channel. Simply assign the track directly to the center channel's output. Figure 11.22 shows the routing of the test track to the center channel directly in Pro Tools.

Figure 11.22

Routing of the test track to the center channel speaker only. Each speaker is tested independently.

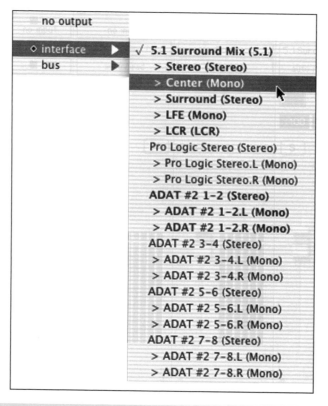

3. Set loop playback mode to play the test signal repeatedly. Press Play.

4. Place the SPL meter right at the mix position at head level. If you're holding the meter in your hand, keep it at arm's length distance to avoid coloration from sound reflected off of your body. Also, hold the meter at an upward angle of roughly 45 degrees. Use this meter position to calibrate all the speakers. If possible, use a microphone stand to hold the SPL meter.

5. Using the SPL meter setup for C weighting and slow response (see Figure 11.20), adjust your monitor level until you get a reading of 85dBC (the C stands for C weighting of the meter).

ROUTING STEREO TEST SIGNALS TO MONO

Be careful when you route the test signal to a mono speaker channel that the left and right channels are not combined to create a higher signal level (+3dB). Otherwise, your calibration will not be correct. Make sure the actual speaker channel's output is −20dBFS RMS using a quality meter plug-in such as Elemental's Inspector XL.

6. Repeat this for both left and right speakers. All front three speakers are calibrated to the same level.

7. When calibrating the surround speakers, set the individual monitor volume to get a reading of 82dBC. With film mixing, the surround speakers are set at a slightly lower volume (–3dB). If you are holding the meter in your hand, turn your back 90 degrees towards the speaker you are calibrating so as to avoid obscuring the sound with your body. Aim the meter at the wall closest to the surround speaker you are calibrating.

8. LFE level adjustment is more complex. To properly calibrate the volume of the LFE channel, it's best to have a real-time analyzer. However, a simple SPL meter can work in a pinch. For film mixing, the LFE channel will play back 10dB louder than any of the front three speakers at the same input level. The reason for this is so that the LFE channel has more headroom for low-frequency sounds such as explosions. Signals sent to the subwoofer should be band-limited from 25 to 120 Hz. When using a simple SPL meter, it should read about 89dBC when feeding pink noise at an RMS level of –20dBFS. Due to the C weighting of the SPL meter and the limited bandwidth of the subwoofer, this level will not quite reach the 10dB increase specified. It is an approximation and can be more accurately determined with a real-time analyzer (RTA).

✳ ADJUSTING VOLUME

When calibrating reference levels for any speaker, make the adjustments so as not to affect the level of a channel in the mix bus. Otherwise, if you make playback monitor calibration adjustments within the DAW, you will be calibrating your recording levels to your speakers and not your speakers to a reference recording level. Doing this would throw away the benefits of calibration: the accurate reproduction of your mix on other calibrated playback systems. Make the level adjustment outside of the mixing environment. Using the volume knobs on your power amps to adjust the monitor level is a very effective way of adjusting the volume and also maintaining the highest degree of signal-to-noise ratio in the playback system.

Nuendo has a Control Room mixer in which you can use metering, bass management, and calibration plug-ins without interfering with the mix bus itself.

If you use bass management and speaker calibration tools in the mix path, be sure to disable them when exporting or recording the final mix.

TV and Home Theater Applications

When mixing material for television, each speaker, including the surrounds, is calibrated to a reference level of 79dBC. This is due to the lower average listening level used by consumers. Referencing at this lower level will provide a better dialogue mix for in-home viewing. The subwoofer should be calibrated 10dB higher, just the same as in theatrical mixing.

SURROUNDS IN A SMALL ROOM

It should be noted that when you are mixing in a very small room where the surround speakers are fewer than six feet away, they should be turned down 2dB to compensate for their proximity to the mix position. This method has proven to be very effective when mixing on location in a remote truck, where space is definitely limited.

This is not the same thing as the film-mixing standard of –3dB for surrounds, because that is a part of the theater calibration system. Normal calibration for television should have the surrounds at the same volume as the front speakers, 79dBC.

Bass Management Setup

The reason bass management systems are needed is because many consumer systems use five small satellite speakers combined with a subwoofer to supplement the low-frequency response of the system *and* act as the LFE channel. The low-frequency information for each of the five satellite speakers is redirected by the bass management system to the subwoofer. Because low-frequency sounds are less directional, the spatial image does not suffer dramatically.

The amount and crossover frequency at which this redirection of low-end occurs is fairly standard among consumer playback systems. Typically, the crossover frequency is 80Hz, meaning that frequencies below 80Hz in any channel are diverted to the subwoofer.

THEATRICAL SOUND SYSTEMS

Sound systems in movie theaters do not have or use bass management. The front three speakers are full-range and can handle deep bass. The surround speakers are full-range as well, but they typically are not as powerful. The subwoofers in theaters reproduce signals only from the LFE channel. No signals from any other channels come through the subwoofer. Consumer systems use bass management for economic and aesthetic reasons, not sonic integrity. 5.1 surround is best heard with five full-range speakers and a dedicated LFE subwoofer.

Bass management can also be used to enhance the performance of smaller speakers used in the studio. Many times, studios will purchase surround and center speakers that are smaller than the main left and right ones and thus are ill equipped to handle lower frequencies. This is usually due to budgetary considerations, because the cost of a full range 5.1 surround speaker system can be formidable. Bass management can compensate for the low-frequency response of the smaller speakers by redirecting the low end to the subwoofer channel. If you must use some smaller speakers in your system, make them the surrounds, and try to keep the Left, Center, and Right speakers matched in response and size.

In addition to this low-frequency content from the five satellite speakers, the subwoofer must also reproduce the signals for the LFE channel. For film mixing, the LFE channel must be regarded as a separate entity from the low-frequency content of the bass management signal. Even though these two signals are reproduced by one subwoofer, they must be treated independently, as two discrete sources.

The way this is done is through the use of a bass management system while you are mixing. Waves offers the 360 degree Surround Toolkit, which, among many tools, has a bass management plug-in that can be used on the master fader to assist in calibrating your system with bass management. There are other software and hardware solutions for bass management, but the Waves plug-in is used here as a common example.

Because bass management is basically acting as a home theater emulation system, it should be used as the last item in your DAW signal path. Consider it a part of your speaker system. And, because you never record the mix by mic'ing the speakers themselves, you must *disable* any bass management before you record your mix. Recording with bass management *on* will yield unpredictable results based solely on your mixing environment and not the real world.

❄ **DISABLE BASS MANAGEMENT WHEN PRINTING FINAL MIXES!**

All bass management does is calibrate your speakers so they react like a home theater system. It does not encode or decode any Dolby or other surround information. *Be sure to disable it when printing your mix to tape or disk!*

Calibration of Bass Management

Using the Waves M360 plug-in shown in Figure 11.23, you can calibrate the bass management system using a process similar to the one outlined earlier in this chapter, with certain exceptions. The Waves M360 plug-in has the capability to divide each speaker channel into frequency bands and divert the low-frequency band to the subwoofer. The amount of signal that goes to the "Sub" channel can be varied independently for each channel. The crossover frequency and slope of the filter used to divide the signals is also adjustable. The LFE or ".1" channel of 5.1 surround mix is dealt with separately from this bass management redirected signal. The result is that the subwoofer *acts* as the low-frequency driver for each speaker in the system in addition to providing discrete LFE signals.

Here's how to set up the Waves M360 plug-in after inserting it on your master surround output:

1. Set the crossover frequency to 80 Hz. This is also the default setting. The default setting for the slope of this crossover filter is set to 24dB/octave for the subwoofer channel and 12dB/octave for all satellite channels, as shown in Figure 11.23. This setting should be fine for most situations. If your satellite speakers are particularly small, you might have to use a higher crossover frequency so that all of the low end that is missing from the satellites is present in the subwoofer. Experiment to find the best setting for your speakers.

2. Engage the high- and low-pass filters on every channel by using the All button (the double-headed arrow button), as shown in Figure 11.23.

Figure 11.23

The pointer is over the "All" button. This button engages all the high- and low-pass filters, thereby directing all low-frequency energy to the subwoofer. For custom setups, you can filter individual channels without affecting the others. This can be helpful when you have one pair of speakers that are full range and several others that require bass enhancement.

3. Route pink noise at –20dBFS to all speaker channels using a signal generator plug-in or recorded audio signal in the DAW.

4. Using the solo buttons on each satellite channel, proceed with the calibration setup as outlined earlier in this chapter. There are some additions and changes to the procedure that relate specifically to the subwoofer channel.

5. When you've calibrated the volume for all five of the satellite speakers to 85dBC, mute every one except the center channel, as shown in Figure 11.24.

CALIBRATE ONE SPEAKER AT A TIME

Remember when you're calibrating, you should hear only one speaker at a time. If you hear more than one speaker, your meter reading will be inaccurate. The Waves plug-in provides convenient Mute and Solo switches to help with this process.

Figure 11.24
Mute buttons are engaged on every satellite channel accept the center channel, where the cursor hand is pointing.

6. Solo the Sub channel, as shown in Figure 11.25. Make sure you don't accidentally solo the LFE channel instead. Remember, the Sub channel and the LFE channel are two distinct *signals*, even though they're both reproduced by the subwoofer *speaker*.

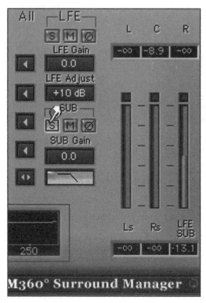

Figure 11.25
Solo the Sub channel, not the LFE channel, which is pictured above the Sub. With all but one satellite speaker muted, the Sub channel will contain only the low-end content from the unmuted satellite speaker. The Sub channel should be calibrated 6dB less than the satellite speaker. Usually, this is 79dBC.

7. With only one satellite speaker unmuted, adjust the Send To Sub control, shown in Figure 11.25, to get a meter reading 6dB lower than its corresponding satellite channel (79dBC if using 85dBC as reference). The 6dB difference is due to the fact that the Sub channel contains less frequency bands and is therefore not as loud.

8. Repeat this Sub channel calibration process for each satellite speaker.

9. Next, mute the Sub channel and all satellite channels.

10. Solo the LFE channel and set the LFE Adjust to +10dB. This adjusts the LFE channel for film mixing, which is 10dB louder than the other speakers.

11. Using the LFE Gain adjustment, shown in Figure 11.26, calibrate level to somewhere between 89 and 92dBC. Again, the SPL meter will not be as accurate as a RTA when calibrating just the low-frequency subwoofer. Some experimentation might be necessary.

Figure 11.26
With the LFE adjust set to + 10dB, use the LFE Gain adjustment to fine-tune the calibration for a SPL meter reading of somewhere between 89 and 92dBC. Make sure to use the slow mode on the SPL meter, because it will swing back and forth when registering low-frequency signals. Use the middle point of the swing as your true reading.

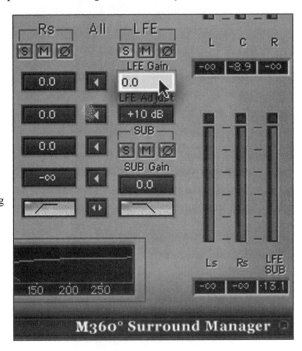

12. Turn off the pink noise generator and un-mute every channel. You should be ready to go.

Voxengo's BMS

Voxengo's BMS provides a simple bass management system in a VST plug-in with some unique features. It can extract low-end information from satellite speakers and redirect it to the subwoofer independently from the LFE channel. This low-end information can be removed from the satellites, left in the satellites, or even auditioned by itself for analysis purposes. BMS, shown in Figure 11.27, is very frugal on DSP resources and can handle channel configurations up to 7.1 surround. Although it lacks some of the sophisticated features of the Waves M360, it accomplishes the task of bass management readily with a minimum of resources.

Figure 11.27
Voxengo's BMS plug-in.

Nuendo's Control Room Mixer

Nuendo offers a unique tool for surround sound mixing: the Control Room Mixer. The Control Room Mixer is a dedicated set of inputs and outputs within Nuendo used specifically for speaker systems and external inputs. You can directly connect various speaker systems to hardware outputs of a Nuendo system and have the software control the speaker volume and routing just like the monitor section of a traditional analog console.

The advantage of the virtual Control Room is the ability to use DSP and plug-ins as part of the monitoring chain. This can facilitate a number of processes, including:

✸ Bass management plug-ins and other speaker calibration tools can be inserted on speaker channels and have no effect on the Main Mix Bus of the DAW.

✸ Various speaker configurations can be auditioned with automatic downmixing between multi-channel formats. For instance, a 5.1 surround mix can be automatically downmixed to stereo when a stereo set of speakers is selected.

✸ Metering of the main mix and soloed channels can be located within the Control Room Mixer.

✸ A calibrated mixing level can be programmed into the mixer strip so that you can quickly set a reference playback level.

✸ **GRAMMY RECORDING ACADEMY RECOMMENDATIONS FOR SURROUND**

For extensive information about surround sound and recommendations from some of the top engineers in the business, please visit:

http://www.grammy.com/pe_wing/guidelines/index.aspx

This valuable site contains information about mixing, speaker calibration, delivery formats, and even Pro Tools session interchange guidelines.

Multi-Channel Encoding and Decoding

In the world of consumer multi-channel playback systems, there are several methods for audio delivery. The DVD has a limited amount of space, which must be allocated between video and audio data. The space limitations have forced manufacturers to create data compression schemes in order to fit multi-channel audio on the DVD.

The emergence of High Definition (HD) broadcasting via satellite, cable, and traditional systems has led to further creation of compressed audio standards. One major concern with these audio standards is backward compatibility with older stereo systems. Many of the broadcast standards are still evolving but there are some systems that have established themselves as standards and others that are emerging as technology advances.

Dolby Stereo (Lt, Rt)

The oldest and most basic surround sound encoding method is known as Dolby Stereo. Dolby Stereo is an analog encoding method that is compatible with all kinds of stereo broadcast and playback systems. Dolby Stereo was invented for the film industry as a way of encoding four channels of audio into the stereo optical tracks used in film prints. The four audio channels are left, center, right, and mono surround. The Dolby Pro Logic home systems use this decoding technique.

The technique involves altering the phase of the surround channel and mixing it directly into the stereo signal. Decoding involves identifying the phase-altered material and extracting it to a discrete rear surround channel. The center channel is derived from all material that is at equal levels in both the left and right channels. When encoded, the channels are labeled Left Total (Lt) and Right Total (Rt).

This type of encoding is relatively simple and can be done with external hardware from Dolby or with a plug-in such as Nuendo's MatrixEncoder shown in Figure 11.28. The encoding is standardized so no options are available. In order to properly mix using Dolby Stereo, you must encode and then decode the signal to hear the results of the process itself. If not, you will not be sure of the outcome when heard on consumer playback systems.

Figure 11.28

Nuendo's MatrixEncoder capable of encoding Dolby Stereo signals.

❊ **MIX TIP: ALWAYS CHECK DOLBY STEREO DECODING**

An interesting phenomenon of the Dolby Stereo decoding is that normal signals not intended to be in the surround channel will get decoded that way anyhow. Any information found in certain mid-band frequencies that is out of phase can be decoded by Pro Logic and other systems to come out of the surround speakers. Often, music mixes can have significant information that will decode incorrectly. Always check your mixes using a Dolby Stereo decoder to know how they will translate. This is especially true for music that will be used in a film production where Dolby Stereo decoding is almost assured at some point.

Dolby Pro Logic II

Dolby Pro Logic II is an updated stereo encoding technique that is backward-compatible with previous Pro Logic systems. It allows the encoding of a 5.1 mix into a stereo Lt/Rt signal that can be used in any stereo-delivery format, including broadcast. Pro Logic II is a very popular encoding method for game consoles, because it does not require any more data space to deliver a complete surround sound experience for the gamer.

Minnetonka Audio Software makes SurCode, a complete set of surround sound encoding tools that includes a Pro Logic II encoder, shown in Figure 11.29. This is not a plug-in but a standalone application that can process five input channels into the composite Lt/Rt stereo output file.

Figure 11.29

Minnetonka's SurCode Pro Logic II encoder.

Dolby Digital

Originally developed for film audio, Dolby Digital has become widely adapted for home viewing and even broadcast use for encoding 5.1 audio into a smaller data stream. Also known as AC3, Dolby Digital does not use analog encoding methods and, as such, each channel is discrete, having no crosstalk with other channels. AC3 also has provisions for downmixing of the 5.1 content into stereo for listening on stereo playback systems.

Nerrynick's SoundCode for Pro Tools

Nerrynick's SoundCode is a plug-in tool for Pro Tools that encodes AC3 files as an Audiosuite plug-in and decodes AC3 files in real-time. The real-time decoding allows the user to preview the results of encoding right away without having to export the mix to a consumer system. Also, downmix functionality is built in to preview the results of automatic downmixing that consumer systems are capable of.

SurCode

Minnetonka's SurCode has a Dolby Digital encoder that runs as a standalone application. SurCode has the ability to adjust all the encoding options for Dolby Digital, as shown in Figure 11.30. These options help the decoder properly deliver the mix as faithfully as possible on various playback systems.

Figure 11.30

Minnetonka's SurCode Dolby Digital encoder options and advanced options.

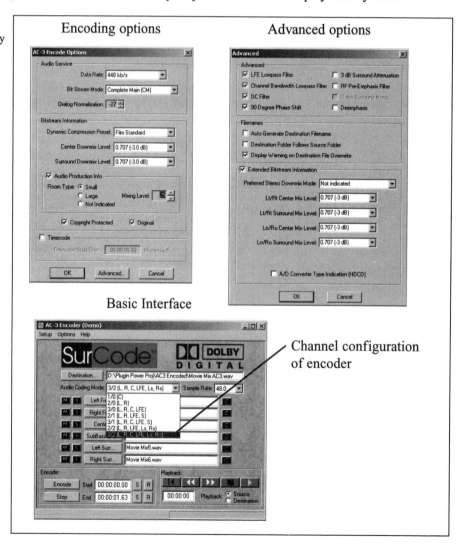

✳ *Audio Coding Mode*—This determines the amount and channel configuration of the encoded bitstream. AC3 is capable of encoding 1–5 channels. The Audio Coding Mode is found in the main interface shown in Figure 11.30.

✳ *Data Rate*—Affords many different rates, depending on the needs of the delivery format. 448kBps is the standard data rate for DVD authoring. The maximum data rate for digital broadcast is 384kBps.

✳ *Bit Stream Mode*—Determines the overall encoding method based on the needs of the program material. The bitstream mode allows you to encode normal audio mixes and additional audio tracks for the hearing or visually impaired, commentary tracks, voice-overs, and even emergency audio for broadcast use.

✳ *Dialog Normalization*—This parameter helps decoders set the average level of the program material from varying sources so that one does not sound louder than the other. Most commercials have a higher dialogue level than films and always sound much louder when heard back to back with a film. Dialogue normalization attempts to minimize those differences in the decoder. This parameter indicates to the decoder what the normal dialogue level will be for this AC3 file. A good starting point is –27dBFS. A long-running film standard is –31dBFS.

✳ *Dynamic Compression*—Determines the amount of data compression in the AC3 file. Less compression is used in "Film Standard" than in "Dialog." Proper setting of the dialogue normalization level affects how dynamic compression is applied.

✳ *Center Downmix Level*—When the 5.1 signal is downmixed to stereo, the pan law must be applied because the center channel will now be represented by two speakers: left and right. The typical setting is –3dB to compensate for this.

✳ *Surround Downmix Level*—When surround speakers are in use, the sound is coming from behind you and usually through smaller speakers. When mixing the surround signals back into a stereo output, adjusting their level down a bit makes for a more natural sounding downmix.

✳ *LFE*—This check box determines whether the LFE channel is to be included in the encoding. For one and two channel streams, this option is not available. In many consumer systems, if the downmixing functions of the decoder are used, it is quite possible for the LFE channel to be ignored. Never mix essential audio information exclusively in the LFE channel, because the consumer might not hear it.

✳ *Audio Production Info*—This optional information can be used by the decoder to properly EQ the output mix to compensate for high-frequency loss typically encountered in large theater mixing rooms.

✳ *Timecode*—The AC3 file can be stamped with timecode for later synchronization with video files in the DVD authoring process.

✳ *Advanced Options*—There are several other options available for bandwidth limiting, surround levels, emphasis, phase shift, and additional downmix settings for more complete control over how the decoder deals with this audio stream.

Nuendo Dolby Digital Encoder

Nuendo offers a dedicated Dolby Digital encoding plug-in that is used during exporting of an audio mix. Figure 11.31 shows the Nuendo Dolby Digital Encoder with most of the same options as SurCode. Some of the advanced options for additional downmixing are not available in the Nuendo encoder.

Figure 11.31

The Nuendo Dolby Digital Encoder.

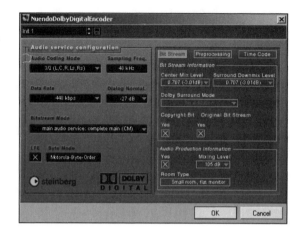

AC3 WAV Format

One feat all of these plug-in are capable of is encoding the Dolby Digital File into either an AC3 file or a special WAV format that can be recorded onto normal digital mediums such as digital VTRs. They can also be transmitted over existing digital audio connections for easy routing and distribution using current technology.

DTS

DTS is another digital multi-channel audio encoding method debuted by the film *Jurassic Park* in 1993. Universal City Studios and Terry Beard created a partnership to bring competition to the theatrical multi-channel audio market that had been dominated by Dolby and THX up to that point. DTS uses the same channel configuration as Dolby Digital. There are now home theater DTS decoding systems available as well.

SurCode offers a standalone DTS encoding application with all the possible options. Nuendo also has a DTS encoder plug-in for use in exporting mixes. Options for DTS encoding include the data rate and whether the surrounds should have the theatrical –3dB gain adjustment. Figure 11.32 shows the Nuendo DTS export window.

MLP

Meridian Lossless Packeting is a technique of data compression that allows bit-accurate reproduction of audio signals after decoding. It is used primarily for DVD-A audio disc encoding of hi-res (96kHz/24-bit) audio for music releases. SurCode offers another standalone tool for encoding MLP files.

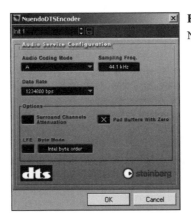

Figure 11.32
Nuendo's DTS export options.

Creating Ambience in Surround

Creating ambience that is enveloping and immersive in surround sound requires some unique processing. Although there are multi-channel reverb plug-ins that are specially designed for surround, more often multiple instances of stereo reverbs are used together to create a surround reverb.

Double-Stereo, Four-Channel Reverb

The most typical surround reverb configuration is a four channel reverb using the front left and right and surround left and right channels. Reverberation in the center channel is not as necessary because the phantom image from the left and right speaker usually suffices. Reverberation of the LFE channel is not a common occurrence.

Just using two of the same reverb plug-ins on the front and rear pairs might not yield the desired results. When the settings are identical, two reverb plug-ins produce almost identical output for the same input signal. This results in an unsatisfactory ambient surround field. Each channel must be unique in order to create the impression of envelopment.

However, the TC Powercore VSS3 ambience plug-in is different in this regard. It uses random algorithm generators in its reverb tail calculations. These random algorithm generators make it possible to use in a surround configuration using two stereo plug-ins to create a discrete four-channel reverb.

There are a couple of techniques for creating a four-channel reverb depending on the DAW that you are using.

❋ *Using multiple stereo aux returns*— This method, common to Pro Tools, uses two stereo aux returns— one for the front left/right pair and the second for the rear surround pair. Each aux track has a stereo reverb inserted on it. The first aux is routed to the front left and right speakers. The second aux is routed to the surround speakers. Create a four-channel bus in Pro Tools with two stereo daughter buses. Each stereo daughter bus is used as the inputs for the two aux tracks. The parent four channel bus can then be used as a destination for aux sends from various other channels. The surround panner on the aux send determines where in the sound field the source is located between the two reverb auxes.

❋ *Using a quad bus*—This technique is a bit simpler and is common to Steinberg Cubase and Nuendo users. Create a quad group channel and insert two stereo reverb plug-ins on it. Using the insert routing options, move the second reverb plug-in to the surround channels, as shown in Figure 11.33. Aux sends routed to that group channel have a surround panner by default. The quad group channel is automatically routed to the front and rear pairs in a 5.1 surround output bus.

Figure 11.33

Nuendo's insert routing view.

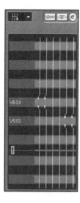

True Multi-Channel Reverbs

Reverbs designed from the ground up for surround will create diffuse reverb in at least four channels. Each channel must have a unique decay character in order to create immersive reverb. Certain surround reverbs also have controls for the center and LFE channels, like the Waves R360, shown in Figure 11.34.

Figure 11.34

The Waves R360 surround reverb with center and LFE controls.

Waves also has IR360 for Pro Tools TDM systems that will create multi-channel convolution reverb. The IR360 has the same controls as the stereo version but accepts multi-channel impulse files. Also, AltiVerb runs as a surround convolution reverb in a four-channel mode. As discussed in Chapter 8, "Convolution," multiple instances of stereo convolution plug-ins can also be used to create a surround impulse reverb using the same techniques as the double-stereo four-channel reverb.

Steinberg's RoomWorks reverb is a true surround four-channel reverb with front/rear balance controls and a CPU usage control to minimize the resources it uses. Figure 11.35 shows RoomWorks with the variation button that generates a new algorithm for the current settings if one particular resonance is causing problems. There are up to 1,000 possible variations for any group of settings in RoomWorks, which should provide enough options for most situations.

Figure 11.35
Steinberg's RoomWorks surround reverb plug-in.

Discrete Front and Rear Reverb

Many engineers find that using two entirely different reverbs for the front and rear pairs is often more desirable than one multi-channel reverb. The ambience in the surround speakers should often be more distant than the front speakers to create the illusion of space. You can accomplish this by using two entirely separate FX chains, one routed to the front pair and the other routed to the rear pair. Feeding various amounts of signals to each reverb creates a sense of placement within the 360 degree sound field. This is probably the most common technique used to create surround ambience and reverb.

Mastering Multi-Channel Audio

Once you have completed a multi-channel mixdown, it might be necessary to adjust the dynamics of the mix and calibrate the reference level to one of the standard delivery formats. Waves provides some dedicated surround dynamics plug-in for basic mastering of multi-channel audio.

❋ *C360*—A true 5.1 compressor with individual threshold and output level controls for each channel, as shown in Figure 11.36. Channels are linkable in various ways for easier operation.

Figure 11.36

Waves C360 surround compressor.

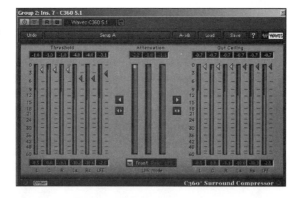

❋ *L360*—A true 5.1 limiter with individual threshold and level controls, as shown in Figure 11.37. Channels are linkable in the same fashion as the C360.

Figure 11.37

The Waves L360 surround limiter.

Be very careful using dynamics plug-ins on multi-channel audio mixes that need to follow industry standards for loudness and reference levels. Having clear control over the dynamics of a surround mix is very important, especially when you're preparing film mixes for release on DVD where the reference levels are different from the original theatrical release.

Summary

The world of surround sound is expanding beyond the movie theater into home viewing and even game consoles. With the merging of the personal computer and the home entertainment system, movies, games, music, and even Web sites will have more and more multi-channel audio content. The need to be fully versed and capable in surround sound practice and technology has never been more important for all audio engineers. Fortunately, DSP developers are coming up with new tools everyday to help with these tasks.

12 } Guitar Processing

Ever since Les Paul started recording his electric guitars on multitrack tape in his home studio, the quest for the ultimate guitar tone goes on in bedrooms, project studios, and world-class facilities everywhere. Recording guitars and guitar amps can be an obsession of a lifetime. If budget is not an issue, the best guitar rig in the world is basically one of everything and perhaps two of some things: every amp, every effects pedal, each make and model of guitar, and of course some quirky specialty toys that make recording so much fun.

It would take a large warehouse to have all these things when recording. In fact, if you were to walk into a major studio recording of a large budget rock album, chances are you would see many amplifiers lined up on the wall with a whole room full of guitars and various pedals strewn about. The best way to get good guitar sounds is to experiment with various setups and audition them with the music without much hassle. If one particular sound does not work well in the song, try another one right away. This makes it easier to choose various tones. Having all the different tones at your fingertips is the ideal way to work.

To be able to package all these amplifiers and guitar pedal effects into a plug-in with instant recall of all parameters would be the panacea of guitar-tone creation. This would give you the ability to try as many guitar tones as you want without even getting out of your seat. Many startlingly believable guitar processing plug-ins are now available, ranging from simple distortion plug-ins to complete guitar performance systems, including external foot controllers and more, from these and other developers:

* ❋ UAD Nigel
* ❋ TC Thirty (AC30 Emulation) and Tubifex
* ❋ Native Instruments Guitar Rig
* ❋ IK Multimedia's Amplitube
* ❋ Waves GTR

All of these plug-ins start with basic amplifier simulation, including tube and solid state types with various popular models such as Fender, Marshall, MesaBoogie, and Vox. Often, the various models are referred to by cryptic descriptions such as *British Tube* or *American Classic*, so as not to infringe upon copyright and trademark issues. But for those who have had a chance to work with great classic guitar amplifiers, the similarities will be obvious. For those who have not had a chance to work with all the different models, the plug-ins provide a great opportunity to become familiar with the various tones that different amplifiers can create.

In addition to amplifier models, there are various speaker cabinet brands and configurations. The difference between a closed-back 2×12" cabinet versus an open-back 4×10" cabinet can be substantial. Also, the microphones used to capture the sound can be modeled to mimic the response of various classic microphone types, such as dynamic (SM57), condenser (Neuman U87), or ribbon (Royer R121). In some plug-ins, you can even change the positions of each microphone from on-axis to off-axis and close or distant positions.

On top of all this comes the fun stuff; the seasoning with every type of guitar effects "pedal" you can think of. This is a guitar player's dreamland. Create endless chains of effects for that perfectly whacked-out solo tone or smooth, ethereal leslie-rotated textures and save all the settings for instant recall later. You can add effects prior to the amplifier stage, as with traditional guitar pedals, or after the amplifier and speakers for another variation.

The DSP technology involved in guitar amplifier modeling is a combination of just about every technique so far covered in this book. There are aspects of frequency, time-domain, and gain processing used together to create the complex simulation of a guitar amplifier. In addition, each guitar effects "pedal" has its own DSP depending on the type of effect. Developers use their own special recipe in order to create each amplifier model.

Using the UAD Nigel Guitar Processor

The UAD Nigel guitar processor, pictured in its complete form in Figure 12.1, is actually made up of eight modules that can be used together or independently. Each module provides a different aspect of the guitar-processing chain. The following list of the modules follows the order in which they are processed in the complete Nigel plug-in. The order follows a logical route that many guitarists typically use and is not adjustable.

Figure 12.1

The UAD Nigel guitar processing plug-in.

❋ *Gate/Comp*—This module processes the guitar signal prior to the amplifier simulator in order to clean up any noise using the gate and control dynamics before the amplifier stage with the compressor.

❋ *Phasor*—Provides a sweeping comb filter effect common to many guitar tones.

❋ *Mod Filter*—This sweepable low-pass filter creates the "wah-wah" effect typically performed with a floor pedal.

❋ *Preflex*—This is the major component of Nigel, creating the amplifier simulation. You can morph together two amplifier types to create a unique tone.

❋ *Cab*—Simulates various speaker cabinet configurations.

❋ *Trem/Fade*—Creates all sorts of tremolo and vibrato effects common to guitar amplifiers.

❋ *Mod Delay*—A standard modulated delay line primarily used for chorusing and flanging.

❋ *Echo*—A secondary delay line for longer echo-type and ping-pong delays.

If you want to use the modules in a different order, they are available as separate plug-ins. The complete Nigel packs them all in one interface for ease of use. You can use each separate module for other things besides guitar.

Preflex

The Preflex is the major component in Nigel. Offering two amplifier modeling paths together with a morphing control, Preflex makes it easy to create just the right tone. Blending a little Marshall ("Marsha" in Nigel) brightness with the chunk of a MesaBoogie Rectifier ("Rectifried" in Nigel) is as easy as moving the morph slider between the two amplifier types.

The Preflex has a basic equalizer that processes the signal before the amplifier modeling, allowing you to "drive" the amplifier with various tones. The color control adjusts the frequency spectrum of distortion from low and chunky to high and sizzly. The Bent knob adjusts the ferocity of the distortion from mild crunch to all-out searing distortion. There is another set of tone controls after the amplifier modeling for final shaping. Each amplifier model reacts to these controls differently. There are twelve amp models in Nigel's Preflex.

Amp models include:

❋ *Marsha*—Better known as the classic Marshall amplifier.

❋ *Big Beaver*—This amp is modeled after vintage Orange amps and also has a deeper and more fuzztone sound created by the Sovtec Big Muff pedal.

❋ *Boutique*—Reminiscent of the Soldano, Matchless, and Rivera amplifiers with a very smooth distortion.

❋ *Custom Blues*—Has a lower gain suited for those hard-to-get blues tones.

❋ *Gemini*—Fender Twin Reverb, clean tone.

❋ *Rectifried*—Modern high-gain amplifier similar to MesaBoogie's Rectifier.

❋ *Supa Clean*—Simulates the direct input of a console channel.

❋ *Super Custom*—The Custom Blues model with more gain and power, modified Fender Super Reverb.

* *Super Sat*—Ultra high gain amplifier that distorts easily in lower frequencies.

* *Big Bottom*—Optimized for bass guitar.

* *Super Tweed*—Models the distinctive sound of small Fender Champ and Princeton Reverb amps at loud volumes.

* *Bassman*—Classic Fender Bassman amplifier model.

Speaker Cabinets

The Cab module is really part of the Preflex and allows the choice of many types of speaker cabinets and microphone positions. The Shure SM57 microphone was used in all instances for analysis. There are 23 choices of speaker cabinets and mic'ing techniques. Also included are speaker emulations from Line 6, ADA, and SansAmp brand guitar pedals.

Phasor

The Phasor module is true filter phaser with up to 12th order filters and an adjustable frequency range. It is actually one of the most adjustable and usable phasers available. You can change the LFO waveform, along with its rate and the "recir" percentage or feedback level, as seen in Figure 12.2.

Figure 12.2

The UAD Nigel Phasor Module is available as a separate plug-in.

Mod Filter

The Mod Filter module is wonderful for setting up an "auto-wah" effect using envelope-based triggering of filters ranging from low-pass and high-pass to band-pass and a special "wah" filter. The frequency ranges and resonance can be adjusted as well. Modulation can come from an LFO, random generator, input envelope, and even external MIDI control for manual "wah" pedal operation or automation.

Trem/Fade

The Trem/Fade module is more than just a tremolo effect. It can do envelope-based fade-ins for bowing effects on guitar. Trem/Fade can change the tremolo rate over time based on the input envelope, having the rate gently speed up after striking a chord or start fast and gradually slow down. This provides some unique functionality. The Onset control, shown in Figure 12.3, determines the amount of time it takes for the effect to kick in after signal has passed the threshold point.

Figure 12.3
The UAD Trem/Fade module with unique envelope options such as onset delay control.

Mod Delay and Echo

The Mod Delay and Echo modules provide complete delay effects for Nigel. Anything from a simple chorus effect to stereo ping-pong delays are possible. The Trem D/U (down/up) and U/D LFO types allow the mod delay to change the LFO speed based on the input envelope. You can achieve many different types of modulation very quickly with these controls.

Using the TC Thirty and Tubifex

TC Electronics PowerCore users have choices for guitar amp processing. The original Tubifex plug-in is a very customizable three-gain stage tube amp simulator with speaker emulation and even tube voltage control. The TC Thirty is a single emulation of the classic Vox AC30 amplifier.

The TC Thirty

The TC Thirty, shown in Figure 12.4, is available for PowerCore users. It features a low-latency mode that improves the plug-in delay time so that live performance is as responsive as possible. There is also an oversampling mode that results in excellent sound quality but more PowerCore CPU usage.

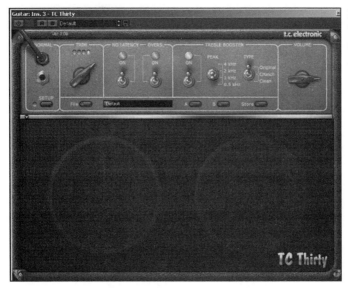

Figure 12.4
TC Electronics's Thirty, available on PowerCore, is a classic Vox AC30 emulation.

The Thirty is a realistic emulation of the classic Vox AC30 used by many artists, including the Beatles. The original amplifier featured a "Top Boost" circuit that was used to create overdriven tones. The TC Thirty has the Treble Booster section that emulates the Top Boost and can tuned to various frequencies, as shown in Figure 12.4. You can specify the type of overdrive, as well as choose between clean, crunch, and original.

This is one of the best sounding guitar amp simulators available. More than just a distortion generator, the TC Thirty seems to do more modeling when distortion and other nonlinearities occur at various signal levels, not just a distortion threshold of some sort. The amplifier response seems more lively and responsive than other amp simulators.

❄ GUITAR TIP: FEEDBACK BELL TONES

The TC Thirty is the one guitar processor that in my experience has been able to generate what are known as "bell tones." A bell tone is a certain type of feedback that occurs at relatively lower volumes and is much more controllable than the normal squeals and high harmonic feedback. Bell tones are usually lower in the frequency spectrum and have a musical quality to them. The real Vox AC30 is a wonderful amp for generating bell tones and the TC Thirty faithfully reproduces this aspect of the amplifier. Creating bell tones does require turning up the monitoring volume to a healthy level (at least above 100dBSPL or so). Wear hearing protection! Try various chords until you strike the right one and you will notice a feedback tone that takes a few seconds to develop but does not accelerate to extremely high volumes too quickly. This is the bell tone. Try moving the guitar around in relation to your monitor speakers to change the pitch and intensity of the resonance.

The TC Thirty does not have many options besides the normal amplifier controls. It is designed to emulate one specific amplifier and does so with great success. If the processing power is available, the oversampling option improves the sound quality even more, allowing more precision in the emulation model. There are some silly options for speaker cone animation and display, but for the most part, the TC Thirty is very straightforward.

Tubifex

Tubifex is most likely the precursor to the Thirty. It is based on three 12AX7 gain stages, a basic speaker cabinet simulator, and a noise reduction system, as shown in Figure 12.5. It uses both native DSP and the dedicated TC PowerCore CPU in a hybrid processing style that is intended to reduce plug-in delays so live performance is not hampered.

Tubifex's Basic Parameters

The basic parameters of Tubifex are all contained in the top portion of the interface. The controls are mostly the standard ones you find on any multi-stage tube amplifier.

Figure 12.5
The TC PowerCore Tubifex amplifier modeling plug-in.

❄ *Trim*—Adjusts the input gain of the plug-in.

❄ *Three Gain Stages*—Two prior to the equalizer and one after.

❄ *Three Band Equalizer*—Low, mid, and high.

❄ *Master Out*—This is not the same as the master volume of a tube amp. It is not intended to be driven into distortion. The indicator above the knob is a clip light that should not light up during normal operation.

❄ *Pres(ence)*—Determines the amount of harmonics added by the speaker cone. Higher values tend to be brighter sounding.

❄ *Distance*—The distance from the speaker to the microphone can be set directly in front of the speaker or at one centimeter which hardly seems like much distance at all. Although a one-centimeter change in distance can have a great effect, how close is "close?" Guitar speakers will move around a centimeter during normal operation. The setting does afford a tonal change, though.

❄ *Axis*—This relates to the microphone's position relative to the speaker. On-axis is placed directly at the center of the cone. Off-axis is at the edge of the speaker, and "mid" is somewhere in between.

❄ *LoFi/HiFi*—This slider has three positions for determining how much CPU resources are consumed for higher fidelity. TC recommends using HiFi when rendering Tubifex processing to disk.

Tubifex's Expert Parameters

When you open the Expert tab, you'll see controls for each tube stage along with several unique variables that almost let you design you own amplifier circuit. The noise reduction controls are found here. Each tube stage has a duplicate set of controls.

❈ *Vgk/Vak*—There are two voltages that affect the linearity of tube amplifier circuits. By adjusting these values, you change the response character of the tube. With these options, you can design amplifiers that have unique responses and distortion curves.

❈ *Character*—This determines how symmetrical the response of the tube is; left being more symmetrical like solid-state circuits and the right being asymmetrical, more like guitar preamplifiers.

❈ *Size*—Sliding this slider to the left will give you a smoother tone with more low-end detail. Moving farther to the left, the signal becomes thinner.

❈ *Strength*—This determines how much the Size parameter affects the tone.

❈ **MIX TIP: RE-AMP'ED BASS GUITAR**

In modern guitar-based music styles, the bass guitar often has to compete with overdriven guitar tones. In order to get that "grinding" bass tone typical of old Ampeg amplifiers pushed to their limits, create a duplicate of the bass track and insert Tubifex or other guitar amplifier plug-in. Dial in the "gank" or drive of the bass with the amplifier plug-in and then mix this with the original bass track to get the best of both worlds. The original track should retain all the low frequencies and size of the bass while the amplifier track will have all the upper harmonics or "gank" that you need to cut through a wall of distorted guitars.

Noise Reduction

The noise reduction in Tubifex is worthy of mention because it uses noise profiling to more accurately detect and remove noise from the signal. This is very helpful when using large amounts of tube gain with single coil pickups that are more susceptible to interference. You can store your noise-reduction settings as separate preset files.

When enabled, the noise-reduction module will learn the noise profile of the input signal and then apply gain reduction based on that and the amount of noise reduction set in dB. Using "inv," you can monitor the removed audio just like the difference function in some noise removal plug-ins. The noise reduction can function as a gate or in the softer expander mode, each with adjustable threshold, range hold and release parameters. The noise-reduction module is very powerful and the result is a more sensitive gate that allows freedom of expression on the guitar without the annoying gate shut-off experienced with actual foot pedal noise gates.

Both Tubifex and the TC Thirty are high-fidelity amplifier processors that make for a very customizable tone generator on the PowerCore platform. What they lack in effects toys, they make up for in pure tone.

Using Native Instruments's Guitar Rig

Native Instruments's has certainly created the most versatile and fun-to-use guitar processing tool thus far. Guitar Rig has the ability to freely rearrange various components within the plug-in to provide the ultimate in flexibility for tone creation. All the graphics and names of the various processing modules hint at the actual vintage devices they are emulating, using clever names for each one.

Additionally, Guitar Rig can use an external foot controller to change settings within the plug-in for use in live performances. It seems that now it is possible to take your guitar, a laptop, and a foot controller without an amplifier to your next gig. I guess I can sell the van now!

Guitar Rig is organized into two main sections. The left side of the interface, or "left view," is a sort of a storage area for all the components available—a preset organization and preference area. The right side, or "control center," shows the current processing chain in a rack-style graphic with signal flow going from top to bottom. See Figure 12.6. You can freely drag modules from the storage side to the rack side and then from one slot in the rack to another at any point in time.

Figure 12.6

Native Instruments Guitar Rig interface.

Left View

The left view has three modes; presets, components, and settings. Each mode is discussed in the following sections.

Presets

Guitar Rig comes with a large amount of presets, which is a nice way to experience all the capabilities of the plug-in. The presets are organized into banks of related settings, such as bass and 70's rock. There is built-in search capability to the interface for fast navigation of many presets. You can also store you own presets with various categorizations for future search results, as you can see in the properties view shown in Figure 12.7.

Figure 12.7

The Properties tab for organizing presets.

Components

The components view shows all the available processing modules that you can use in the rack. Once you have found the right effect or amp, simply drag it into the control center area at a point in the rack where the signal flow is appropriate. Signal flows from top to bottom in the rack.

Components are grouped by type and each has its own creative graphic that distinguishes it from the others. Besides being fun, this helps you visually inspect the processing chain from a slight distance, such as from the front of the stage to the backline.

* *Amps*—Has all of the amplifier models, including the speaker cabinet tool that allows multiple speaker cabinets and various microphones and placement techniques for each cabinet.

* *Distort*—If tubes are not enough, this category contains models of popular distortion foot pedals that you can use to drive an amplifier into harder distortion.

* *Mod*—Contains all the modulated effects such as chorusing, flanging, leslie speaker simulator, and octave generator.

❋ *Filter*—Filters include manual and auto-wah pedals and various equalizers.

❋ *Volume*—Includes a volume pedal for external control and assorted gain processors such as a compressor and limiter.

❋ *Other*—A grab-bag of leftover effects, including spring and digital reverbs, various delays, and the signal split component.

Split Signal Chains

Besides all the various signal chains you can create with the multitude of components, the Split component offers the most intriguing options. Inserting the split component divides the signal into two isolated paths. The split mix component, which can combine the two signal paths after processing, is automatically inserted. You can place various components in the A or B signal path to create parallel processing chains. The split mix offers a crossfade control to balance the two sounds together.

You can use splits to create a dual amplifier setup, such as the one shown in Figure 12.8. One chain could have a clean Fender-type of sound and the other could have a MesaBoogie modern distortion sound, each with its own effects. Once the signals are combined by split mix, you can then add other effects. Using a foot controller to adjust the blend between the two amplifier chains, you can have a very complex rig without the need for roadies!

Figure 12.8

A dual-amplifier chain created in Guitar Rig.

Settings

The settings tab offers global preferences, preset folders, and external foot controller settings. The external foot controller can be a dedicated unit such as the one made by Native Instruments and shown in Figure 12.9. This controller not only transmits the MIDI data to Guitar Rig for changing settings, but also has an audio interface optimized for guitar and bass pickups that can function as the input converter for the software. You can also add other MIDI controllers to augment the six buttons and single foot controller of the Rig Kontrol.

Figure 12.9

Native Instrument's Rig Kontrol audio interface and MIDI control for Guitar Rig.

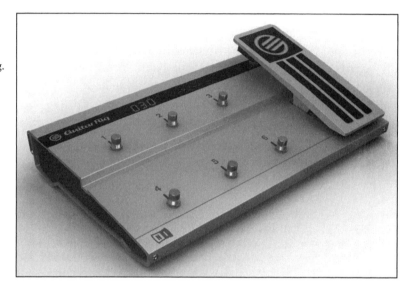

Control Center (Right View)

The Control Center side of Guitar Rig displays the current signal processing chain with all the parameters for adjustment. The plus and minus icons at the right of each component allow you to open and close the parameter's display. When several components are inserted, it is easy to have the rack extend beyond the window, thus requiring you to scroll to see the settings. By closing some components using the minus buttons, you can see more pertinent controls.

> ❋ **GUI TIP: ADVANCED HIDDEN CONTROLS**
>
> As with any guitar amplifier or pedal, many musicians tinker around with internal settings in order to create unique tones for the guitar. Native Instruments has strived to make those "mods" available in the software model. If a plus button is visible on any component, it means there are controls that are not displayed. All of the amplifier models and many of the effects have additional expert parameters so you can tweak your sound even more. Figure 12.10 shows the hidden controls for the Twang Reverb model.

Figure 12.10
The hidden controls for the Twang Reverb model in Guitar Rig.

Control Center also provides some practical functions that are always available. Some of these functions are useful in the standalone configuration and some are also useful when Guitar Rig is within a DAW.

❊ *Two virtual "tape decks" for recording audio within Guitar Rig*—One captures the source at the top of the signal chain and the second captures the output at the end of the signal chain.

❊ *Digital Tuner*—Offering chromatic, bass, guitar, and open tuning presets.

❊ *Metronome*—Can run independently or synchronized with the host DAW's tempo map.

With a wide array of configuration possibilities and attention to detail within each component, Guitar Rig has the most versatile tone-creation scheme for both studio and live performance. Additionally, the various components can function on their own as effects for other sounds during mixing or sound design creation.

Using IK Multimedia's Amplitube

IK Multimedia's Amplitube was the first plug-in guitar amplifier emulation. Amplitube innovated the idea that tube nonlinear distortion could be recreated by DSP.

Amplitube has a very simple and easy-to-operate interface shown in Figure 12.11. There are three pages to the interface that access the "stomp" pedals, amplifier controls, and post effects such as reverb. Each effect, besides the amplifier section, can be bypassed but the signal chain order remains constant. The stomp pedals are first, then comes the amplifier section, and then the FX.

Figure 12.11
IK Multimedia's Amplitube.

Stomp Page

There are five "stomps" or foot pedal effects that are processed before the signal enters the amplifier modeling stage. Each one has an activation button that looks like a real floor pedal, as you can see in Figure 12.12. The various parameters are shown above the pedal, where they can be edited.

* Wah-Wah
* Delay
* Chorus
* Flanger
* Overdrive

Figure 12.12

Amplitube's stomp section.

Amp Page

The amplifier section of Amplitube has all of the standard controls including, gain, a three-band equalizer with presence control, output volume, and spring reverb level. In addition, Amplitube separates the modeling of the pre-amp stage from the filter and power amp stages in a guitar amp. This allows you to mix and match various combinations of pre-amps, filter sections, and power amp characteristics to come up with unique tones.

* Seven pre-amp models, ranging from Solid State Clean and British Crunch to Fuzz.
* Five filter or EQ models, from Tube American to Tube British.
* Four power amp models, including both solid state and various tube wattages.

In the speaker cabinet section, you can choose from nine cabinet variations ranging from small combo to vintage 4×12 and even no speaker at all. Once you choose a cabinet, you can select the microphone type and position for the best tonal match possible.

Amplitube has so many combinations between pre-amp and filter models to power amp and speaker models that it can get overwhelming just to try them all at once. There are two "matching" functions that allow one-touch changing of the pre-amp that triggers the corresponding EQ model, power amp, and cabinet choice that most originally matches an actual amplifier. The Amp Match switch automatically changes the EQ model and amp model to the appropriate selections that best mimic the sound of the various pre-amp models. The Cab Match switch does the same thing for the speaker cabinet setup.

FX Page

The third page of Amplitube contains three processors typically used in the studio. The parametric equalizer can certainly come in handy. There is also a stereo delay and stereo reverb module. These are not processed until after the guitar tone has come through the amp modeling stage first.

Amplitube has a variety of presets that you can use in some interesting ways. Of course there are normal guitar and bass guitar presets for various tones, but there are also presets designed to be used with other instruments and as elements in a mix. Under the MultiFX submenu in the Presets pull-down menu, there are two categories—Insert FX and Send FX. Here, you can store presets to process all sorts of sounds with guitar amplifier modeling. Insert FX are designed to be used on one audio track in the same fashion as a compressor or equalizer. Send FX are designed to be inserted on auxiliary tracks so that several audio tracks can be routed via aux sends to create effects such as spring reverb and other "lo-fi" effects.

❊ **MIX TIP: LO-FI VOCALS**

In the world of heavy metal, post-punk, and "screamo" styles, vocals often are processed to sound like megaphones or other distorted tones. To do this conveniently, create a second "screamo" vocal track and insert Amplitube or other guitar amp modeling plug-in. In the DAW, edit portions of the vocal you want to be distorted and move those regions to the "screamo" track. Adjust the amp modeling to taste and, voila, instant "screamo" lo-fi track.

Using Waves GTR

Waves teamed up with legendary guitar maker Paul Reed Smith to create guitar processing tools in the Waves product line. The result: Waves Amp and Waves Stomp. The two plug-ins work in concert to create a multitude of various guitar tones. Having two plug-ins offers you the routing flexibility of NI's Guitar Rig when used within a DAW. You can place stomps before or after the Guitar Amp plug-in just like any other plug-in. There is also a tuner plug-in that has all the available open and drop tunings.

Guitar Amp

The Guitar Amp plug-in comes in four forms:

* *Guitar Amp Mono*—For mono guitar signals through one cabinet.
* *Guitar Amp Mono to Stereo*—Creates a stereo output for further processing after the amp.
* *Guitar Amp Mono 2Cab*—Has two speaker cabinets, each with its own settings.
* *Guitar Amp Stereo*—Offers true stereo inputs and stereo outputs.

The amplifier controls are very straightforward. There are seven amp model types, ranging from "direct" all the way to "modern" for extreme overdrive. The tone and presence controls react differently to each amplifier type. The amplifier types have generic names such as clean and crunch. Each one is modeled after a classic type of amplifier.

Depending on the plug-in form used, there are controls for one or two speaker cabinets featuring microphone choice and placement plus phase and volume adjustments. See Figure 12.13.

Figure 12.13

The Waves Guitar Amp 2Cab plug-in.

Stomp

After you have created a quality tone with the Waves Amp, the Stomp plug-ins provide all the toys you need to get creative with guitar sounds. Stomp comes with several virtual PedalBoards for conservation of DSP. There are two-, four-, and six-slot PedalBoards; each slot can hold any one of the Waves Stomp effects, as you can see in Figure 12.14.

Figure 12.14
Waves Stomp 6 with pedals installed.

All of the Stomp pedals are high-quality effects that have enough control to facilitate creating many unique guitar tones. Some Stomp effects are better placed after the amplifier and Waves has recommendations on how best to set up the GTR system.

The Waves/PRS Guitar Interface

Waves GTR is also combined with a special guitar interface that functions as a direct input for your DAW. The Waves/PRS Guitar Interface, shown in Figure 12.15, has a specially designed input circuit that better matches the high impedance of passive guitar pickups. This more closely emulates the behavior of tube amplifier input circuits. The result is better guitar tone before the signal enters the digital domain.

The Guitar Interface is not a digital converter. It is a guitar optimized direct input with a preamp that converts guitar signals into low-impedance line level signals suitable for connection with analog to digital converters.

Figure 12.15
The Waves/PRS Guitar Interface high-impedance DI preamp.

347
❄❄❄

Summary

The ability to accurately reproduce classic guitar tones that normally require thousands of dollars worth of temperamental tube equipment, a studio full of microphones, and the isolation needed to crank up vintage amplifiers has freed the modern guitarist. Now, the ability to create new and interesting guitar tones is at your fingertips. Although there might not be a true substitute for plugging in a '59 Les Paul into a "dime'd" Marshall stack and letting a big A chord fly, the ability to get real recording done without lugging a truck full of equipment and damaging your hearing at the same time seems like a bargain.

One very beneficial effect of this is the ability for producers to alter the guitar tones after recording is complete. Because only the direct sound of the electric guitar is actually recorded, an infinite amount of tonal variations can be auditioned within the context of a mix without too much trouble. The search for the perfect tone goes on!

13 } Virtual Instruments

One of the important plug-in areas not covered in this book so far is sound creation using virtual instrument technology. The scope of this topic far exceeds the realm of this book, but many of the basic principles involved have relevance to digital signal processing. This chapter covers some of the basic techniques used to create sounds in a plug-in environment and surveys some of the popular virtual instruments available today.

There are several ways that computers can generate musical sounds through DSP. Virtual instruments are typically combinations of various techniques blended together to create the final sound, as follows:

* Subtractive synthesis
* Additive synthesis
* Wavetable synthesis
* Granular synthesis
* FM synthesis
* Sample playback instruments

Subtractive Synthesis

Subtractive synthesis is the oldest method traditionally used by analog synths such as the Moog, ARP, and other models. Their digital counterparts in the world of virtual instruments include Steinberg's a1 Analog Synth Unit shown in Figure 13.1, the Access Virus synth, and TC's PowerCore 01.

Figure 13.1

Steinberg's a1 Analog Synth Unit uses subtractive synthesis.

The process begins with oscillators that generate various waveforms at frequencies determined by the keys you press on the keyboard. Once the initial raw waveform is created, it is run through a series of filters to remove any undesired components and harmonics. Next, amplitude filters or envelopes are applied to the sound to give it attack, sustain, and release properties.

Subtractive synthesis starts with a complete waveform with all the desired elements and harmonics included and then progressively removes or subtracts undesired elements with filters until the desired sound is all that is left.

Additive Synthesis

Additive synthesis works in the opposite fashion of subtractive synthesis. Using Fourier analysis, complex waveforms are broken down into a series of simple sine waves combined together in various ways. Using this idea, additive synthesis recreates sounds by generating all the component sine waves needed for a particular sound and then adding them together to finish the composite sound.

A pipe organ is an example of natural additive synthesis. Each pipe in the organ makes a basic sine wave tone (including harmonics, but for the sake of discussion we'll consider the sine wave), and when you add many multiples of pipes at harmonic frequencies related to the first pipe, a very rich harmonic tone is created. Modifying which harmonic pipes are active and the blend of them all together determines the tonality of the organ.

An additive synth needs oscillators for each element of the composite sound. This method involves hundreds of components, or "partials," to create certain natural sounds, so is not well suited for recreating acoustic instruments.

The Hammond organs are a very early example of additive synthesis. A modern digital version of additive synthesis from White Noise, the White Noise Additive Synth, is shown in Figure 13.2.

Figure 13.2

The White Noise Additive Synth.

Instead of having multiple oscillators to generate the fundamental and each partial, the White Noise Additive Synth uses a library of noise spectra as the basis for each oscillator. Each spectrum contains fundamental tones and various partials that evolve over time. Additionally, you can load spectra into the formant filter window. The formant filter processes the output of the additive oscillators, removing various frequencies based on its spectrum. The formant filter can remain constant or can shift its bias based on keyboard MIDI input or LFO modulation.

Each spectrum contains partials that vary over time. These are represented by the color displays on the left side of the interface. You can alter or create spectra by drawing freehand in the display. The spectra are the basis for each oscillator and formant filter, creating fundamentals and partials or harmonics for the rest of the synthesizer to process. The envelopes can modulate where in the spectrum the source oscillation comes from, shifting it over time.

This novel method of sound creation offers unique possibilities, especially in texture and sound design areas. There are not too many other examples of strict additive synthesis available besides the Camel Audio Chameleon 5000, shown in Figure 13.3. Notice the series of partials shown at the top of the display.

Figure 13.3

Camel Audio's Chameleon 5000 additive synthesizer plug-in.

FM Synthesis

FM synthesis was popularized by the famed Yamaha DX7. It uses a process known as *frequency modulation* (FM). Although the name has for years implied this type of synthesis, it is not technically correct. The process involves modulating the phase of a carrier frequency in order to add harmonic spectra to the carrier tone. This should technically be called *phase modulation* instead of frequency modulation.

By controlling the type of modulation (shape, frequency, and amplitude), various harmonics are added to the carrier frequency, thereby changing its spectrum and creating a new tone. For example, if the modulator's frequency is below the range of human hearing, the result heard is vibrato. As the modulator's frequency increases into the audible band, the result is the generation of harmonics around the carrier frequency. By applying envelopes to both the carrier and the modulator, you can control these effects dynamically in order to create realistic musical sounds.

The FM7 from Native Instruments, shown in Figure 13.4, is a fine example of digital FM synthesis emulation. With a GUI that resembles the DX7 of yesteryear, the FM7 has up to eight operators (modulators) to add harmonic content to the carrier frequency. Each operator can have its own envelope and filter settings that offer a multitude of possible FM sounds.

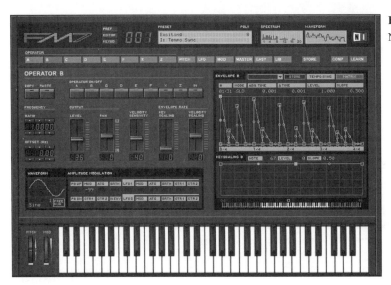

Figure 13.4
Native Instruments FM7.

Wavetable Synthesis

Wavetable synthesis is probably the most common technique used to emulate acoustic and electric instruments. Wavetable synthesizers use a library of waveforms from which to build sounds. Usually, the library consists of samples of initial attacks of various types of instruments. These samples are used as foundations for building a complete sound. For example, you might use the attack of an acoustic guitar to create a harpsichord sound. The sustained tones are often created through other methods such as FM or subtractive techniques.

You can also use additional samples to create the sustained portions of sounds by looping them and using filters to alter their tonality. You can filter and loop the sustain of a piano, for example, to create an altogether new sound.

The advantage of Wavetable synthesis is its capability to create many natural sounds without using too much memory. You can optimize the samples in the waveform library for size and store them in a portable device such as the classic Proteus sound module. With virtual instruments, DSP usage can be minimized while still providing many voices for the instrument.

An example of Wavetable synthesis in a virtual instrument is Steinberg's Hypersonic shown in Figure 13.5. This virtual instrument is capable of playing many sounds simultaneously without using too many CPU resources due to the Wavetable synthesis efficiency.

Figure 13.5

Steinberg's Hypersonic Wavetable synthesizer.

Granular Synthesis

Granular synthesis is based on a different view of sound than the traditional Fourier analysis of composite sine waves. The granular model suggests that sound is made up of a series of small sound events that are collected in a cloud to form a larger body of sound that humans recognize.

STOCHASTIC PROCESS

The granular model of sound implies a *stochastic process* whereby individual elements within a system do not have specific properties or behavior. However, the overall view of the system has certain characteristics. Control over individual "grains" is random, but the control over the whole system is somewhat predictable. This type of process is applied in granular synthesis.

Native Instruments Absynth, shown in Figure 13.6, offers a granular synthesis module among many others. Samples are loaded in Absynth and played using a granular model where pitch and time elements are controlled separately. You can use various modulators to alter the pitch or time of the sample in order to create entirely new sounds from an existing sample.

Figure 13.6

Native Instruments Absynth is capable of granular sample processing.

Another interesting example of granular synthesis is seen in Tweakbench's Dropout, shown in Figure 13.7. This sample payback tool allows you to chop up the sample and vary each segment's pitch. This creates some interesting results. Additionally, you can reverse each sample chunk for more variations. Best of all, Dropout is a free plug-in.

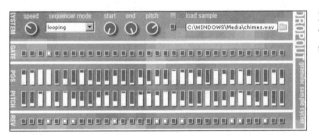

Figure 13.7

Tweakbench's Dropout, a free granular sample playback tool.

❄ **FREE PLUG-INS**

There are many small developers who offer free virtual instruments and other plug-ins. Often, these free plug-ins are available to entice you to buy more complete versions or other tools made by the same developer. Regardless of the intention, there are many high-quality plug-ins available for free. Searching KVR (www.KVRaudio.com) and other resources will allow you to find many of these plug-ins.

Sample Playback Instruments

Samplers are basically audio playback devices that can vary the pitch of sample playback as a function of the various notes played on a keyboard. One recording of a flute can be played back at various pitch intervals to create a virtual flute instrument from one recording. This is sampling at its most basic level.

In the past, hardware-based samplers, such as the classic Akai S1000, had limitations based on the amount of memory that could be installed in the unit. Each sample had to be stored in RAM (random access memory) in order to be available for playback. Various techniques were used to increase the amount of realistic sounds a sampler could play back through the use of looping and time stretching.

The result of all of this was a limited realism of the sampled instruments. Pianos are notoriously difficult to sample because there are so many dynamic levels for each note in the piano that the memory needed to play back all the samples is impractical for hardware units. The looping of sustained notes of a piano only works to a limited extent and the realism is compromised.

With the advent of the computer audio workstation, the hardware-memory limitation is a thing of the past. Virtual samplers such as Native Instruments Kontakt, shown in Figure 13.8, can use the hard drive to stream samples from disk just like DAW software. The sample size is now only limited by the size of your hard disk. This provided an enormous opportunity for sample library designers to go "hog wild" in sampling acoustic instruments. Kontakt even boasts complete surround-sound support, expanding the amount of samples used for each note.

Figure 13.8

Native Instruments Kontakt 2 sampler.

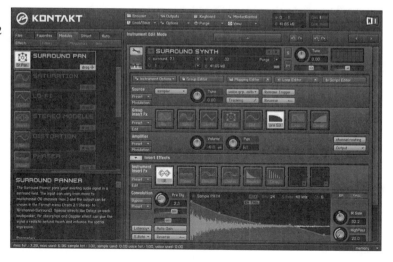

❄ Q & A WITH NATIVE INSTRUMENTS'S SYNTHESIS TECHNOLOGY DIRECTOR MICHAEL KURZ

Q: How and when did you first get involved with virtual instrument creation?

A: My first real-time software synthesis project was a physical modeling string simulation that I developed for my Masters degree in Electronic Engineering. After that, I joined Native Instruments as one of the first members, and started out with improving and extending the synthesis algorithms of Reaktor.

Q: What is your background? Musical? Technical?

A: I have played piano and keyboards since age 6, synthesizers since age 15, and a couple of other instruments as well. I am an amateur musician but a professional engineer, and I'm fortunate to be able to combine both passions into one career.

Q: What was the first virtual instrument that NI created?

A: Apart from Reaktor, which is a modular environment and a virtual instrument construction kit, our first software instrument with a distinct identity was the Pro-Five virtual analog synth, released in 1999.

Q: What motivates you to create a new instrument?

A: The challenge to come up with the best possible technology and the best product design to satisfy musicians' needs, desires, and dreams. And the satisfaction when everything comes together, works as intended, and is received with praise by musicians with all different backgrounds.

Q: What was the hardest thing about creating your first virtual instrument?

A: With the Pro-Five, we were trying to achieve a number of things for the first time, like programming a plug-in for the then-new VST plug-in instrument interface, and designing a vintage-style Graphical User Interface. And, of course, developing a software synthesis engine to be equivalent to an established classic electronic instrument was a challenge in itself.

Q: Where do you think the future of virtual instrument technology lies?

A: I think in the future, virtual instruments will just be a normal part of music making, taken for granted by everybody involved with music recording and production. Creative people everywhere will continue to design and develop new instruments, some of which will fall by the wayside, but some which will become classics in their own right.

(continued on next page)

Q: What is the single biggest limitation in virtual instrument technology today?

A: The limiting factor is not the technology. It all depends on the creativity of people to come up with new ideas, new designs, and new ways of doing things. The power to innovate doesn't come from a computer or a compiler, but from having a deep understanding of principles and concepts relating to music, creativity, and information science.

Q: What is your favorite Native Instrument?

A: The instruments which are closest do my heart are the ones which I have been most involved in designing and developing: Pro-53, B4 II, FM7, and Guitar Rig. Of these I would say that my favorite is the B4, because its design is most focused on being an actual musical instrument, as opposed to being a product of music technology.

The result is a plethora of sample libraries from various developers covering everything from pianos and orchestral instruments to bizarre ethnic instruments and one-of-a-kind items such as built-in pipe organs that cannot be easily recorded. If you can play it, they have sampled it.

One of the earlier examples of streaming-from-disk samplers is GigaSampler and now GigaStudio, shown in Figure 13.9. GigaStudio uses a hybrid approach by storing the initial portions of samples in

Figure 13.9

Tascam's GigaStudio sampler.

RAM so that playback can be instantaneous, following the initial portion with the remainder of the sample streaming from disk. This technique offered less latency and more playability for the samples. GigaStudio and other virtual samplers have also integrated various other forms of DSP to modify the samples being played back. You can add equalizers, compressors, reverbs, and other processing types within the instrument itself, offering more sonic possibilities in one tool.

Another area in which virtual sample playback has really altered the creative approach to music is the use of drum loops. Instruments such as Stylus RMX, shown in Figure 13.10, offer a unique approach to rhythmic creation on-the-fly. Stylus RMX can segment drum loops and process various chunks to alter the pitch of the snare drum by itself, for example. You can time-stretch and even reverse various bits of the drum loop. Combine that with many real-time DSP effects, including filters and delays, and you have quite a versatile toolbox for rhythmic creation.

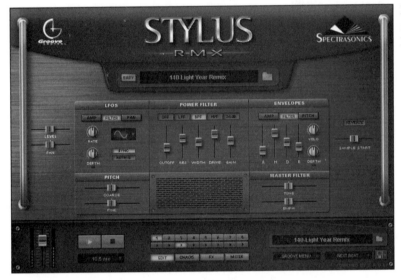

Figure 13.10
Spectrasonic's Stylus Virtual Rhythm instrument.

The ability to stream samples from disk instantaneously created a whole other dimension for electronic musicians who perform live. Now, electronic music can have improvisational aspects to it in the form of virtual instrument technology, including sample playback. Performers can switch drum grooves on-the-fly as the mood changes. Software such as Abelton Live, shown in Figure 13.11, allows fast and intuitive sample loop playback with real-time changes that do not interrupt the sound.

Figure 13.11

Abelton Live real-time sample loop playback and recording software.

Using Live, the musician can switch loops in each channel as inspiration strikes. Live takes care that the sounds remain in sync with one another and that transitions are smooth when samples are changed over. In the past, synchronizing two drum loops that were not at the same tempo took a certain amount of time. Now, with DSP tools such as Live or Stylus, the process is instantaneous. Improvisation has moved into the computer age.

Summary

The world of music will never be the same now that the era of the virtual instrument has begun. If only some of the classic composers of the past could have access to the tools of today. It sounds cliché, but what would Mozart do with this technology? We will never know.

We can, however, explore more musical territory than ever before without the need for an orchestra or even another musician. Nothing can ever completely substitute for real humans playing real instruments, but at least you can explore musical ideas without expending massive effort to get individuals together to perform a complex piece of music. You can quietly sit in front of your computer and score an entire movie. It is a brave new world.

The frontier lies in sounds that come from the imagination. New techniques in synthesis provide ways of creating sounds that have never been heard before. Granted, some of those sounds do not need to be heard (read: bad synth programming), but there also are wonderful sounds that could not have existed without the world of digital audio synthesis.

14 } Author's Picks

Having started my career on a two-inch analog machine with a large format console and racks of outboard gear, my perspective on the revolution of digital processing has been interesting. The studio I was working at had the first Sound Designer II system in the area, and we were all amazed at how we could edit the two track master in the computer and not use any razor blades or grease pencils. When I bought my first one gigabyte hard drive for $1,000, I was so happy to be able to store an entire album worth of mixes on one hard drive. Times have changed.

Times Have Changed

The ability to process audio in a high-quality manner on a personal computer has changed so many things about the way audio is produced. The equipment it would take to do what I can do in my personal studio would not even fit in the room where I work. These are amazing feats of technology that will continue to evolve into the future.

The one element that I am sorry to see go is the teamwork that arises from the large studio tradition. Working with other engineers, producers, musicians, and artists in a collective environment is one of the best sources of information, inspiration, and friendship. It does not occur as often in the world of home studios and laptop music production.

The idea of an engineering apprenticeship that in the past was the vehicle for education in audio engineering is no longer a valid paradigm. Today, with the purchase of a computer and some basic software, many of the tools that were only available in top-line studios can be used by anyone. This is a good thing. However, a new method of passing the tried-and-true techniques of the studio on to new audio engineers is needed.

Hopefully, this book can provide one aspect of that lost education of the studio apprentice tradition. The background in theory for audio processing is much more valuable than knowledge of each tool. The theory allows you to learn how to use any audio tool with ease.

My Favorite Picks

After reviewing so many plug-ins, many of which I have used everyday for years, and discovering so many new and interesting tools, there are some that stand out for their outstanding quality or uniqueness. Some are just plain too much fun to mess around with. Although all of the plug-ins mentioned in this book provide quality processing, each one has strengths that other might not have, some of them have intrigued me more than others. Here are some of my favorite picks.

* *Spectron*—This is the wildest delay plug-in I've ever messed with. Being able to delay various frequency bands independently with all sorts of modulation and feedback possibilities makes Spectron one of the most interesting plug-ins around.

* *TC's VSS3*—This plug-in stands out for its incredible quality. For dealing with single sources, I have never heard more realistic reverb and ambience from either a hardware or software processor. Placing sounds in VSS3 takes you there immediately.

* *PSP MasterQ*—This equalizer stunned me when I first hit the Fat processing button that engages the oversampling process. It is not a transparent EQ and that is what I like so much about this plug-in. It has a character that I find attractive, reminding me of the Millennia Media NSEQ-2 hardware equalizer.

* *Algorithmix reNOVAtor*—This plug-in is almost uncanny in its ability to remove very specific noises without leaving any trace of processing. It enters the realm of Star Trek in being able to do the impossible. I found that using reNOVAtor gave me insight into audio and sound that I did not have before.

* *Native Instruments Guitar Rig*—This is simply the most fun you can have with a plug-in. It is as if somebody has let me loose in a vintage guitar store with all my favorite guitar pedals and amps and a technician to rip it all apart and customize it to my desires—a guitar players dream. And I'm a bass player!

These picks do not negate the quality of other plug-ins. Each one of these had a surprise for me; something I did not expect. These surprises made me realize that the potential for plug-in processing is still expanding and this expansion is creating new and unique methods of working with sound everyday.

Index

Numbers

A

X-Z